BARRON'S

Encyclopedia of Dog Breeds

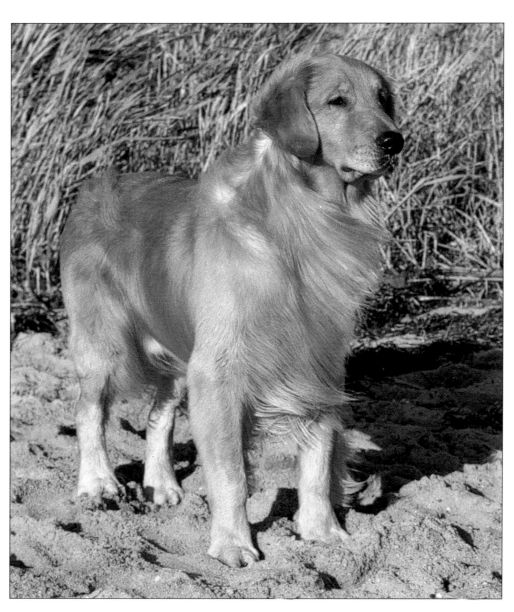

BARRON'S

Encyclopedia of Dog Breeds

D. CAROLINE COILE, Ph.D.

ILLUSTRATIONS BY MICHELE EARLE-BRIDGES

PHOTO CREDITS

Kent & Donna Dannen: pages vi, 1, 2, 11, 22, 23, 25, 28, 33, 36, 49, 50, 56, 64, 69, 70, 74, 76, 77, 83, 84, 91, 98–102, 107, 111, 112, 116, 117, 127, 130, 134–138, 145, 154, 160, 162, 176, 177, 183, 187, 191, 198, 212, 222–225, 230, 234, 235, 237, 240, 244, 254–257, 260, 266, 268, 270, 278, 279, 290, 304; Tara Darling: pages i, 3, 6, 8, 9, 12, 14, 17, 18, 20, 26, 31, 34, 38, 39, 46, 47, 48, 54, 55, 57–63, 65–68, 71–73, 75, 78–82, 86–89, 93–97, 108–110, 113, 114, 118, 119, 121, 123, 124, 126, 128, 129, 131, 133, 141, 144, 146–153, 155, 157–159, 163–165, 167–173, 175, 180, 181, 184, 185, 188–190, 192–195, 200–202, 204–211, 213–215, 217–219, 221, 228, 229, 233, 242, 244–246, 250, 253, 258, 261–264, 267, 271–273, 281–284, 286, 288, 291, 293–303, 305, 306; Judith E. Strom: pages iii, 4, 13, 15, 27, 29, 37, 40–45, 51, 105, 122, 125, 247, 285, 308; Winter/Churchill: cover photos and pages 5, 7, 10, 16, 19, 24, 32, 35, 85, 90, 103, 106, 139, 162, 163, 166, 199, 203, 227, 243, 252, 259, 280, 287, 292, 309; Dee Ross/Pure Images: pages 21, 115, 140; Pets by Paulette: pages 30, 96, 104, 120, 132, 156, 161, 182, 186, 204, 216, 226, 231, 232, 236, 248, 251, 276, 307; M. Agramonte: page 92; Pam Ross: pages 174, 220; Elizabeth Flynn: pages 178, 179; Norvia Behling: pages 269, 289

Text: D. Caroline Coile
Photos and illustrations: Barron's Educational Series, Inc.

© Copyright 1998 by Barron's Educational Series, Inc.

All inquiries should be addressed to:
Barron's Educational Series, Inc.
250 Wireless Boulevard
Hauppauge, NY 11788
http://www.barronseduc.com

International Standard Book No. 0-7641-5097-9

Library of Congress Catalog Card No. 98-20368

Library of Congress Cataloging-in-Publication Data
Coile, D. Caroline.
    Encyclopedia of dog breeds / D. Caroline Coile ;
illustrations by Michele Earle-Bridges.
        p.   cm.
    ISBN 0-7641-5097-9
    1. Dog breeds—Encyclopedias. 2. Dog breeds—Pictorial
works. I. Title.
SF442.C65   1998
636.7'1'03—dc21   98-20368
                                                             CIP

Printed in Hong Kong
15 14 13 12

CONTENTS

The Right Dog

You can choose your friends, but you can't choose your family—except, of course, for the family dog. In fact, humans have been choosing the dog's family for it for thousands of years, since the first time an arranged breeding between dogs with favored characteristics was carried out in an effort to produce more dogs of the same. In so doing, they gradually created from wolf ancestors the most diverse species in the world: *Canis familaris*, the domestic dog.

From the Dog Family to the Family Dog
The circumstances of the dog's initial domestication are forever lost in time. Early in the course of domestication, selection for traits that enabled this formerly wild species to share its life with humans was molding the dog that is such an integral part of human life today. Traits such as lack of fear, low reactivity, and dependence helped the first domestic dogs to live among members of another species. These traits are also found in juvenile wolves, and one theory of dog domestication suggests that dogs represent a sort of "arrested development" of the wolf. Fossil evidence of even the earliest domesticated dogs show them to have smaller brains, smaller teeth, more rounded heads, and smaller stature than wolves of the time, more like juvenile wolves. Many of the herding, hunting, and playing behaviors humans have found so useful and entertaining in modern dogs can be found in immature forms of

hunting behavior in wolves. Barking is not seen in adult wolves, but is a trait of juveniles—as well as a well-known trait of adult dogs.

The earliest "domestic" dogs may have proven useful by cleaning up debris around living areas, alerting to intruders, or running down food. No matter what the forces were that drew humans and canines together, no doubt the relationship continued mostly because early humans found the dog useful. It is doubtful that food was available for dogs that did not earn their keep, so generation by generation, selection for only the most useful dogs occurred.

These forces—selection for tameness and for function—formed the initial basis for the vast array of modern breeds. As humans came to realize that "like begat like," they purposefully bred their best hunting dogs together, and their best guarding dogs together, creating the first canine specialists. Even in prehistoric times, considerable diversity in dogs existed, with distinct types or families—"breeds"—of domestic dogs arising at least by 3000 to 4000 years ago. Ancient Egypt was home to at least two distinct types of dogs, Greyhound and Mastiff, each specialized for a different job. By Roman times, most of the main types of modern breeds were in existence, with dogs specifically bred as guard, sheep, hunting, and lap dogs. The variety of dog breeds expanded greatly in Europe in the Middle Ages, with many breeds taking on importance as specialized hunters for either the aristocracy or poachers. Europe was not the only home of new dog breeds. Wherever humans lived, they shaped their dogs to do their bidding. Just as the needs of people change throughout history, breeds of dogs are not static. Many breeds have been born only to disappear into history, lost either because their work was no longer needed or another breed was developed that could do it better.

In the mid 1800s, a new pastime caught the attention of the European upper class: the exhibition of dogs. Before this time, it had been common to arrange contests between dogs based on coursing, fighting, or hauling ability, but the idea that any dog's worth could be estimated by its physical appearance was relatively new. As competition among breeds grew, the search for "new and exotic" breeds began. Travelers and dog buyers would spot prospective breed candidates, acquire a few, and exhibit them. The dogs selected to found a breed often represented a small minority of that breed's total population, a fact that has led to decreased genetic variation within breeds. Some breeds caught on, whereas others did not. Those that attracted fanciers needed an objective means by which to evaluate them, a description of the ideal for that breed—the breed standard.

The sport of purebred dogs spread quickly to America, where the American Kennel Club (AKC) was formed to register and promote pure-bred dogs. The requirements for breed recognition have changed somewhat through the years, but in general a breed must be backed by a national club that can demonstrate a sustained interest in the breed. New breeds are initially admitted into the Miscellaneous Class, and then later, pending demonstration of continued interest in the breed, admitted into one of the AKC's seven regular groups. The AKC breeds represent only a fraction of the world's breeds, but they are the most popular dogs in America.

Many breeds continue to be used for their original purposes, whereas for other breeds that purpose has long since vanished. Nonetheless, these breeds are prevented from becoming extinct by breeding them to the same traditional standards that would enable them to do their original job. Each breed standard has been forged to describe a dog that can best do its specific job—whether that dog will ever get the chance to do it or not.

Body and Soul

The breeds of dog differ in many ways: body size, body proportion, musculature, head shape, ear shape, coat length, coat texture, and even color. In many cases these differences arose from selection for the physical traits that were best suited for the job at hand, whether that job was hunting over rough terrain, swimming through icy water, or simply adorning the lap of aristocracy. Yet, as important as conformation to function is, behavior is even more important. The fastest Greyhound is of no use to the coursing enthusiast if it is not interested in chasing the rabbit. The quickest terrier is of no use to the farmer if it is afraid of the rat. The largest stock guard is of no use to the shepherd if it kills the sheep. The toughest home guard is of no use if it falls asleep on the job. It should thus come as no surprise that dogs display just as many breed-related behavioral differences as physical differences. It should come as no surprise—but it does.

Too often prospective dog owners select a breed based upon its physical characteristics, with the assumption that all dogs act alike. They don't. Thousands of generations of selection have seen to that. Behavior is

THE RIGHT DOG ix

malleable, but dogs are born with a propensity to act in certain ways dictated by their genes. Not all dogs within a breed act the same, but most dogs within a breed have a tendency to act in certain ways, especially if those traits were important ones for doing the job for which it was developed.

The domestic dog is a marvel of selection, unsurpassed in its variety of physical and behavioral traits. Yet one behavioral trait that seems constantly present in all dogs is that of selfless love, devotion, and loyalty. Unscientific traits, perhaps, but they are so integral to the nature of the dog that its scientific name, *Canis familaris*, literally means faithful dog. And it is the job of faithful dog that is, after all, the most important job a dog can have. Luckily, that is the job at which the dog is at its very best.

Are They Good with Children?

Every breed of dog can, in general, be good with children if raised with them the right way, and every breed can be bad with children if not adequately socialized with them or raised with them the wrong way. Every breed has its own qualities, and sometimes the job for which a breed was developed strongly affects its interaction with children. For example, some herding breeds tend to herd anything, including children. Some breeds naturally herd by nipping, which can be frightening to some children. Some guarding breeds will tend to be protective of the children in their family. They often do not understand that a visiting child playing roughly with their child is not a threat, however, and precautions must sometimes be taken.

Size of any dog should be considered. A large dog can accidentally knock a small child down. Large dogs have large teeth and powerful jaws and can do more damage if they did bite. Small dogs can be hurt by children, either through rough play or careless behavior around the house.

Activity level is also a consideration. Excitable dogs may become overly excited by the activity of children. An overly boisterous dog can jump on children in play or simply annoy parents by adding to the activity level in the house. Inactive dogs are more likely to ignore children and perhaps even leave the room. Though they may help keep excitement levels down in the home, they may not be satisfying for children needing a playmate.

Playful, attentive, obedient dogs can make excellent playmates for children. Dogs that tend to be independent can be frustrating for children and may themselves be endangered by living with a child. Children may have difficulty taking an independent dog for a walk because it may tend to wander away in search of adventure or game. Active, independent dogs may tend to run through gates and doors that children may inadvertently leave open. Children should not be given the responsibility of walking the dog.

How to Use the Breed Profiles

Choosing a breed entails more than looking at pictures, although esthetics certainly plays a role. But looks aren't everything. The range of behavioral attributes is every bit as wide as the range of physical attributes, but it is not as outwardly obvious. The ideal dog for one person is not necessarily the ideal dog for another. The breed profiles are designed not only to inform you about a breed but also to provide information that will help you choose your best of breeds.

Each breed profile is divided into several sections.

History

The history of a breed not only is interesting but also describes the forces that molded the distinct features of that breed. Knowing the other breeds that have contributed to a new breed can help you understand the traits that new breed displays; knowing what features a breed's creators were interested in preserving or accentuating can also help explain why a breed looks and acts as it does. A dog that has been bred to hunt at long range will have a lot of energy and tend to run at a great distance from its owner, even if the owner has no interest in hunting. A breed developed to dig out vermin will dig every chance it gets—it's in its genes! Understanding a breed's history will help you decide whether a breed's innate characteristics will blend harmoniously into your lifestyle.

Note that there is a box in this section that lists a number of "facts" about each breed. The "Area of Origin" and "Date of Origin" are many times just educated guesses; because of the fact that there are no written records for the origins of most breeds, there is much disagreement as to when and where they originated.

Temperament

The breed's background also influences its temperament. The same forces that shaped the differences in physical attributes have shaped its behavior and temperament. In fact, more often than not, the behavior of the dog was the initial trait that caused it to eventually become a breed. A dog may be built to do a job, but unless it wants to do a job, it is worthless to the working dog breeder. The temperament described here assumes that the dog has received proper socialization and an average amount of training.

Every breed of dog should learn basic obedience. Obedience training is absolutely essential in large, strong, or domineering breeds. It is also helpful in breeds that tend to be shy or independent. In all cases, obe-

dience training can have its desired effects only if done properly. Great advances in obedience training methods have been made in the past decade. The major change involves the use of food, play, or praise as motivational techniques in place of harsh force training. Many of the breeds that have gained a reputation of being "stubborn" or difficult to train simply do not respond well to force training; when trained with food or play, these same dogs can be very willing obedience pupils. Obedience training, done properly, offers a dog the chance to exercise its mental capacities, which in many breeds is every bit as essential as physical exercise.

Upkeep

Dogs are always there for you, but will you be there for them? Even though a breed may act and look just like your ideal dog, you must evaluate that breed's needs in terms of your circumstances.

There is no such thing as a breed that requires no exercise. Most breeds require far more exercise than people are willing to give. Conversely, it's not fair or healthy to push a naturally sedate breed into being your marathon partner. The exercise requirements suggested here are average; dogs would usually do better with more but are usually given less. Note also that the requirements stated here are for adult dogs; never push a puppy to exercise beyond the time it is the least bit tired. Especially in giant breeds, such a practice can cause irreparable harm. Old dogs require considerably less exercise.

Some people want a dog that can live in an apartment. Apartment living is suggested only for very small dogs and a few larger dogs with lower energy levels, or for owners who are committed to a vigorous and regular exercise schedule. Some people want a dog that can live exclusively outdoors. No dog should ever be expected to live outside without human or canine companionship. Prospective dog owners who intend to keep their dog outside and separated from their family should seriously reconsider their reasons for acquiring a dog. Dogs are social animals; to a dog, solitary living is frustrating and so adverse that it can be considered severe punishment. In many breeds it creates behavior problems, including aggression. Most breeds depend upon close bonding with their human families In order to live up to their potentials as companions, guardians, or competitors. It is strongly suggested that all dogs be allowed access to the home and family. Even those breeds that can physically withstand outdoor life during the daytime must be furnished with shade and draft-free shelter. Any time outdoor living or a yard is mentioned in this text, it is assumed to be a securely fenced area; running at large, chaining, or constant confinement in a small pen are not humane options.

Coat care is another important consideration. Owners tend to underestimate the need for coat care, and overestimate their willingness to keep up a regular coat care regime. Even within a breed, coat texture can vary considerably, so that some individuals' needs may be considerably more or less than average. The dogs pictured in this book display the result of the maximum level of coat care. The coat care suggested here is average for the maintenance of an attractive coat typical of the breed; maintenance of a show-quality coat will require more commitment. In addition, preparation of a dog for the show ring often requires considerable attention to minute details; the specifics of show grooming for each breed are not outlined. Many wire coats require hand-plucking to maintain the correct harsh texture and deep coloration; clipping the coat will cause the coat to become soft and faded.

Professional groomers seldom have the time or experience to hand-pluck a dog, so unless the owner wishes to learn the technique, they will need to have their dog clipped. Though incorrect for the show ring, a soft coat in these breeds is seldom objectionable to the pet owner. Many breeds may require professional grooming; consider that this can be very expensive and stressful to some dogs. Pet owners can usually buy the proper grooming equipment and learn to groom their own dogs adequately. In all breeds, puppies should be introduced to grooming at a young age in order to be cooperative as adults. Some people fall in love with a long-coated breed and then clip it to avoid coat care. Consider that a clipped dog will not resemble the dog you were attracted to, and decide whether it might be better to get a short-haired dog to begin with.

Grooming that is mandatory for all breeds is not specifically mentioned. All dogs need occasional bathing; long coats generally need bathing more often than short coats. Bathing removes oil and debris that can create matting; long show-quality coats usually require bathing once a week. All dogs need occasional ear cleaning; only those in which ears are prone to problems are specifically mentioned as needing frequent cleaning. All dogs need tooth care, though many toy breeds suffer from tooth loss and periodontal disease and will need more attention to dental care. All dogs need regular nail clipping.

Many people are interested in finding a dog that doesn't shed. There is no such thing. All dogs lose their hair; in some dogs, typically those with very curly coats (such as the Poodle), the hair is trapped by the other hairs instead of falling to the floor. It must be brushed out or it will mat the hair. In general, thick, double coats tend to shed in great amounts periodically; short, single coats shed just as much but because less hair is involved, the mess is less noticeable. Of course, a hairless breed scarcely sheds at all! Note also that it is the dander of the dog, not the hair, that causes human allergies, and that a clean dog generally creates fewer problems for an allergic person.

Some dogs are just plain messy. Dogs that have pendulous lips tend to drip water after drinking; many also tend to drool. Dogs with hairy feet tend to track mud and debris into the house.

Although not specifically mentioned, food costs are higher for larger and more active dogs and for dogs that are outdoors in cold weather. Boarding and veterinary costs are also usually higher for larger dogs. Owners of giant dogs must take their size into consideration when buying a car, or even a home. Tiny dogs need special precautions to avoid being injured, especially by other strange dogs. Obedience training is essential for all breeds of dogs; it tends to be more critical in larger or more active dogs.

Health

Pure-bred dogs are prone to different health problems for various reasons. In some breeds, selection for particular traits may also inadvertently cause some health problems. Thus, flat-faced (brachycephalic) breeds have difficulty cooling themselves in hot weather and, sometimes, breathing. In other cases, a small number of dogs were used to found a breed, and if one of those dogs happened to carry a gene for a health problem, that undesirable gene could have become widespread throughout the breed because of the restricted gene pool. Finally, in breeds that have been extremely popular, careless breeding by owners not aware of health problems can cause genetic disor-

ders to become more widespread. The health concerns listed here are subject to the problem of reporting; thus, rare breeds may be beset with certain problems but because these dogs are rare and seldom seen at veterinary clinics, these problems go unreported. Common breeds probably have overreported health problems simply because so many of them are seen at veterinary clinics. Thus, the health guide should be only a guide; a reported disorder does not doom a dog to having that problem nor does the absence of a reported disorder guarantee that the breed is free of it. The disorders are ranked as being of major concern (prevalent and serious), minor concern (either rare and serious or prevalent but not serious), and occasionally seen (reported more than in other breeds, but not enough that it should dissuade anyone from choosing that breed). Note that the placement in one category versus another is at times a close or arbitrary decision. For disorders in which breed statistics are available, prevalent means that the disorder is reported in 10 percent or more of the individuals within a breed. Please refer to the Appendix at the back of this book for definitions of medical conditions.

Several health problems are so widespread in all breeds that they are not included here. Foremost among these are hypothyroidism, cancer (unless a specific type of cancer is prevalent), and allergies (unless especially severe). This is not to imply that a hereditary component does not exist for these conditions, and a potential buyer is well advised to inquire about such problems in a prospective puppy's ancestors, no matter what the breed.

Recommended tests refer to tests that the parents of any prospective puppy you may be considering should have had. Tests reported in parentheses are suggested and preferred, but are not absolutely essential.

Several health registries exist for pure-bred dogs, and some breed parent clubs maintain their own breed-specific registries. The Orthopedic Foundation for Animals (OFA) maintains a registry for dogs evaluated as normal for several hereditary problems, including canine hip dysplasia (CHD), elbow dysplasia, patellar luxation, craniomandibular osteopathy, and several breed-specific disorders. PennHip also provides hip dysplasia evaluation and certification. The Canine Eye Registry Foundation (CERF) provides registration for dogs evaluated with normal eyes; because some eye problems may not be evident until later in life, CERF evaluation should be periodically renewed. The Institute for Genetic Disease Control in Animals (GDC) is an open registry for all dogs and all diseases. The list of DNA tests for disorders within a breed is growing and represents an exciting advancement. Even when specific tests are not available for a disorder, a breeder should be cognizant of a problem in the breed and be willing to discuss it with you. Health problems can cut short the enjoyable times you and your dog can spend together and can also be extremely expensive. As such, they should be realistically considered when choosing a breed or puppy within that breed.

Form and Function
The physical features typical of a breed more often than not have their roots in functional requirements. This section describes the overall look, general proportions, substance, gait, coat, and expression of the breed, whenever possible explaining how that feature relates to the breed's function. Much of the information for this section is taken directly from the AKC standard for the breed. Note that when overall proportions are available, unless otherwise specified, they refer to the proportion of the distance of height at the withers to the distance from the point of the breastbone to the point of the rump. Most breeds, when measured in this way, are very slightly longer than tall.

Illustrated Standard
The AKC standard for each breed is long and exacting. The illustrated standards point out some of the details that distinguish each breed. This is not a complete list of traits, and the reader is urged to consult the entire breed standard before evaluating a dog. Any breed is far more than the sum of its parts, and more general breed attributes are described under the Form and Function section. Accepted colors are listed here, as well as breed specific disqualifications (DQ). These disqualifications (unless based on temperament or health) will in no way affect a dog's ability to function as a pet, but they do indicate that a dog is not show or breeding quality. It can still (in most cases) be AKC registered, however. Note that many disqualifications apply to all breeds and are not specifically mentioned; examples of all-breed disqualifications include the failure of one or both testicles to descend normally into the scrotum, or changing a dog's appearance through artificial means in ways not specifically allowed in that breed's standard.

Note that many breeds traditionally may have docked tails and/or cropped ears. Tail docking is usually performed at a few days of age, so puppy buyers have little input if they do not wish this procedure performed on their prospective dog. If not performed at that time, it should never be performed. Ear cropping is usually performed at several months of age. It requires general anesthesia and extensive postoperative care, as well as some pain for the puppy. Many pet owners elect not to have their puppy's ears cropped; however, this should be mutually agreed upon by the owner and breeder at the time the puppy is acquired. The ears of some breeds, especially those requiring an erect ear that tips forward near the top, may require some taping or gluing in puppyhood in order to train the ears to stand or bend properly; the techniques involved should be explained by the breeder.

At a Glance

Entries in this section range from *low* (represented by one box) to *high* (represented by five boxes). Most breeds vary over several rankings, and as such each ranking should be considered to be approximate for that breed. Individual dogs, like people, can show marked deviations from the average.

Energy level. Most people think they want an energetic dog. Think twice before you choose a high-energy breed, however, because a dog in constant motion may be unnerving or annoying to you. A very low-energy dog, however, may be frustrating for children or to an owner who wants an enthusiastic jogging companion. Note that even in breeds with low energy levels as adults, puppies will have high energy. There is no such thing as a low-energy puppy (or even adolescent), and buyers who need a low-energy dog from the outset are advised to consider a mature dog.

Exercise requirements. Exercise requirements are a combination of a dog's energy requirements and size or athleticism. The Greyhound is athletic, but quiet; its requirements can be met with short running bursts. The Miniature Pinscher is small, but energetic, and can get a lot of exercise indoors. Even a dog with very low requirements needs daily exercise.

Playfulness. Playfulness is related to energy level but focuses on whether that energy is aimed at interacting with people. Most people want a playful dog; however, the constant thud of a tennis ball dropped in your lap may be too demanding for busy people.

Affection level. Not everybody wants a dog that jumps all over them and licks them in the face. Some dogs, although devoted to their owners, are less demonstrative or fawning. People differ in which type of dog they prefer. A dog that ranks lower in this category does not mean that it does not need or thrive on attention and affection; it simply means that it may be less extroverted in its exhibition of it.

Friendliness toward dogs. Almost any dog can be aggressive toward strange dogs; those in which it is noted are a little more so than others. Similarly, in almost any breed, dogs may fight within a household, particularly dogs of the same sex. Dogs with higher ratings in this section tend to be less likely to fight than others, but they are not immune from it.

Friendliness toward other pets. All dogs can chase cats, and all dogs can learn to live peacefully with cats if they are raised with them. Some breeds, however, were bred to chase and kill small mammals, and these breeds are more likely to chase cats or other animals outside.

Friendliness toward strangers. Some breeds have never met a stranger. Some tend to be naturally aloof, or tend to be shy, or tend to be suspicious. Not everybody wants to see their darling dog seemingly adoring a complete stranger as much as it loves them! A friendly dog is a great way to meet people, however.

Ease of training. Training ease does not necessarily reflect intelligence. Some dogs combine intelligence with a high energy level and a willingness to please that, taken together, result in a dog that learns quickly. Such dogs may be hard to live with if not trained, however, because they enjoy mental stimulation and need it in order to avoid boredom.

Watchdog ability. A dog that is alert enough to detect a stranger and will bark in response is given a high rating here, regardless of its size or protectiveness. Note that very high rankings may reflect a breed that tends to bark a lot.

Protection ability. The ability of a dog to be protective is a combination of its desire to act in a protective fashion, including its boldness, and its physical ability to enforce that desire.

Grooming requirements. This ranking is determined by coat type as well as size of the dog. A tiny dog with a lot of hair would generally get a lower ranking than a large dog with a lot of hair.

Cold tolerance. This ability is important if you intend to keep your dog outside a lot or live in a cold climate. Small dogs and short-haired dogs are less heat tolerant than large, bulky dogs or dogs with thick, double coats.

Heat tolerance. Dogs, in general, are not heat tolerant. As a rule, the shorter the nose, the bulkier the body, and the thicker the coat, the less heat tolerant a dog will be.

Important note: In all cases these ratings are based upon the assumption that a dog has been acquired from a reputable, qualified breeder. Qualified breeders will be willing to discuss temperament and health problems of their breed and will have proven their breeding stock in some sort of competitive area as well as screening it for breed typical health problems. They will have pictures of many of your potential puppy's ancestors. They will raise your puppy with plenty of human contact and proper health care. They will stand behind their dog and be available to you for advice for the rest of that puppy's life. They will screen potential buyers and make it clear that you will not be able to recoup your money by breeding your pup in the future.

Height and weight are the suggested values given in the AKC standards. Height is measured as the distance from the ground to the top of the withers. Weight is considered to be that of a dog in ideal weight for its bone structure; that is, neither thin nor fat. Those with an asterisk (*) indicate that no requirement was listed in the standard; these measurements are either average reported values or values from the breed standard of another registry. Note that in any case, average values within a breed may differ from suggested values. Some breeders boast of weights or sizes that differ markedly from the AKC standard weights; such breeders should generally be avoided. See the section on upkeep to interpret the significance of size when evaluating a breed.

The information supplied in this section pertains to adult dogs. Even dogs of the calmest and least playful breeds, for example, are energetic and playful (and destructive) as puppies.

With the dog, you can choose both your family and your friend. Choose well!

The Sporting Group

The Sporting breeds are the modern hunters in that they hunt in concert with a hunter armed with a gun. Their roots often lay in hunters armed with nets, however. They work with the hunter to extend the hunter's abilities by either locating, moving, or bringing back birds. The group that locates game is composed of pointing and setting breeds, which freeze in mid stride and "point" to game. The group that moves game is the spaniels, which range back and forth close to the hunter, flushing game so that the hunter can shoot it. The group that brings back downed game is the retrievers, which mark where game falls and return with it over land or through water. Many breeds combine talents and are termed versatile hunters.

Brittany

History

In the mid 1800s, French sportsmen crossed their small land spaniels with English Setters in attempts to produce a dog better suited for their needs. Some of the offspring were tailless, and their descendents continued to be tailless or stub-tailed. More importantly, they were excellent woodcock hunters with strong noses. These dogs soon became popular not only with the French gentry but also with poachers because they would both point and retrieve and were extremely obedient—essential qualities for the clandestine activities of the poachers. The first Brittany (or "Epagneul Breton") was registered in France in 1907. The Brittany came to America (Mexico) around 1925 and was AKC recognized in 1925. The breed took a while to be accepted, mostly because hunters expected a pointing dog to have a long tail. When the dogs were given a chance, however, they proved their mettle and have since become the most popular of all pointing

AKC Ranking: 33
Family: Gundog, Setter, Pointer, Versatile Hunting Dog
Area of Origin: France
Date of Origin: 1800s
Original Function: Pointing & retrieving
Today's Function: Pointing & retrieving, pointing field trials
Other Name: Epagneul Breton, Brittany Spaniel

breeds at field trials. In fact, registrations eventually soared to place the Brittany among the top 20 in popularity, no doubt because of its bird-hunting abilities, close-ranging hunting style, small size, and tractable nature. Although registered as the Brittany Spaniel with the AKC from 1934, the word spaniel was dropped in 1982 in recognition of the dog's hunting style, which is more like that of a setter than a spaniel.

Temperament

The Brittany is quick and curious, always on the lookout for birds or fun. It loves to run, scout, hunt, and play. It has an independent nature, befitting any pointing breed, yet it is sensitive and very responsive to human direction. The Brittany makes a good house pet as long as it receives daily mental and physical exercise. If not given sufficient exercise, it can become destructive.

Upkeep

The Brittany is generally a hardy dog that requires little maintenance. Its major requirement is for abundant exercise, at least an hour of exertion—not just walking—every day. For this reason, it is not suited for apartment life. It can live outdoors in temperate weather, but it is a social dog that needs human interaction. Its coat is not particularly thick or long, but it does require brushing once or twice weekly.

Health

- Major concerns: CHD
- Minor concerns: epilepsy, lipfold pyoderma
- Occasionally seen: spinal paralysis
- Suggested tests: hip
- Life span: 12–13 years

Form and Function

The leggiest of the Sporting breeds, the Brittany is square-proportioned, the height at the shoulder equaling the length of the body. It stands slightly higher at the withers than at the rump. It is medium-sized with light bone. The combination of long legs and light bones endows

the Brittany with remarkable agility and speed. In fact, the breed is very quick and is noted for its ground-covering side movement at the trot. The Brittany may be born tailless or have the tail docked to about 4 inches. The breed's coat is far less profuse than that of spaniels and is either flat or wavy. An overly profuse

coat is detrimental when hunting in briars and is considered a severe fault. The Brittany's expression is alert and eager, but soft. The eyes are protected from briars by a fairly heavy eyebrow. The Brittany is an extremely athletic, eager dog that should be ready and able to run in the field for extended periods.

Illustrated Standard

1. Nose some shade of brown or pink
2. Medium length, rounded skull
3. Short, triangular ears, set high
4. Short, straight back
5. Tailless to about 4 inches long

❏ **Color:** orange and white, liver and white, or tricolored
❏ **DQ:** under 17.5" or over 20.5" tall; black nose; black in coat

At a Glance

Energy level:	▢▢▢□
Exercise requirements:	▢▢▢▢□
Playfulness:	▢▢▢□
Affection level:	▢▢▢▢□
Friendliness toward dogs:	▢▢□
Friendliness toward other pets:	▢▢□
Friendliness toward strangers:	▢▢▢▢□
Ease of training:	▢▢▢□
Watchdog ability:	▢▢▢□
Protection ability:	▢
Grooming requirements:	▢
Cold tolerance:	▢▢□
Heat tolerance:	▢▢□

Weight:	30–40 lb
Height	17.5–20.5"

Pointer

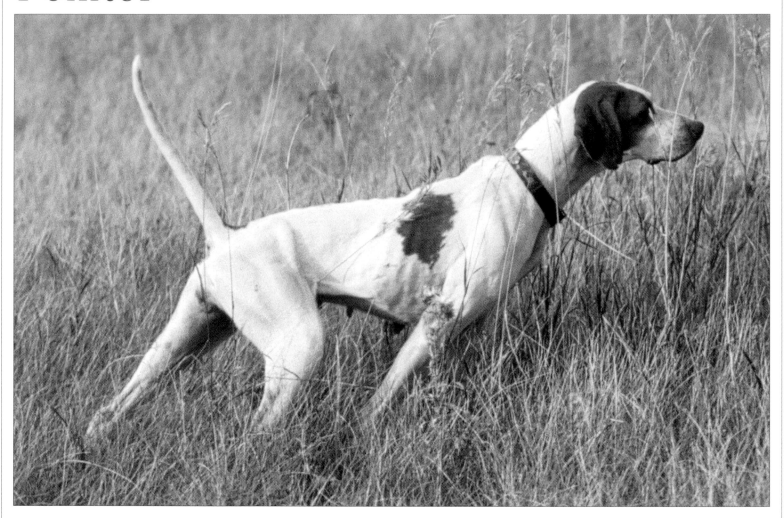

History

The earliest Pointers were used in the seventeenth century not to point birds, but to point hare, which coursing Greyhounds were then unleashed to pursue. When wing-shooting became popular in the eighteenth century, the Pointer found its place as an adept bird locator. The ideal dog would find game, indicate its location, and remain still until the hunter could get ready to shoot—a task that was somewhat slow with the old flintlock guns. The early Pointer probably included in its genetic makeup some of the most talented breeds in existence: Greyhounds, Foxhounds, and Bloodhounds, as well as an old type of setting spaniel. Different countries developed different Pointer breeds. The large, ponderous Spanish Pointer was crossed with the English Pointer to increase pointing ability, but at the expense of agility. With the advent of self-loading guns in the nineteenth century, the slower working traits of the Spanish Pointer became undesirable, so the crosses were discontinued. In the nineteenth century, crosses with setters were made, perhaps to improve disposition and make the dogs more amenable to training and less prone to try to catch

AKC Ranking: 92
Family: Gundog, Pointer
Area of Origin: England
Date of Origin: 1600s
Original Function: Pointing
Today's Function: Pointing, pointing
  field trials, companion
Other Name: English Pointer

the game. Pointers became popular for recreational hunting on large estates. Ideally, two Pointers were used so that the hunter could locate the bird precisely by cross-referencing the dogs' points. When dog shows came in vogue in the late nineteenth century, Pointers were among the most prominent of the breeds shown. Pointers remain very popular as competitive field trial dogs and recreational hunters; however, they are not as popular as pets as many other sporting breeds.

Temperament

The Pointer is a true wide-ranging hunter, which means that it not only is an excellent bird dog but also has the stamina to run for hours. Consequently, it needs lots of exercise or it can become frustrated and destructive. Because it is ever on the lookout for birds, it is easily distracted from everyday matters—but it is nearly impossible to distract once on point. It is gentle and sweet but may be too energetic and boisterous at times for very small children. Like many sporting breeds, it can be found in field or show types; the field type is generally smaller and perhaps more active.

Upkeep

The Pointer needs exercise, and lots of it. It needs at least an hour of exertion every day. It is best when it has a regular opportunity to hunt, but it also enjoys running and searching the wilds on long jaunts afield. At home it needs space to exercise outdoors and should not be expected to sit inside all day. The Pointer can live outdoors in temperate to warm climates as long as it is given a soft bed and warm shelter. It needs canine or human companionship, however, and does far better when allowed to spend time with its family. It requires only an occasional brushing to remove dead hair.

Health

- Major concerns: entropion
- Minor concerns: CHD
- Occasionally seen: cataract, deafness
- Suggested tests: (hip), eye
- Life span: 12–15 years
- Note: prone to tail-tip injuries

Form and Function

The Pointer combines athletic grace and power with a lean, muscular body, noble head, alert expression, and noble

Illustrated Standard

1. Square, deep muzzle; nose slightly higher at tip than at stop
2. Long head with pronounced stop
3. Rounded eyes
4. Thin, soft, hanging ears, somewhat pointed at tip
5. Tail tapering, straight, carried near the line of the back
6. Muscular body
7. Oval feet

❑ **Color:** liver, lemon, black, orange, either solid or mixed with white
❑ **DQ:** none

carriage. The gait is smooth and powerful, with head held high and nostrils wide, enabling it to cover a lot of ground while searching for airborne scent. The tail lashes from side to side when the dog gaits. The Pointer's close coat is short and dense, giving a clean stream-lined appearance. Field type pointers tend to hold their tails upright when on point.

At a Glance

Energy level:	❑❑❑❑
Exercise requirements:	❑❑❑❑
Playfulness:	❑❑❑❑
Affection level:	❑❑❑
Friendliness toward dogs:	❑❑❑❑
Friendliness toward other pets:	❑❑❑
Friendliness toward strangers:	❑❑❑
Ease of training:	❑❑❑
Watchdog ability:	❑❑❑❑
Protection ability:	❑❑❑
Grooming requirements:	❑
Cold tolerance:	❑❑❑
Heat tolerance:	❑❑❑

Weight:	male: 55–75 lb; female: 45–65 lb
Height:	male: 25–28"; female: 23–26"

German Shorthaired Pointer

History

The German Shorthaired Pointer is one of the most versatile of hunting breeds, combining pointing, retrieving, trailing, and even game-killing abilities. This versatility arose through the purposeful blending of various breeds beginning as early as the seventeenth century. Crosses of the Spanish Pointer (a heavy type of pointer) with the Hannover Hound (a strain of scenthounds) resulted in a heavy houndlike dog that could both trail and point and was interested in both birds and mammals. When trailing, these dogs would bay; if needed, they would dispatch wounded game and even fox. Although all the early breeders agreed upon the goal of an all-purpose hunting dog, not all agreed upon how to achieve it. Crosses with the English Pointer were controversial but bestowed upon the breed a more stylish look and nose-up hunting mode. It also imparted a dislike of water and an aversion to attacking quarry. Further breeding eliminated these shnwanted pointer character-

AKC Ranking: 24
Family: Gundog, Pointer, Versatile Hunting Dog
Area of Origin: Germany
Date of Origin: 1600s
Original Function: General hunting
Today's Function: Pointing, pointing field trials
Other Name: German Pointer (Shorthaired), Deutscher, Kurzhaariger Vortsehund, Kurzhaar

istics. In the early 1800s two Deutsch Kurzhaars (as the breed was originally known), Nero and Treff, distinguished themselves against other pointing breeds at the German Derby and, through the success of their descendents, are often credited as the modern Shorthaired's foundation. The breed was recognized in the late 1800s in Germany with the first Shorthaired coming to America in the 1920s. The German Shorthaired Pointer gained AKC recognition in 1930. The breed soon gained a reputation as the ideal dog for the hunter who wanted only one dog that could do it all. Besides being a gifted and versatile hunter, it is a handsome dog and obedient companion. These attributes helped the German Shorthaired Pointer become popular today.

Temperament

The German Shorthaired Pointer's idea of heaven is a day hunting in the field and an evening curled up by its owner's side. This is an active dog that can become frustrated and "creative" if not given ample daily exercise, both mental and physical. It is a devoted family pet, although at times it is overly boisterous for small children. Because part of its heritage includes hunting mammals, some can be aggressive to small pets unless raised with them. It is a sensitive breed, responsive to gentle training. Some can whine or bark a lot.

Upkeep

Bred to be an active hunting companion, this breed has a good deal of energy and requires a good deal of exercise. It thrives on mental and physical stimulation and can get both by hunting, hiking, or playing with its owner for a long period—at least an hour—every day. They like water and will swim if given the chance. Although physically able to live outside in mild weather, this is a companionable breed that does best when allowed to live in the house with access to a yard. Its grooming needs are minimal, consisting only of occasional brushing to remove dead hair.

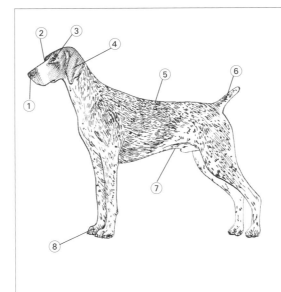

Illustrated Standard

1. Large brown nose
2. Stop not as defined as in the Pointer
3. Almond-shaped eye
4. Broad, high set, rounded ears
5. Short, strong back
6. Tail docked to 40 percent of length, carried down when relaxed or horizontally when moving
7. Defined tuck-up
8. Rounded feet

❏ **Color:** liver or combinations of liver and white*
❏ **DQ:** china or wall eyes; flesh-colored nose; extreme overshot or undershot; any area of black, red, orange, lemon, or tan or solid white

Health

- Major concerns: lymphedema
- Minor concerns: CHD, entropion, gastric torsion, vWD, pannus, OCD
- Occasionally seen: gastric torsion, ectropion, PRA
- Suggested tests: hip, eye, (blood)
- Life span: 12–14 years

Form and Function

The Shorthaired is an all-purpose close-working gundog that combines agility, power, and endurance. It is square or slightly longer than tall; although it has a short back, it should stand over plenty of ground. It should have a clean-cut head, graceful outline, strong quarters, and an athletic physique. The gait is smooth, light, and ground covering. The coat is short and tough.

At a Glance

Energy level:	❏❏❏❏
Exercise requirements:	❏❏❏❏❏
Playfulness:	❏❏❏❏
Affection level:	❏❏❏❏
Friendliness toward dogs:	❏❏❏
Friendliness toward other pets:	❏❏
Friendliness toward strangers:	❏❏❏
Ease of training:	❏❏❏
Watchdog ability:	❏❏❏❏❏
Protection ability:	❏❏❏
Grooming requirements:	❏
Cold tolerance:	❏❏❏
Heat tolerance:	❏❏❏

Weight:	male: 55–70 lb; female: 45–60 lb
Height:	male: 23–25"; female: 21–23"

German Wirehaired Pointer

History

When game-bird shooting became accessible to persons of average means, demand for both specialist and versatile hunting breeds soared. The quest for versatile breeds reached its height in Germany, and the German Wirehaired Pointer represents one of its most successful results. Hunters wanted a dog that would locate and point upland game, track wounded game, confront tough vermin, retrieve water-fowl from land or water, and also function as companion and watchdog. It was developed to be a close worker over any kind of terrain. A rough wiry coat was needed to hunt through dense brambles. Its most important ancestor was the Pudelpointer (itself a combination of the old German Pudel and the Pointer), which was crossed with the early

AKC Ranking: 73
Family: Gundog, Pointer, Versatile Hunting Dog
Area of Origin: Germany
Date of Origin: 1800s
Original Function: General hunting, watchdog
Today's Function: Pointing, pointing field trials, companion
Other Name: Deutscher Drahthaariger, Vorstehund, German Pointer (Wirehaired), Drahthaar

German Shorthaired Pointer, Griffon, Stichelhaar, and Polish Water Dog. The breed, known as the Drahthaar in Germany, has since become the most popular hunting breed in Germany. Nonetheless, it was not recognized there officially until the 1920s, the same time the first Wirehaired came to America. The German Wirehaired Pointer was recognized in America in 1959 but has never gained the popularity that they enjoy in their native land.

Temperament

The German Wirehaired Pointer is both a rugged bird dog and amiable companion. It has the energy to hunt for hours, so it must be given a daily outlet lest it becomes destructive. It is a responsive breed, although it tends to be stubborn. It retains a

At a Glance

Energy level:	☐☐☐☐☐
Exercise requirements:	☐☐☐☐☐
Playfulness:	☐☐☐
Affection level:	☐☐☐
Friendliness toward dogs:	☐☐
Friendliness toward other pets:	☐☐☐
Friendliness toward strangers:	☐☐
Ease of training:	☐☐☐
Watchdog ability:	☐☐☐☐☐
Protection ability:	☐☐☐☐
Grooming requirements:	☐☐☐
Cold tolerance:	☐☐☐
Heat tolerance:	☐☐☐

Weight:	45–75 lb*
Height:	male: 24–26"; female: smaller, but not under 22"

Illustrated Standard

① Beard and whiskers of medium length
② Medium stop
③ Oval eyes, with medium length eyebrows
④ Short, straight, strong back
⑤ Tail docked to about two fifths of the original length; carried at or above horizontal
⑥ Defined tuck-up
⑦ Round, webbed feet

❏ **Color:** liver and white, with ears and head solid liver, sometimes with a white blaze
❏ **DQ:** none

Form and Function

A sturdily built hunter, the German Wirehaired Pointer should be able to hunt all day through all types of cover. It is slightly longer than it is tall, enabling the gait to be free and smooth. The weather-resistant, straight wiry coat is an essential breed characteristic.

The outer coat is about 1 to 2 inches long, long enough to protect against brambles but not so long that the outline of the dog is obscured. The eyebrows, beard, and whiskers are of medium length. The undercoat is thick in winter for warmth but thin in summer.

guarding instinct, so it tends to be aloof, even protective, toward strangers as well as strange dogs. It is generally good, if sometimes overly boisterous, with children. It is ideal for the outdoor-oriented person wanting a tireless, weather-proof, intelligent partner.

Upkeep

Exercise is a daily requirement for this energetic hunter. At least an hour a day of exertion is recommended, and the ideal situation would combine exercise with hunting or a chance to run and explore afield. As a breed that thrives on human companionship, it does best as a house-dog with access to the outdoors. Like most harsh coats, some minimal hand-stripping may occasionally be needed to maintain a sleek outline; otherwise, brushing about once a week will suffice.

Health

• Major concerns: CHD
• Minor concerns: elbow dysplasia
• Occasionally seen: none
• Suggested tests: hip, elbow
• Life span: 12–14 years

Chesapeake Bay Retriever

History

The history of the Chesapeake Bay Retriever is one of the most fascinating—and fortunate—in dogdom. In 1807, an American ship rescued the crew and cargo from a shipwrecked English brig off the coast of Maryland. Among the rescued were two presumably Newfoundland pups that were given to the rescuers. These pups (one black and one red) later proved to be skilled water retrievers, and as their reputations grew, many local retrievers of uncertain background came to be bred to them. It is also thought that Irish Water Spaniel, Newfoundland, Bloodhound, and other local hound crosses added to the development of the breed. Gradually a distinct local breed emerged, a dog that would repeatedly swim through the rough icy waters of the Chesapeake Bay and unerringly retrieve duck after duck. Even today, the Chessie is renowned for its remarkable ability to mark and remember where a bird has fallen. Its reputation spread well beyond the Chesapeake Bay area. By 1885, the breed was thoroughly established and recognized by the AKC. Despite being one of the oldest AKC recognized breeds, as well as one of the few

AKC Ranking: 42
Family: Gundog, Retriever
Area of Origin: United States
Date of Origin: 1800s
Original function: Water retriever
Today's function: Water retriever, retriever field trials, companion
Other Name: None

breeds that can boast of being made in the United States, the Chessie's popularity has remained modest.

Temperament

The Chesapeake Bay Retriever is hardy enough to not only withstand, but also relish, repeated plunges into icy water. It loves to swim and retrieve. Despite an active life when outdoors, inside it tends to be calm. The Chessie tends to be independent, although it is eager to learn. It is reserved with strangers and can be protective; it also can be aggressive toward strange dogs if challenged. This is the hardiest, most strong-willed, and protective of the retriever breeds.

Upkeep

The Chessie is a large active dog that needs a daily chance to exercise. It enjoys a good walk or swim. It can live outside in temperate conditions, but more than anything it prefers to spend time with its family. The oily, wavy coat needs weekly brushing but is generally easily maintained. It seldom needs washing; in fact, it's hard to get a Chessie wet! Bathing destroys the coat's oils and thus, its water resistance.

Health

- Major concerns: CHD, gastric torsion
- Minor concerns: PRA
- Occasionally seen: entropion, OCD, elbow dysplasia, cerebellar abiotrophy
- Suggested tests: hip, eye
- Life span: 10–13 years

Form and Function

The Chesapeake Bay Retriever was developed to hunt waterfowl under adverse conditions, facing strong tides in rough water, high winds, and sometimes even having to break through ice. It is an extraordinary swimmer, with a strong, yet tender, bite enabling it to carry birds. It has powerful limbs and webbed feet. The Chessie is slightly longer than tall, with its hindquarters as high, or higher, than its forequarters. Its coat is rendered virtually waterproof by virtue of its oily, harsh outer coat and dense wooly undercoat. The color matches its working surroundings: any shade of brown, sedge, or dead grass.

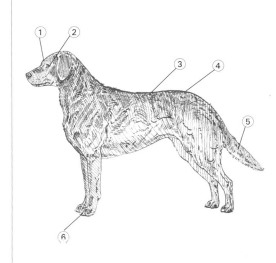

Illustrated Standard

1. Broad round skull with medium stop
2. Eyes amber
3. Hindquarters as high or slightly higher than shoulder
4. Especially powerful hindquarters for swimming
5. Tail straight or slightly curved
6. Webbed hare feet

❏ **Color:** any color of brown, sedge, or dead-grass
❏ **DQ:** lacking in breed characteristics; teeth overshot or undershot; dewclaws on hind legs; coat curly or with a tendency to curl all over the body; feathering on the tail or legs over 1-3/4″ long; black colored; white on any part of the body except breast, belly, toes, or back of feet

At a Glance

Energy level:	❑❑❑
Exercise requirements:	❑❑❑
Playfulness:	❑❑❑
Affection level:	❑❑❑❑
Friendliness toward dogs:	❑❑❑
Friendliness toward other pets:	❑❑❑
Friendliness toward strangers:	❑❑
Ease of training:	❑❑❑
Watchdog ability:	❑❑❑❑
Protection ability:	❑❑❑
Grooming requirements:	❑❑
Cold tolerance:	❑❑❑❑
Heat tolerance:	❑❑❑

Weight:	male: 65–80 lb; female: 55–70 lb
Height:	male: 23–26″; female: 21–24″

Curly-Coated Retriever

History

One of the oldest and most distinctive of the retriever breeds, the Curly-Coated Retriever may have been used in England for retrieving as long ago as the late eighteenth century. Although its exact origin remains conjectural, it probably stems from crosses of the descendents of the Old English Water Dog with the Irish Water Spaniel, and a small type of Newfoundland. These breeds together combined some of the finest water dogs in existence into one animal. Later crosses to the Poodle, a fine water retriever in its own right, served to further enhance the tight curls. By the mid 1800s, the Curly-Coated Retriever was the most popular retriever in England, prized not only for its unsurpassed retrieving abilities but also as a staunch and trustworthy companion. It was among the first breeds to be exhibited at English dog shows. Exports to Australia and New Zealand were well received, and the breed still enjoys great popularity there. The first exports to America were in 1907, with the breed receiving AKC recognition in 1924. The breed

AKC Ranking: 129
Family: Gundog, Retriever
Area of Origin: England
Date of Origin: 1700s
Original Function: Water retrieving
Today's Function: Water retrieving, retriever field trials, companion
Other Name: None

never became particularly popular in America, however. Even popularity of the Curly in England waned during the 1900s. One theory about its fall in popularity is that several atypical Curlies gave the breed the undeserved reputation as hard-mouthed retrievers, causing newer hunters to choose other retrievers. Those who give the Curly a chance have found that the breed is actually quite soft-mouthed. They also find that it makes a versatile family companion.

Temperament

The Curly-Coated Retriever is an eager and tireless land and, especially, water retriever outdoors, but a calm companion indoors. It is sensitive and gentle, very good with children, and responsive to commands. It is reserved with strangers. One of the most courageous of the retrievers, it is nonetheless quite sensitive. It makes an ideal partner for an active, outdoor-oriented person who also wants a loyal family companion.

At a Glance

Energy level:	☐☐☐
Exercise requirements:	☐☐☐
Playfulness:	☐☐☐
Affection level:	☐☐☐
Friendliness toward dogs:	☐☐☐
Friendliness toward other pets:	☐☐☐☐
Friendliness toward strangers:	☐☐
Ease of training:	☐☐☐
Watchdog ability:	☐☐☐☐
Protection ability:	☐☐
Grooming requirements:	☐
Cold tolerance:	☐☐☐☐
Heat tolerance:	☐☐☐

Weight:	60–70 lb*
Height:	male: 25–27"; female: 23–25"

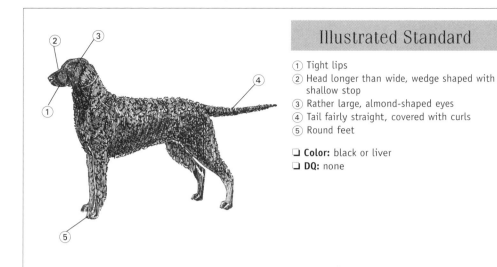

Illustrated Standard

① Tight lips
② Head longer than wide, wedge shaped with shallow stop
③ Rather large, almond-shaped eyes
④ Tail fairly straight, covered with curls
⑤ Round feet

❏ **Color:** black or liver
❏ **DQ:** none

Upkeep

The Curly is an easy dog to maintain, requiring no unusual care. It needs daily exercise, preferably involving swimming and retrieving. It can live outdoors in temperate weather, but it does best as an indoor–outdoor dog. Because brushing diminishes the tight curls, it should be combed only occasionally, preferably before getting wet. Some very minimal scissoring may be desirable to tidy up scraggly hairs. It does need regular brushing during its shedding seasons.

Health

• Major concerns: CHD
• Minor concerns: none
• Occasionally seen: distichiasis, cataract
• Suggested tests: hip
• Life span: 8–12 years

Form and Function

The Curly is the most graceful and elegant of the retrievers, appearing longer legged and more agile than the others. It has an alert upright carriage, enabling it to mark downed animals easily, be they fur or feather. It is an active land retriever and a hardy water retriever, able to withstand the rigors of repeated retrieves into heavy thickets or cold waters. Its distinctive coat provides protection from cold and briars and is made up of a dense mass of tight curls.

Flat-Coated Retriever

History

One of the earliest uses of retrieving dogs was to help fishermen retrieve fish and objects from the water. In the nineteenth century, such retrieving dogs were especially popular with the cod fisheries around Newfoundland. Of these dogs, the most popular breeds were the Labrador (not to be confused with the present Labrador Retriever) and several sizes of Newfoundlands. With the development of more advanced firearms, hunters were increasingly able to shoot "on the wing," but they needed a dog to mark the fallen bird and bring it back. The fishery dogs were unrivaled swimmers and natural retrievers, and crosses between them and British breeds such as setters or pointers honed the dog's bird sense. The result was the Wavy-Coated Retriever, and it became quite popular in America and England. In fact, it was among the earliest breeds to be shown at English dog shows. Near the end of the 1800s, crosses with a straighter-haired breed were made because the wavy coat was thought to be less water repellant. The resulting Flat-Coated Retrievers became tremendously popular. The breed was not recognized by the

AKC Ranking: 102
Family: Gundog, Retriever, Water Dog
Area of Origin: England
Date of Origin: 1800s
Original Function: Water retrieving
Today's Function: Water retrieving, retriever field trials
Other Name: None

AKC until 1915, by which time it had already begun to drop in popularity. By the end of the Second World War, the number of Flat-Coats had dwindled to the point that the breed was threatened with extinction. Concerted efforts to bring the breed back slowly succeeded, and the Flat-Coat now enjoys modest popularity.

Temperament

The Flat-Coated Retriever is a sweet, exuberant, lively dog that loves to play and retrieve. It is on the go outdoors, but quiet indoors. This breed is among the most devoted and companionable of dogs, a true family dog. It needs regular exercise to be on its best behavior, however. It is a sensitive breed and very responsive to training. Its hallmark is its wagging tail.

Upkeep

This active dog needs daily exercise and fun, and especially enjoys the chance to hunt or swim. This is a family-oriented dog that does best when allowed to live inside and play outside. Its coat needs only weekly brushing and little, if any, minor trimming occasionally.

Health

- Major concerns: none
- Minor concerns: CHD
- Occasionally seen: PRA, epilepsy, diabetes
- Suggested tests: (hip), (knee), (eye)
- Life span: 10–14 years

Form and Function

"Power without lumber and raciness without weediness" is the traditional description of the Flat-Coated Retriever. It is strong but elegant, never cobby, among the most streamlined of the retrievers. It is slightly longer than tall, of moderate substance. The head is distinctive, long and of "one piece," all parts flowing smoothly into each other. The gait is ground covering, smooth, and efficient. The coat is thick and flat, of only moderate length, providing protection without adding weight. These attributes have resulted in a versatile and athletic hunter capable of retrieving over land and water.

Illustrated Standard

① Long deep muzzle
② Long head with slight stop
③ Almond-shaped eyes
④ Small, hanging, thickly feathered ears
⑤ Fairly straight tail, carried near horizontal

❏ **Color:** solid black or liver
❏ **DQ:** any color other than black or liver

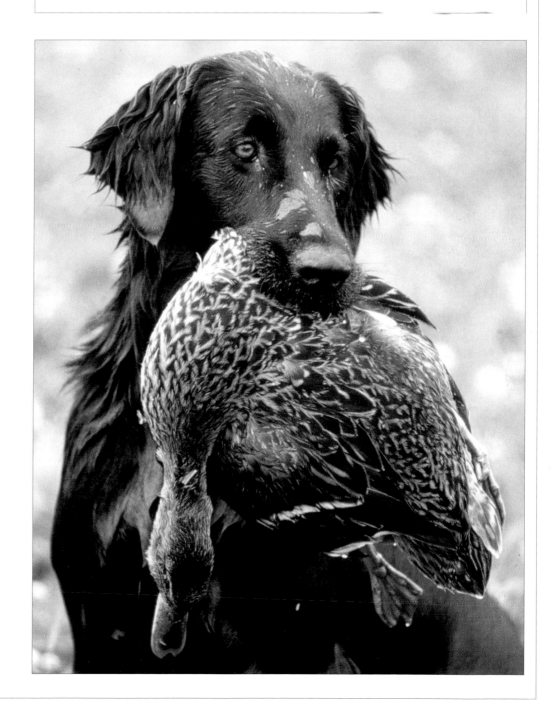

At a Glance

Energy level:	☐☐☐
Exercise requirements:	☐☐☐
Playfulness:	☐☐☐☐
Affection level:	☐☐☐☐☐
Friendliness toward dogs:	☐☐☐
Friendliness toward other pets:	☐☐☐☐
Friendliness toward strangers:	☐☐☐☐
Ease of training:	☐☐☐☐☐
Watchdog ability:	☐☐☐☐
Protection ability:	☐☐
Grooming requirements:	☐☐
Cold tolerance:	☐☐☐
Heat tolerance:	☐☐☐

Weight:	60–70 lb*
Height:	male: 23–24.5"; female: 22–23.5"

Golden Retriever

History

One of the best documented and most fortuitous efforts to produce a breed resulted in the Golden Retriever. The man responsible for the breed was Lord Tweedmouth, who lived just north of the Scottish border along the Tweed River. With an increasing interest in retrieving dogs in the mid 1800s, a dog that could push through heavy vegetation, brave cold water, swim strongly, and retrieve gently was in demand. Lord Tweedmouth bred Nous, a yellow Wavy-Coated Retriever (a descendent of the small Newfoundland and the earlier Labrador breeds used by fisherman) to Belle, a Tweed Water Spaniel (a popular liver-colored retriever with tightly curled coat). They produced four puppies, which showed promise of being outstanding upland bird dogs. Subsequent judicious crosses were made with other black retrievers, Tweed Spaniels, setters, and even a Bloodhound. The breed was first considered to be a yellow variety of Flat-Coated Retrievers, but was recognized as a separate breed, the Yellow or Golden Retriever, in 1912. A few of these dogs had

> AKC Ranking: 4
> Family: Gundog, Retriever
> Area of Origin: England
> Date of Origin: 1800s
> Original Function: Retrieving
> Today's Function: Retrieving, assistance, obedience competition, retriever field trials
> Other Name: Yellow Retriever

come to America by way of Lord Tweedmouth's sons by 1900, but the AKC did not register them as a separate breed until 1927. The breed was valued for the hunting abilities so ably produced by the careful blending of foundation stock. It only later became popular as a pet, show dog, and obedience competitor. After it made the transition, however, its rise to the height of popularity was meteoric, and it remains one of the most popular of all breeds in America.

Temperament

Everybody's friend, the Golden Retriever is known for its devoted and obedient nature as a family companion. It is an apt sporting retriever as well and yearns for a day in the field. Ignoring its active nature and powerful physique can lead to behavior problems, and it needs daily physical and mental exercise. It tends to be overly exuberant and boisterous, and its enthusiasm for everything often distracts it during training; however, it is eager to please and enjoys learning. The Golden's achievements in competitive obedience are remarkable. It especially enjoys games that involve retrieving and loves to carry items in its mouth.

Upkeep

The Golden Retriever needs daily exercise and human interaction. Challenging obedience lessons, active games, or retrieving sessions are all good ways to exercise the Golden's mind and body. Although it is capable of living outdoors, it is such a social dog that it is best when it shares its life with its family. The coat does not tend to mat but needs twice weekly brushing.

Health

- Major concerns: CHD, elbow dysplasia, cataract
- Minor concerns: entropion, distchiasis, trichiasis, cataract, pyotraumatic dermatitis, subvalvular aortic stenosis, OCD, allergies, vWD, cardiomyopathy
- Occasionally seen: gastric torsion, epilepsy, CPRA, osteosarcoma
- Suggested tests: hip, elbow, eye, cardiac, (blood)
- Life span: 10–13 years

Illustrated Standard

1. Stop well defined
2. Broad skull, slightly rounded
3. Rather short ears
4. Thick tail, carried near horizontal
5. Little tuck-up
6. Round feet

❏ **Color:** various shades of gold
❏ **DQ:** deviation from height of more than 1"; undershot or overshot bite

Form and Function

The Golden Retriever is an athletic, strong dog, capable of carrying heavy game over land and water. For this, it needs a broad, powerful head with strong neck and well-developed fore- and hindquarters. It is just slightly longer than tall. The gait is smooth, powerful, and ground covering. The water-repellant coat is dense, with the outer coat straight or wavy.

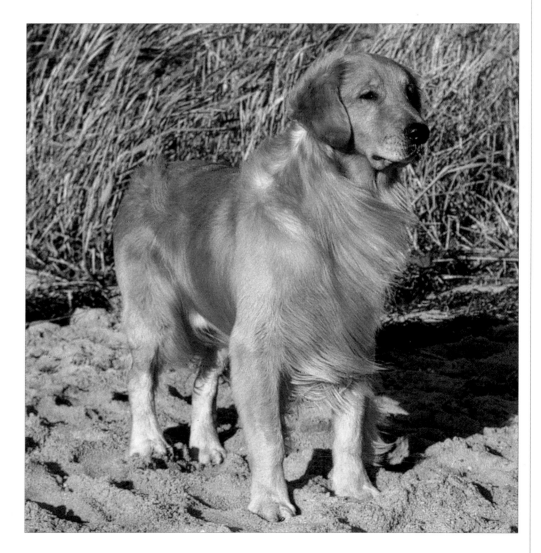

At a Glance

Energy level:	❏❏❏
Exercise requirements:	❏❏❏
Playfulness:	❏❏❏❏❏
Affection level:	❏❏❏❏❏
Friendliness toward dogs:	❏❏❏❏❏
Friendliness toward other pets:	❏❏❏❏❏
Friendliness toward strangers:	❏❏❏❏❏
Ease of training:	❏❏❏❏❏
Watchdog ability:	❏❏❏
Protection ability:	❏❏
Grooming requirements:	❏❏❏
Cold tolerance:	❏❏❏
Heat tolerance:	❏❏❏

Weight:	male: 65–75 lb; female: 55–65 lb
Height:	male: 23–24"; female: 21.5–22.5"

Labrador Retriever

History

The original Labradors were all-purpose
water dogs originating in Newfoundland,
not Labrador. Not only did the breed not
originate in Labrador, but it also was not
originally called the Labrador Retriever. The
Newfoundland of the early 1800s came in different sizes, one of which was the "Lesser" or
"St. John's" Newfoundland—the earliest incarnation of the Labrador. These dogs—medium-sized black dogs
with close hair—not only retrieved game but also retrieved fish,
pulled small fishing boats through icy water, and helped the fisherman in any task involving swimming. Eventually the breed died
out in Newfoundland in large part because of a heavy dog tax.
However, a core of Labradors had been taken to England in the
early 1800s, and it is from these dogs, along with crosses to other
retrievers, that the breed continued. It was also in England that
the breed earned its reputation as an extraordinary retriever of

AKC Ranking: 1
Family: Gundog, Retriever
Area of Origin: Canada
Date of Origin: 1800s
Original Function: Water retrieving
Today's Function: Water retrieving,
    assistance, obedience competition,
    retriever field trials
Other Name: None

upland game. Initially breeders favored black
Labs, and culled yellow or chocolate colors. By
the early 1900s, the other colors had become
acceptable, although still not as widely favored
as the blacks. The breed was recognized by the
English Kennel Club in 1903 and by the AKC in
1917. The popularity of this breed has grown
steadily until it became the most popular breed
in America in 1991 and remains so today.

Temperament

Few breeds so richly deserve their popularity as does the
Labrador Retriever. Devoted, obedient, and amiable, the Lab
is good with children, other dogs, and other pets. It will be a
calm housedog, playful yard dog, and intense field dog, all on
the same day. It is eager to please, enjoys learning, and excels
in obedience. It is á powerful breed that loves to swim and
retrieve. It needs daily physical and mental challenges to keep

it occupied, however; a bored Lab can get into trouble.

Upkeep

Labradors are active and sociable dogs. They need daily exercise, preferably in the form of retrieving and swimming. Owners with swimming pools either must fence them out or be prepared to share the pool with dog. The Lab coat sheds water easily. It needs weekly brushing to remove dead hair. Although Labs can live outdoors in temperate climates, they are much happier indoors with their family.

Health

- Major concerns: CHD, gastric torsion, retinal dysplasia/skeletal dwarfism, muscular dystrophy, elbow dysplasia
- Minor concerns: cataract, OCD, CPRA, pyotraumatic dermatitis
- Occasionally seen: diabetes, entropion, distichiasis
- Suggested tests: hip, elbow, eye
- Life span: 10–12 years

Form and Function

The Labrador is a moderate dog, not extreme in any way. It is square or

Illustrated Standard

① Kind, intelligent eyes
① Broad backskull with moderate stop
③ Tail very thick toward base, with a rounded "otter-like" appearance, carried in line with topline
④ Little or no tuck-up; short-coupled

❑ **Color:** solid black, yellow, or chocolate
❑ **DQ:** deviation from prescribed height; thoroughly pink or pigmentless nose or eye rims; alteration of length or carriage of tail; any color other than solid black, yellow, or chocolate (a small white spot on the chest is permissible)

slightly longer than tall, of fairly large bone and substance. Its broad head and strong jaws should enable it to carry the largest game birds, such as Canada geese. Its heavy body set and strong legs enable it to swim and run powerfully. Its coat, which is short, straight, and dense with a soft undercoat, is weatherproof and helps to protect it from icy waters. The Lab is a working retriever and should possess style without over refinement and substance without clumsiness.

At a Glance

Energy level:	❑❑❑❑
Exercise requirements:	❑❑❑
Playfulness:	❑❑❑❑❑
Affection level:	❑❑❑❑❑
Friendliness toward dogs:	❑❑❑❑
Friendliness toward other pets:	❑❑❑❑❑
Friendliness toward strangers:	❑❑❑❑❑
Ease of training:	❑❑❑❑❑
Watchdog ability:	❑❑❑❑
Protection ability:	❑❑
Grooming requirements:	❑❑
Cold tolerance:	❑❑❑❑
Heat tolerance:	❑❑❑

Weight: male: 65–80 lb; female: 55–70 lb
Height: male: 22.5–24.5"; female: 21.5–23.5"

English Setter

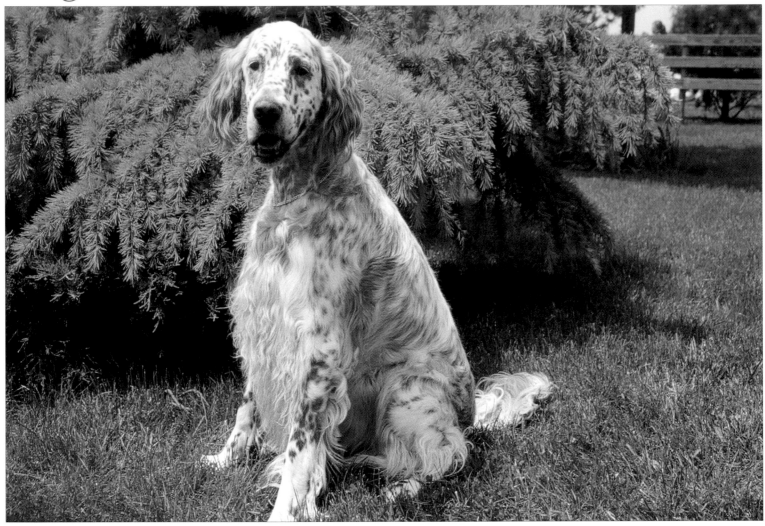

History

Even before the advent of the shotgun, when birds were often caught with a net, dogs were trained to crouch when they pointed game. These "setters" were the forerunners of today's setters. The English Setter is the oldest known of this group, perhaps dating back to the fourteenth century. It was developed to locate game on the moors and then to freeze until the game was dispatched. The English Setter's ancestors probably included the Spanish Pointer, Springer Spaniel, and large Water Spaniel. The cultivation of the English Setter through concerted pure breeding was undertaken by Edward Laverack beginning around 1825 and continuing for over 35 years. These dogs formed the basis of all English Setters today. Incidentally, the term *belton* was coined by Laverack to describe the roan or ticked flecks of color and comes from the town of Belton, where Laverack hunted. The other most influential breeder, Purcell Llewellin, obtained his foundation stock from Laverack but based his breeding on field

AKC Ranking: 86
Family: Gundog, Setter, Pointer
Area of Origin: England
Date of Origin: 1300s
Original Function: Bird setting & retrieving
Today's Function: Pointing, pointing field trials
Other Name: None

ability alone. Llewellin crossed his Laveracks with unrelated English Setters to produce such outstanding field dogs that many were imported to America. The Laverack and Llewellin setters diverged, with the Laverack providing the foundation for the show setters and the Llewellin forming the foundation for the field setters. Both types have enjoyed steady popularity in America.

Temperament

Bred to cover a lot of area when hunting, the English Setter is a lively dog that loves to hunt and run. This is especially true of dogs from field lines. If not given sufficient exercise, they can be overly lively inside, but with daily exertion, they are calm and tractable housedogs. Those from conformation lines are particularly laid back and gentle and excel with children and less active adults. This is an amiable, easygoing breed that gets along well with children, strangers, and other dogs.

At a Glance

Energy level:	☐☐☐☐
Exercise requirements:	☐☐☐☐
Playfulness:	☐☐☐
Affection level:	☐☐☐☐
Friendliness toward dogs:	☐☐☐
Friendliness toward other pets:	☐☐☐☐
Friendliness toward strangers:	☐☐☐☐☐
Ease of training:	☐☐☐
Watchdog ability:	☐☐☐☐
Protection ability:	☐☐
Grooming requirements:	☐☐☐
Cold tolerance:	☐☐☐
Heat tolerance:	☐☐☐

Weight:	male: 60–65 lb; female: 50–55 lb* (field types about 10 lb less)
Height:	male: about 25"; female: about 24"

Illustrated Standard

① Muzzle long and square, with fairly pendant flews
② Head long and lean with a well-defined stop
③ Eyes large and nearly round
④ Occiput moderately defined
⑤ Lowset ears
⑥ Topline level or sloping slightly to rear
⑦ Tail carried straight, and level with topline, tapering to a fine point

❏ **Color:** orange, liver, lemon, or black ("blue") flecks over a white ground color; also a combination of black and tan flecks on white ("tricolor"). Liver and lemon colors are rarely seen today. Puppies are born white, except for those with solid patches.
❏ **DQ:** none

backs of legs, underside of thighs, and tail. Its markings are distinctive, consisting of flecks of color, sometimes with patches, on a white background. The combination of good looks and hunting ability make the English Setter a perfect gentleman's hunting companion. The Laveracks tend to be larger, carry more feathering, often have deeper muzzle, and usually hold their tails nearly level when on point. The Llewellins tend to be smaller, faster, with less coat and often larger patches of color. They tend to hold their tails straight up when on point.

Upkeep

The English Setter needs a lot of exercise every day, requiring at least an hour of hard exertion. It is best when it can live inside and play outside. The long coat needs regular brushing every two or three days. The white coat may be difficult to keep gleaming in some areas. Some clipping and trimming every month or two is advisable for optimal good looks.

Health

• Major concerns: deafness, CHD, elbow dysplasia
• Minor concerns: PRA, OCD
• Occasionally seen: epilepsy
• Suggested tests: hip, elbow, hearing, eye
• Life span: 10–14 years

Form and Function

The English Setter is an elegant and athletic hunting dog with the ability to run tirelessly at a good pace. Its trot is ground covering and effortless, with the head held proudly and a lively tail. The coat is flat, with feathering on the ears, underside,

Gordon Setter

History

Black and Tan Setters existed in Scotland at least by the 1600s, but it was not until the late 1700s that the breed became established as the Gordon Castle Setter. The Fourth Duke of Gordon kept many of these dogs at his Gordon Castle, thus lending the breed its name. Efforts to breed the finest setters at Gordon Castle continued through the efforts of the Duke of Richmond after the Fourth Duke's death. Although the breed's name was changed back to Black and Tan Setter around 1900, the name Gordon Setter was restored when the English Kennel Club registered the breed. Gordon Setters are the heaviest and slowest working of the setter breeds, and this distinction was accentuated when Gordons first entered the show ring. In 1875, the trend toward an overly ponderous show Gordon was halted largely through the efforts of one man, Robert Chapman. Unlike many sporting breeds, little division between show- and field-type

AKC Ranking: 79
Family: Gundog, Setter, Pointer
Area of Origin: Great Britain
  (Scotland)
Date of Origin: 1600s
Original Function: Bird setting &
  retrieving
Today's Function: Pointing, pointing
  field trials
Other Name: None

Gordons exists. Gordon Setters first arrived in America in the middle 1800s and were among the first breeds recognized by the AKC, receiving the nod in 1892. The breed is a favorite among hunters demanding a one-man shooting dog, though it generally lacks the flash and speed of the other setter breeds. Although it has a steady following, it has never been as popular as the other setters as a pet.

Temperament

The Gordon Setter is a capable, close-working bird dog. It can run and hunt all day, and this kind of energy needs a regular outlet or the dog is apt to become frustrated. Gordons make lively, enthusiastic companions, and need the company of lively people. Somewhat more protective than the other setters, it is reserved toward strangers and sometimes aggressive toward strange dogs. The Gordon has earned its reputation as a devoted family dog.

Upkeep

The Gordon needs much strenuous exercise every day in order to stay in shape. It can live outdoors in temperate climates, but it must be able to spend ample time with people and does best dividing its time between inside and outside. Its coat needs regular brushing and combing every two to three days. In addition, some clipping and trimming is needed for optimal good looks.

Health

• Major concerns: CHD, gastric torsion
• Minor concerns: PRA, elbow dysplasia
• Occasionally seen: cerebellar abiotrophy
• Suggested tests: hip, elbow, eye
• Life span: 10–12 years

Form and Function

The heaviest of the setters, the Gordon is sturdily built with plenty of substance and bone. The suggestion should be one of strength and stamina rather than speed. It is square-proportioned, upstanding and stylish. The gait is bold, smooth, and effortless, with head carried proudly and tail constantly flagging. The Gordon Setter

Illustrated Standard

1 Well-defined stop
2 Low-set ears
3 Short from shoulder to hips
4 Tail carried near horizontal, tapering
5 Cat feet
6 Pronounced forechest

❑ **Color:** black and tan
❑ **DQ:** predominantly tan, red, or buff dogs lacking the typical black and tan markings

carries a thicker coat than the other setters. The hair is straight or slightly wavy, always soft and shiny. Longer feathering is on the ears, underside, backs of legs, and tail. The whole impression should be of a rugged dog capable of withstanding a long, active day in the field under a variety of conditions.

At a Glance

Energy level:	❑❑❑❑
Exercise requirements:	❑❑❑❑
Playfulness:	❑❑❑
Affection level:	❑❑❑❑
Friendliness toward dogs:	❑❑
Friendliness toward other pets:	❑❑❑❑
Friendliness toward strangers:	❑❑
Ease of training:	❑❑❑
Watchdog ability:	❑❑❑❑
Protection ability:	❑❑❑
Grooming requirements:	❑❑❑
Cold tolerance:	❑❑❑
Heat tolerance:	❑❑❑

Weight:	male: 55–80 lb; female: 45–70 lb
Height:	male: 24–27"; female: 23–26"

Irish Setter

History

The precise origins of the Irish Setter are
obscure, but the most reasonable theories
consider it to have resulted from a blend of
spaniels, pointers, and other setters—mostly
the English but, to a lesser extent, the Gordon.
Irish hunters needed a fast-working, keen-
nosed dog, large enough to be seen from a
distance. They found their dog in the red and
white setters produced from these crosses. The first kennels of
solid red setters appeared around 1800. In only a few years,
these dogs had gained a reputation for their rich mahogany color.
By the mid 1800s, Irish Red Setters (as they were originally
known) had come to America, proving themselves as effective
on American game birds as Irish ones. Back in Ireland, around
1862, a dog that was to forever change the breed, Champion
Palmerston, was born. With an unusually long head and slender
build, he was considered too refined for the field, so his owner
ordered him drowned. Another fancier interceded, and the dog
became a sensation as a show dog, going on to sire an incredible
number of offspring. Virtually every modern Irish Setter can be

AKC Ranking: 59
Family: Gundog, Setter, Pointer
Area of Origin: Ireland
Date of Origin: 1700s
Original Function: Bird setting &
  retrieving
Today's Function: Pointing, pointing
  field trials
Other Name: Red Setter

traced to Palmerston. Interest changed from
field trials to dog shows, and emphasis changed
from hunting ability to glamour. Despite this,
the Irish Setter remained a capable hunter, and
dedicated breeders took steps to retain the
breed's dual abilities. The breed increased principally in popularity as a show dog, however,
and later as a pet. It eventually rose to a place
among the most popular breeds in America in
the 1970s, but has since plummeted in the rankings.

Temperament

The Irish Setter was bred to be a tireless and enthusiastic hunter,
and it approaches everything in life with a rollicking, good
natured attitude, full of gusto and fervor. Given a daily outlet
for its energy, it makes a pleasant companion. Without ample
exercise, it can be overly active inside or become frustrated.
It is an amiable breed, eager to please and be part of its family's
activities. It is good with children, but can be too rambunctious
for small children. It is less popular as a hunter than the other
setters.

Upkeep

The Irish needs exercise, and lots of it. It is not fair to take a dog selected for boundless energy and expect it to sit inside. A minimum of one hour of hard strenuous games and exertion a day is recommended. Because of its energy, it is not suited as an apartment dog. It can live outside in temperate or warm weather, but it needs warm shelter and needs to come inside in colder weather. It is such a sociable dog that it does best living with its family. The coat needs regular brushing and combing every two to three days, plus some clipping and trimming to looks its best.

Health

- Major concerns: PRA, CHD, gastric torsion
- Minor concerns: epilepsy, megaesophagus, OCD, panosteitis, HOD
- Occasionally seen: OCD, epilepsy, hemophilia A
- Suggested tests: DNA for PRA, hip, eye, cardiac
- Life span: 12–14 years
- Note: With the advent of DNA testing for PRA, this problem should no longer be a concern if both parents have been tested.

Illustrated Standard

1. Muzzle moderately deep
2. Medium-size, almond-shaped eyes
3. Long, lean head with distinct stop and well-defined occiput
4. Low-set ears
5. Topline slopes to rear
6. Tail carried straight or slightly curving upward, nearly level with the back
7. Small feet

❏ **Color:** mahogany or rich chestnut red
❏ **DQ:** none

Form and Function

Among the most breathtaking of dogs, the Irish Setter's beauty is in part the result of necessity. Its elegant, yet substantial build enables it to hunt with speed and stamina. Its build is slightly longer than tall, giving ample room for movement without interference between fore and hind legs. The trot is ground covering and efficient. The coat is flat, straight, and of moderate length, with longer feathering on ears, backs of legs, belly, chest, and tail, providing protection from briars without becoming entangled in them. The rich mahogany color is just beautiful.

At a Glance

Energy level:	☐☐☐☐☐
Exercise requirements:	☐☐☐☐☐
Playfulness:	☐☐☐☐☐
Affection level:	☐☐☐☐☐
Friendliness toward dogs:	☐☐☐☐
Friendliness toward other pets:	☐☐☐☐
Friendliness toward strangers:	☐☐☐☐☐
Ease of training:	☐☐☐
Watchdog ability:	☐☐☐
Protection ability:	☐
Grooming requirements:	☐☐☐
Cold tolerance:	☐☐☐
Heat tolerance:	☐☐☐

Weight: male: about 70 lb; female: about 60 lb
Height: male: about 27"; female: about 25"

American Water Spaniel

History

Exactly when and where, or from what the American Water Spaniel was developed was never recorded. Its appearance strongly suggests a smaller version of the Irish Water Spaniel, and it is likely that it is derived from that breed or its earlier versions, the Northern, Southern, and Tweed Water Spaniels. The Curly-Coated Retriever and its forebear, the English Water Spaniel, may also have played a role. Some theories even credit the American Indians who lived in the Great Lakes regions as the creators of the breed. Whatever its origin, the American Water Spaniel first became established as a recognizable breed in the midwestern parts of the United States, where it was unsurpassed as a hunting companion. This small dog with the waterproof coat and keen nose could hunt through rough thickets, spring game, and retrieve all manner of game from land and water, often marking several fallen birds before retrieving them all unfailingly. Until it was recognized by the AKC in 1940, no one ever considered breeding these dogs for anything but hunting ability. Even after recognition, the breed's forte

AKC Ranking: 117
Family: Gundog, Water Dog, Spaniel
Area of Origin: United States
Date of Origin: 1800s
Original Function: Bird flushing & retrieving
Today's Function: Bird flushing & retrieving, spaniel field trials
Other Name: None

remained in the field, and it is a rarity in the show ring or even the home. Today the American Water Spaniel is among the least known of AKC recognized breeds, despite being one of only two sporting breeds developed in America. In fact, the American Water Spaniel is the State Dog of Wisconsin.

Temperament

As its name implies, the American Water Spaniel is a natural lover of water. Not only is it a skilled retriever and versatile hunter, but it is also a tractable fun-loving family dog—as long as it gets regular physical and mental exercise. It is sensitive and willing to please. Some can be timid. Generally good with other dogs in the household, some are aggressive toward strange dogs. Barking can be a definite problem; some also whine or drool.

Upkeep

Like all hunting dogs, the American Water Spaniel needs daily exercise, although these requirements can be met with a long

At a Glance

Energy level:	☐☐☐☐
Exercise requirements:	☐☐☐
Playfulness:	☐☐☐☐
Affection level:	☐☐☐
Friendliness toward dogs:	☐☐
Friendliness toward other pets:	☐☐☐
Friendliness toward strangers:	☐☐
Ease of training:	☐☐☐
Watchdog ability:	☐☐☐☐
Protection ability:	☐☐☐
Grooming requirements:	☐☐☐
Cold tolerance:	☐☐☐
Heat tolerance:	☐☐☐

Weight:	male: 30–45 lb; female: 25–40 lb
Height:	15–18"

Illustrated Standard

1. Slightly rounded eyes, color harmonizing with coat
2. Broad skull, stop moderately defined
3. Long, wide ears
4. Tail curved in a rocker fashion, carried near the level of the back

❏ **Color:** solid liver, brown, or dark chocolate
❏ **DQ:** yellow eyes

walk. The coat is oily and needs weekly brushing. Hair may be clipped from the feet and topknot. Ears should be checked regularly.

Health

- Major concerns: none
- Minor concerns: lenticular opacities, CHD
- Occasionally seen: patellar luxation, PRA
- Suggested tests: (hip), (eye)
- Life span: 10–12 years

Form and Function

The American Water Spaniel packs a lot of ability into a comparatively small dog. Its muzzle is long and strong enough to carry a large goose, and it has strong quarters to propel it through water and over land. It is slightly longer than tall, solidly built and muscular. The coat can range from uniform waves (marcel) to close curls, with a dense undercoat. This combination provides protection against weather, water, or briars. The ears are well covered with hair, which should not grow into the ear canal. The gait is balanced, with reach and drive.

Clumber Spaniel

History

The stockiest of the spaniels, the Clumber is also one of the oldest, dating to the late 1700s. Although the exact derivation of the breed is unknown, it is likely that the old heavy-headed Alpine Spaniel and the low-bodied Basset Hound played prominent roles in its development. The breed did not get its name until around the time of the French Revolution, when it is believed that the Duc de Noailles of France moved his spaniel kennels to the Duke of Newcastle's English estate, Clumber Park. Clumber Spaniels appealed to the English nobility, who appreciated this slow-moving but especially keen-nosed hunter that was also an adept retriever. The breed was not readily available to commoners because the nobility discouraged its popularity except among high-er society. As befitting their high status, Clumbers were among the earliest breeds to be shown. They came to America in the late 1800s. Their popularity has remained strongest in the field, although Clumbers have attained high show honors. They remain

AKC Ranking: 122
Family: Gundog, Spaniel
Area of Origin: England
Date of Origin: 1700s
Original Function: Bird flushing & retrieving
Today's Function: Bird flushing & retrieving, spaniel field trials
Other Name: None

generally unknown to the public despite their many attributes.

Temperament

Among the most low-keyed and easygoing of sporting breeds, the Clumber Spaniel is nonetheless a hunter at heart, ever ready for a day in the field. At home it tends to be quiet and may even need to be goaded into exercise. It is one of the few sporting breeds suitable for city life, although it will relish walks and outings. The Clumber makes a good pet, especially devoted to one person.

Upkeep

The Clumber enjoys a daily outing, but its exercise requirements can be met with a long walk on leash or a leisurely hike in the field. The coat needs brushing two to three times weekly, although in dirty areas it may need more frequent bathing in order to keep its coat a gleaming white. Clumbers tend to drool and, at times, snore.

Health

- Major concerns: CHD, entropion
- Minor concerns: intervertebral disc problems, ectropion
- Occasionally seen: epilepsy
- Suggested tests: hip, eye
- Life span: 10–12 years

Form and Function

The Clumber Spaniel is a long, low dog, rectangular in shape and with massive bone. This build, in combination with a deep chest, heavy brow, and powerful hindquarters, enables the dog to move through thick underbrush when hunting. The coat is straight, flat, soft, and dense, imparting resistance to weather. The white color helps the hunter locate the dog. The Clumber tends to hunt close. It moves easily, tending to roll slightly because of its wide body and short legs. The expression is soft.

Illustrated Standard

1. Well-developed flews
2. Nose colored any shade of brown
3. Eyes large, deep-set, diamond shaped; some haw may show
4. Pronounced stop and occiput
5. Massive head
6. Low-set ears
7. Tail docked and carried near horizontal*
8. Large feet

❏ **Color:** white dog with lemon or orange markings (the fewer the markings on body, the better)
❏ **DQ:** none

* Clumbers in some European countries may have undocked tails.

At a Glance

Energy level:	❏❏
Exercise requirements:	❏❏
Playfulness:	❏❏❏
Affection level:	❏❏❏❏
Friendliness toward dogs:	❏❏❏
Friendliness toward other pets:	❏❏❏❏
Friendliness toward strangers:	❏❏❏
Ease of training:	❏❏❏
Watchdog ability:	❏❏
Protection ability:	❏
Grooming requirements:	❏❏❏
Cold tolerance:	❏❏❏
Heat tolerance:	❏❏

Weight:	male: 70–85 lb; female: 55–70 lb
Height:	male: 19–20"; female: 17–19"

American Cocker Spaniel

History

The American version of the Cocker Spaniel is derived from the English Cocker Spaniel. In the late 1800s, many English Cockers were brought to America, but American hunters preferred a slightly smaller dog to hunt quail and other small game birds. Just how this smaller Cocker was developed is not entirely clear; some credit the dog Obo 2nd, born around 1880, as the first true American Cocker. But other evidence points to crosses of the English Cocker with even smaller toy spaniels (that nonetheless arose from the same ancestral stock). Initially the English and American Cocker Spaniels were considered varieties of the same breed, but they were officially separated by the AKC in 1935. Although Cockers were already popular, after the separation the American Cocker surged in popularity and has remained one of the most popular breeds of all time in America. In fact, it was the most popular breed for many years. So popular was it that it was eventually divided into three color varieties: black, particolor, and ASCOB, which stands for Any Solid Color Other than Black. Only recently has its popularity spread to

AKC Ranking: 8
Family: Gundog, Spaniel
Area of Origin: United States
Date of Origin: 1800s
Original Function: Bird flushing & retrieving
Today's Function: Spaniel field trials
Other Name: Cocker Spaniel

England, where it was recognized by the English Kennel Club in 1968, and it has gained admirers steadily since.

Temperament

This breed is known as the "merry" Cocker, and the name is most fitting. It is playful, cheerful, amiable, sweet, sensitive, willing to please, and responsive to its family's wishes. It is not known for retaining its hunting instincts, but it is inquisitive and will appreciate a country outing. It is equally at home in the city and will happily walk on leash for its exercise needs. Some bark a lot; some are overly submissive.

Upkeep

Although it enjoys a romp, the Cocker can receive adequate exercise with a long daily walk on leash. The coat of the Cocker requires a greater commitment than that of most breeds, although pets can be clipped short. In order to maintain a nice coat, it will need to be brushed and combed two to three times a week, in addition to professional clipping and scissoring every two to three months.

Special attention must be paid to ear and eye cleanliness in this breed. The profusely coated feet tend to carry debris. The Cocker is physically able to live outside in temperate climates (given adequate shelter), but it is not mentally able to do so; this is such a social dog that to banish it outdoors would not be acceptable. Cockers have a tendency to become overweight.

Health
- Major concerns: cataracts, glaucoma, patellar luxation
- Minor concerns: CHD, ectropion, entropion, PRA, allergies, seborrhea, lip fold pyoderma, otitis externa, liver disease, urolithiasis, prolapse of nictitans gland, CHF, phosphofructokinase deficiency, cardiomyopathy
- Occasionally seen: gastric torsion, elbow dysplasia
- Suggested tests: eye, knee, DNA for phosphofructokinase deficiency, (hip)
- Life span: 12–15 years

Form and Function
The smallest member of the Sporting Group, the Cocker should be compact and

❏ **DQ:** males over 15.5"; females over 14.5"; colors other than those specified; white markings (other than on the chest and throat) in the black or ASCOB; primary color of more than 90% in the particolor in tan-pointed dogs, absence of tan markings in any normally tan-marked places or tan markings in excess of 10%

Illustrated Standard
① Expression alert, soft, and appealing
② Rounded skull with pronounced stop
③ Long, low-set, lobular ears
④ Topline slopes slightly to rear
⑤ Tail docked and carried in line or slightly higher than the topline
⑥ Round feet

❏ **Color:** Black variety: solid black or black and tan; ASCOB variety: any solid color other than black, including cream, red, brown, and brown with tan points; Particolor variety: any of the allowed solid colors broken up on a white background; also roans

sturdy. Its gait is ground covering, strong, and effortless. The coat is silky, flat or slightly wavy, not overly long. Excessive coat can hinder the dog in the field. The head and expression are hallmarks of the breed; the expression is soft and appeal- ing. Though seldom used for its original purpose, the Cocker should still be able to spend a day in the field and should be balanced and athletic. It is true, however, that most Cockers now have too much coat for field work.

At a Glance

Energy level:	☐☐☐
Exercise requirements:	☐☐☐
Playfulness:	☐☐☐☐
Affection level:	☐☐☐☐☐
Friendliness toward dogs:	☐☐☐☐☐
Friendliness toward other pets:	☐☐☐☐
Friendliness toward strangers:	☐☐☐☐
Ease of training:	☐☐☐
Watchdog ability:	☐☐☐☐
Protection ability:	☐
Grooming requirements:	☐☐☐☐
Cold tolerance:	☐☐☐
Heat tolerance:	☐☐☐

Weight:	24–28 lb*
Height:	male: 14.5–15.5"; female: 13.5–14.5"

English Cocker Spaniel

History

The spaniel family is one of the largest groups of dogs, and one of the most specialized. The English Cocker Spaniel is one of the land spaniels. The land spaniels consisted of larger spaniels that were better for springing game, and smaller spaniels that were better for hunting woodcock. These different sizes appeared in the same litters and were essentially two variations of the same breed. Only in 1892 were the two sizes considered separate breeds, with the smaller size (under 25 lb) designated as the Cocker Spaniel. In fact, because both breeds shared the same gene pool, they still share many of the same hunting talents. In 1901, the weight limit was abolished. Cocker Spaniels became extremely pop-

AKC Ranking: 75
Family: Gundog, Spaniel
Area of Origin: England
Date of Origin: 1800s
Original Function: Bird flushing & retrieving
Today's Function: Bird flushing & retrieving, spaniel field trials
Other Name: Cocker Spaniel

ular in England, but American breeders strove to change the breed in ways that traditional English Cocker Spaniel enthusiasts objected to. English and American Cocker Spaniels were shown together until 1936, when English Cocker Spaniel Club of America was formed and the English Cocker received status as a separate variety. The English Cocker Spaniel Club discouraged the interbreeding of the American and English Cockers, and in 1946 the English Cocker was designated a separate breed. After the breeds were separated, the American Cocker eclipsed the English in popularity—but only in America. Throughout the rest of the world, the English Cocker is by far the more popular of the two breeds and is known simply as the Cocker Spaniel.

At a Glance

Energy level:	☐☐☐
Exercise requirements:	☐☐☐
Playfulness:	☐☐☐☐
Affection level:	☐☐☐☐☐
Friendliness toward dogs:	☐☐☐☐☐
Friendliness toward other pets:	☐☐☐☐☐
Friendliness toward strangers:	☐☐☐☐
Ease of training:	☐☐☐☐
Watchdog ability:	☐☐☐☐
Protection ability:	☐☐
Grooming requirements:	☐☐☐
Cold tolerance:	☐☐☐
Heat tolerance:	☐☐☐

Weight:	male: 28–34 lb; female: 26–32 lb
Height:	male: 16–17"; female: 15–16"

Temperament

The English Cocker Spaniel retains more of its hunting nature than does the American version, and it also needs a little more exercise. It is cheerful, inquisitive, demonstrative, devoted, biddable, loyal, and sensitive. This is a sociable dog that likes to stay close to its human family.

Upkeep

Daily exercise is a necessity, either in the form of a long walk on leash, a good run in the field, or a lively game in the yard. Although the English Cocker could physically live outside in temperate to warm weather, it is such a social dog that it does best living inside and playing outside. The medium-length coat needs brushing two to three times per week, plus clipping around the head and ears scissoring around the feet and tail every two months. The ears should be cleaned weekly.

Health

- Major concerns: PRA
- Minor concerns: cataracts, CHD, familial nephropathy
- Occasionally seen: glaucoma, cardiomyopathy

- Suggested tests: hearing (for particolors), eye, hip, (knee)
- Life span: 12–14 years
- Note: deafness is a major concern in particolors; CHD is more common in solid colors; PRA is of PRCD type

Form and Function

The English Cocker must be able to find, flush, and retrieve upland game birds for a full day of hunting. It must be small enough to penetrate dense cover, but of sufficient size to retrieve larger game. The broad muzzle helps when retrieving.

Illustrated Standard

1. Slightly oval eyes
2. Slightly flattened skull, with moderate stop
3. Softly contoured head, with soft expression
4. Low-set ears
5. Topline slopes slightly to rear
6. Docked tail, carried horizontally
7. Cat feet

❏ **Color:** solid black, liver, or red, black and tan, liver and tan, and any of these colors on a white background either particolored, ticked, or roan.
❏ **DQ:** none

The dog is slightly taller than long, compactly built, and short coupled. This breed loves to hunt and shows it by the wagging of its tail when on the job. The English Cocker has a driving, powerful gait that covers ground effortlessly. The coat is of medium length, silky in texture, and either flat or slightly wavy. The feathering should not be so profuse that it becomes a hindrance in the field, but it should be long enough to protect the underside of the dog. The expression is soft and melting, yet dignified.

English Springer Spaniel

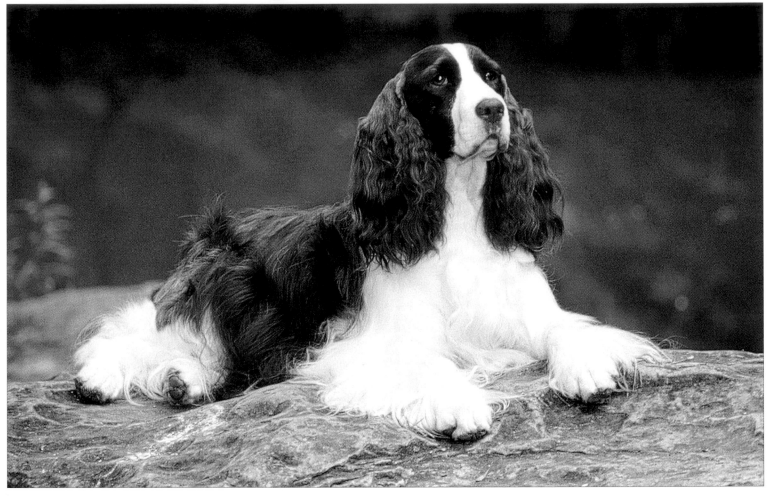

History

As the spaniels became increasingly special-ized, the larger land spaniels that ranged far-ther afield became extremely useful at flushing or "springing" game. Before the advent of shot-guns, the game was flushed into nets or then chased by falcons or Greyhounds. The first ref-erence to springers referred to land spaniels in the late 1500s. Around 1800, distinct strains of carefully bred springers began to develop; one of the best known were those bred by the Duke of Norfolk. His dogs so heavily influ-enced the breed that for a while the breed was called Norfolk Spaniels. The name was changed to Springer Spaniel in 1900. The matter is complicated by the fact that the larger Springer and smaller Cocker Spaniels were simply size variations of the same breed. Only in 1902 did the English Kennel Club recognize the Springer as a distinct breed. In America, the American Spaniel Club was formed in 1880 and began the task of separating the Springer and Cocker sizes. After separation, the Springer contin-ued to thrive. It has remained popular with hunters demanding a versatile gundog that ranges fast snd far and that can also flush

AKC Ranking: 25
Family: Gundog, Spaniel
Area of Origin: England
Date of Origin: 1800s
Original Function: Bird flushing & retrieving
Today's Function: Bird flushing & retrieving, spaniel field trials
Other Name: None

and retrieve. It is also a popular show dog and pet.

Temperament

The English Springer Spaniel is cheerful, play-ful, and energetic, ready for a day in the field and an evening by the hearth. It does every-thing with gusto and can be overly enthusiastic unless given plenty of exercise. The typical Springer is the ideal family companion.

Upkeep

As an energetic and inquisitive dog, the Springer needs daily mental and physical exertion. Hunting is the first choice to satisfy both needs, but an outing in the field, long walk on leash, and good obedience lesson can go far to making the Springer a calm and well-behaved house dog. This breed does best if allowed to live in the house with access to a yard. Its coat needs brushing or combing one or two times weekly plus clipping and scissoring every three months. Springers from field, rather than show, lines tend to have less coat.

Health

- Major concerns: otitis externa, CHD, PRA, elbow dysplasia
- Minor concerns: ectropion, entropion
- Occasionally seen: phosphofructokinase deficiency, skin fragility, gastric torsion, rage syndrome
- Suggested tests: hip, elbow, eye, DNA for phosphofructokinase deficiency
- Life span: 10–14 years

Form and Function

The English Springer Spaniel is compactly built, upstanding with proud carriage, slightly longer than tall but with fairly long legs and a deep body. Its build should suggest a combination of strength, agility, and endurance, a dog capable of hunting tirelessly under the most difficult of conditions. The outer coat is medium length, either flat or wavy, and the undercoat is soft and dense. This combination protects the dog from weather, water, and thorns. The gait is long and ground covering. The expression—alert, kindly, and trusting—is an essential feature of Springer type.

Illustrated Standard

1. Full lips
2. Oval eyes of medium size
3. Moderate stop
4. Long ears
5. Topline slopes slightly to rear
6. Docked tail carried horizontally or slightly elevated

❏ **Color:** black or liver with white, black or liver roan, or tricolored (black or liver and white with tan markings); also white with black or liver markings
❏ **DQ:** none

At a Glance

Energy level:	▢▢▢◻
Exercise requirements:	▢▢▢◻
Playfulness:	▢▢▢◻
Affection level:	▢▢▢▢▢
Friendliness toward dogs:	▢▢◻
Friendliness toward other pets:	▢▢▢◻
Friendliness toward strangers:	▢▢▢◻
Ease of training:	▢▢▢▢▢
Watchdog ability:	▢▢▢◻
Protection ability:	▢◻
Grooming requirements:	▢▢▢◻
Cold tolerance:	▢▢◻
Heat tolerance:	▢▢◻

Weight: male: about 50 lb; female: about 40 lb
Height: male: 19–21"; female 18–20"

Field Spaniel

History

The Field Spaniel shares its early history with the English Cocker Spaniel, the only difference between the two breeds initially being one of size. The Field Spaniel was composed of those land spaniels weighing over 25 pounds. These larger Field Spaniels were derived from the Cocker, Sussex, and English Water Spaniels and were initially required to be black. After becoming recognized as a separate breed in the late 1800s, the Field Spaniel succumbed to breeding for exaggeration, and the repeated infusion of Sussex Spaniel blood resulted in dogs of excessive length, overly heavy bones, and short legs. The breed lost its usefulness as a hunter, and although it enjoyed a short vogue in the early 1900s, it ultimately teetered on the brink of extinction. Crosses to English Springer Spaniels were made in an effort to recreate the original Field Spaniel. The crosses were successful, and the modern Field Spaniel is not only a handsome replica of its former self but also an able hunter. All modern Field Spaniels can be traced back to four Field Spaniels from the 1950s: Ronayne Regal, Gormac Teal, Colombina of Teffont, and Elmbury

AKC Ranking: 135
Family: Gundog, Spaniel
Area of Origin: England
Date of Origin: 1800s
Original Function: Bird flushing & retrieving
Today's Function: Bird flushing & retrieving, spaniel field trials
Other Name: None

Morwena of Rhiwlas. Despite the fact that Field Spaniels were being shown in America in the late 1800s, no champions were made up between 1916 and 1966; in fact, the breed was essentially extinct in America for much of that time. The breed was reintroduced into America in the late 1960s. The Field Spaniel remains among the rarest of breeds in America.

Temperament

The Field Spaniel is happiest when it has a job to do. Although independent in nature, it is devoted, sensitive, and willing to please. Always cheerful and affectionate, it is an excellent family companion as long as it is given regular exercise. The Field Spaniel is especially known for its tractable nature. It is typical for a Field Spaniel to be somewhat reserved with strangers.

Upkeep

The Field Spaniel needs daily exercise, and even though it is happiest when given the chance to run and explore, its needs can be met with a long walk on leash. It can live outside in temperate climates if given warm shelter, but it does best when allowed to divide its time between house and yard. It thrives on human companionship and should not be deprived of its family. Its coat needs brushing and combing once or twice weekly. Straggling hairs should be scissored every few months, and some clipping and thinning is needed for show dogs. The ears should be checked and cleaned regularly. Some can be somewhat sloppy, and some snore.

Health

- Major concerns: CHD
- Minor concerns: otitis externa, patellar luxation
- Occasionally seen: PRA, SAS
- Suggested tests: hip, eye
- Life span: 12–14 years

Form and Function

Somewhat longer than tall, solidly built with moderate bone, the Field Spaniel is a dog without exaggeration, a combination of beauty and utility. Its stride is long and low, with head held proudly and

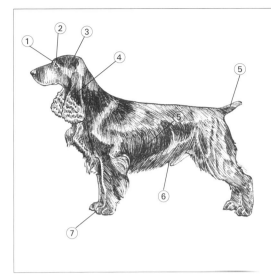

Illustrated Standard

① Moderate stop
② Almond-shaped, medium-sized eyes
③ Distinct occiput
④ Low-set ears, long and wide
⑤ Docked tail slanting downward when at rest
⑥ Little or no tuck-up
⑦ Large round webbed feet

❑ **Color:** black, liver, roan, or any of these with tan points
❑ **DQ:** none

alertly and the tail wagging but not carried high. The Field Spaniel is built for both activity and stamina, enabling it to hunt in dense cover or water. It has a single coat, which is flat or slightly wavy and moderately long, giving it protection from thorns and water. The expression is grave and gentle.

At a Glance

Energy level:	❑❑❑□
Exercise requirements:	❑❑❑□
Playfulness:	❑❑❑□
Affection level:	❑❑❑❑❑
Friendliness toward dogs:	❑❑❑
Friendliness toward other pets:	❑❑❑❑❑
Friendliness toward strangers:	❑❑❑❑❑
Ease of training:	❑❑❑❑
Watchdog ability:	❑❑❑❑
Protection ability:	❑❑
Grooming requirements:	❑❑❑
Cold tolerance:	❑❑❑
Heat tolerance:	❑❑❑

Weight:	35–50 lb*
Height:	male: 18"; female: 17" (±1 inch)

Irish Water Spaniel

History

The Irish Water Spaniel is one of the oldest and most distinctive spaniels. Dogs resembling them are depicted in manuscripts from 1000 years ago. In the 1100s, mention is made of dogs called Shannon Spaniels, Rat-Tail Spaniels, Whip-Tail Spaniels, or Irish Water Spaniels. Continued references to the Irish Water Spaniel can be found from 1600 on. Around that time, the King of France is said to have been presented with an Irish Water Spaniel. Whether the breed was at one time found in different varieties or whether several similar breeds were its forebears is a matter of conjecture. What is agreed upon is that several similar spaniels existed in Ireland: the Northern Irish, Southern Irish, and Tweed Spaniels. The Southern Irish Spaniel, also called McCarthy's Breed, is credited with being the eventual major forebear of today's dogs. In the mid 1800s, the appearance of the prolific sire Boatswain so influenced the breed that he is often credited as being the progenitor of the modern Irish Water Spaniel. The breed entered the show ring in both Britain and America by the late 1800s. In 1875, it was the third most popular

AKC Ranking: 132
Family: Gundog, Spaniel
Area of Origin: Ireland
Date of Origin: 1800s
Original Function: Water retrieving
Today's Function: Water retrieving, retriever field trials
Other Name: None

sporting dog. Despite its enchantingly clownish appearance and adept water-retrieving ability, the Irish Water Spaniel lost popularity and is only rarely seen in the show ring or found as the family pet.

Temperament

The Irish Water Spaniel goes at everything in life with gusto and enthusiasm. It loves to swim, run, hunt, and play and needs a lot of exercise. A clown at heart, it can be stubborn and independent, so it needs to be trained with patience, firmness, and a sense of humor. It tends to be reserved with strangers. It is generally good with children, though some can be timid.

Upkeep

This active, athletic, inquisitive breed needs lots of mental and physical exertion to keep it from becoming frustrated or bored. An hour of free-running or strenuous playing a day is necessary to satisfy its needs. Obedience work can also be helpful in giving it the mental challenges it enjoys. The curly coat needs brushing and

At a Glance

Energy level:	▢▢▢
Exercise requirements:	▢▢▢
Playfulness:	▢▢▢▢▢
Affection level:	▢▢▢
Friendliness toward dogs:	▢▢▢
Friendliness toward other pets:	▢▢▢
Friendliness toward strangers:	▢▢
Ease of training:	▢▢▢
Watchdog ability:	▢▢▢▢
Protection ability:	▢▢▢
Grooming requirements:	▢▢▢
Cold tolerance:	▢▢▢
Heat tolerance:	▢▢▢

Weight:	male: 55–65 lb; female: 45–58 lb
Height:	male: 22–24"; female: 21–23"

Illustrated Standard

1. Medium-sized almond-shaped eyes, hazel in color
2. Topknot consisting of long loose curls
3. Prominent occiput and gradual stop
4. Low-set, long ears
5. Topline level or slightly higher in rear
6. "Rat" tail, thick and covered with curls at base only, tapering to a fine point at end, carried nearly level with back
7. Large feet

❑ **Color:** solid liver
❑ **DQ:** none

combing two to three times a week, plus scissoring every few months. Like all dogs, it loses its coat periodically; however, the hairs tend to become trapped in the other hairs rather than fall off. If not combed out, they will form mats and cords.

Health

- Major concerns: CHD
- Minor concerns: none
- Occasionally seen: none
- Suggested tests: hip
- Life span: 10–12 years

Form and Function

The Irish Water Spaniel is built like no other spaniel, being much taller and racier. The body is of medium length, the whole dog being slightly rectangular in appearance. The general appearance suggests both dash and endurance. The gait is smooth and ground covering. The coat is one of the breed's distinctive features. The body is covered with a double coat consisting of crisp ringlets. This combination imparts water, weather, and thorn resistance to the dog, enabling it to hunt in the harshest of conditions. The Irish Water Spaniel's expression says it all: alert, intelligent, and quizzical.

Sussex Spaniel

History

The "Spaniels of Sussex" are mentioned in a sporting publication of 1820 as good working dogs. The name was adopted from Sussex, England, the home of the first important kennel (established in 1795) of these small land spaniels. The breed soon became popular among the estates around Sussex County. They were adept as upland shooting dogs, slow working but with a good nose and apt to give tongue when on scent. This latter trait hurt the breed at field trials in the early 1900s, when quiet hunters were preferred. In addition, American hunters usually preferred a faster hunter. Although one of the first ten AKC-recognized breeds and among the earliest breeds to compete at dog shows, the Sussex has never been a particularly popular or competitive show dog. Perhaps because of these reasons, the Sussex Spaniel has been perilously close to extinction throughout most of the twentieth century. At times the breed has had so few individuals that inbreeding had to be practiced to a greater extent that otherwise desirable. In 1954, a successful cross was made

> AKC Ranking: 142
> Family: Gundog, Spaniel
> Area of Origin: England
> Date of Origin: 1800s
> Original Function: Small game tracking & flushing
> Today's Function: Bird flushing & retrieving
> Other Name: None

with the Clumber Spaniel in an effort to expand the gene pool. The Sussex gene pool remains limited because the breed is still among the rarest of AKC breeds.

Temperament

The Sussex Spaniel tends to be less playful and demonstrative than other spaniels, with a lower energy level. This makes it better suited for city life, but it still appreciates the chance to take to the wilds and hunt up birds. It tends to bark when hunting, which has made it less popular with hunters than other breeds; some also bark or howl when not hunting. At home it is calm, steady, and easygoing, although it may be aggressive to strange dogs. Its somber expression is misleading because it is quite cheerful.

Upkeep

The Sussex needs daily exercise, but its needs can be met with a good walk on lead or a short romp in the yard. Given the chance, it will appreciate a longer foray into the field. It can live outdoors

At a Glance

Energy level:	☐☐☐
Exercise requirements:	☐☐☐
Playfulness:	☐☐☐
Affection level:	☐☐☐☐
Friendliness toward dogs:	☐☐☐
Friendliness toward other pets:	☐☐☐☐
Friendliness toward strangers:	☐☐☐
Ease of training:	☐☐
Watchdog ability:	☐☐☐☐
Protection ability:	☐☐☐
Grooming requirements:	☐☐☐
Cold tolerance:	☐☐☐
Heat tolerance:	☐☐☐

Weight:	35–45 lb
Height:	13–15"

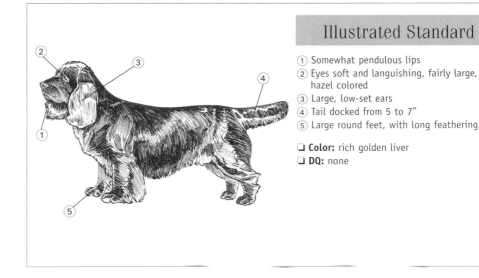

Illustrated Standard

① Somewhat pendulous lips
② Eyes soft and languishing, fairly large, hazel colored
③ Large, low-set ears
④ Tail docked from 5 to 7"
⑤ Large round feet, with long feathering

❏ **Color:** rich golden liver
❏ **DQ:** none

Health

- Major concerns: none
- Minor concerns: intervertebral disc syndrome, otitis externa, heart murmur and enlarged heart
- Occasionally seen: none
- Suggested tests: cardiac
- Life span: 12–14 years

Form and Function

The long, low, "rectangular" body, coupled with a muscular and rather massive physique, allows the Sussex to penetrate dense cover when hunting. Its movement is deliberate and rolling because of its short legs and comparatively wide body, a gait that emphasizes power over speed. The abundant body coat is flat or slightly wavy, giving protection from thorns. A distinctive feature is the long feather between the toes, which should be long enough to cover the toenails. The expression is somber and serious, even frowning, but the wagging tail belies its true nature. The Sussex tends to bark when hunting, which helps the hunter locate it in thick cover.

in temperate climates, as long as it has a warm shelter, but it generally does better as a house dog that also has access to a yard. The coat needs brushing and combing two to three times a week, plus scissoring every few months.

Welsh Springer Spaniel

History

A dog identified as a Welsh Springer Spaniel is mentioned in some of the earliest records of the Laws of Wales dating around 1300. Whether this dog is the forebear of today's Welsh Springer is in dispute, however. Other evidence indicates the possibility that the Welsh Springer either developed alongside the English Springer or resulted from crosses of English Springers to Clumber Spaniels. Although land spaniels were used in Wales for some time before the Welsh Springer emerged as a recognized breed, the early dogs were probably not a uniform lot. At the first dog shows in England, English and Welsh Springers were shown together as one breed because the only difference at that time was in their color. The Welsh grew in popularity, and the breed came to America and was recognized by the AKC in 1906. But the breed failed to gain the support it needed, and by the end of World War II it may have totally disappeared from America. New imports and, luckily, new supporters, arrived and the Welsh has since enjoyed a steady, if modest, pop-

AKC Ranking: 117
Family: Gundog, Spaniel
Area of Origin: Wales
Date of Origin: 1600s
Original Function: Bird flushing & retrieving
Today's Function: Bird flushing & retrieving
Other Name: None

ularity. Not as flashy in the show ring as the English Springer, the Welsh makes up for it in the field. It is an all-purpose, all-terrain hunter with a keen nose that can flush and retrieve over land and water.

Temperament

Less exuberant that the English Springer, the Welsh Springer Spaniel is steady and easygoing. It still needs plenty of hard exercise, however, as it loves to hunt for birds. It is extremely devoted to its family, but it is independent in nature. It is reserved with strangers; some may even be timid.

Upkeep

The Welsh needs daily exercise, which can be met with long walks on leash combined with strenuous games in the yard. It especially likes jaunts afield and makes a good hiking companion. It can live outdoors in temperate climates if given warm shelter, but it does better living inside with its family. The coat needs brushing once or twice weekly and also needs occasional scissoring to neaten stragglers.

Health

- Major concerns: CHD
- Minor concerns: glaucoma, otitis externa, epilepsy
- Occasionally seen: cataract
- Suggested tests: hip, (eye)
- Life span: 12–15 years

Form and Function

The Welsh Springer Spaniel is a hunting dog and should be in hard muscular condition. It is in no way a breed of exaggeration. It is very slightly longer than tall, compact, and possessing substance without coarseness. Its strides are powerful and ground covering. The coat is flat and straight, dense enough to protect it from water, weather, and thorns but not so excessive as to be a hindrance in the dog's work as a flushing spaniel. The expression is soft.

Illustrated Standard

① Oval eye
② Slightly domed skull with moderate stop
③ Low-set, somewhat short ears
④ Docked tail carried near horizontal
⑤ Round feet

❏ **Color:** rich red and white
❏ **DQ:** none

At a Glance

Energy level:	▢▢▢
Exercise requirements:	▢▢▢
Playfulness:	▢▢▢
Affection level:	▢▢▢
Friendliness toward dogs:	▢▢▢
Friendliness toward other pets:	▢▢▢▢
Friendliness toward strangers:	▢▢
Ease of training:	▢▢▢
Watchdog ability:	▢▢▢▢
Protection ability:	▢▢
Grooming requirements:	▢▢▢
Cold tolerance:	▢▢▢
Heat tolerance:	▢▢▢

Weight:	35–45 lb*
Height:	male: 18–19"; female: 17–18"

Spinone Italiano

History

The Spinone is one of the earliest breeds developed as a pointing dog, with evidence of wire-haired pointing dogs dating as far back as 500 B.C. Dogs resembling the Spinone can be found in artwork of fifteenth- and sixteenth-century Italy. Still, its exact origin remains a mystery, although some believe it arose from Celtic wirehaired stock, whereas others place its origins with Greek traders who brought it to Italy during the times of the Roman Empire. Unfortunately, few records remain of the breed's subsequent development, even though present day Spinoni trace back principally to Italy's Piedmont region. It proved itself adept at penetrating thorny cover and finding feathered or fur game. During World War II, the Spinone further distinguished itself by tracking German patrols. The end of the war found the breed in trouble, however, because its numbers had been decimated and many of the remaining dogs crossed with other breeds. The Spinone was in danger of being lost. In the 1950s, breeders began a concerted effort to recon-

AKC Ranking: N/A
Family: Gundog, Pointer
Area of Origin: Italy
Date of Origin: 1200s
Original Function: Pointing & retrieving
Today's Function: Pointing & retrieving
Other Name: Italian Spinone

struct the Spinone Italiano. Its hunting abilities are well worth the effort. This is a dog that can point, set, and retrieve, aided by a good nose and good sense. It is noted for hunting at a fast trot in a diagonal pattern that keeps it fairly close to the hunter and is classified as a versatile hunting breed. It is now a popular dog in Italy and some other European countries, but it has been slower to attract attention in America. The Spinone Italiano is also known as the Italian Griffon. The word *Spinone* is derived from *pino*, an Italian thorn bush through which these tough-skinned dogs could hunt in search of the small game often hiding within. The plural form is Spinoni (Spi-no-ni); the singular is Spinone (Spi-no-nay).

Temperament

This is a devoted and gentle dog, very willing to please. It is affectionate and gets along well with other dogs and pets and children. It is also courageous. The Spinone is calmer and easier going than most pointing breeds.

Upkeep

Like all sporting dogs, the Spinone needs daily exercise. This can take the form of a long walk or good run off leash. It can live outdoors in temperate to cool climates, but it is a family dog and prefers to share time with its people. Coat care consists of weekly brushing, plus occasional hand-stripping to neaten the face and feet.

Health

- Major concerns: CHD
- Minor concerns: ectropion, gastric torsion, otitis externa
- Occasionally seen: cerebral ataxis
- Suggested tests: hip, (eye)
- Life span: 12–14 years

Form and Function

The Spinone Italiano has a hound look about it, with a fairly long head and muzzle, large, dropped ears, and somewhat pendulous lips. It is a strong, muscular dog, able to trot at fast pace all day and then retrieve over water or land. Its dense wiry coat allows it to hunt under any conditions. The coat is generally single, consisting of rough, dry, thick hair

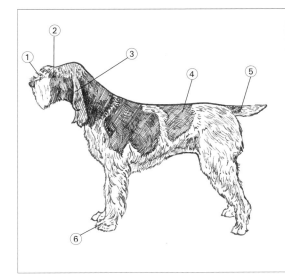

Illustrated Standard

1. Muzzle long and square, with bridge straight or slightly Roman
2. Eyes ochre colored
3. Ears large and dropped
4. Well-arched loin
5. Tail carried down or horizontal; docked to 5½ to 8"
6. Rounded feet

❏ **Color:** all white or white with orange or chestnut markings
❏ **DQ:** none

about 1.5 to 2.5" in length. Longer hair garnishing the lips and eyebrows adds further protection in addition to adding to its intelligent and gentle expression.

At a Glance

Energy level:	▢▢▢
Exercise requirements:	▢▢▢
Playfulness:	▢▢▢
Affection level:	▢▢▢▢
Friendliness toward dogs:	▢▢▢
Friendliness toward other pets:	▢▢▢▢
Friendliness toward strangers:	▢▢▢▢
Ease of training:	▢▢▢
Watchdog ability:	▢▢▢▢
Protection ability:	▢
Grooming requirements:	▢▢
Cold tolerance:	▢▢▢
Heat tolerance:	▢▢▢

Weight:	male: 71–82 lb; female: 62–71 lb*
Height:	male: 23.5–27.5"; female: 22.5–25.5"

Vizsla

History

The Vizsla's forebears may have included breeds that the Magyars collected as they swarmed across Europe before settling in Hungary over a thousand years ago. Writings on falconry from the Middle Ages describe dogs of Vizsla type. The Hungarian plains were rich in game, and hunters wanted a fast but close-working dog that could not only point and retrieve birds but trail mammals over thick ground cover. The breed was unquestionably established by the eighteenth century, having found special favor with barons and warlords of the time. By the end of the nineteenth century, however, the breed had greatly declined in numbers. It was revived through the discovery and careful breeding of about a dozen good specimens. World War II spread the Vizsla throughout the world. Hungarians fleeing Russian occupation took their pointing dogs to

AKC Ranking: 50
Family: Gundog, Pointer, Versatile
  Hunting Dog
Area of Origin: Hungary
Date of Origin: Middle Ages
Original Function: Pointing, falconry,
  trailing
Today's Function: Pointing, pointing
  field trials
Other Name: Hungarian Vizsla,
  Magyar Vizsla, Hungarian Pointer,
  Drotszoru Magyar Vizsla

various other countries, including America, where their handsome appearance and exceptional hunting abilities were soon appreciated. AKC recognition came in 1960. Once again, the Viszla quickly gained admirers, and the breed is now regularly seen in the field, show ring, and home. It is also sometimes called the Hungarian Vizsla or Hungarian Pointer.

Temperament

Bred to be a close-working gundog, the Viszla has the energy to range all day. It is a true hunter at heart, a talented pointer, and always on the lookout for bird scent. It can become frustrated and destructive if not given adequate exercise. Most can be stubborn, some can be timid, and others can be overly excitable. It is gentle, affectionate, and sensitive, and can be protective. The Vizsla makes a good companion

At a Glance

Energy level:	☐☐☐
Exercise requirements:	☐☐☐
Playfulness:	☐☐☐☐
Affection level:	☐☐☐☐☐
Friendliness toward dogs:	☐☐☐
Friendliness toward other pets:	☐☐☐☐
Friendliness toward strangers:	☐☐☐☐☐
Ease of training:	☐☐☐
Watchdog ability:	☐☐☐☐
Protection ability:	☐
Grooming requirements:	☐
Cold tolerance:	☐☐
Heat tolerance:	☐☐☐

Weight:	45–65 lb*
Height:	male: 22–24"; female: 21–23"

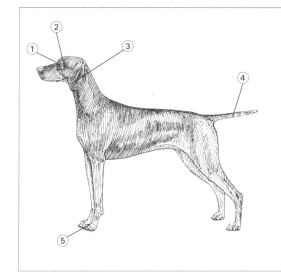

for an active owner who spends a lot of time outdoors.

Upkeep

The Vizsla needs a lot of strenuous exercise every day. This is an active breed that cannot be expected to meet its energy requirements with a short walk or within a small yard. It needs to be jogged or allowed to run in a large enclosed area. Otherwise, its needs are minimal. Its coat requires little care except an occasional brushing to remove dead hair. It can live outside in warm climates, given adequate shelter, but should sleep indoors on cold nights. It needs a soft bed.

Health

• Major concerns: none
• Minor concerns: hemophilia A, CMO, CHD
• Occasionally seen: none
• Suggested tests: (hip)
• Life span: 10–14 years

Form and Function

The Vizsla is lightly built but muscular, giving it speed and endurance in the field. Its gait is light, graceful, smooth, and ground covering. Its short smooth coat is dense, providing some protection from the elements. The golden rust color is a hallmark of the breed.

Weimaraner

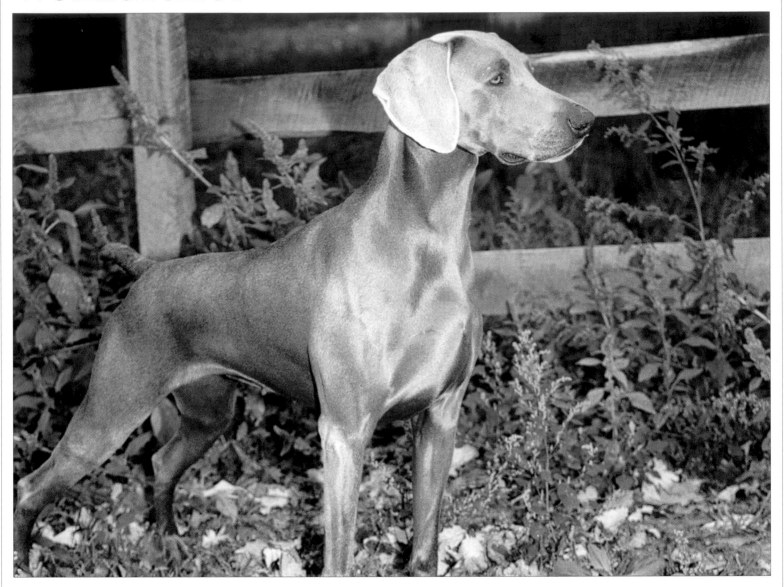

History

Germany has always been a country rich in wildlife, and German dog breeds have gained the reputation as some of the best in the world. The Weimaraner was produced in the nineteenth century by a concerted effort to create the ideal all-around gundog that could hunt game of all sizes, including deer and bear. This effort was sponsored by the court of Weimer, and the breed was initially known as the Weimar Pointer. Some of the breed's forebears include the Bloodhound, Red Schweisshund, and early pointing breeds. The origin of the Weimaraner's distinctive gray color is unknown, but it was an early feature of the breed. The breed's progress was strictly overseen by the German Weimaraner Club. Dogs could not be sold to nonmembers, and membership was hard to obtain. Dogs from nonapproved breedings could not be registered, and poor specimens had to be

AKC Ranking: 39
Family: Gundog, Pointer, Versatile
  Hunting Dog
Area of Origin: Germany
Date of Origin: 1800s
Original Function: Large game trailing
Today's Function: Pointing, pointing
  field trials
Other Name: Weimaraner Vorstehhund

destroyed. Only when an American gained entry to the club and was allowed to take two dogs back to America in 1929 did the Weimaraner leave its native land. Early American Weimaraners performed so extraordinarily in obedience competitions that they aroused great interest. As more enthusiasts were attracted to the breed, they discovered its great worth as a hunting companion. AKC recognition came in 1943. The breed's beauty and versatility as personal gundog, pet, and competition dog have earned it a steady following.

Temperament

The Weimaraner is bold and rambunctious, sometimes too much so for small children. It loves to run and hunt and can become frustrated and destructive if kept penned up. It can be stubborn or headstrong. It functions best with an active owner who enjoys outdoor activities and wants a fun-loving companion.

Upkeep

Daily strenuous exertion is a must for the Weimaraner. This is not a breed for city life unless its owner is a jogger. It needs to stretch its legs, run, and explore in a large, safe area. It needs a yard at home, and although it can live outdoors in warm climates, it is not suited for cold nights outside. As a social dog, it does best when it can divide its time between indoors and out. Coat care is minimal: occasional brushing to remove dead hair.

Health

- Major concerns: gastric torsion
- Minor concerns: spinal dysraphism, CHD, entropion, distichiasis, vWD, hemophilia A, hypertrophic osteodystrophy*
- Occasionally seen: ununited anconeal process, eversion of nictitating membrane

*To avoid this autoimmune reaction, it is best to avoid combination vaccines.

Illustrated Standard

1. Nose gray
2. Eyes shaded light amber, gray, or blue-gray
3. Prominent occipit
4. High-set, long ears
5. Topline slopes slightly to rear
6. Tail docked to 6"
7. Webbed feet

❏ **Color:** mouse-gray to silver-gray
❏ **DQ:** deviation in height of more than 1" from standard in either way; distinctly long, blue, or black coat

- Suggested tests: (hip), (eye), (blood)
- Life span: 10–13 years

Form and Function

The Weimaraner is built to hunt with great speed and endurance and combines grace, stamina, raciness, and an alert demeanor. It has find aristocratic features, with a kind expression. The gait is smooth and effortless. The short sleek coat is noted for its unique gray color.

At a Glance

Energy level:	❏❏❏❏❏
Exercise requirements:	❏❏❏❏❏
Playfulness:	❏❏❏❏
Affection level:	❏❏❏
Friendliness toward dogs:	❏❏
Friendliness toward other pets:	❏❏
Friendliness toward strangers:	❏❏
Ease of training:	❏❏
Watchdog ability:	❏❏❏❏❏
Protection ability:	❏❏❏❏
Grooming requirements:	❏
Cold tolerance:	❏❏
Heat tolerance:	❏❏❏

Weight:	70–85 lb*
Height:	male: 25–27"; female: 23–25"

Wirehaired Pointing Griffon

History

Unlike the development of most breeds, most of the development of the Wirehaired Pointing Griffon was deliberate and fairly well documented, beginning in the middle 1800s with the creation of the Cherville Griffon, which was subsequently crossed with the setter and pointer. It was Edward Korthals of Holland, however, who is credited with developing and refining the breed. In fact, the Griffon is still known as the Korthals Griffon throughout most of the world. He began his mission in 1874, crossing twenty dogs representing seven breeds (griffons, spaniels, water spaniels, German and French pointers, and setter). Korthals traveled extensively in France and popularized his new breed wherever he went, whether it was a field activity, bench show, or business meeting. Through his French connections, his new breed became adopted in France, where it gained a reputation as a deliberate, careful hunter with a good nose. It was in France that the breed found a stronghold, causing people to consider it as a French breed despite its Dutch roots. By 1887, the breed type was stable, and a breed standard

AKC Ranking: 123
Family: Gundog, Pointer, Versatile
   Hunting Dog
Area of Origin: France
Date of Origin: 1800s
Original Function: Pointing, retrieving
Today's Function: Pointing, retrieving,
   pointing field trials
Other Name: Korthals Griffon, Pointing
   Wirehaired Griffon, Griffon D'Arrêt a
   Poil Dur

was published. The first show classes for the breed were offered in 1888 in England, although at that time it was referred to as a Russian Setter or Retriever (apparently any well-furred dog was assumed to be of Siberian origin). In fact, the first Griffon registered in America was registered as a Russian Setter in 1887. Its popularity grew steadily, only to be halted by the Second World War. After the war, its reputation as an ideal dog for the walking hunter again gained it new popularity, but the initiation of competitive field trials, in which faster paced breeds dominated, caused many competitive hunters to turn away from the Griffon. Despite its low numbers, the Wirehaired Pointing Griffon has loyal followers who value its excellent abilities not only as a pointer and retriever but also as a versatile and loyal companion. In fact, it is often called "the supreme gundog."

Temperament

The Wirehaired Pointing Griffon is a skilled field dog, pointing and retrieving with a deliberate style, generally staying within the hunter's gun range. It combines independent action with the ability to be directed by the hunter. It is an equally adept family pet, absolutely devoted, willing to please, amiable, and often, comical. It is generally friendly toward strangers, other dogs, and pets.

Upkeep

The Wirehaired Pointing Griffon needs daily exertion, either in the form of jogging, games, or a run in the field. It particularly enjoys swimming. It can live outdoors in temperate weather as long as it has warm shelter, but it does best when allowed to be both an indoor and outdoor dog. Its harsh coat needs combing or brushing once or twice a week, plus hand-stripping to remove dead hair twice a year. Its ears need regular cleaning and plucking of hair within the canal in order to avoid ear problems.

Health

- Major concerns: none
- Minor concerns: CHD, otitis externa, entropion, ectropion
- Occasionally seen: none

Illustrated Standard

1. Eyes large and rounded, in all shades of yellow and brown
2. Nose brown
3. Abundant mustache and eyebrows
4. High-set, medium-sized ears
5. Topline slopes slightly to rear
6. Tail docked to two-thirds to one-half length, carried straight or slightly raised
7. Round webbed feet

❏ **Color:** preferably steel gray with brown markings, also chestnut brown, or roan, white and brown. Less desirable is solid brown, solid white, or white and orange.
❏ **DQ:** nose any color but brown; black coat

- Suggested tests: (hip), (eye)
- Life span: 12–14 years

Form and Function

This strong breed can cope with any terrain. It should be slightly longer than tall, of medium substance. It functions as both a retriever and pointer, and its size and conformation reflects a compromise between the requirements of these jobs. Its gait is efficient and tireless, with low, catlike strides. The coat is of medium length, straight and wiry, with a fine, downy, thick undercoat. The combination provides protection in the swampy country in which it was developed, as well as insulation from cold and water. The abundant facial furnishings contribute to its friendly expression.

At a Glance

Energy level:	◻◻◻◻
Exercise requirements:	◻◻◻◻
Playfulness:	◻◻◻
Affection level:	◻◻◻
Friendliness toward dogs:	◻◻◻
Friendliness toward other pets:	◻◻◻
Friendliness toward strangers:	◻◻◻
Ease of training:	◻◻◻
Watchdog ability:	◻◻◻◻◻
Protection ability:	◻◻◻
Grooming requirements:	◻◻◻
Cold tolerance:	◻◻◻
Heat tolerance:	◻◻

Weight:	50–60 lb*
Height:	male: 22–24"; female: 20–22"

The Hound Group

The hounds are one of the oldest groups of dogs, aiding humans by pursuing and catching their quarry. The sighthounds pursue by sight and include the fast running dogs of greyhound build, whereas the scenthounds pursue by scent and include the more solidly built dogs of general foxhound build. Some breeds hunt by both sight and scent, and a few breeds don't seem like hounds at all. Again, all hound breeds have in common the independent pursuit of mammalian quarry. As such, they traditionally could not wait for the hunter's direction; they led the way.

Afghan Hound

History

With roots dating to the Egyptian pharaohs, the Afghan Hound is an ancient breed derived from the group of Middle Eastern sighthounds. Despite such illustrious roots, most of the Afghan Hound's development is the result of its use by nomadic tribes as a coursing hound capable of providing hare and gazelle meat for the pot. The dogs often hunted with the aid of falcons, which were trained to swoop at the quarry. Generations of hunting in the harsh mountainous terrain of Afghanistan produced a fast dog that also had a good deal of stamina, but most of all, had incredible leaping ability and nimbleness. Its long coat protected it from the cold climate. These dogs remained isolated for centuries, hidden in the impenetrable Afghanistan Mountains. The first Afghan Hound came to England in the early 1900s; at that time these dogs were called Persian Greyhounds or Barukhzy Hounds. These dogs were a diverse lot so a standard of perfection—modeled on Zardin, a particularly striking dog—that

AKC Ranking: 83
Family: Sighthound, Southern (sighthound)
Area of Origin: Afghanistan
Date of Origin: Ancient times
Original Function: Coursing hare and gazelle
Today's Function: Lure coursing
Other Name: Tazi, Baluchi Hound

described the more elegant, racy dog of today was created. Popularity grew slowly, with the dog appealing mostly to the glamour set. Popularity in the show ring was faster coming, with the Afghan quickly becoming one of the most competitive and glamorous dogs in the rings. In the 1970s the Afghan became a fad breed with the public, but it has since dwindled in popularity.

Temperament

Despite its glamorous reputation, the Afghan Hound is a hunter at heart, bred to chase down game over rugged terrain. While it maintains its regal bearings inside, it needs a daily chance to stretch its legs in a safe area. Its worst trait is a reluctance to come when called. It will chase small animals outside; inside, it will coexist peacefully. Though gentle with children, it may not be playful and interactive enough with them. Described by some as "catlike," it is independent yet sensitive, and not overly demonstrative. It is reserved with strangers; some can be timid. It has a gay, clownish side.

Upkeep

The Afghan needs daily exertion, either in the form of a long walk followed by a short sprint, or preferably, a chance to run full speed in a safe enclosed area. Although its coat might make it amenable to outdoor living in temperate areas, it needs a soft bed and is better suited as a housedog. The coat requires some commitment, especially when shedding the puppy coat; most adult coats need brushing or combing every two to three days.

Health

- Major concerns: none
- Minor concerns: cataract
- Occasionally seen: necrotic myelopathy, CHD
- Suggested tests: (eye)
- Life span: 12–14 years
- Note: sensitive to anesthesia; prone to tail injuries

Form and Function

The Afghan is built along greyhound-like lines, enabling it to execute a double-suspension gallop and run down fleet game. The comparatively short back and steep pelvis helped it to leap great heights and to turn almost in place, essential attributes for coursing in rocky mountainous terrain. The large feet gave it better foothold and were more resistant to injury on rough ground. The silky coat protected the dog from cold nights at high altitudes. The Afghan appears dignified and aloof, with an exotic expression and proud carriage. The gait shows great elasticity and spring, and the dog moves with head and tail high.

Illustrated Standard

1. Long refined head
2. Almond-shaped eyes
3. Topknot of long, silky hair
4. Long ears
5. Short-haired saddle
6. Pronounced hipbones
7. Ring on the end of tail
8. Large feet

❏ **Color:** all colors permissible except spotted
❏ **DQ:** none

At a Glance

Energy level:	❏❏
Exercise requirements:	❏❏❏
Playfulness:	❏❏❏
Affection level:	❏
Friendliness toward dogs:	❏❏❏
Friendliness toward other pets:	❏❏❏
Friendliness toward strangers:	❏
Ease of training:	❏❏
Watchdog ability:	❏❏❏❏
Protection ability:	❏
Grooming requirements:	❏❏❏❏
Cold tolerance:	❏❏❏
Heat tolerance:	❏❏❏

Weight:	male: 60 lb; female: 50 lb
Height:	male: 27"; female: 25" (±1")

Basenji

History

The Basenji is among the most primitive of breeds, discovered in the African Congo with Pygmy hunters. Early explorers called the dogs after the tribes that owned them or the area in which they were found, such as Zande dogs or Congo terriers. The native tribes used the dogs (which often wore a large bell) as pack hunters, driving game into nets. Early attempts to bring the dogs to England in the late 1800s and early 1900s were unsuc- cessful because they all succumbed to distemper. In the 1930s, a few dogs were successfully brought back to England and became

AKC Ranking: 69
Family: Sighthound, Scenthound,
   Primitive, Southern (Pariah)
Area of Origin: Central Africa (Zaire
   and the Congo)
Date of Origin: Ancient
Original Function: Hunting small game
Today's Function: Lure coursing
Other Name: Congo Dog, Congo Terrier

the foundation (along with subsequent imports from the Congo and Sudan) of the breed outside of Africa. The name "Basenji," meaning "bush thing," was chosen. The early imports attracted much attention, and soon after dogs were brought to America. The breed's popularity as both a pet and show dog grew modestly but steadily. In the 1950s, a surge of popularity occurred as a result of a book and movie featur- ing a Basenji. The 1980s saw two important but controversial events for the Basenji in America. First, several Basenjis were brought from Africa in an attempt to widen the gene pool and combat some widespread hereditary health problems; some of these introduced the previously unrecognized brindle color into the breed. Second, the Basenji was recognized by the American Sighthound Field Association as a sighthound and allowed to compete in lure-coursing trials. Its body structure and hunting style had previously been deemed too un-sighthound-like. The Basenji has always been hard to categorize. It retains several primitive characteristics, most notably its lack of barking ability and its yearly, rather than twice yearly, estrus cycle.

Temperament

Some consider the Basenji to have terrier-like mannerisms because it is feisty for a hound. More often it is considered catlike in mannerisms: clever, inquisitive, stubborn, independent, and reserved. Its hunting roots are very evident, as it loves to chase and trail. It needs regular mental and physical stimulation lest it become frustrated and destructive. Basenjis may be barkless, but they are not mute. They do make a sort of yodel, howl, and shriek—and occasionally bark, but just one or two "fox barks" at a time.

Illustrated Standard

1. Almond-shaped eyes
2. Fine, profuse wrinkles on forehead, visible when ears are erect
3. Small erect ears
4. Short back
5. Tail bends acutely forward and lies well curled over to either side
6. Small oval feet

❏ **Color:** red, black, black and tan, or brindle, all with white feet, chest and tail tips; white legs, blaze, and collar optional
❏ **DQ:** none

Upkeep

The Basenji is an active dog that needs daily mental and physical exercise. Its needs can be met by a long walk followed by a vigorous game or by free-running in a safe enclosed area. It can live outdoors only in warm climates and generally does best as an indoor dog with access to a yard. Coat care is minimal, consisting of only occasional brushing to remove dead hair.

Health

- Major concerns: Fanconi syndrome, PRA, Basenji enteropathy
- Minor concerns: PPM, PK
- Occasionally seen: CHD
- Suggested tests: eye, DNA test for PK, Fanconi urine test
- Life span: 12–14 years

Form and Function

The Basenji is square-proportioned and high on leg. It is far more slightly built and longer legged than most other primitive breeds, giving it a good amount of speed and the ability to perform the double-suspension gallop. Its erect ears help it locate prey in thick bush and may act as heat dissipaters. Its short coat also aids in dealing with the hot climate of Africa.

At a Glance

Energy level:	❏❏❏
Exercise requirements:	❏❏
Playfulness:	❏❏
Affection level:	❏❏
Friendliness toward dogs:	❏
Friendliness toward other pets:	❏
Friendliness toward strangers:	❏❏
Ease of training:	❏
Watchdog ability:	❏❏❏❏
Protection ability:	❏
Grooming requirements:	❏
Cold tolerance:	❏
Heat tolerance:	❏❏

Weight:	male: 24 lb; female: 22 lb
Height:	male: 17"; female: 16"

Basset Hound

History

The first mention of the "Basset" dog is found in a sixteenth-century text about badger hunting. Dwarfed short-legged specimens occur in many breeds and have been known since ancient times, but it is difficult to know at what point such dogs were purposefully bred and which ones led to the present Basset Hound. The word *Basset* is derived from the French *bas* meaning low thing or dwarf, so that definitive evidence of the breed may be hard to follow. Short-legged dogs were used by the pre-Revolutionary French for hunting at a slower pace, but most of these dogs were dispersed, and their fates undocumented, during the French Revolution. The history becomes clearer after the Revolution, when greater numbers of commoners took up hunting, often aided by guns. They needed a dog that they could follow on foot, but that still had great scenting ability and strong heavy bone—in essence, a short-legged version of the pack hounds popular with the aristocracy. Because the Basset could not pursue its quarry at speed, the quarry was less likely to be on the run and thus presented an easier target for the gunman. The dogs would

AKC Ranking: 23
Family: Scenthound
Area of Origin: France
Date of Origin: 1500s
Original Function: Trailing rabbits and hare
Today's Function: Trailing rabbits and hare, field trials, Basset field trials
Other Name: None

hunt all mammals but were especially suited for rabbits and hares. Four different versions of short-legged hounds were created, with the Basset Artesien Normand most closely resembling today's Basset. In the late 1800s (and again in 1930), crosses with Bloodhounds were made to increase size; the results were then tempered with subsequent crosses to the Artesien Normand. The first Bassets were brought to England and America in the late 1800s, and interest in the breed grew gradually. By the mid 1900s, the Basset's droll expression had won it a place in advertising and entertainment and in many new pet owner's hearts.

Temperament

The Basset Hound is among the most good natured and easygoing of breeds. It is amiable with dogs, other pets, and children, although children must be cautioned not to put strain on its back with their games. It is calm inside, but it needs regular exercise in order to keep fit. It prefers to investigate slowly, and loves to sniff and trail. It is a talented and determined tracker, not easily dissuaded from its course. Because of this, it may get on a trail and follow it until it becomes lost. It tends to be stubborn and slow moving. It has a loud bay that it uses when excited on the trail.

Upkeep

The Basset needs mild daily exercise, which can be satisfied by walking on leash or playing in the yard. It does best as a housedog with access to a yard. The coat needs only minimal grooming, but the face may need regular cleaning around the mouth and wrinkles. Bassets tend to drool.

Health

- Major concerns: foreleg lameness, OCD, entropion, ectropion, otitis externa, intervertebral disc disease, glaucoma, vWD, CTP, gastric torsion
- Minor concerns: foot cysts and infection
- Occasionally seen: patellar luxation
- Suggested tests: eye, blood
- Life span: 8–12 years
- Note: Obesity is a problem in the breed, especially because it contributes to intervertebral disk disease

Illustrated Standard

1. Pendulous lips with hanging flews
2. Soft, sad eyes, showing prominent haw
3. Loose skin falling in distinct wrinkles over the brow when the head is lowered
4. Skull domed with prominent occiput
5. Extremely long, low-set ears
6. Straight topline
7. Tail slightly curved and carried gaily
8. Massive, round feet
9. Short, powerful forelegs with wrinkled skin

❏ **Color:** any recognized hound color
❏ **DQ:** over 15" in height, knuckled over forelegs, distinctly long coat

Form and Function

The Basset's long, heavy body and short legs make it easy to follow on foot, and give it an edge in dense cover. The Basset Hound has heavier bone, in proportion to its total size, than any other breed. Its thick, tight coat protects it from brambles without becoming caught in them. It is speculated that the long ears may stir up ground scent, and the wrinkles trap the scent around the face. The large muzzle gives ample room for the olfactory apparatus. Such room would not be available in a miniature dog; only a large dog with shortened legs can combine the short height with large muzzle size. Its movement is smooth and powerful; it tends to move with nose to the ground.

At a Glance

Energy level:	❏
Exercise requirements:	❏
Playfulness:	❏
Affection level:	❏❏❏
Friendliness toward dogs:	❏❏❏
Friendliness toward other pets:	❏❏❏
Friendliness toward strangers:	❏❏❏
Ease of training:	❏❏
Watchdog ability:	❏❏❏❏
Protection ability:	❏
Grooming requirements:	❏❏
Cold tolerance:	❏❏❏
Heat tolerance:	❏❏❏

Weight:	40–60 lb*
Height:	preferably not over 14"

Beagle

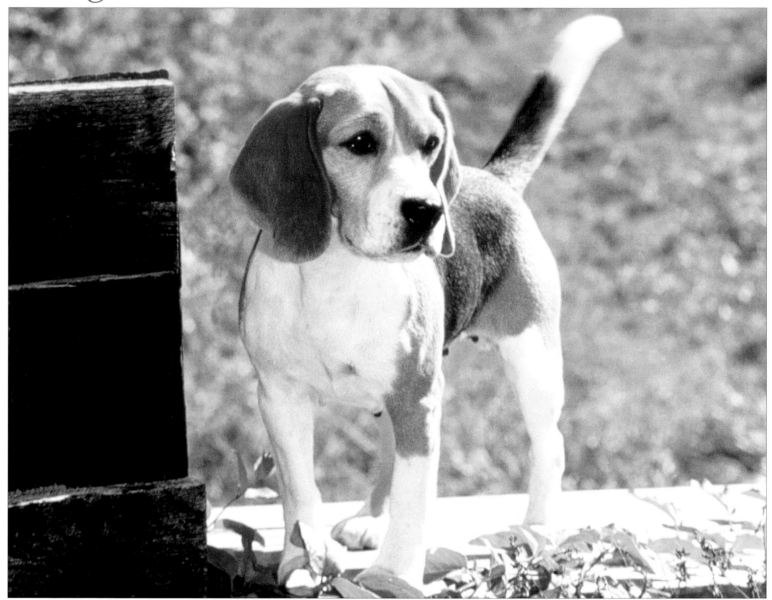

History

By the fourteenth century, hare-hunting had become a popular sport in England, and the dogs used were probably of Beagle type. The origin of the name Beagle may be from old French words meaning open throat in reference to the breed's melodious bay, or from the Celtic, old English, or old French words for small. The word *Beagle* was not used until 1475, however, but can then be found frequently in writings from the sixteenth century on. Hunters could follow these dogs on foot and could even carry one in a pocket if the need arose. By the 1800s, Beagles existed in several sizes, but the smaller "pocket-size" dogs were particularly popular. These dogs measured only about 9 inches and often needed the hunter's assistance in crossing

AKC Ranking: 6
Family: Scenthound
Area of Origin: England
Date of Origin: 1300s
Original Function: Trailing rabbits
Today's Function: Trailing rabbits, field trials, contraband detection, Beagle field trials
Other Name: English Beagle

rough fields. One of the special appeals of the smaller Beagles was that the hunt could be followed even by "ladies, the aged, or the infirm," as they slowly followed the winding path of the hare. The first mention of the Beagle in America was in 1642. Beagles were used in the South prior to the Civil War, but these dogs bore little resemblance to their English counterparts. After the war, English imports formed the basis of the modern American Beagle. By the end of the nineteenth century, Beagles were popular competitors in both field and conformation exhibitions. But the merry little scenthound did not stop there: it continued to become one of America's all-time favorite breeds, finding its special niche as family pet.

At a Glance

Energy level:	☐☐☐
Exercise requirements:	☐☐☐
Playfulness:	☐☐☐
Affection level:	☐☐☐☐☐
Friendliness toward dogs:	☐☐☐☐☐
Friendliness toward other pets:	☐☐☐☐☐
Friendliness toward strangers:	☐☐☐☐☐
Ease of training:	☐
Watchdog ability:	☐☐☐☐
Protection ability:	☐
Grooming requirements:	☐
Cold tolerance:	☐☐☐
Heat tolerance:	☐☐☐

Weight:	18–30 lb*
Height:	13" variety: not exceeding 13"
	15" variety: over 13" but under 15"

Illustrated Standard

1. Square muzzle
2. Gentle pleading expression
3. Stop moderately defined
4. Rounded ears
5. Short back
6. Slightly curved tail, carried gaily
7. Round feet

❑ **Color:** any true hound color
❑ **DQ:** taller than 15"

Temperament

One of the most amiable hounds, the Beagle was bred as a pack hunter and needs companionship, whether human or canine. It loves to explore the outdoors and is an enthusiastic trailer. Given adequate exercise, it is a calm, tractable house pet. It is an excellent child's dog, gentle, incredibly tolerant, and always ready to join in a game or adventure. It is an independent breed, however, and may run off if a trail beckons. It barks and howls.

Upkeep

The Beagle needs daily exercise, either a long walk on leash or a romp in a safe area. It can live outdoors in temperate climates as long as it is given warm shelter and bedding. It is a social dog, however, and needs the companionship of either other dogs or its human family; as such, it is usually happiest if it can divide its time between the house and yard.

Health

* Major concerns: intervertebral disc disease, CHD
* Minor concerns: glaucoma, epilepsy
* Occasionally seen: deafness, hemophilia A, cataract
* Suggested tests: hip, (eye)
* Life span: 12–15 years

Form and Function

The Beagle should look like a miniature Foxhound, solid for its size. The Beagle's moderate size enables it to be followed on foot. It can also be carried to the hunt, and once there, can scurry around in thick underbrush. Its close hard coat protects it from underbrush. Its moderate build enables it to nimbly traverse rough terrain. The Beagle's amiable personality allows it to get along with other dogs and to be a successful pack hunter. The Beagle is noted for its melodious bay, which helps hunters locate it from a distance.

Black and Tan Coonhound

History

A true American breed, the Black and Tan Coonhound probably originated from crosses of the Bloodhound and the Foxhound, particularly the black and tan Virginia Foxhound. The Black and Tan Coonhound developed mostly in the Appalachian, Blue Ridge, Ozark, and Smokey Mountains, where these dogs were used to hunt raccoons and bears over fairly rugged terrain. They trailed in the fashion of their Bloodhound ancestors, with nose to ground but at a somewhat swifter pace. Although they will trail any mammal, they specialize in raccoons and opossums, often trailing at night. When the quarry is treed, the dogs bay until the hunter arrives and shoots the animal. The AKC recognized the breed in 1945, but the Black and Tan has always been much more popular as a hunting dog than as a show dog or pet. Organized night hunts are extremely competitive and popular, and the United Kennel Club holds many bench shows for coonhounds only, in which Black and Tan Coonhounds, Blue Tick Coonhounds, Redbone Coonhounds, English Coonhounds, Plott Hounds, and Treeing Walkers compete.

AKC Ranking: 121
Family: Scenthound
Area of Origin: United States
Date of Origin: 1700s
Original Function: Hunting raccoons
Today's Function: Hunting raccoons, night hunts
Other Name: American Black and Tan Coonhound

Temperament

Not the prototypical housedog, the Black and Tan Coonhound, nonetheless, makes an exemplary pet. It is mellow, amiable, calm, and unobtrusive indoors. Outdoors, its strong hunting instincts take over, and it can be difficult, if not impossible, to turn from a track after it starts trailing. As befitting a dog with its heritage, it is strong, independent, and stubborn. It is gentle and tolerant with children, but it may be too independent to satisfy a playful child. It is reserved with strangers. It may bay and howl.

Upkeep

The Black and Tan is a dog that can run for miles, although it is usually content with a moderate jog or long walk, with an occasional excursion into the field. It can wander if it catches a scent, so a safe area is mandatory. Its coat needs only occasional brushing. Most Coonhounds drool to some extent, and the face may need regular wiping. The ears should also be checked regularly.

At a Glance

Energy level:	▢▢
Exercise requirements:	▢▢▢▢
Playfulness:	▢▢▢
Affection level:	▢▢▢
Friendliness toward dogs:	▢▢▢
Friendliness toward other pets:	▢▢▢
Friendliness toward strangers:	▢▢
Ease of training:	▢
Watchdog ability:	▢▢▢▢
Protection ability:	▢▢▢
Grooming requirements:	▢
Cold tolerance:	▢▢▢
Heat tolerance:	▢▢▢

Weight:	55–75 lb*
Height:	male: 25–27"; female: 23–25"

Illustrated Standard

① Well-developed flews
② Skin devoid of folds
③ Almost round eyes
④ Low-set, long ears hanging in folds
⑤ Tail carried high, nearly perpendicular to back

❑ **Color:** black and tan
❑ **DQ:** solid patch of white extending more than 1" in any direction

Health
- Major concerns: CHD
- Minor concerns: ectropion
- Occasionally seen: hemophilia B
- Suggested tests: hip, (eye)
- Life span: 10–12 years

Form and Function
The Black and Tan Coonhound's moderate build gives it a blend of strength, speed and agility. It is square or slightly longer than tall, with moderate bone. Its long ears may help stir up ground scents. Its deep muzzle allows room for olfactory apparatus. The deep voice enables the hunter to locate the dog when it has treed its quarry. Its hair is short but dense, providing an all-weather-protective coat. Its expression is alert, friendly, and eager. The stride is easy and graceful, with head and tail held high.

Bloodhound

History

The quintessential scenthound, the Bloodhound traces its roots to ancient times. Their earliest ancestor may have been the black St. Huberts hound documented in Europe by the eighth century. William the Conqueror is credited with bringing these hounds to England in 1066. In the twelfth century, many Church dignitaries were interested in hunting with these dogs, and most monasteries kept carefully bred packs. So highly bred were these dogs that they came to be known as "blooded hounds," referring to their pure blood and noble breeding. Bloodhounds have been known in America since the mid 1800s. Even though they gained a reputation as slave trailers, many of those dogs were mixed scenthounds. The Bloodhound has since proved itself to be one of the most useful of breeds, using its unrivaled sense of smell to trail lost persons and criminals alike. After the person is located, the Bloodhound's job is over because it is never inclined to attack. The Bloodhound holds many trailing records (for both length and age of trail), and at one time it was the only breed of dog whose identifications were accepted in a court of law. Ironically, the Bloodhound's name and bad press scared many people away from the breed because they believed stories that claimed the dogs trailed people out of a lust for blood. Nothing, of course, could be farther from the truth. The breed is well known to all but not particularly popular as a pet; it is a competitive show dog and unsurpassed working trailer, however.

AKC Ranking: 55
Family: Scenthound
Area of Origin: Belgium, England
Date of Origin: Middle Ages
Original Function: Trailing
Today's Function: Trailing humans, search and rescue
Other Name: St. Hubert's Hound, Chien St. Hubert

Temperament

For all its calm manners at home, the Bloodhound is a tireless trailer once on the track. It is tough, stubborn, and independent, yet it is so gentle and placid that it is extremely trustworthy around children—although it may not be playful enough for some children's needs. Nonetheless, it is not the lazy ol' hound dog portrayed in folklore but instead an active, playful companion. Although not the easiest breed to train for traditional obedience, it is exceptionally easy to train in tasks involving trailing. The Bloodhound is reserved with strangers.

Upkeep

As a hunting hound, the Bloodhound needs a good deal of daily exercise. It was bred to trail through any hardship, and once on a trail it cannot be called off. It thus must be exercised in a safe area. The Bloodhound drools a lot, so its facial wrinkles require daily cleaning; the ear tips drag in food and must also be kept clean. The ear canals also need regular cleaning for good health. Coat care is minimal, requiring only occasional brushing or wiping. The Bloodhound can live outside in temperate climates if they are given plenty of shelter and soft, warm,

bedding. Most do best as indoor/outdoor dogs; note, however, that this is not the breed for people obsessed with cleanliness in the house!

Health
- Major concerns: ectropion, entropion, gastric torsion, otitis externa, skin-fold dermatitis, CHD, elbow dysplasia
- Minor concerns: none
- Occasionally seen: none
- Suggested tests: hip, elbow, eye
- Life span: 7–10 years

Form and Function

The Bloodhound is a steadfast trailer, built for endurance rather than speed. The skin is thin and loose, falling in wrinkles around the head and throat. Its long ears are supposed to stir up scents as the ears rake along the ground, and its profuse wrinkles are said to trap the odors around the face, although neither of these assertions has ever been scientifically verified. Its dense short coat protects it from being caught in brambles. Its docile temperament makes it non-threatening to the humans

it is sometimes now called upon to trail. The gait is elastic and free, with the tail held high. The expression is noble and dignified.

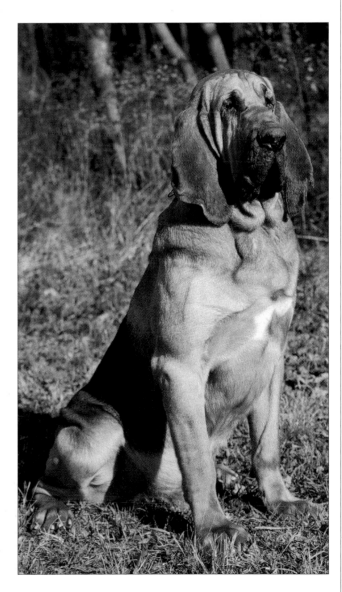

At a Glance

Energy level:	❏❏❏
Exercise requirements:	❏❏❏
Playfulness:	❏
Affection level:	❏❏❏❏❏
Friendliness toward dogs:	❏❏❏
Friendliness toward other pets:	❏❏❏❏❏
Friendliness toward strangers:	❏❏❏
Ease of training:	❏
Watchdog ability:	❏❏❏❏
Protection ability:	❏
Grooming requirements:	❏
Cold tolerance:	❏❏❏
Heat tolerance:	❏❏

Weight:	male: average 90 lb, up to 110 lb; female: average 80 lb, up to 100 lb (Note: Most Bloodhounds are actually heavier than this.)
Height:	male: 25–27"; female: 23–25"

Borzoi

History

The Borzoi (also known as the Russian Wolf-hound) was bred by the Russian aristocracy for hundreds of years. Coursing of hare for sport was known in Russia as early as the thirteenth century. In the fifteenth and sixteenth centuries, crosses of coursing hounds with bearhounds and with tall Russian sheepdogs were made to increase size and coat, both necessary for hunting wolves in the cold climate. The first standard was written in the 1600s in a book of Borzoi hunting rules. Perhaps no other breed has ever been the focus of hunting on such a grand scale. Hundreds of serfs worked in the upkeep of the hounds on huge estates; the hunts themselves were grand events. One account describes the hounds, horses, beaters, and hunters arriving in a train of over 40 cars, with another train bringing the Grand Duke and other nobility. Over 100 Borzoi might partake in a hunt. Beaters and scenthounds initially trailed the wolf, followed by hunters on horseback. A pair or trio (consisting of two males and

AKC Ranking: 80
Family: Sighthound, Southern (sighthound)
Area of Origin: Russia
Date of Origin: Middle Ages
Original Function: Coursing wolves
Today's Function: Lure coursing
Other Name: Russian Wolfhound

a female) of matched Borzoi was then unleashed when the wolf was sighted. The dogs would strike at the same time, forcing the wolf down and holding it until the hunter arrived to bind the wolf—and then, often, set it free. By the 1800s, seven distinct subtypes of Borzoi existed in Russia. Most present Borzoi descend from the Perchino type kept by the Grand Duke Nicolai Nicolayevitch, and many of the early American imports came directly from the Perchino kennels. The Russian Czar would often present Borzoi as gifts to visiting royalty. After the Russian Revolution, the days of the nobility were over, and many Borzoi were killed. The fate of the breed was left in the hands of foreign royalty who had been given Borzoi and of a few remaining Borzoi kennels. In America, the Borzoi soon gained the reputation as the ultimate glamour dog, often seen at the sides of movie stars. Although only enjoying modest popularity as a pet, the breed remains a popular show dog, coursing dog, and model.

Temperament

A breed of quiet elegance, the Borzoi exemplifies the well-mannered housedog indoors. Outdoors, it races with wild abandon, and it will chase any small animal that runs. It is independent but very sensitive. Although generally good with children, it may not be playful enough to satisfy some children. Some can be timid. It is reserved with strangers.

Upkeep

The Borzoi needs the chance to exert itself daily. Although a long walk can satisfy most of its needs, it should be combined with a sprint in a large safe area. The coat, which is characteristically fuller on males, needs brushing or combing two or three times a week; at times it sheds a lot. Borzoi can live outdoors in temperate climates as long as they have soft bedding and good shelter, but most do best as housedogs with access to a yard.

Health

- Major concerns: gastric torsion
- Minor concerns: none
- Occasionally seen: none

- Suggested tests: none
- Life span: 10–12 years
- Note: sensitive to anesthesia

Form and Function

The Borzoi is a running hound capable of hunting large, fierce game in a very cold climate. As such, it retains the greyhound build necessary for running at great speed, but it is larger and stronger than the greyhound. Its jaws should be strong enough to hold down a wolf. The long, silky coat, which can be either flat, wavy, or rather curly, provides protection against cold weather and snow. The Borzoi should possess elegance and grace, with flowing lines, whether standing or moving.

At a Glance

Energy level:	▢▢▢
Exercise requirements:	▢▢▢
Playfulness:	▢▢▢
Affection level:	▢▢▢
Friendliness toward dogs:	▢▢▢
Friendliness toward other pets:	▢▢
Friendliness toward strangers:	▢▢
Ease of training:	▢▢▢
Watchdog ability:	▢▢
Protection ability:	▢▢▢
Grooming requirements:	▢▢▢
Cold tolerance:	▢▢▢▢
Heat tolerance:	▢▢

Weight: male: 75–105 lb; female: 60–85 lb

Height: male: at least 28"; female: at least 26"

Dachshund

History

Definitive evidence of the Dachshund as a breed isn't found until the sixteenth century, when reference was made to a "low crooked legged" dog called a Little Burrow Dog, Dacksel, or Badger Dog. The modern name "Dachshund" means simply badger *(dachs)* dog *(hund)* in German. These tenacious hunters would follow their quarry, enter its burrow, pull it out, and kill it. The Dachshund comes in three coat varieties and two sizes. The original Dachshunds were smooth coated and arose from crosses of the Bracke, a miniature French pointer, with the Pinscher, a vermin killer of terrier type. Some evidence exists of longer-haired Dachshund-like dogs in sixteenth-century woodcuts. It is also possible that smooth Dachshunds were later crossed with spaniels and the German Stoberhund (a gundog) to produce the long-haired variety. Mention is made of wire-coated Dachshunds as early as 1797, but these dogs were not carefully bred and most modern wires were created around the end of the

AKC Ranking: 7
Family: Scenthound, Terrier, Dachshund
Area of Origin: Germany
Date of Origin: 1500s
Original Function: Flushing badgers
Today's Function: Earthdog trials, Dachshund field trials
Other Name: Teckel (Miniature: Zwergteckel)

nineteenth century by crossing smooth Dachshunds with German Wire-haired Pinschers and the Dandie Dinmont Terrier. Each of these varieties was best suited for hunting under slightly different terrain and climatic conditions, but all were tough, strong dogs capable of dispatching badger, fox, and other small mammals. Before 1900, very small Dachshunds were kept for going to ground after small quarry, such as rabbits. Although some were simply runts, others were intentionally produced by crosses with toy terriers or pinschers. Most of the resulting miniatures lacked Dachshund type, however. By 1910, stricter criteria were adopted for type, and each coat type was crossed with different breeds to achieve the best results: smooths were bred with the Miniature Pinscher, longs with the Papillon, and wires with the Miniature Schnauzer. The Dachshund has since found its real niche as a family pet, steadily rising in popularity to hold a place as one of the most popular hounds in America.

Temperament

The Dachshund is bold, curious, and always up for adventure. It likes to hunt and dig, tracking by scent and going to ground after game. It is independent but will join in its family's activities whenever given a chance. It is good with children in its own family, but some may snap at strange children. Most are reserved with strangers. Some bark. The longhaired variety may be quieter and less terrier-like; the wires may be more outgoing. Some miniatures are more prone to be timid.

Upkeep

Although active, the Dachshund's exercise requirements can be met with moderate walks on leash and games in the yard. It is amenable to city life or apartment living, but it is still a hunter at heart and enjoys forays into the wilds. Although it can live outdoors in warm weather, it does best sleeping inside. The smooth coat requires minimal grooming. The long coat requires brushing or combing once

or twice weekly and occasional trimming of stray hairs. The wire coat requires brushing or combing about once a week, with occasional trimming of stray hairs and stripping to remove dead hair twice a year.

Health

- Major concerns: intervertebral disc disease
- Minor concerns: KCS
- Occasionally seen: diabetes, epilepsy, patellar luxation, deafness, gastric torsion
- Suggested tests: (eye)
- Life span: 12–14 years
- Note: Obesity is a major problem for the Dachshund. Many dachshunds tend to be overweight, which in turn predisposes them to intervertebral disc disease.

Form and Function

The Dachshund's long low-slung body enables it to enter and move freely inside the confines of a den or tunnel, without sacrificing the necessary jaw and body strength to overcome its quarry. Its confidence, hunting instinct, keen nose, and loud voice also are of significant aid in hunting underground. Agility, freedom of movement, and endurance are necessary for the Dachshund's work, and its gait is fluid and smooth. The Dachshund has an energetic, pleasant expression. Each of the three coat varieties has special attributes: the smooth is short and shining, imparting some protection against the elements; the long hair is sleek, sometimes slightly wavy, providing somewhat more protection; the wire has tight, thick, and hard hair with a finer undercoat, providing maximal protection.

At a Glance

Energy level:	❏❏❏□
Exercise requirements:	❏❏
Playfulness:	❏❏❏
Affection level:	❏❏❏
Friendliness toward dogs:	❏❏❏
Friendliness toward other pets:	❏❏
Friendliness toward strangers:	❏
Ease of training:	❏❏
Watchdog ability:	❏❏❏❏❏
Protection ability:	❏❏
Grooming requirements: Smooth:	❏
Long:	❏❏
Wire:	❏❏❏
Cold tolerance:	❏❏❏
Heat tolerance:	❏❏❏

Weight:	Miniature: 11 lb and under Standard: over 11 lb (usually 16–32 lb)
Height:	Miniature: 5–6"; Standard: 8–9"*

American Foxhound

History

This most American of breeds dates back to 1650, with the first record of fox-chasing hounds arriving from England. By the 1700s, riding to the hounds had become extremely popular with the upper class; even George Washington found it a favorite pastime. Imports from England, France, and Ireland helped shape the breed. Foxhound pedigrees have been recorded in America since 1850. Around this same time, the sport spread to the southern United States, particularly the mountains of Kentucky and Tennessee, and hunters there preferred a faster dog with the ability to start, chase, and kill a fox alone, and also to give chase to deer. The dogs became more streamlined than their English counterparts. The dogs further developed into different strains, the most popular being the Walker. This strain descends from a dog named Tennessee Lead, alleged to have been stolen from a deerchase by a dog trader, who subsequently sold him to George Washington Mauphin, who is sometimes called the father

AKC Ranking: 139
Family: Scenthound
Area of Origin: United States
Date of Origin: 1600s
Original Function: Trailing fox
Today's Function: Trailing fox
Other Name: None

of the breed. His breedings to this fast running foxhound produced some of the best running dogs seen to that time. Dogs from that strain were subsequently called Walker hounds because the Walker brothers kept careful records of dogs produced from this strain. Other strains of foxhounds include Trigg, Goodman, July, Calhoun, and Hudspeth. These dogs eventually became specialized as either running hounds or show hounds, with the former being even further specialized as competitive field trial hounds and pack hounds. The pack type is generally considered the prototypical Foxhound. These dogs combine great speed, endurance, and jumping ability with a strong nose and willingness to give chase as a pack member. The American Foxhound was one of the earliest breeds to be registered by the AKC, although registrations have never been particularly high. The low AKC registration numbers belie the Foxhound's popularity, however, because most Foxhounds are kept in large packs by hunters with little interest in AKC registration. Their dogs are instead registered with Foxhound specialty studbooks, most notably the International Foxhunter's Studbook, published by the Chase. The Foxhound can thus lay claim to being one of the most unpopular popular breeds in America.

Temperament

Although by tradition the Foxhound is not a house pet, it is actually well mannered in the home. It gets along best with human or canine companionship. It is a tolerant, amiable, and gentle dog, even though it is not very demonstrative. Most are reserved with strangers. It is first and foremost a hunter, ever ready to hit the trail. It needs daily exercise in a safe area. Once on a scent, it will follow gleefully, heedless of commands. This is a dog that likes the outdoors; it is not a city dog. It bays.

Upkeep

The Foxhound needs daily exercise, preferably in the form of a long walk or jog. If allowed to run off leash, it should only be in a safe enclosed area.

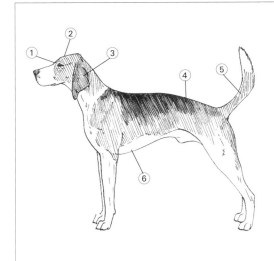

Foxhounds traditionally live outside, although only with warm shelter and bedding and in temperate climates. They are highly sociable, however, and should never be expected to live alone. The coat is easily maintained, requiring only occasional brushing to remove dead hair.

Health
• Major concerns: none
• Minor concerns: thrombocytopathy
• Occasionally seen: none
• Suggested tests: (blood)
• Life span: 10–13 years

Form and Function

The American Foxhound is slighter of bone and higher on leg that the English Foxhound, with more rear angulation and arch over the loin. These attributes give it greater speed and agility for hunting over rough terrain. It has a melodious voice when on the trail. The coat is hard and of medium length. The expression is gentle and pleading.

At a Glance

Energy level:	❏❏❏
Exercise requirements:	❏❏❏
Playfulness:	❏❏
Affection level:	❏❏
Friendliness toward dogs:	❏❏❏❏
Friendliness toward other pets:	❏❏
Friendliness toward strangers:	❏❏❏
Ease of training:	❏
Watchdog ability:	❏❏❏
Protection ability:	❏
Grooming requirements:	❏
Cold tolerance:	❏❏
Heat tolerance:	❏❏

Weight:	21–24 lb
Height:	22–25"

English Foxhound

History

Careful pedigrees have been kept of English Foxhounds since the late 1700s—longer than for any other breed. Still, the exact origin of the breed is unknown. At the time of its inception, coursing the stag with Greyhounds was still the favored dog sport of the gentry. Around 1750, a few men envisioned hunting foxes with swift horses and hounds. The hounds would have to be able to track a faint scent while on the run and to maintain their chase for hours. Foxhunting gained its appeal as a pastime of the wealthy, and packs of hounds were tended to by Masters of Foxhounds, who looked to the care and breeding of the dogs. Riding to the hounds became an affair steeped in ceremony, with the actual killing of the fox anticlimatic. As the esthetic aspects of the hunt increased in significance, care was taken to produce dogs that looked good not only individually but also as a pack. Thus, pack members would usually share the same coat coloration, most often the black saddle over a tan body with white points. Foxhunting became so popular that by the

AKC Ranking: 145
Family: Scenthound
Area of Origin: Great Britain
Date of Origin: 1700s
Original Function: Trailing fox
Today's Function: Trailing fox
Other Name: Foxhound

late 1800s, 140 packs (each with about 50 hounds) were registered in England alone. Foxhounds came to America in the 1700s, although in time a good percentage of these dogs were bred with other dogs to produce the American Foxhound. The latter has since surpassed the English Foxhound in popularity in America, although neither is popular as a pet or show dog. The English Foxhound is still the first choice of hunters wishing a traditional outing on horseback, riding to the melodious bay of this most classic of breeds.

Temperament

Traditionally a pack hound, the English Foxhound nonetheless makes a stately housedog, as long as it has human or canine companionship. It gets along well with horses, dogs, children, and other pets. It is an avid sniffer and trailer, however, and needs daily exercise in a safe area. It is a tolerant, amiable, and gentle dog even though it is not very demonstrative. Most are reserved

At a Glance

Energy level:	☐☐☐☐
Exercise requirements:	☐☐☐☐
Playfulness:	☐☐☐
Affection level:	☐☐☐
Friendliness toward dogs:	☐☐☐☐☐
Friendliness toward other pets:	☐☐☐
Friendliness toward strangers:	☐☐☐☐
Ease of training:	☐☐
Watchdog ability:	☐☐☐☐
Protection ability:	☐
Grooming requirements:	☐
Cold tolerance:	☐☐☐
Heat tolerance:	☐☐☐

Weight:	55–75 lb*
Height:	23–27"*

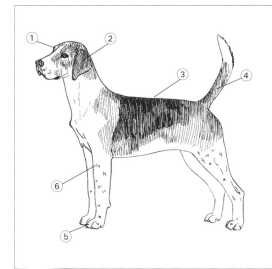

with strangers. It is not well suited for city life. It bays.

Upkeep

The Foxhound is an easygoing dog that nonetheless needs plenty of exercise. It is bred to run for miles, and it can make a good jogging companion on leash or a hiking companion in a safe area. It can live outdoors in temperate climates as long as it has warm shelter and bedding and, preferably, another Foxhound. The coat needs only occasional brushing to remove dead hair.

Health

• Major concerns: none
• Minor concerns: none
• Occasionally seen: CHD, renal disease
• Suggested tests: none
• Life span: 10–13 years

Form and Function

The English Foxhound is of powerful build, with large bone. The size of bone at the ankle is considered especially important. This build, along with comparatively straight angulation of the stifles, favors stamina over speed. The rich, deep voice is prized for the hunt. Many English Foxhounds have "rounded" ears, in which about 1½" are surgically removed from the end of the ear.

Greyhound

History

One of the first types of dogs selectively bred by humans was the sighthound, a dog that could run after and catch game by outrunning it. The prototypical sighthound has always been the Greyhound. Greyhound-like dogs have been depicted since ancient Egyptian, Greek, and Roman times. The name Greyhound may come from *Graius*, meaning Greek, or from the Latin *gradus*, denoting high grade. By Saxon time, Greyhounds were well established in Britain and were valued by both commoners for their ability to put food on the table and by nobility for the sport of the chase. In 1014 the Forest Laws prohibited all but nobility from keeping Greyhounds near royal forests unless they had been "lamed"; these laws remained in effect for four hundred years. Even when they were repealed, Greyhounds remained the dogs of nobility because with the growing importance of agriculture and domestic animal food sources, the running dog was not economically advantageous. Instead, Greyhounds were used for coursing hare for sport, and during the 1800s coursing became a consuming pastime of the upper class. Early American immigrants often

AKC Ranking: 128
Family: Sighthound, Southern (sighthound)
Area of Origin: Great Britain
Date of Origin: Ancient times
Original Function: Coursing hares
Today's Function: Racing, lure coursing, open-field coursing
Other Name: None

brought Greyhounds with them to the New World; here they proved adept at coursing on the open plains. When coursing was made available to the masses by staging it first in closed parks and then on tracks after a mechanical lure, the Greyhound's fate was sealed. Track racing proved so popular that dogs were bred specifically for short bursts of speed, ultimately resulting in the fastest breed of dog. At the same time, Greyhounds entered the show ring. The breed soon became divided into show and racing types, which were seldom interbred. In America, the Greyhound is one of the least popular breeds according to AKC registrations of show stock. The National Greyhound Association (NGA) registers many thousands of Greyhounds annually; however, recently retired racers from NGA stock have become popular as pets.

Temperament

Known as "the world's fastest couch potato," the Greyhound is quiet, calm, and extremely well-mannered indoors. They are good with other dogs, and with other pets if raised with them; out-

At a Glance

Energy level:	❑❑
Exercise requirements:	❑❑❑
Playfulness:	❑❑❑
Affection level:	❑❑❑
Friendliness toward dogs:	❑❑❑
Friendliness toward other pets:	❑❑
Friendliness toward strangers:	❑❑❑
Ease of training:	❑❑❑
Watchdog ability:	❑❑❑❑
Protection ability:	❑❑
Grooming requirements:	❑
Cold tolerance:	❑
Heat tolerance:	❑❑

Weight: male: 65–70 lb; female: 60–65 lb
Height: 27–30"*

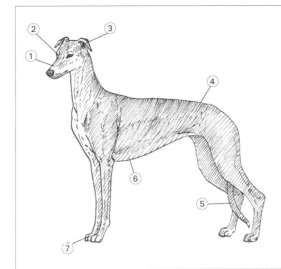

doors, they tend to chase any small thing that moves. They are reserved with strangers, very sensitive, and sometimes timid. Despite their independent nature, they are eager to please.

Upkeep

The Greyhound needs daily exercise, but it is a sprinter, not an endurance runner. Its needs can thus be met with a chance to run, or by a longer walk on leash. It loves to run and chase outdoors, and can easily run into danger at great speed unless exercised in a safe area. It is not generally amenable to living outdoors. Greyhounds relish creature comforts and must have soft bedding and warmth. The coat is extremely easy to care for, needing only occasional brushing to remove dead hair.

Health

- Major concerns: none
- Minor concerns: esophageal achalasia, gastric torsion, osteosarcoma
- Occasionally seen: none
- Suggested tests: none
- Life span: 10–13 years
- Note: Racing injuries, especially toe, hock, and muscle injuries, are common

in retired NGA dogs. Both NGA and AKC Greyhounds are sensitive to anesthesia and are prone to lacerations and tail-tip injuries.

Form and Function

The ultimate running dog, the Greyhound is built for speed. Its long legs and arched back enable it to contract and stretch maximally while executing the double-suspension gallop. It has tremendous muscle mass and light legs, further enhancing speed. The feet are long and narrow, giving maximum leverage. The long tail serves as a rudder and brake when running at high speed. The coat is short and smooth. Two types of Greyhounds are available: AKC (show) and NGA (racing). Retired NGA Greyhounds are smaller, sturdier, and faster than show dogs and may be more inclined to chase small animals.

Harrier

History

The word *harier* was Norman for dog or hound, so that it is difficult to unravel the ancient history of the Harrier from the history of hounds in general. Nonetheless, the Harrier may be one of the older scenthounds still in existence today, with references dating from thirteenth-century England. They probably stem from the long-extinct Talbot and St. Hubert hounds, and perhaps the Brachet and later, the French Basset. This lineage produced a dog that tracked hare by scent at a pace that enabled hunters to follow on foot. Thus, although Harrier packs were kept by the gentry, poorer hunters without horses could also hunt with Harriers, often combining the few dogs each individual had to form an impromptu pack. Smaller English Foxhounds may have been bred with these dogs in the early 1800s to develop a longer legged, faster dog also capable of running with mounted hunters. The Harrier has been known in America since colonial times.

AKC Ranking: 144
Family: Scenthound
Area of Origin: Great Britain
Date of Origin: Middle Ages
Original Function: Trailing hares
Today's Function: Trailing hare and fox
Other Name: None

Despite its classic proportions and handy size, it has never been popular as a show dog or pet.

Temperament

The Harrier is somewhat more playful and outgoing than the Foxhound, but not as much as the Beagle. It is amiable, tolerant, and good with children. Its first love is for the hunt, and it loves to sniff and trail. It needs daily exercise in a safe area. Most are reserved with strangers. It tends to bay.

Upkeep

The Harrier needs daily exercise, but its needs can be met with a long walk or jog and a vigorous game in the yard. It can live outdoors in temperate climates as long as it is given warm shelter and bedding. The coat is easily cared for, needing only occasional brushing to remove dead hair.

At a Glance

Energy level:	☐☐☐☐
Exercise requirements:	☐☐☐☐
Playfulness:	☐☐☐
Affection level:	☐☐☐
Friendliness toward dogs:	☐☐☐☐☐
Friendliness toward other pets:	☐☐☐
Friendliness toward strangers:	☐☐
Ease of training:	☐☐
Watchdog ability:	☐☐☐☐☐
Protection ability:	☐
Grooming requirements:	☐
Cold tolerance:	☐☐☐
Heat tolerance:	☐☐☐

Weight:	50–60 lb*
Height:	19–21″

Illustrated Standard

1. Moderately defined stop
2. Low-set ears with round tips
3. Level topline
4. Long tail, carried gaily but not curled over back, with a brush
5. Cat feet
6. Inclined to knuckle over slightly

❏ **Color:** any
❏ **DQ:** none

Health
- Major concerns: none
- Minor concerns: none
- Occasionally seen: none
- Suggested tests: none
- Life span: 10–12 years

Form and Function
The Harrier is a smaller version of the English Foxhound, more suited for hunting hares. It has large bone for its size, and is slightly longer than tall. It is a scenting pack hound and should be capable of running with other dogs, scenting its quarry, and hunting tirelessly over any terrain for long periods. It has a gentle expression when relaxed and alert when aroused. The coat is short and hard.

Ibizan Hound

History

The Ibizan Hound probably shares the same roots as the Pharaoh Hound, bearing uncanny resemblance to the dogs depicted in Egyptian tombs and to the jackal god Anubis. Phoenician sea traders may have taken the dogs to the island of Ibiza in ancient times, where they remained in relative seclusion. Ibiza saw many rulers through the ages, coming under the auspices of the Egyptians, Chaldeans, Carthaginians, Romans, Vandals, Arabs, and, most recently, Spanish. Hannibal was born on a neighboring island, and some say the Ibizan Hound was the dog that accompanied him across the Alps. With little outside influence, the dogs of Ibiza remain uncontaminated by crosses to other breeds. The hard conditions on the island imposed stringent selection by islanders because only the best rabbit hunters could be allowed to procreate or, for that matter, survive. These factors produced a hardy, true breeding dog little changed from its ancestral stock. The first Ibizan Hound came to America in the 1950s.

AKC Ranking: 136
Family: Sighthound, Southern (pariah), Primitive
Area of Origin: Ibiza (Balaeric Islands)
Date of Origin: Ancient times
Original Function: Hunting rabbits
Today's Function: Lure coursing
Other Name: Podenco Ibicenco, Ca Eibisenc, Balaeric Dog

The breed's striking appearance aroused much attention but has failed to attract a great number of pet owners. It gradually gained enough popularity to warrant AKC recognition in 1979, but the Ibizan Hound remains one of the rarer breeds.

Temperament

The graceful Ibizan Hound retains great hunting instinct, using its acute senses of hearing and smell to locate small animals, and relishing the opportunity to chase anything that moves. Unlike most sighthounds, it barks when chasing. It is reserved with strangers; some can be timid. It is gentle, mild-mannered, even-tempered, and loyal, and makes a quiet, trustworthy house pet.

Upkeep

As an independent and athletic dog, the Ibizan Hound needs daily exercise in a safe area. Ideal exercise allows the dog to stretch out at full speed, but its needs can also be met with long walks or jogs on leash, combined with an occasional chance to run full out. The Ibizan is not generally kept as an outside dog, although it can live outdoors in temperate climates given warm shelter and soft bedding. It is a skilled jumper, which should be taken into consideration when designing an enclosure. The smooth coat requires only occasional brushing, whereas the wire coat requires weekly brushing as well as occasional hand-plucking of dead hairs.

Health

- Major concerns: none
- Minor concerns: none
- Occasionally seen: deafness
- Suggested tests: none
- Life span: 12–14 years
- Note: sensitive to anesthesia

Form and Function

The Ibizan should possess a deer-like elegance and expression, and its movement reflects these qualities. Its lithe build enables it to perform the double-suspension gallop with great speed, agility, and

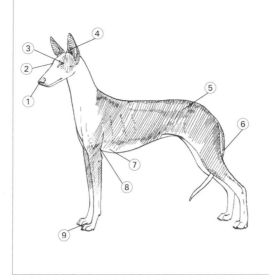

Illustrated Standard

① Rosy flesh-colored nose
② Long, narrow, cone-shaped head with prominent occiput, little-defined stop
③ Small light eyes
④ Large pointed ears, held erect when alert
⑤ Slightly arched loin
⑥ Tail set low and carried in a sickle, ring, or saber position
⑦ Brisket about 2½" above elbow
⑧ Rather upright upper arm, with elbow in front of deepest part of chest
⑨ Hare feet

❏ **Color:** white or red (from light yellowish red to deep red), solid or in any combination
❏ **DQ:** any color other than white or red

endurance. It is a superb jumper, able to spring to great heights from a standstill. It is racy, slightly longer than tall. With the exception of its large ears, it should not be exaggerated in any way. The trot is light and graceful. The coat can be hard, either short or wire, the latter from one to three inches in length.

At a Glance

Energy level:	❏❏❏
Exercise requirements:	❏❏❏
Playfulness:	❏❏❏
Affection level:	❏❏
Friendliness toward dogs:	❏❏❏❏
Friendliness toward other pets:	❏❏❏
Friendliness toward strangers:	❏❏❏
Ease of training:	❏❏
Watchdog ability:	❏❏❏❏
Protection ability:	❏
Grooming requirements: Smooth:	❏
Wire:	❏❏❏
Cold tolerance:	❏❏
Heat tolerance:	❏❏❏

Weight:	male: 50 lb; female: 45 lb
Height:	male: 23.5–27.5"; female: 22.5–26"

Irish Wolfhound

History

Dogs of great size are believed to have come to Ireland from Greece by 1500 B.C. In Ireland they became even more imposing, and gifts of these great dogs were made to Rome. The first definite mention of the Irish Wolfhound occurred in Rome in A.D. 391. The breed gained fame for its imposing stature and ability in fighting wild animals in arena sports. It was so acclaimed in Ireland that it became the subject of many legends recounting its valor in battle and chase. All large hounds were once known as *Cu*, a term implying bravery. The Irish name for the breed is Cu Faoil. Favored by Irish chieftains for the hunt, it gained its reputation as an unparalleled hunter of wolves and Irish elk. Illustrations of these dogs from the seventeenth century look very similar to modern Irish Wolfhounds. The impressive hounds (often seven at a time) were traditionally given to foreign nobility. This practice, along with the extinction of the wolf in Ireland in the eighteenth century, contributed to the decline of the breed's numbers. By the nineteenth century, Irish Wolfhounds were almost extinct in Ireland, and the

AKC Ranking: 77
Family: Sighthound, Southern (sighthound)
Area of Origin: Ireland
Date of Origin: Ancient times
Original Function: Coursing wolves and elk
Today's Function: Lure coursing
Other Name: None

famine of 1845 virtually decimated the breed. In 1869, Captain G. A. Graham determined to resurrect the Irish Wolfhound, a task he set about by crossing the few existing Wolfhounds—in particular one named Bran, thought to be the last true Wolfhound in Ireland—with such breeds as Scottish Deerhound as well as Great Dane, Borzoi, and even Tibetan Wolfdog. When first exhibited at a dog show in the 1870s, the reborn Wolfhound created a sensation—the same reaction it inspires to this day when first seen. Its commanding appearance draws many admirers, but its popularity is tempered by the practicalities of keeping such a large dog.

Temperament

Known as the gentle giant, this is an apt description of this soft-natured, easygoing breed. It is calm around the house, sensitive, patient, easygoing, and sweet. Despite its great size, it is good with children, pets, and other dogs. It is reserved with strangers, and courageous when the need arises.

Upkeep

The Irish Wolfhound enjoys a long walk and a chance to stretch its legs, so it needs daily exercise. At home it needs ample room to stretch out on a soft surface and should not be required to live in cramped quarters. It can develop callouses if allowed to lie on hard surfaces too often. Its coat needs to be brushed or combed once or twice weekly, plus occasional slight scissoring to neaten up straggly hairs. Dead hairs should be stripped twice a year.

Health

- Major concerns: gastric torsion
- Minor concerns: cardiomyopathy, OCD, osteosarcoma, CHD
- Occasionally seen: none
- Suggested tests: (hip), (heart)
- Life span: 5–7 years
- Note: sensitive to anesthesia; prone to tail-tip injuries

Form and Function

The tallest of the sighthounds, the Irish Wolfhound resembles a rough-coated Greyhound, although of more powerful build. Great size is especially valued in

Illustrated Standard

1. Long head and muzzle
2. Small, folded ears
3. Rather long back with arched loins
4. Very deep chest
5. Large round feet

❏ **Color:** gray, brindle, red, black, white, or fawn
❏ **DQ:** none

the breed. This combination of speed, power, and size enables the Irish Wolfhound to run down and overpower large prey. Despite its size, the breed should be gracefully built, its gait easy and active, its head held proudly. The rough coat, which provides protection against the cold and damp, as well as its opponents' teeth, is especially wiry and long over the eyes and under the jaw.

At a Glance

Energy level:	❏
Exercise requirements:	❏❏❏
Playfulness:	❏
Affection level:	❏❏❏
Friendliness toward dogs:	❏❏❏
Friendliness toward other pets:	❏❏❏
Friendliness toward strangers:	❏❏❏
Ease of training:	❏❏
Watchdog ability:	❏❏❏
Protection ability:	❏❏
Grooming requirements:	❏❏❏
Cold tolerance:	❏❏❏❏
Heat tolerance:	❏

Weight:	male: at least 120 lb; female: at least 105 lb
Height:	male: at least 32"; female: at least 30"

Norwegian Elkhound

History

The Elkhound is an unusual hound because its roots lie in the spitz breeds, which it still closely resembles. Its placement in the Hound Group reflects its hunting ability because the breed hunts like a hound. Still, this is a breed of many skills. The Elkhound has served humans as a hunter, guardian, herder, and defender at least since the time of the Vikings. In a land of subzero temperatures, deep snow, thick forests, and rugged mountains, only the hardiest of breeds could evolve to perform the variety of jobs at which the Elkhound excels. Of all its roles, hunting the elk (actually, moose) is this breed's forte. Two hunting-style Elkhounds are used: the bandhund is attached by a long line to the hunter while trailing the elk, while the loshund runs ahead trailing until it is within striking range. Its goal is to hold the elk at bay, and it will hunt quietly if the animal begins to run away. If the elk stops, the dog begins barking furiously to alert the hunter. Nimbly jumping

AKC Ranking: 72
Family: Spitz, Northern (hunting)
Area of Origin: Norway
Date of Origin: Ancient times
Original Function: Hunting elk
  (moose)
Today's Function: Companion
Other Name: Elkhound, Norsk Elghund

in and out toward the elk, it deftly avoids the swinging antlers. Either way, the Elkhound's job is not to kill the elk, but to locate it and hold it at bay until the hunter can shoot it. Although the breed had been carefully bred for centuries, only since the late 1800s were pedigrees kept and breeding according to standard performed. The breed has been exhibited in Scandinavian dog shows since that time and was brought to England and America shortly thereafter. The AKC recognized the breed around 1930, and it has enjoyed moderate popularity since then. In Scandinavia, the Elkhound is still tested by grueling elk hunts that may entail an entire day of trailing.

Temperament

The Norwegian Elkhound combines traits of hounds and spitz-like dogs, resulting in a breed that is bold, playful, independent, alert, boisterous, and—unlike most hounds—even protective. This is a dog ready for adventure and happiest if that adventure takes place outdoors in cold weather. It needs daily exercise lest it become frustrated or even destructive. It is friendly with strangers but may quarrel with strange dogs. It tends to pull when on leash unless trained, and it may bark a lot.

Upkeep

The Elkhound was developed to hunt all day under grueling conditions. It needs daily exertion in order to feel satisfied. This can be in the form of a good jog, very long walk, or invigorating play session. It can live outdoors in temperate or cool climates, but it is happiest living with its family. Its double coat needs brushing twice a week, and daily during main shedding season when it sheds a lot.

Health

- Major concerns: CHD
- Minor concerns: pyotraumatic dermatitis, PRA
- Occasionally seen: Fanconi syndrome
- Suggested tests: hip, eye
- Life span: 10–12 years

Illustrated Standard

1. Defined stop
2. Oval eyes
3. Wedge-shaped head, broad at ears
4. High-set, erect, fairly small ears with pointed tips
5. Tail tightly curved and carried over the centerline of the back
6. Small oval feet

❏ **Color:** gray, with lighter undercoat and undersides. Muzzle, ears, and tail tip are black.
❏ **DQ:** an overall color other than gray

Form and Function

A typical northern spitz-like breed, the Norwegian Elkhound is square-proportioned, close coupled, with substantial bone, broad head, pricked ears, and tightly curled tail. It is constructed for agility and endurance, rather than speed, enabling it to trail for hours and then hold big game at bay by barking and dodging attack. Its trot is effortless. It has a thick, smooth-lying coat consisting of straight outer hairs and a wooly undercoat. This combination presents the best protection against cold and snow.

At a Glance

Energy level:	▫▫▫▫
Exercise requirements:	▫▫▫
Playfulness:	▫▫▫▫
Affection level:	▫▫▫
Friendliness toward dogs:	▫▫
Friendliness toward other pets:	▫▫
Friendliness toward strangers:	▫▫▫
Ease of training:	▫
Watchdog ability:	▫▫▫▫▫
Protection ability:	▫▫▫▫
Grooming requirements:	▫▫▫
Cold tolerance:	▫▫▫▫▫
Heat tolerance:	▫

Weight:	male: 55 lb; female: 48 lb
Height:	male: 20.5"; female: 19.5"

Otterhound

History

One of the most unusual members of the Hound Group is the Otterhound, a hardy, tousled scenthound of uncertain origin. The breed may have originated in France, and it closely resembles the old French Vendeen hound. Other breeds that may have played a part in its origin were the Welsh Harrier, Southern Hound (a foxhound-like breed), Bloodhound, or a type of water spaniel. Whatever the genetic makeup, the Otterhound came to fill a unique niche as a hunter of otters in England and is thus most associated with that country. King John kept the first documented packs of Otterhounds in 1212. The breed was useful for finding otters that were depleting fish in local streams. They would trail the otter to its den and bay when locating it. The hunters would then remove the Otterhounds and send small terriers to dispatch the otter. Otterhunting was never among the most popular of sports, lacking the formal trappings of foxhunting and taking place under wet and uncomfortable conditions. Nonetheless, the sport reached its peak during the latter half of the nineteenth century, when over twenty packs were hunting in Britain, but it essentially died out after the Second World

AKC Ranking: 143
Family: Scenthound
Area of Origin: England
Date of Origin: Ancient times
Original Function: Hunting otters
Today's Function: Companion
Other Name: None

War. The first Otterhound came to America at the beginning of the twentieth century and was recognized by the AKC soon after. Otterhound aficionados have been especially adamant that the breed retain its functional characteristics, without succumbing to exaggerated grooming practices or the temptation to breed only for a competitive show dog. Even though this practice has maintained the true Otterhound type, the breed has never been especially popular as a show dog or pet. Despite the fact that the Otterhound is one of the most ancient of the English breeds, it is one of the rarest of English Kennel Club or AKC recognized breeds, verging perilously close to extinction.

Temperament

As a packhound, the Otterhound is amiable with other dogs. As a hunter, it has an innate urge to follow the trails of mammals. Once on the trail, it is determined, single-minded, and nearly impossible to dissuade from its task. Even though the Otterhound's job was not to kill its quarry, it will nonetheless give chase to small animals. The Otterhound loves to hunt, sniff, trail, and, especially, swim. At home it is boisterous, amiable, and easygoing (although stubborn), affectionate with its family, and quite good with children. Because the Otterhound was never traditionally kept as a pet, it is not among the most responsive of breeds. However, the Otterhound is a low-key dog that can function as a quiet companion.

Upkeep

The Otterhound needs daily exercise in a safe area or on a leash. It has a loud, melodious voice that carries for long distances. The Otterhound's coat requires only weekly brushing or combing. It may need its beard washed more frequently. Tidiness is not one of its virtues; the large, hairy feet tend to hold debris and mud, and the long hair around the mouth can hold water and food. It can sleep outdoors in temperate or cool climates, given good shelter.

Health

- Major concerns: CHD, CTP, gastric torsion
- Minor concerns: elbow dysplasia
- Occasionally seen: none

Illustrated Standard

1. Square muzzle with deep flews
2. Deep-set eyes
3. Large, fairly narrow head, well covered with hair
4. Long, pendulous, low-set ears
5. Tail carried saber fashion when moving
6. Large webbed feet

❏ **Color:** any
❏ **DQ:** none

- Suggested tests: hip, elbow, blood
- Life span: 10–13 years

Form and Function

The Otterhound is a large dog with a somewhat stocky build, slightly longer than tall, not exaggerated in any way, enabling it to trot at a slow steady pace for long distances without tiring. Its coat, which consists of a rough, coarse outer coat combined with a soft wooly slightly oily undercoat, is essential for protecting it from brambles and cold water. It has a fairly large nose and muzzle, allowing ample room for olfactory receptors. Its large feet provide traction over rough and slippery terrain. This is a strong athletic breed that can withstand harsh weather and long strenuous hunts. Its expression is open and amiable, reflecting its temperament. The Otterhound is noted for its steadfast pursuit of its quarry despite the roughest of conditions. It has an acute sense of smell and can trail unerringly through running water and over all sorts of terrain.

At a Glance

Energy level:	❑❑
Exercise requirements:	❑❑❑
Playfulness:	❑❑❑
Affection level:	❑❑❑❑❑
Friendliness toward dogs:	❑❑❑
Friendliness toward other pets:	❑❑❑
Friendliness toward strangers:	❑❑❑❑❑
Fase of training:	❑❑
Watchdog ability:	❑❑❑❑
Protection ability:	❑
Grooming requirements:	❑❑❑
Cold tolerance:	❑❑❑❑
Heat tolerance:	❑❑

Weight:	male: 115 lb; female: 80 lb
Height:	male: 27"; female: 24"

Petit Basset Griffon Vendéen

History

The PBGV, as it is affectionately known, is a comparative newcomer to the AKC world, but it is an ancient breed with roots in sixteenth-century Europe. The long French name provides an accurate description of the breed: Petit (small) Basset (low) Griffon (rough-coated) Vendéen (its area of origin in France). This area, on the west coast of France, is filled with thick brambles, underbrush, and rocky terrain. Hunting in such terrain demanded a dog that had a coat that could withstand thorns and brambles, short legs that could enable it to wind its way through the underbrush in pursuit of rabbits, but nimbleness that allowed it to run over rocks and logs without tiring. Thus, the PBGV is more than a wire-coated Basset Hound, and more than a dwarf Grand Basset Griffon Vendéen (a breed that resembles a slightly taller PBGV), even though it is closely related to both breeds. In England in the mid 1800s, the PBGV was shown with the Basset Hound as a

AKC Ranking: 114
Family: Scenthound
Area of Origin: France
Date of Origin: 1700s
Original Function: Trailing hare
Today's Function: Companion
Other Name: Little Griffon Vendeen
  Basset

wire-coated variety, but the PBGV is a longer legged, more nimble hound. In France, the Griffon Vendéen was considered to be one breed with two sizes until the 1950s. The two sizes were still interbred until the 1970s. The AKC recognized the PBGV in 1990, and since then the PBGV has attracted many new admirers because of its merry disposition and tousled carefree appearance.

Temperament

Despite its appearance, the PBGV is not a Basset Hound in a wire coat, but is in many ways more terrier-like in temperament. It is a merry, inquisitive, tough, busy dog, always on the lookout for excitement and fun. It loves to sniff, explore, trail, and dig, a true hunter at heart. Amiable and playful, it is good with children, other dogs, and pets, and it is friendly toward strangers. It is stubborn and independent. It tends to dig and bark.

At a Glance

Energy level:	▢▢▢▢
Exercise requirements:	▢▢▢
Playfulness:	▢▢▢▢
Affection level:	▢▢▢▢▢
Friendliness toward dogs:	▢▢▢▢
Friendliness toward other pets:	▢▢▢
Friendliness toward strangers:	▢▢▢▢
Ease of training:	▢
Watchdog ability:	▢▢▢▢
Protection ability:	▢
Grooming requirements:	▢▢
Cold tolerance:	▢▢▢
Heat tolerance:	▢▢▢

Weight:	25–35 lb*
Height:	13–15"

Illustrated Standard

① Long beard and mustache
② Large eyes surmounted by long eyebrows
③ Domed skull with well-defined occiput and stop
④ Proudly carried, long head
⑤ Low-set, long ears
⑥ Level back with slight arch over loin
⑦ Medium-length tail, carried proudly

❏ **Color:** white with any combination of lemon, orange, tricolor, or grizzle markings
❏ **DQ:** height over 15.5"

Upkeep

The PBGV is not content to lie around. Its exercise requirements can be easily fulfilled, however, by a good walk on leash or a vigorous romp in the yard. It can sleep outdoors in temperate climates, given adequate shelter, but it is happiest when dividing its time between house and yard. The coat needs weekly brushing and occasional tidying of straggling hairs.

Health

• Major concerns: none
• Minor concerns: otitis externa, CHD
• Occasionally seen: meningitis, patellar luxation, epilepsy
• Suggested tests: (hip)
• Life span: 11–14 years

Form and Function

A correctly proportioned PBGV is about 50 percent longer than it is tall, enabling it to push its way through dense thickets. It has strong bone and surprising nimbleness. The gait is free, giving the appearance of a dog that is capable of a full day in the field. The tousled appearance results in part from its rough coat, with long facial furnishings. This, in combination with its thick shorter undercoat, gives the PBGV ample protection against brambles and the elements. Its expression—alert and friendly—reflects its nature.

Pharaoh Hound

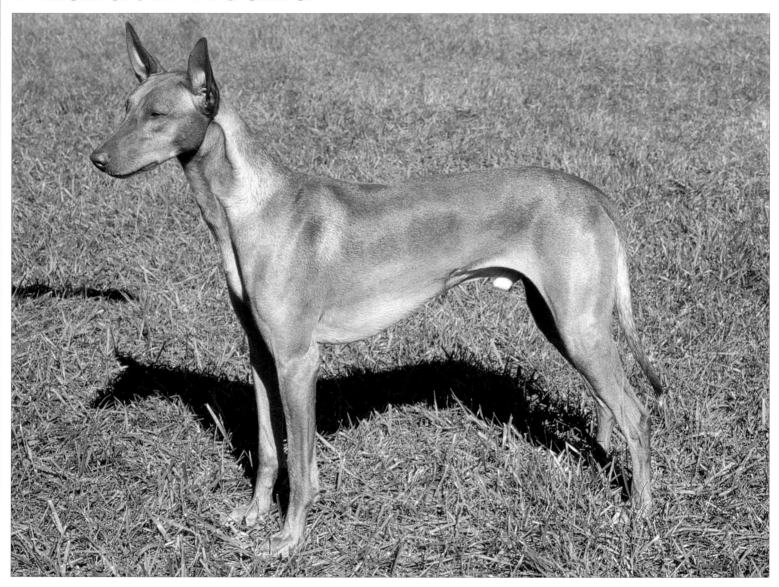

History

A hunting account from the XIX Egyptian dynasty supplies an apt description of the modern Pharaoh Hound: "The red, long-tailed dog goes at night into the stalls of the hills. He makes no delay in hunting, his face glows like a God and he delights to do his work." Even today, the Pharaoh Hound is noted for "blushing": the tendency of its nose and ears to flush with blood and "glow" when the dog is excited. The breed is one of several with a legitimate claim of most-ancient breed and appears to have changed little in the last 3000 years. It bears an uncanny resemblance to the jackal god Anubis and to dogs depicted on the tombs of the Egyptian pharaohs, and later, dogs featured in ancient Greek art. Phoenician traders may have introduced the dogs from Greece and North Africa to the islands of Malta and Gozo, where they became essentially secluded

AKC Ranking: 134
Family: Sighthound, Southern
    (pariah), Primitive
Area of Origin: Malta
Date of Origin: Ancient times
Original Function: Hunting rabbits
Today's Function: Lure coursing
Other Name: Kelb-tal Fenek

from the rest of the world. Here they flourished as rabbit dogs, or Kelb-tal Fenek. Several hounds would be released (often at night) to find the scent of a rabbit; they would bark once the rabbit went to ground (usually in a stone wall or rocky crevice). A belled ferret would then be sent after the rabbit, and one hound would follow its progress by sound, until the rabbit was flushed and caught by the dog. The Pharaoh Hound is now the National Dog of Malta. In the 1960s, the breed was redis-covered and imported to England and later America. The AKC recognized it in 1983.

Temperament

The svelte Pharaoh Hound is more than a gracious addition to the home (though it surely is that)—it is a keen hunter and an exuberant chaser. Although it is calm indoors, it loves to run. It is sensitive, loving, gentle, and good with children and other dogs, but it may chase strange animals. It tends to be reserved with strangers; some are even timid. It is independent but willing to please. The breed has the unique characteristic of "blushing" when excited, with the nose and ears turning a rosy color.

Upkeep

The Pharaoh Hound relishes the opportunity to stretch its legs in a safe area, although it can manage with long daily walks on leash and occasional sprints. It needs soft bedding and warmth and generally should not be expected to sleep outside except in warm climates—but it would still prefer to sleep with its family. Its coat is low maintenance, requiring only occasional brushing to remove dead hair.

Health

- Major concerns: none
- Minor concerns: none
- Occasionally seen: none
- Suggested tests: none
- Life span: 11–14 years

Illustrated Standard

1. Flesh-covered nose
2. Amber-colored eyes
3. Slight stop
4. Long chiseled head
5. Large ears, carried erect when alert
6. Whip-like tail

❏ **Color:** tan or chestnut, with a white tail-tip desired
❏ **DQ:** any solid white spot on the back of neck, shoulder, or any part of the back or sides

Form and Function

Although considered a sighthound in America, the Pharaoh Hound hunts by both sight and scent—as well as hearing. It has an unexaggerated greyhound-like build, combining grace, power, and speed, enabling it to run nimbly along rocky walls and ground. It has a good nose. Its large, mobile ears help it follow animals underground. Slightly longer than tall, its gait is free and flowing, with head held high. The coat is short and glossy.

At a Glance

Energy level:	❏❏❏
Exercise requirements:	❏❏❏❏
Playfulness:	❏❏❏
Affection level:	❏❏❏
Friendliness toward dogs:	❏❏❏❏
Friendliness toward other pets:	❏❏
Friendliness toward strangers:	❏❏
Ease of training:	❏❏❏
Watchdog ability:	❏❏❏❏
Protection ability:	❏
Grooming requirements:	❏
Cold tolerance:	❏❏
Heat tolerance:	❏❏❏

Weight:	45–55 lb*
Height:	male: 23–25"; female: 21–24"

Rhodesian Ridgeback

History

When European Boer settlers arrived in South Africa in the sixteenth and seventeenth centuries, they brought with them such breeds as the Mastiff, Great Dane, Bloodhound, Pointer, Staghound, and Greyhound, among others. These settlers needed a dog that could withstand both hot and cold temperatures, limited water, and rough bush, while performing the duties of guard dog and hunting dog. By breeding their European dogs with native Hottentot tribal hunting dogs (which were distinguished by a ridge of hair growing in the opposite direction along the top of their back) they produced just such a dog. These dogs hunted by both sight and scent and were devoted protectors of the entire family. In the 1870s, several of these dogs were taken to Rhodesia to hunt lions, chasing and harassing the lion until the hunter could shoot it. The dogs were so successful that the "Lion Dogs" became popular, their distinctive ridge becoming a trademark of quality. By the 1920s, so many different types of ridged Lion Dogs existed in Rhodesia that a meeting was held to elucidate the most desirable points of the breed, which became the basis for the current standard. Dogs

> AKC Ranking: 56
> Family: Sighthound, Scenthound, Southern (sight)
> Area of Origin: South Africa
> Date of Origin: 1800s
> Original Function: Large game (including lion) hunting, guardian
> Today's Function: Lure coursing
> Other Name: African Lion Hound

meeting the standard criteria were known as Rhodesian Ridgebacks (the dogs' former designation as Lion Dogs was deemed to sound too savage). The breed was introduced into England in the 1930s and to America soon after. In both cases, it gained recognition in the 1950s and quickly attracted admirers. In the 1980s, the breed received recognition as a sighthound and became eligible to compete in sighthound field trials. Today it is among the more popular hounds, undoubtedly because it combines the abilities of hunter, protector, and companion in a sleek handsome body.

Temperament

The Rhodesian Ridgeback is the Hound Group's answer to a somewhat protective dog. Not only is it a keen and versatile hunter, but it is a loyal guardian. It is good with children, especially protective of those in its family, but it is sometimes overly boisterous in play for small children. It is strong-willed and powerful; some can become domineering. It is reserved with strangers and can be aggressive toward strange dogs and animals.

Upkeep

The Ridgeback loves to run, and it needs daily mental and physical exercise to keep it from becoming frustrated. It can be a good jogging or hiking companion. The Ridgeback can live outdoors in temperate or warm climates, but it is usually much happier sleeping indoors and dividing its time between the house and yard during the day. Coat care is minimal, consisting only of occasional brushing to remove dead hair.

Health

- Major concerns: dermoid sinus
- Minor concerns: CHD
- Occasionally seen: deafness, elbow dysplasia
- Suggested tests: breeder check for dermoid sinus, (hip)
- Life span: 10–13 years

Form and Function

Slightly longer than tall, the Ridgeback combines features of speed, power, and endurance. The Rhodesian Ridgeback must have an athletic build to enable it to catch up to a lion and then harass it without being hurt. Because the

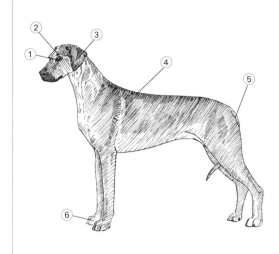

Illustrated Standard

1. Round eyes
2. Flat skull, rather broad between ears
3. High-set ears of medium size
4. Ridge on back
5. Tapering tail, carried with a slight curve
6. Feet compact

☐ **Color:** light wheaten to red wheaten; nose can be black, brown or liver
☐ **DQ:** ridgelessness

lion is not the only quarry of the Ridgeback, the dog must also be strong enough to bring down other large game. Its stride is efficient and long. The short glossy coat is adapted for working in hot climates. A distinctive feature is the clearly defined ridge, which should start with two identical whorls just behind the shoulders and taper to a point between the hipbones.

At a Glance

Energy level:	☐☐☐
Exercise requirements:	☐☐☐
Playfulness:	☐☐☐
Affection level:	☐☐☐
Friendliness toward dogs:	☐
Friendliness toward other pets:	☐☐
Friendliness toward strangers:	☐
Ease of training:	☐☐☐
Watchdog ability:	☐☐☐☐☐
Protection ability:	☐☐☐☐☐
Grooming requirements:	☐
Cold tolerance:	☐☐☐
Heat tolerance:	☐☐☐

Weight:	male: 85 lb; female: 70 lb
Height:	male: 25–27"; female: 24–26"

Saluki

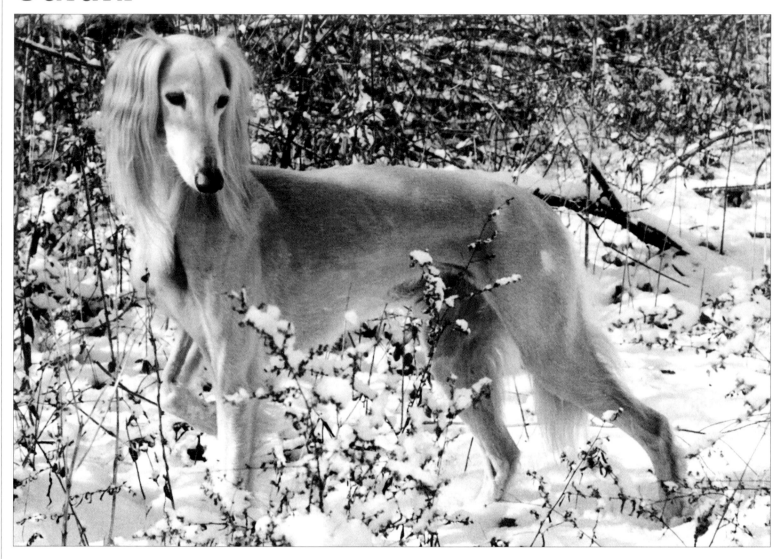

History

The Saluki is perhaps the most ancient breed of domestic dog. Evidence of the Saluki can be found on Egyptian tombs dating several thousand years B.C. The name Saluki may come from the ancient civilization of Seleucia. Arab nomads used Salukis to run down gazelles, foxes, and hares in the desert, often with the aid of falcons. Although the Muslim religion considered the dog to be unclean, an exception was made for the Saluki, which was referred to as *el hor*, the noble one. As the provider of meat, the Saluki was allowed to sleep in the tents and enjoy the tender attention of its Bedouin master. Salukis were not allowed to breed with non-Salukis, accounting for their purity throughout the centuries. Because they ranged with their nomadic owners over a wide area of the Middle East, Salukis became widely distributed with great local variation, resulting in the breed's variability today. The Saluki came to the attention of the Western world around 1900 and was recognized

AKC Ranking: 107
Family: Sighthound, Southern (sighthound)
Area of Origin: Middle East
Date of Origin: Ancient times
Original Function: Coursing hare and gazelles
Today's Function: Lure coursing, open-field coursing
Other Name: Gazelle Hound, Persian Greyhound

by the AKC in 1928. Their numbers have decreased in the lands of their origin as a result of the advent of hunting with guns from jeeps. The primary role of the Saluki today is as an exotic companion and show dog, although many are still used for hare coursing. The Saluki is also called the Persian Greyhound, Gazelle Hound, or Tazi.

Temperament

The Saluki tends to be aloof and reserved with strangers. It is extremely devoted to its own family, but it is not particularly demonstrative. The Saluki is very gentle with children, but it may not be playful enough to satisfy most children. The Saluki is extremely sensitive and does not take to rough and tumble play or deal well with harsh corrections. Some can be shy. It is very quiet and sedate inside, seeking out a soft warm spot. Outside, it runs in great circles at tremendous speeds and will chase any small running animals or fast-moving objects. It may not come when called.

At a Glance

Energy level:	☐☐
Exercise requirements:	☐☐☐
Playfulness:	☐☐☐
Affection level:	☐☐☐
Friendliness toward dogs:	☐☐☐
Friendliness toward other pets:	☐☐☐
Friendliness toward strangers:	☐
Ease of training:	☐☐☐
Watchdog ability:	☐☐☐☐
Protection ability:	☐☐
Grooming requirements: Smooth:	☐
Feathered:	☐☐
Cold tolerance:	☐☐
Heat tolerance:	☐☐☐

Weight:	35–65 lb*
Height:	male: 23–28";
	female: may be considerably smaller

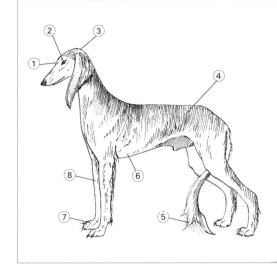

Illustrated Standard

① Stop not pronounced
② Large oval eyes
③ Long narrow head, moderately wide backskull
④ Slightly arched loin
⑤ Long tail, well feathered underneath*
⑥ Deep, moderately narrow chest
⑦ Long toes, well feathered between them*
⑧ Long legs

❑ **Color:** white, cream, fawn, golden, red, grizzle, black and tan, tricolor, or any of these on a white background
❑ **DQ:** none

*no feathering appears in smooth variety.

- Suggested tests: none
- Life span: 12–14 years
- Note: sensitive to anesthesia

Form and Function

The Saluki has a general greyhound-like build and should combine the aspects of grace, symmetry, great speed, and endurance coupled with strength to enable it to kill gazelle or other quarry over deep sand or rocky mountains.

The expression should be dignified and gentle with deep, faithful, far-seeing eyes. Its movement is light. The coat is smooth and silky; the feathered variety has long hair on ears, tail, between its toes, and sometimes on the backs of its legs; the smooth variety has no long feathering. This breed has a wide range of equally acceptable types, reflecting the wide area over which it was developed.

Upkeep

Daily exercise is essential, preferably in the form of free-running in a safe enclosed area. Its needs can also be met with long leash walks or jogging. They should sleep inside in all but the warmest climates, and do best as an indoor dog with access to a yard. They can play in snow and cold weather but should not be expected to spend extended time in the cold. The Saluki must have a soft bed, or it can develop callouses. A Saluki in proper weight is naturally thin, but many tend to be picky eaters, which can result in a very thin-looking dog. Many people not familiar with the breed wrongly assume that the dog is not being fed properly! The smooth coat needs only occasional brushing to remove dead hair, but the longer feathering needs combing once or twice a week to prevent matting.

Health

- Major concerns: none
- Minor concerns: none
- Occasionally seen: cardiomyopathy

Scottish Deerhound

History

Among the most aristocratic of breeds, the Scottish Deerhound has been valued by nobility for its prowess in running down deer at least since the sixteenth century. Confusion regarding names makes tracing its exact history before that time difficult, but it probably is a very ancient breed, deriving from ancestral Greyhound roots. Like its smooth-coated Greyhound relative, the rough-coated Deerhound could not be owned by anyone ranked lower than an Earl during the Age of Chivalry. As the stag population declined in England, the larger, rough-coated dogs suited for hunting stag became concentrated where the stag remained plentiful—namely, the Scottish Highlands—where they were valued and hoarded by Highland chieftains. This hoarding resulted in the decline of the breed in the mid 1700s following the collapse of the clan system of Culloden. Further decline occurred with the advent of breech-loading rifles in the 1800s because hunting deer with guns supplanted coursing in popularity. By the mid 1800s, however, a concerted effort to restore the breed had

AKC Ranking: 119
Family: Sighthound, Southern (sighthound)
Area of Origin: Scotland
Date of Origin: Middle Ages
Original Function: Coursing stag
Today's Function: Lure coursing
Other Name: Deerhound

proved successful, and although its numbers were never great, the quality of the dogs was high. The first Deerhound club was formed in England in the 1860s, around the same time the first Deerhounds were exhibited in dog shows. The First World War again decimated the breed's numbers because most of the dogs had been the property of a limited number of large estates, most of which did not survive the war intact. Since then, the Deerhound has remained low in number but high in quality, a classic in every sense.

Temperament

The Scottish Deerhound is mellow, low-key, and easygoing, a gracious and well-mannered addition to the home. Outdoors, it loves to run and chase anything that moves. Indoors, it needs plenty of room to stretch on a soft surface. It is independent but willing to please; it is extremely sensitive. It is amiable toward but often reserved with strangers. It is good with children, other dogs, and usually other pets, although it may give chase to strange animals.

Upkeep

The Deerhound needs a good amount of daily exercise, either a long walk or a romp in a safe area. Although physically suited to outdoor living in temperate or cool climates, it prefers to live inside with its family and needs human companionship. Regardless, it needs soft bedding to avoid callouses. The crisp coat needs combing one or two times weekly. Some scissoring is optional to neaten up straggling hair, plus minimal stripping around the face and ears.

Health

- Major concerns: gastric torsion, osteosarcoma
- Minor concerns: cardiomyopathy
- Occasionally seen: none
- Suggested tests: cardiac
- Life span: 8–11 years
- Note: sensitive to anesthesia

Form and Function

The Scottish Deerhound has a body like that of a Greyhound but is of larger size and bone, enabling it to run at great speed using the double-suspension

Illustrated Standard

1. Good mustache and beard of silky hair
2. Long head with flat skull
3. Small, folded ears, dark in color
4. Arched loin drooping to the tail
5. Wide, drooping hindquarters
6. Long, tapering tail
7. Deep chest
8. Compact feet

❏ **Color:** all shades of gray and gray brindle, with dark blue-gray preferred; yellow, red, and fawn are permitted but not seen today
❏ **DQ:** white blaze on head, or a white collar

gallop without sacrificing strength and endurance. Its trotting gait is easy and true. The hair is harsh and crisp, about three to four inches long on the body, ideally close lying. Such a coat imparts a weather- (and dirt-) resistant quality, an essential asset in cold, damp climates.

At a Glance

Energy level:	❏❏
Exercise requirements:	❏❏❏
Playfulness:	❏❏
Affection level:	❏❏❏
Friendliness toward dogs:	❏❏❏❏
Friendliness toward other pets:	❏❏❏
Friendliness toward strangers:	❏❏❏
Ease of training:	❏❏
Watchdog ability:	❏
Protection ability:	❏❏
Grooming requirements:	❏❏❏
Cold tolerance:	❏❏❏
Heat tolerance:	❏❏

Weight:	male: 85–110 lb; female: 75–95 lb
Height:	male: 30–32"; female: at least 28"

Whippet

History

A medium-sized sighthound, the Whippet stems
from Greyhound roots. The Whippet's progenitors
may have come from crosses between small
Greyhounds and even smaller dogs, to be used
by peasants for poaching rabbits and other small
game in the eighteenth century. The peasants
also found entertainment in "snap dog" contests,
in which bets were made on which dog could
"snap up" as many rabbits as possible before
they escaped from a circle. Crosses with ratting terriers were probably made to increase quickness and gameness. It was the advent
of the Industrial Revolution, however, that spurred the development
of the true Whippet breed. Masses of rural workers moved to indus-
trialized areas, bringing with them their snap dogs and a need for
entertainment. Without a supply of rabbits, they found their dogs
would just as readily race toward a waving rag. Rag racing became
the sport of coal miners; in fact, the Whippet was dubbed the "poor
man's race horse." A family's Whippet was not only an immense
source of pride but sometimes also a source of extra income and

AKC Ranking: 66
Family: Sighthound, Southern
  (sighthound)
Area of Origin: England
Date of Origin: 1700s
Original Function: Racing, rabbit
  coursing
Today's Function: Racing, lure
  coursing
Other Name: None

procurer of food for the pot. As a valued family
member, it shared the family rations and often,
the children's beds, and came to be valued as a
companion as well. Whippet racing is still popular today, but it never gained the commercial
appeal of Greyhound racing and so remains
strictly an amateur sport. After the Whippet
was officially recognized as a breed in 1888, it
began to be appreciated for its aesthetic appeal,
and crosses with the Italian Greyhound further
refined its appearance. The Whippet gained popularity only slowly,
but its unequaled combination of lithe elegance and gracious
companionship gradually created a devoted following. Today the
Whippet is the most popular of the sighthounds and is highly valued
as a show dog, lure-courser, racer, and family companion.

Temperament

Perhaps the most demonstrative and obedient of the true
sighthounds, the Whippet makes an ideal pet for people who want
a quiet housedog and absolutely devoted companion. The Whippet

is extremely gentle with children and can make an excellent companion for them. It is calm indoors but loves to run and play outdoors. It is extremely sensitive (both physically and mentally) and cannot take rough treatment or harsh corrections.

Upkeep

The Whippet can make a good apartment dog if it is taken for a long walk or run daily. Grooming is minimal. The Whippet must have a warm, soft bed. It dislikes cold weather intensely and cannot be expected to live outside. The Whippet can play and run in snow and cold weather but should spend inactive times in warmer temperatures. The hair is extremely short and fine, and the Whippet is virtually free of "doggy odor."

Health

- Major concerns: none
- Minor concerns: none
- Occasionally seen: deafness, some eye defects
- Suggested tests: none
- Life span: 12–15 years
- Note: sensitive to anesthesia; prone to lacerations

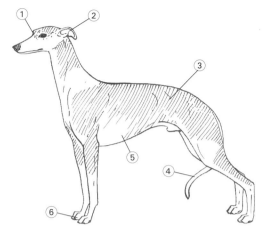

Illustrated Standard

① Long lean skull with scarcely perceptible stop
② Small folded ears
③ Gracefully arched loin
④ Long tail carried low
⑤ Deep chest with definite tuckup
⑥ Hare feet

❏ **Color:** immaterial
❏ **DQ:** over ½" above or below stated height limits; blue or wall eyes; undershot, overshot ¼" or more; any coat other than short

Form and Function

A Greyhound in miniature, the Whippet is among the sleekest of dogs, with a curvaceous, streamlined silhouette, long legs, and a lean physique. The Whippet is the ultimate sprinter, unsurpassed by any other breed in its ability to accelerate to top speed and to twist and turn with unequaled agility. It is a lightweight version of the Greyhound, with an especially supple topline and powerful hindquarters enabling it to execute the double-suspension gallop at its most extreme. It is square or slightly longer than tall. The gait is low and free-moving. The expression is keen and alert.

At a Glance

Energy level:	❏❏❏
Exercise requirements:	❏❏❏
Playfulness:	❏❏❏
Affection level:	❏❏❏❏
Friendliness toward dogs:	❏❏❏❏❏
Friendliness toward other pets:	❏❏❏❏
Friendliness toward strangers:	❏❏❏
Ease of training:	❏❏❏
Watchdog ability:	❏❏❏❏
Protection ability:	❏
Grooming requirements:	❏
Cold tolerance:	❏
Heat tolerance:	❏❏❏

Weight:	20–40 lb*
Height:	male: 19–22"; female: 18–21"

The Working Group

The Working dogs are those that put their bravery or brawn into the service of humans. They can be broadly divided into guarding or protecting breeds, sledding breeds, carting breeds, and rescue breeds. In general, the Working breeds are known for their intelligence and hardiness.

Akita

History

The Akita is perhaps the most renowned and venerated of the native Japanese breeds. Although it bears a likeness to dogs from ancient Japanese tombs, the modern Akita traces back to the seventeenth century, when a nobleman with a keen interest in dogs was exiled to the Akita Prefecture of the island of Honshu, a rugged area with intensely cold winters. He challenged the landowners there to compete in breeding a race of powerful hunting dogs. These dogs distinguished themselves in the hunting of bear, deer, and wild boar, holding the game at bay for the hunter. These Akita forebears were called Matagi-inu (hunting dog). The breed's numbers and quality varied over the next 300 years. In the late 1800s, it underwent a period when it was used as a fighting dog, and some were even crossed

AKC Ranking: 34
Family: Spitz, Northern (hunting)
Area of Origin: Japan
Date of Origin: 1600s
Original Function: Large game hunting, dog fighting
Today's Function: Security
Other Name: Akita Inu, Japanese Akita

with other breeds in an attempt to enhance its fighting prowess. In 1927, the Akita-inu Hozankai Society of Japan was formed to preserve the original Akita, and in 1931 the Akita was designated as one of Japan's natural treasures. The most honored Akita of all time was Hachiko, who greeted his master every evening at the train station to accompany him home. When his master died at work one day, Haichiko waited for him, and continued to return and wait for his master every day until he died nine years later on March 8, 1935. Today, a statue and annual ceremony pay homage to Haichiko's loyalty. The first Akita arrived in America in 1937, when Helen Keller returned from Japan with one. Following World War II, servicemen returned home with Akitas from Japan. The breed's popularity grew slowly until it received AKC recognition in 1972.

Since then, it has steadily gained admirers and continues to grow in popularity. The Akita is now used as a guard and police dog in Japan.

Temperament

As befitting its spitz-like heritage, the Akita is bold, independent, stubborn, and tenacious. Demonstrative to its family, it is utterly devoted and will protect family members. It is reserved with strangers and can be aggressive toward other dogs. It can be domineering. Though not the breed for everyone, in the right hands the Akita is an excellent companion.

Upkeep

The Akita appreciates mental and physical exercise every day. It needs the chance to run in a safe area or on leash for a long jog. Given ample exercise and training, it can be a quiet and well-mannered house dog. The Akita is able to live outdoors in temperate or cool climates, but it is happiest if it can spend most of its time with its family. The coat needs brushing about once a week to remove dead hair, much more often when shedding. They tend to be somewhat messy drinkers!

Health

- Major concerns: CHD, PRA
- Minor concerns: elbow dysplasia, pemphigus, sebaceous adenitis, gastric torsion
- Occasionally seen: PRA, patellar luxation, VKH-like syndrome, entropion, epilepsy, cataract, polyneuropathy, renal cortical hypoplasia
- Suggested tests: hip, elbow, eye
- Life span: 10–12 years
- Note: Onions have been documented to cause changes in red blood cells of Akitas.

Form and Function

This is a large and powerful breed, with much substance and heavy bone; it is slightly longer than tall. The Akita's build reflects its original job of hunting big game through deep snow and rugged terrain. Its double coat consists of a dense undercoat and straight, harsh, outer coat standing off from the body, about 2 inches or less in length. Such a combination provides ample insulation from water and weather. The gait is brisk and powerful. The Akita is a versatile dog of large spitz type, able to perform as hunting companion and protector.

At a Glance

Energy level:	☐☐☐
Exercise requirements:	☐☐☐
Playfulness:	☐☐☐
Affection level:	☐☐☐
Friendliness toward dogs:	☐☐☐
Friendliness toward other pets:	☐☐☐
Friendliness toward strangers:	☐☐
Ease of training:	☐☐☐
Watchdog ability:	☐☐☐☐☐
Protection ability:	☐☐☐☐
Grooming requirements:	☐☐
Cold tolerance:	☐☐☐☐☐
Heat tolerance:	☐

Height:	*male: 85–130 lb; female: 65–110 lb
Weight:	male: 25–28"; female: 23–26"

Alaskan Malamute

History

Like most of the dogs of the spitz family, the Alaskan Malamute evolved in the Arctic regions, shaped by the adverse climatic conditions. Its origin is unknown, but it was first described living among the native Inuit people known as the Mahlemuts, who lived along Norton Sound on Alaska's northwest coast. The word *Mahlemut* comes from *Mahle*, an Inuit tribe name, and *mut*, meaning village. The dogs served as hunting partners for big game (such as seals and polar bears), and hauled the heavy carcasses back home. These dogs were, of necessity, large and strong rather than fast, enabling one dog to do the work of many smaller dogs. They were an essential cog in these people's lives and were treated almost as one of the family, although they were never pampered as pets. The unforgiving environment meant that a less than optimal dog would probably not have been kept. When the first outside explorers came to the region in the 1700s, they were impressed not only by the

AKC Ranking: 46
Family: Spitz, Northern (draft)
Area of Origin: Alaska
Date of Origin: Ancient times
Original Function: Heavy sled pulling, large game hunting
Today's Function: Sled pulling
Other Name: None

hardy dog but also by their owners' obvious attachment to them. With the discovery of gold in 1896, a flood of outsiders came to Alaska; for entertainment, they staged weight-pulling contests and races among their dogs. The native breeds were interbred with each other and those brought by settlers, often in an attempt to create a faster racer or simply supply the vast numbers of dogs needed to supply the gold rush. The pure Malamute was in danger of being lost. In the 1920s, a New England dog racing enthusiast obtained some good specimens, and began to breed the traditional Malamutes. As the breed's reputation grew, some were chosen to help Admiral Byrd in his 1933 trek to the South Pole. During World War II, the Malamute was once again called into service, this time to serve as freight haulers, pack animals, and search-and-rescue dogs. In 1935, the breed received AKC recognition and began a new phase as an imposing show dog and loyal pet.

At a Glance

Energy level:	☐☐☐
Exercise requirements:	☐☐☐☐
Playfulness:	☐☐☐
Affection level:	☐☐☐☐☐
Friendliness toward dogs:	☐
Friendliness toward other pets:	☐
Friendliness toward strangers:	☐☐☐☐
Ease of training:	☐
Watchdog ability:	☐☐☐
Protection ability:	☐☐☐
Grooming requirements:	☐☐☐
Cold tolerance:	☐☐☐☐☐
Heat tolerance:	☐

Weight:	male: 85 lb; female 75 lb
Height:	male: 25″; female: 23″

Temperament

The Alaskan Malamute is powerful, independent, strong willed, and fun loving. Its idea of great fun is to pull a sled or cart, but it also loves to run and roam. It is family oriented, and as long as it is given daily exercise, it is well-mannered in the home. Without proper exercise, it can become frustrated and destructive. It is friendly and sociable toward people, but it may be aggressive to strange dogs, pets, or livestock. Some can be domineering. It tends to dig and howl.

Upkeep

The Alaskan Malamute loves cold weather, and especially loves to haul a sled through the snow. It can run for miles and needs to have adequate exercise every day, either in the form of a long walk on leash or the opportunity to run or mush. It can live outdoors in temperate to cold climates, but it does better inside during warm weather. Its coat needs brushing once or twice a week, more when shedding.

Health

- Major concerns: CHD, ChD, cataract
- Minor concerns: renal cortical hypoplasia

- Occasionally seen: gastric torsion
- Suggested tests: hip, eye, ChD clear rating
- Life span: 10–12 years

Form and Function

The Alaskan Malamute is a powerfully built dog of Nordic breed type, developed to haul heavy loads rather than race. It is slightly longer than it is tall. It is heavy boned and compact, designed for strength and endurance. Its gait is steady, balanced, and tireless. Its coat is thick and double, with a coarse outer coat and dense, wooly, oily undercoat, providing the ultimate in insulation. Although the eyes have a "wolf-like" appearance, the expression is soft.

Anatolian Shepherd

History

The Anatolian Shepherd is an ancient guardian breed with a long working history. Its roots probably lie in the Tibetan Mastiff and Roman Mollosian war dogs that came to Turkey more than 4000 years ago. Here they proved invaluable as staunch defenders of livestock against formidable predators, including wolves and bears. They accompanied the nomadic shepherds and became widespread over a large geographical region, accounting for the Anatolian's great variation in size, coat type, and color. Several traits that remained constant throughout all the breed, however, are loyalty, independence, and hardiness. The name Shepherd is a misnomer because the breed was never used as a herder. Its Turkish name, *koban copek*, means shepherd's dog. The first of the breed did not come to America until the 1950s, where although it proved itself as an effective livestock guard against coyotes and other predators, it remained unknown to most dog fanciers. Only in the late 1970s

AKC Ranking: 124
Family: Livestock Dog, Mastiff, Flock Guard
Area of Origin: Turkey
Date of Origin: Ancient times
Original Function: Flock guard
Today's Function: Flock guard, security
Other Name: Coban Kopegi, Karabash Dog, Kara bas, Kangal Dog

and 1980s did the Anatolian Shepherd begin to be more widely appreciated, still valued for its utilitarian, rather than cosmetic, attributes. Pet owners desiring a loyal and effective guardian began to acquire the breed. In 1996, the Anatolian Shepherd was accepted in the AKC Miscellaneous class; Anatolian fanciers are adamant about retaining the dog's working instincts above all else. Upon official recognition as a regular breed, the Anatolian Shepherd will be in the Working Group.

Temperament

This is a serious dog, devoted to its family and its duty as family protector. At the same time, it is laid back and easygoing, never on the lookout for trouble. It is suspicious of strangers and is territorial. It is good with children, but it may not be playful enough to satisfy children's desires. As a serious watch dog, it tends to bark a lot when its suspicions are aroused.

Upkeep

The Anatolian Shepherd needs a chance to exercise every day, either with a long walk or brisk run. It can live outside in temperate to cool climates. Coat care is minimal, consisting only of a weekly brushing to remove dead hair.

Health

- Major concerns: CHD
- Minor concerns: entropion
- Occasionally seen: none
- Suggested tests: hip, (eye)
- Life span: 10–13 years
- Note: sensitive to anesthesia

Form and Function

The Anatolian is built tough to do a tough job. It is a large, powerful, rugged dog, having both great agility and endurance. It has good bone and a large head. Its gait is powerful, smooth, and fluid. Its coat consists of a thick undercoat and an outer coat that ranges from short (about 1 inch) to rough (about 4 inches), slightly longer around the neck and mane. The expression is intelligent, and the general impression is one of a bold yet calm protector.

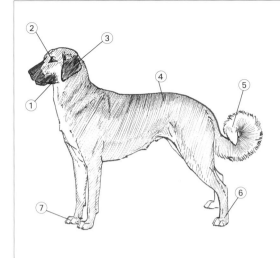

Illustrated Standard

1. Dewlap not excessive
2. Eyes almond-shaped
3. V-shaped ears with rounded apex
4. Gradual arch over loin
5. Tail long, highset, with a curl in the end; carried in a wheel when alert
6. Double dewclaws optional on rear feet
7. Oval feet

- ❏ **Color:** any, most common is fawn with black mask
- ❏ **DQ:** blue eyes or eyes of two different colors, erect ears, overshot, undershot, or wry bite

At a Glance

Energy level:	❏
Exercise requirements:	❏❏❏
Playfulness:	❏❏❏
Affection level:	❏❏❏
Friendliness toward dogs:	❏
Friendliness toward other pets:	❏❏❏
Friendliness toward strangers:	❏
Ease of training:	❏❏❏
Watchdog ability:	❏❏❏❏❏
Protection ability:	❏❏❏❏❏
Grooming requirements:	❏❏
Cold tolerance:	❏❏❏❏
Heat tolerance:	❏❏❏

Weight: male: 110–150 lb; female: 80–120 lb

Height: male: from 29" up; female: from 27" up

Bernese Mountain Dog

History

The most well known of the Sennehunde, or Swiss mountain dogs, the Bernese is distinguished by being the only one to have a fairly long, silky coat. The origin of the breed is speculative at best. Some experts believe its history traces to the Roman invasion of Switzerland, when the Roman mastiffs were crossed with native flock-guarding dogs. This cross produced a strong dog that was able to withstand the Alpine weather and that could serve as draft dog, flock guard, drover, herder, and general farm dog. Despite their utility, little attempt was made to perpetuate them as a breed purposefully. By the late 1800s, the breed was in danger of being lost. At that time, Professor Albert Heim initiated a study of Swiss dogs that led to the identification of the Bernese Mountain Dog as one of the existing types. These dogs were found

AKC Ranking: 62
Family: Livestock Dog, Mountain Dog, Mastiff (draft/cattle)
Area of Origin: Switzerland
Date of Origin: Ancient times
Original Function: Draft
Today's Function: Companion
Other Name: Berner Sennenhund, Bernese Cattle Dog

only in the valleys of the lower Alps. Through Dr. Heim's efforts, these dogs were promoted throughout Switzerland and even Europe. The finest specimens came to be found in the Durrbach area, at one time giving the breed the name Durrbachler. With the breed's spread, the name was changed to Bernese Mountain Dog. The first Bernese came to America in 1926; official AKC recognition was granted in 1937.

Temperament

The Bernese Mountain Dog is an easygoing, calm family companion (that is, after it leaves its adolescent stage). It is sensitive, loyal, and extremely devoted. It is gentle with children and often reserved with strangers. It generally gets along well with other dogs and pets.

Upkeep

This dog enjoys the outdoors, especially in cold weather. It needs daily but moderate exercise, either a good hike or walk on leash. It enjoys pulling. Although it can physically live outdoors in temperate to cold climates, it is so in tune with its human family that it cannot be relegated to life alone in the yard. Inside, it needs plenty of room to stretch out. Its coat needs brushing one or two times weekly, much more often when shedding. The Bernese life span is described by a Swiss expression: "Three years a young dog, three years a good dog, and three years an old dog. All else is a gift from God."

Health

- Major concerns: CHD, elbow dysplasia, histicytosis, OCD
- Minor concerns: fragmented coronoid process, gastric torsion, PRA
- Occasionally seen: hypomyelination
- Suggested tests: hip, elbow, eye
- Life span: 7–9 years
- Note: Extra care must be taken to avoid heat stroke.

Illustrated Standard

1. Well-defined stop
2. Skull flat
3. Ears medium sized, triangular with rounded tips, hanging close to head
4. Tail bushy, carried low
5. Feet round

❏ **Color:** tricolored; black with tan markings and white flashings
❏ **DQ:** blue eyes, any ground color other than black

Form and Function

The Bernese Mountain Dog is slightly longer than tall, though appearing square. It is a sturdy, large, hardy dog capable of both draft and droving work. This requires a combination of strength, speed, and agility. Its natural working gait is a slow trot, but with good reach and drive. Its thick coat is moderately long, and slightly wavy or straight, providing insulation from the cold. The expression is gentle, and the color is striking.

At a Glance

Energy level:	❏
Exercise requirements:	❏❏
Playfulness:	❏❏
Affection level:	❏❏❏
Friendliness toward dogs:	❏❏❏
Friendliness toward other pets:	❏❏❏❏
Friendliness toward strangers:	❏❏❏
Ease of training:	❏❏❏
Watchdog ability:	❏❏❏
Protection ability:	❏❏
Grooming requirements:	❏❏❏
Cold tolerance:	❏❏❏❏❏
Heat tolerance:	❏

Weight: male: 90–120 lb; female: 70–100 lb*
Height: male: 25–27.5"; female: 23–26"

Boxer

History

The Boxer derives from two central European breeds of dog that no longer exist: the larger Danziger Bullenbaiser and smaller Brabenter Bullenbaiser. *Bullenbaiser* means bull-biter, and these dogs were used to grab large game (wild boar, deer, and small bear) after it was at bay, hanging onto it until the hunter arrived to kill it. This required a strong but agile dog with a broad powerful jaw and a recessed nose to enable the dog to breathe while its jaws were clamped onto an animal. Similar attributes were required of dogs used in bull baiting, a popular sport in many European countries. In England, the Bulldog was the favored breed

AKC Ranking: 13
Family: Livestock Dog, Mastiff (Bulldog)
Area of Origin: Germany
Date of Origin: 1800s
Original Function: Bullbaiting, guardian
Today's Function: Guardian
Other Name: None

for the sport, whereas in Germany large mastiff-type dogs were used. Around the 1830s, German hunters began a concerted effort to create a new breed, crossing their Bullenbaisers with mastiff-type dogs for size, terriers for tenacity, and, finally, Bulldogs. The result was a tough agile dog with a streamlined body and strong grip. When bull baiting was outlawed, the dogs were mostly used as butcher's dogs in Germany, controlling cattle in slaughteryards. By 1895, an entirely new breed, the Boxer, had been established. Although the exact origin of the name Boxer is obscure, it may have been derived from the German *Boxl*, as they were called in the slaughterhouses. The

Boxer was one of the first breeds to be employed as a police and military dog in Germany. By 1900, the breed had become established as a general utility dog, family pet, and even show dog. The AKC recognized the breed soon after, but only in the 1940s did the breed begin its steady rise to the top of the popularity charts, eventually peaking as the fourth most popular breed in America.

Temperament

The Boxer is playful, exuberant, inquisitive, attentive, demonstrative, devoted, and outgoing; it is a perfect companion for an active family. It can be stubborn, but it is sensitive and responsive to commands. It may be aggressive toward strange dogs, but it is generally good with other household dogs and pets.

Upkeep

The Boxer needs daily mental and physical exertion. It likes to run, but its exercise needs can also be met with a good jog or long walk on leash. It does not do well in hot weather and is generally unsuited to live outdoors. It does best when allowed to divide its time between a

*Ears may be uncropped, although this may be faulted in the show ring.

Illustrated Standard

1. Broad, blunt muzzle
2. Undershot bite
3. Shallow wrinkles on forehead when alert
4. Distinct stop
5. Slightly arched skull
6. Ears cropped long and tapering*
7. Slightly sloping topline
8. Tail set high, docked and carried upward
9. Stomach slightly tucked up

❑ **Color:** fawn and brindle, both with or without white flashing and black mask
❑ **DQ:** any color other than fawn or brindle; white markings exceeding one third of entire coat

house and yard. Some snore. Its coat needs only occasional brushing to remove dead hair.

Health

- Major concerns: cardiomyopathy, SAS, CHD
- Minor concerns: gastric torsion, tumors, intervertebral disc degeneration, corneal erosion, colitis
- Occasionally seen: none
- Suggested tests: cardiac, hip
- Life span: 8–10 years

- Note: sensitive to heat and anesthesia; white Boxers may be deaf.

Form and Function

The Boxer is exemplary in its combination of stylish elegance with strength and agility. It is square-proportioned with good substance and musculature. Its stride is free and ground covering, with proud carriage. Its head is distinctive, with a broad, blunt muzzle and alert expression. Its coat is short and shiny. It is perfectly suited to serve as a working watchdog.

At a Glance

Energy level:	❑❑❑❑
Exercise requirements:	❑❑❑
Playfulness:	❑❑❑❑
Affection level:	❑❑❑❑❑
Friendliness toward dogs:	❑❑❑
Friendliness toward other pets:	❑❑❑
Friendliness toward strangers:	❑❑❑
Ease of training:	❑❑❑
Watchdog ability:	❑❑❑
Protection ability:	❑❑❑
Grooming requirements:	❑
Cold tolerance:	❑❑
Heat tolerance:	❑

Weight:	male: 65–80 lb; female: 50–65 lb*
Height:	male: 22.5–25"; female: 21–23.5"

Bullmastiff

History

Although the Mastiff is one of Britain's oldest
breeds, its immediate descendant, the Bullmastiff, is probably a fairly recent development.
It is true that occasional references to the
Bullmastiff, or crosses of the Mastiff and
Bulldog, can be found as early as 1791; however, no evidence exists that these strains were
bred on. The documented history of the Bullmastiff begins near the
end of the nineteenth century, when poaching game from the large
estates had become such a problem that the gamekeeper's lives
were endangered. They needed a tough courageous dog that could
wait silently as a poacher approached, attack on command, and
subdue but not maul the poacher. The Mastiff was not fast enough,
and the Bulldog was not large enough, so they crossed the breeds
in an attempt to create their perfect dog; the aptly named
"Gamekeeper's Night Dog." The preferred color was dark brindle,

AKC Ranking: 53
Family: Livestock Dog, Mastiff
  (Bulldog)
Area of Origin: England
Date of Origin: 1800s
Original Function: Estate guardian
Today's Function: Companion
Other Name: None

as it faded into the night. As the breed's reputation grew, however, many estate owners chose
the dogs as estate sentries and preferred the
lighter fawns, especially those with black masks,
a coloration reminiscent of their Mastiff ancestry. Breeders began to aim for a pure-breeding
strain rather than relying upon repeating crosses between the Mastiff and Bulldog. They worked
for an ideal animal that appeared to be 60 percent Mastiff and
40 percent Bulldog. By 1924, the breed was deemed to be pure
and was recognized by the English Kennel Club. AKC recognition
followed in 1933.

Temperament

The Bullmastiff is gentle and quiet, a devoted companion and
guardian. It is not easily roused, but once threatened it is fearless.
It is stubborn and cannot easily be goaded into action against its

will. Some can be aggressive toward strange dogs, but it is generally good with other household dogs and pets. It is good with children, but it may not be playful enough to satisfy some children. The Bullmastiff needs a firm but loving home. It is not for fragile or timid owners.

Upkeep

The Bullmastiff is a big dog and needs daily exercise to stay in shape. Its needs are moderate, however, and can be met with walks on leash and short romps. It does not do well in hot, humid weather and generally should be kept as an indoor dog. It needs a soft bed and plenty of room to stretch out. It drools; some snore. Coat care is minimal.

Health

- Major concerns: gastric torsion, CHD, elbow dysplasia
- Minor concerns: entropion
- Occasionally seen: PRA
- Suggested tests: hip, elbow, (eye)
- Life span: 8–10 years

Illustrated Standard

① Muzzle broad, dark preferred
② Stop moderate
③ Eyes medium size
④ Skull large, with fair amount of wrinkle when alert
⑤ V-shaped ears carried close to cheeks
⑥ Topline straight and level
⑦ Tail set high, not carried over back

❑ **Color:** red, fawn, or brindle
❑ **DQ:** none

Form and Function

This nearly square breed should be powerful and active, a combination of strength, endurance, and alertness. It should appear to be 60 percent Mastiff and 40 percent Bulldog. Its gait is smooth and powerful, but its angulation is moderate. Its coat is short and dense, and its expression keen and alert. These attributes allowed the Bullmastiff to both overtake and overpower intruders.

At a Glance

Energy level:	❑
Exercise requirements:	❑❑
Playfulness:	❑
Affection level:	❑❑❑
Friendliness toward dogs:	❑❑
Friendliness toward other pets:	❑❑❑❑
Friendliness toward strangers:	❑
Ease of training:	❑
Watchdog ability:	❑❑❑❑❑
Protection ability:	❑❑❑❑❑
Grooming requirements:	❑
Cold tolerance:	❑❑❑
Heat tolerance:	❑

Weight: male: 110–130 lb; female: 100–120 lb
Height: male: 25–27"; female: 24–26"

Doberman Pinscher

History

Few people can claim to have had so great an impact upon the dog world as Louis Dobermann of Thuringen, Germany. Herr Doberman was a door-to-door tax collector who needed a watchful guard dog to accompany him on his rounds. In the late 1800s he set about to create an alert streamlined guard dog, most likely by crossing the old German Shepherd and German Pinscher, with later crosses to the Black and Tan Manchester Terrier, Greyhound, and Weimaraner. He soon obtained the prototype of the breed that now bears his name. The original Dobermans were still somewhat heavy boned and round-headed; subsequent breeders selected for a more racy-looking dog. The breed evolved in remarkable time; by 1899 the first breed club was formed. The breed continued to attract acclaim, and the first Doberman arrived in America in 1908. It

AKC Ranking: 22
Family: Mastiff
Area of Origin: Germany
Date of Origin: 1800s
Original Function: Guardian
Today's Function: Security, police, military, Schutzhund
Other Name: Dobermann

soon found favor throughout Europe and America as a police and guard dog, and later as a war dog. Its prowess in these areas soon brought more admirers, and the Doberman quickly became a valued family protector. Its chiseled silhouette and fearless alert demeanor has made the Doberman a top contender as a show dog. As its fame grew, many families grew to appreciate the breed as a family pet, and the Doberman eventually rose to be the second most popular breed in America in 1977. During this same time period, a new challenge arose for the breed, the emergence of the albinistic white Doberman. In an effort to decrease the chance of producing these dogs, the Doberman Pinscher Club of America convinced the AKC to tag the registration numbers of dogs with the likelihood of carrying the albino gene with the letter Z.

At a Glance

Energy level:	▢▢▢▢
Exercise requirements:	▢▢▢
Playfulness:	▢▢▢
Affection level:	▢▢▢
Friendliness toward dogs:	▢
Friendliness toward other pets:	▢▢▢
Friendliness toward strangers:	▢
Ease of training:	▢▢▢▢▢
Watchdog ability:	▢▢▢▢▢
Protection ability:	▢▢▢▢▢
Grooming requirements:	▢
Cold tolerance:	▢▢▢
Heat tolerance:	▢▢▢

Weight:	65–90 lb*
Height:	male: 26–28"; female: 24–26"

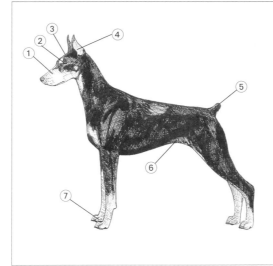

Illustrated Standard

① Head long and dry, resembling a blunt wedge from front and side
② Almond-shaped eyes
③ Skull flat
④ Ears normally cropped and carried erect*
⑤ Tail docked near second joint, carried slightly above horizontal
⑥ Stomach well tucked up
⑦ Feet catlike

❏ **Color:** black, red, blue, and fawn, all with tan markings
❏ **DQ:** overshot more than 3/16", undershot more than 1/8", dog of non-allowed color

*Ears may be uncropped.

Temperament

The Doberman Pinscher is an intelligent capable guardian, ever on the alert and ready to protect its family or home. It is also a loyal and adventurous companion. It likes to be mentally challenged, and is a gifted obedience pupil. It is sensitive, and very responsive to its owner's wishes, though some can be domineering. It is generally reserved with strangers. It can be aggressive with strange dogs.

Upkeep

This is an active breed that needs daily mental and physical exercise lest it become frustrated or destructive. Its exercise requirements can be met with a long jog or walk on leash, or a strenuous run in a safe area. The Doberman can live outside in temperate climates, but it is a much better companion and effective guardian if it shares its human home. Coat care is minimal.

Health

- Major concerns: CVI (wobbler's syndrome), cardiomyopathy
- Minor concerns: vWD, demodicosis, osteosarcoma, narcolepsy, gastric torsion, CHD
- Occasionally seen: albinism
- Suggested tests: DNA for vWD, cardiac, (hip)
- Life span: 10–12 years
- Note: Blue Dobermans often have alopecia; white Dobermans suffer from several serious health problems.

Form and Function

The Doberman is compactly built, muscular, powerful, and square-proportioned. It combines elegance and strength, speed and endurance. Its carriage is proud and alert, and its gait is free and vigorous. Its coat is short, smooth, and hard, showing off the exceptionally clean-cut lines of this athletic breed.

Giant Schnauzer

History

The Giant Schnauzer originated in the country-side of Bavaria and Wurrtemburg. Cattlemen there were impressed by the smaller Standard Schnauzer, and sought to emulate it on a larger scale that would be suitable for driving cattle. It is likely, though not documented, that they crossed the Standard Schnauzer with their larger smooth-coated cattle-driving dogs in an attempt to create a wire-haired drover. Later crosses with rough-coated Sheepdogs and the Great Dane and Bouvier des Flandres probably occurred, and even crosses with the black Poodle, Wolf Spitz, and Wirehaired Pinscher have been suggested. The result was a weather-resistant, smart-looking dog capable of handling cattle, then known as the Munchener. They later became more popular as butcher's or stockyard dogs, and even later, brewery guard dogs. The dogs maintained a low profile, with little expo-

AKC Ranking: 81
Family: Livestock Dog, Herding
Area of Origin: Germany
Date of Origin: Middle Ages
Original Function: Cattle herding, guardian
Today's Function: Security, police, Schutzhund
Other Name: Riesenschnauzer

sure until just before World War I, when it was suggested that they could be trained as police dogs. They excelled at their new assignment but have not been well accepted outside of Germany in that capacity. They have gained more headway as a pet in recent years, however, and now enjoy modest popularity in America.

Temperament

The playful, rambunctious Giant Schnauzer may be too boisterous for small children, even though it is otherwise very good with children in its own family. It is bold and protective of its family and reserved with strangers. It may be aggressive toward other dogs. This intelligent and exuberant breed is a good choice for an active person wanting a partner in adventure, although at times the Giant may try to be the leader.

Upkeep

The Giant Schnauzer needs daily exercise and daily fun. Its exercise requirements can be met with vigorous games and long hikes or walks. It can live outside in temperate to cool climates, but it is best when allowed to divide its time between house and yard. Its harsh coat needs combing once or twice weekly, plus shaping two to four times yearly. Shaping is best done by professional scissoring and hand-stripping, but clipping is acceptable for pets.

Health

- Major concerns: CHD
- Minor concerns: OCD, gastric torsion
- Occasionally seen: none
- Suggested tests: hip
- Life span: 10–12 years

Form and Function

This is a larger, more powerful version of the Standard Schnauzer. Its body is strong, compact, and nearly square, combining great power with agility. The stride is free and vigorous, with good reach and drive. Its double coat consists of a soft undercoat and a harsh, wiry, dense outer

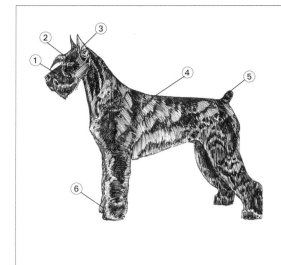

Illustrated Standard

1. Rectangular head
2. Oval deep-set eyes
3. Ears may be cropped or uncropped; when uncropped, ears are V-shaped
4. Short, straight back
5. Tail docked to second or third joint, carried high
6. Cat feet

❏ **Color:** solid black or pepper and salt
❏ **DQ:** overshot or undershot, markings other than specified

coat, a combination that enables it to withstand harsh, alpine conditions. Its hallmark harsh beard and eyebrows, coupled with its smart outline, make a striking figure. The combination of rugged build, reliable temperament, and weather-resistant coat make for a powerful and versatile worker.

At a Glance

Energy level:	❑❑❑
Exercise requirements:	❑❑❑❑
Playfulness:	❑❑❑
Affection level:	❑
Friendliness toward dogs:	❑
Friendliness toward other pets:	❑❑
Friendliness toward strangers:	❑
Ease of training:	❑❑❑
Watchdog ability:	❑❑❑❑❑
Protection ability:	❑❑❑❑❑
Grooming requirements:	❑❑❑
Cold tolerance:	❑❑❑
Heat tolerance:	❑❑❑

Weight:	65–90 lb*
Height: male: 25.5–27.5"; female: 23.5–25.5"	

Great Dane

History

Dubbed the "Apollo of Dogs," the Great Dane is probably the product of two other magnificent breeds, the old English Mastiff and the Irish Wolfhound. Its ancestors were used as war dogs and hunting dogs; thus, its ability as a fearless big game hunter seemed only natural. By the fourteenth century, these dogs were proving themselves as able hunters in Germany, combining speed, stamina, strength, and courage in order to bring down the tough wild boar. The dogs became popular with the landed gentry not only because of their hunting ability but also because of their imposing yet graceful appearance. These noble dogs made gracious additions to any estate. British familiar with the breed first referred to them as German Boarhounds. Exactly when and why the breed was later dubbed the Great Dane is a mystery because, although undeniably great, it is not Danish.

AKC Ranking: 29
Family: Livestock Dog, Mastiff
Area of Origin: Germany
Date of Origin: Middle Ages
Original Function: Guardian, hunting large game
Today's Function: Companion
Other Name: Deutsche Dogge, German Mastiff

It is a German breed, and in 1880 German authorities declared that the dog should only be referred to as the Deutsche Dogge, the name by which it still goes in Germany. The English paid no heed, and the old name stuck for the English-speaking world. By the late 1800s, the Great Dane had come to America. It quickly attracted attention, as it does to this very day. The breed has since achieved great popularity in spite of some of the difficulties owning a giant dog entails.

Temperament

The Great Dane is gentle, loving, easygoing, and sensitive. It is generally good with children (although its friendly overtures may overwhelm a small child) and usually friendly toward other dogs and pets. It is powerful but sensitive and responsive to training. It makes a pleasant, well-mannered family companion.

At a Glance

Energy level:	▢▢
Exercise requirements:	▢▢▢
Playfulness:	▢▢
Affection level:	▢▢▢▢
Friendliness toward dogs:	▢▢▢
Friendliness toward other pets:	▢▢▢
Friendliness toward strangers:	▢▢▢
Ease of training:	▢▢▢▢
Watchdog ability:	▢▢▢
Protection ability:	▢▢▢
Grooming requirements:	▢
Cold tolerance:	▢▢
Heat tolerance:	▢▢

Weight:	100–120 lb*
Height: male: at least 30", preferably 32" or more; female: at least 28", preferably 30" or more	

Illustrated Standard

1. Square jaw with deep muzzle
2. Almond-shaped, medium-sized eyes
3. Head long and rectangular, stop pronounced
4. Ears medium size; if cropped, carried uniformly erect
5. Short level back
6. Tail set high, not carried over level of back
7. Well-defined tuck-up
8. Round feet

❏ **Color:** brindle, black-masked fawn, blue, black, harlequin (white with irregular black patches)
❏ **DQ:** under minimum height, split nose, docked tail, any color other than those specified

in a dog required to overtake and then overpower relatively swift but formidable quarry. Its coat is short, thick, and glossy.

The Great Dane is most noteworthy for its majestic carriage and appearance—the Apollo of Dogs.

Upkeep

The Great Dane needs daily moderate exercise. Its needs can be met with a good walk or romp. Despite its sturdy appearance, it is not well suited to living outdoors and is best suited to divide its time between indoors and out. Inside, it needs soft bedding and sufficient room to stretch out when sleeping. Some tend to drool. Coat care is minimal.

Health

- Major concerns: gastric torsion, CHD, cardiomyopathy
- Minor concerns: CVI (wobbler's syndrome), cataract, elbow dysplasia, osteosarcoma, OCD, HOD
- Occasionally seen: glaucoma, vWD
- Suggested tests: cardiac, elbow, hip, eye, blood
- Life span: 6–8 years

Form and Function

This regal breed combines great size and power with elegance. It is square proportioned and well balanced. Its gait is strong and powerful with long, easy strides. These attributes are necessary

Great Pyrenees

History

Also known as the Pyrenean Mountain Dog, the Great Pyrenees is a very old breed probably descending from the Tibetan Mastiff. It may have come to Europe with the Aryans from Central Asia, as well as with Phoenician sea traders. They settled in the Spanish Pyrenees and in various mountain valleys in Europe. It was used from earliest times to guard flocks. A painting of the times shows a pair of these guards, each wearing a spiked iron collar to protect its throat from animal or human adversaries. In medieval France, the Pyrenees became a formidable fortress guard, and eventually a band of these imposing dogs was the pride of many large chateaus. In the late 1600s, the breed caught the eye of French nobility, and for a brief time they were in great demand in the court of Louis XIV. In fact, in 1675 the Great Pyrenees was decreed the "Royal Dog of France" by Louis XIV. Around the same time Great Pyrenees came to Newfoundland, where they may have played a role in the development of the

AKC Ranking: 44
Family: Livestock Dog, Flockguard
Area of Origin: France
Date of Origin: Ancient times
Original Function: Sheep guardian
Today's Function: Companion
Other Name: Pyrenean Mountain Dog,
  Chien des Pyrenees, Chien de
  Montagne des Pyrenees

Newfoundland breed, but it did not itself continue as a pure breed. The first documented Pyrenees came to America with General Lafayette in 1824. By the 1900s, the breed had disappeared from French court life, and the remaining dogs were those found still working in the isolated Basque countryside. Many of the poorer puppies were sold to tourists who brought them back to England and other countries. These dogs bore little resemblance to the magnificent Pyrenees that had once been so admired, however. Interest in the breed declined in England, but fortunately the breed still existed in sufficient numbers and quality in its native mountain land that later fanciers were able to obtain good breeding stock. These dogs served as the foundation of the modern Pyrenees. Serious importation of the breed to America occurred in the 1930s, and by 1933 the Great Pyrenees received AKC recognition. It attracted great attention as well as new owners, and today the Great Pyrenees enjoys moderate popularity.

At a Glance

Energy level:	❑
Exercise requirements:	❑❑❑
Playfulness:	❑❑
Affection level:	❑❑❑
Friendliness toward dogs:	❑❑
Friendliness toward other pets:	❑❑❑
Friendliness toward strangers:	❑❑
Ease of training:	❑
Watchdog ability:	❑❑❑❑❑
Protection ability:	❑❑❑❑
Grooming requirements:	❑❑❑
Cold tolerance:	❑❑❑❑❑
Heat tolerance:	❑

Weight:	male: 100 lb; female: 85 lb
Height:	male: 27–32"; female: 25–29"

Temperament

The Great Pyrenees is a capable and imposing guardian, devoted to its family and somewhat wary of strangers—human or canine. When not provoked, it is calm, well-mannered, and somewhat serious. It is very gentle with its family and children. It has an independent, somewhat stubborn, nature, and may try to dominate a less secure owner. Some are not good off leash and may wander away. The Great Pyrenees tends to bark a lot.

Upkeep

The Great Pyrenees needs daily exercise to stay in shape, though its needs are not excessive. A moderate walk will usually suffice. It enjoys hiking, especially in cold weather and snow. It does not do well in hot weather. This breed can live outdoors in temperate to cold weather, although it enjoys being with its family indoors. Its coat needs brushing once or twice weekly, daily when shedding. It may drool at times, and it tends to be a messy drinker.

Health

• Major concerns: CHD, patellar luxation

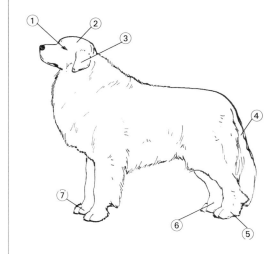

Illustrated Standard

① Eyes medium sized, almond shaped
② Head wedge shaped, not heavy, slightly rounded crown
③ Ears small to medium, V-shaped with rounded tips
④ Tail well plumed
⑤ Rear feet tend to toe out
⑥ Double dewclaws on each hind leg
⑦ Round feet

❑ **Color:** white or white with markings of gray, badger, reddish brown, or tan
❑ **DQ:** none

• Minor concerns: entropion, OCD, skin problems, osteosarcoma
• Occasionally seen: ChD, gastric torsion, otitis externa, panosteitis
• Suggested tests: hip, knee, (eye)
• Life span: 10–12 years

Form and Function

Elegant, imposing, and majestic, the Great Pyrenees is a large dog of medium substance that is slightly longer than tall. Its thick coat gives the impression of heavier bone and stature. This breed was developed to guard flocks on steep mountain slopes and so must combine strength with agility. It moves smoothly, with good reach and drive. The weather-resistant double coat consists of a dense, wooly undercoat and a long, flat, coarse outer coat, imparting great insulation from the Pyrenean cold. Its expression is elegant and contemplative.

Greater Swiss Mountain Dog

History

The Greater Swiss Mountain Dog is the oldest and largest of four varieties of Sennenhunde, or Swiss Mountain Dogs, the other three being the Appenzeller, Entlebucher, and Bernese. The breeds share a common heritage, probably derived from the Mastiff or Molossian dogs of the Romans. These dogs were probably introduced when the Romans crossed through Switzerland. Another theory is that the Phoenicians brought them to Spain around 1100 B.C. Whatever their origin, they spread over Europe and interbred with native dogs, eventually developing along independent lines in isolated communities. They shared the same working ethic, dividing their duties between acting as guardian of livestock and home, herder, and draft dog. Many came to be known as Metzgerhunde, or butcher's dogs. Until the late 1800s, all these dogs, which share a common coat color pattern, were generally assumed to be of one breed or type. Only when Professor A. Heim

AKC Ranking: 112
Family: Livestock Dog, Mastiff
 (draft/cattle)
Area of Origin: Switzerland
Date of Origin: Ancient times
Original Function: Draft dog, guardian
Today's Function: Companion
Other Name: Grosser Schweizer
 Sennenhund, Great Swiss Cattle Dog

endeavored to study the native Swiss mountain breeds seriously did he discern consistent differences that allowed them to be categorized as four distinct breeds. The year 1908 can be regarded as the birth date of the Greater Swiss; in this year Professor Heim spotted a magnificent short-haired dog entered in a Bernese Mountain Dog contest. He considered the dog a separate breed, and dubbed it the Greater Swiss because of its resemblance to the sturdy Swiss butcher's dogs he had also seen. The breed grew very slowly in popularity, additionally thwarted by two World Wars. Only in 1968 did the Greater Swiss come to America, with the first litter born in 1970. In 1985 the breed was admitted into the AKC Miscellaneous class, achieving full recognition in 1995.

Temperament

The Greater Swiss Mountain Dog is a sensitive, loyal, and extremely devoted family companion. It is calm and easygoing, very gentle with children as well as other pets. It is territorial, alert, bold, and vigilant.

Upkeep

As befitting of a dog with working roots, this breed likes the outdoors, especially in cold weather. It needs daily exercise, either a good long walk or vigorous romp. It especially enjoys pulling. It can live outside in temperate to cool climates but would prefer to be with its family. When indoors, it needs plenty of room to stretch out. Its coat needs brushing once weekly, more often when shedding.

Health

- Major concerns: CHD, gastric torsion, elbow dysplasia
- Minor concerns: panosteitis, OCD, distichiasis, entropion
- Occasionally seen: ectropion
- Suggested tests: hip, elbow, (eye)
- Life span: 10–12 years

Form and Function

This is a strong draft breed. It is large and powerful, slightly longer than tall. Its movement displays good reach and drive. Its double coat consists of a thick under-

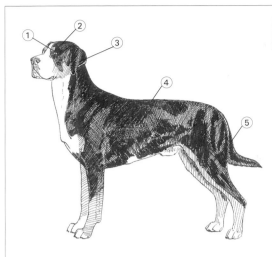

Illustrated Standard

① Eyes medium sized
② Skull flat and broad
③ Ears set high, triangular with rounded tip
④ Topline level
⑤ Tail carried down in repose, raised when excited

❏ **Color:** black and rust, with white feet, chest, tail tip, muzzle, blaze, and possibly collar; rust color present on legs between white and black
❏ **DQ:** any ground color other than black, blue eye color

coat and dense outer coat, about 1 to 1¾ inches long. Its expression is gentle and animated.

At a Glance

Energy level:	❏❏
Exercise requirements:	❏❏❏
Playfulness:	❏❏
Affection level:	❏❏❏
Friendliness toward dogs:	❏❏❏
Friendliness toward other pets:	❏❏❏❏
Friendliness toward strangers:	❏❏
Ease of training:	❏❏❏❏
Watchdog ability:	❏❏❏❏
Protection ability:	❏❏❏
Grooming requirements:	❏
Cold tolerance:	❏❏❏
Heat tolerance:	❏❏

Weight: male: 105–140 lb; female: 85–110 lb*
Height: male: 25.5–28.5"; female: 23.5–27"

Komondor

History

When the Huns came to Hungary, they brought with them the large, long-legged, Russian Owtcharka, which became the progenitor of the Komondor (plural: Komondorok). These dogs bore a close resemblance to the Magyar sheep known as Racka, which had a proud "dog-like" carriage and masses of curly wool. Thus, the dogs easily intermingled with the sheep and at first glance appeared to be one of the flock. Greatly valued by the Magyar shepherds, the Komondorok were not allowed to interbreed with other breeds. The earliest documentation of the breed dates back to 1555, although the breed is certain to have existed long before then. The Komondor earned its keep by guarding the flocks against marauding animals. So effective was it that some claim it is responsible for wiping out the wolf in Hungary. The Komondor was still used as a guard into the twentieth century. The first Komondor came to America in 1933, and the AKC recog-

> AKC Ranking: 133
> Family: Livestock Dog, Sheepdog, Flockguard
> Area of Origin: Hungary
> Date of Origin: Ancient times
> Original Function: Sheep guardian
> Today's Function: Sheep guardian
> Other Name: None

nized the breed in 1937. World War II almost decimated the breed in Europe, but through the concerted efforts of breeders, the Komondor was saved. Although one of the most impressive dogs to ever grace the show ring, the difficulty of preparing its coat has usually dictated that none but the very finest be shown. As a result, the Komondor remains an uncommon breed everywhere but in its native Hungary. Recent attempts to use the breed as a guardian of flocks in the western United States have yielded promising results, attracting the attention of a new generation of shepherds.

Temperament

Bred as an independent protector of livestock, the Komondor is true to its heritage. It is an independent thinker and can be stubborn or domineering. It is not for meek owners who can be dominated; socialization is essential. It is reserved with strangers and possibly aggressive toward strange dogs. It is good with other pets and especially livestock. In fact, it is happiest when it has something or someone to watch over. Although usually calm and quiet, it is utterly fearless when the need arises. As a natural guardian, it is protective of children in its own family, but it may at times misunderstand rough and tumble games of visiting children.

Upkeep

The Komondor needs daily exercise in the form of long walks or short romps. Swimming is not a good idea because of the time it takes the coat to dry. It may also be difficult to keep the coat clean in some areas. This breed does not like warm weather. It can live outdoors in temperate to cool weather. The Komondor is nonshedding but not carefree. Its cords must be regularly separated or they will look like flat mats, and its coat tends to hold dirt; bathing is time-consuming and drying takes as much as a day. Care of the coat in non-show dogs is far less extensive. Pets can be clipped but then lose part of the breed's unique appeal. Note that it may take a dog up to two years of age before cords form.

Health

- Major concerns: CHD, gastric torsion
- Minor concerns: otitis externa, acute moist dermatitis
- Occasionally seen: entropion
- Suggested tests: hip
- Life span: 10–12 years

Form and Function

The Komondor is a large, muscular dog, with plenty of bone and substance; it is slightly longer than tall. Its gait is light and leisurely, with long strides. Its hallmark coat is double, consisting of a dense wooly undercoat and a coarser outer coat that is wavy or curly. The undercoat is trapped in the outer coat so that it forms strong, felty, tassel-like cords. This coat helped protect the dog from the elements as well as the teeth of tough adversaries. It also helped the dog to blend in with its flock.

At a Glance

Energy level:	❏❏❏
Exercise requirements:	❏❏❏
Playfulness:	❏❏❏
Affection level:	❏❏❏❏
Friendliness toward dogs:	❏
Friendliness toward other pets:	❏❏❏❏
Friendliness toward strangers:	❏
Ease of training:	❏❏❏
Watchdog ability:	❏❏❏❏❏
Protection ability:	❏❏❏❏❏
Grooming requirements:	❏❏❏
Cold tolerance:	❏❏❏❏
Heat tolerance:	❏❏

Weight: male: avg. 80 lb; female: avg. 70 lb*

Height: male: 27.5" and up; female: 25.5" and up

Kuvasz

History

Although considered a Hungarian breed, the Kuvasz has its roots in giant dogs of Tibet. It came to Hungary from Tibet by way of Turkey. Nor is its name Hungarian, but probably a corruption of the Turkish *kawasz*, meaning armed guard of the nobility. At one time only those nobility in favor with the royal family were allowed to keep one. This is a very old breed; in the latter fifteenth century, the Kuvasz was held in highest esteem. Breedings were carefully planned and recorded, and the dogs were a fixture of most large Hungarian estates. They served as both guard and hunting dog, capable of defending the estate against marauders and of pulling down large game such as bear and wolf. King Matthias I was a special patron of the breed, keeping a large kennel and doing much to improve the quality of the breed. In the succeeding centuries, the Kuvasz gradually came into the hands of commoners, who found them to be capable livestock dogs. During this period, the name was

AKC Ranking: 110
Family: Livestock Dog, Sheepdog, Flockguard
Area of Origin: Hungary
Date of Origin: Middle Ages
Original Function: Guardian, hunting large game
Today's Function: Sheep guardian, security
Other Name: Hungarian Kuvasz

corrupted to its present spelling, which ironically, translates as mongrel. Incidentally, the plural form of Kuvasz is Kuvaszok. The breed seriously declined as a result of two World Wars, but German stock formed a basis for the breed to continue through these hard times. Some dogs had also been imported to America in the 1930s. The AKC recognized the Kuvasz in 1935.

Temperament

Despite its sweet looks, the Kuvasz is a tough protector, fearlessly defending its family or home. It is gentle with and protective of children in its own family, but it may misinterpret a child's rough and tumble games with other children as attacks on its child. It is reserved with strangers and may be aggressive toward strange dogs; however, it tends to be very gentle with other pets and livestock. It is devoted and loyal but not very demonstrative. Some can be domineering.

At a Glance

Energy level:	▢▢▢
Exercise requirements:	▢▢▢▢
Playfulness:	▢▢
Affection level:	▢
Friendliness toward dogs:	▢
Friendliness toward other pets:	▢▢▢▢
Friendliness toward strangers:	▢
Ease of training:	▢
Watchdog ability:	▢▢▢▢
Protection ability:	▢▢▢▢▢
Grooming requirements:	▢▢
Cold tolerance:	▢▢▢
Heat tolerance:	▢

Weight:	male: 100–115 lb; female: 70–90 lb
Height:	male: 28–30"; female: 26–28"

Upkeep

The Kuvasz needs daily exercise and enjoys a long walk or good run in a safe area. It especially enjoys cold weather and can live outdoors in temperate to cool climates. It does best when allowed access to both house and yard. Its coat needs brushing one or two times weekly, more during heavy shedding periods.

Health

- Major concerns: CHD, OCD
- Minor concerns: none
- Occasionally seen: panosteitis, HOD
- Suggested tests: hip
- Life span: 9–12 years

Illustrated Standard

① Eyes almond shaped
② Skull elongated but not pointed
③ V-shaped ears, tip slightly rounded
④ Back straight and broad
⑤ Stomach well tucked-up
⑥ Cat feet

❑ **Color:** white
❑ **DQ:** overshot or undershot bite, males smaller than 26" or females smaller than 24", any color other than white

Form and Function

The Kuvasz is a large dog, slightly longer than tall, with medium bone. It is not bulky, but instead it is light footed, with a free, easy gait. The breed's combination of power and agility stems from its versatile roots as a guardian, hunter, and herder. Its double coat is medium coarse, ranging from wavy to straight.

Mastiff

History

The Mastiff is the prototypical breed of the ancient mastiff group of dogs. The confusion between the Mastiff breed and the mastiff family makes it very difficult to trace the history of the breed. Even though the mastiff family is one of the oldest and most influential in dogdom, the breed is undoubtedly of more recent, though still ancient, origin. By the time of Caesar, mastiffs were used as war dogs and gladiators. In medieval times, they were used as guard dogs and hunting dogs and became so widespread as to become commonplace. Mastiffs later stepped into the arena of dog fighting, bull baiting, and bear baiting. Even when these cruel sports were banned in England in 1835, they continued to be popular events. The modern Mastiff descends not only from these pit dogs but also from more noble lines, being descendants of one of the most famous Mastiffs of all time: the Mastiff of Sir Peers Legh. When Sir Legh was wounded in the battle of Agincourt, his Mastiff stood over him and protected him for many hours through the battle.

AKC Ranking: 41
Family: Livestock Dog, Sheepdog, Mastiff
Area of Origin: England
Date of Origin: Ancient times
Original Function: Guardian
Today's Function: Guardian
Other Name: English Mastiff

Although he later died, the Mastiff returned to Legh's home and was the foundation of the Lyme Hall Mastiffs. Five centuries later the Lyme Hall Mastiffs figured prominently in founding the modern breed. Some evidence exists that the Mastiff came to America on the Mayflower, but the breed's documented entry to America did not occur until the late 1800s. The breed was nearly decimated in England by World War II, but sufficient numbers had been brought to America by that time to keep the breed going. Since that time, it has gradually risen in popularity.

Temperament

The Mastiff is innately good natured, calm, easygoing, and surprisingly gentle. It is a well-mannered house pet but needs sufficient room to stretch out. This is an extremely loyal breed, and though not excessively demonstrative, it is devoted to its family and good with children.

Upkeep

The adult Mastiff needs daily moderate exercise, consisting of either a good walk or game. It does not enjoy hot weather. It can live outdoors in temperate or cool weather, but it does not do well in warm weather; in fact, even though it may be physically able to live outside, it is a breed that should live inside with its family so that it will be inclined to fulfill its role of devoted guardian. It tends to drool. Coat care is minimal.

Health

- Major concerns: CHD, gastric torsion
- Minor concerns: ectropion, PPM, vaginal hyperplasia, elbow dysplasia, PRA
- Occasionally seen: cardiomyopathy
- Suggested tests: hip, elbow, eye
- Life span: 8–10 years
- Note: obesity can be a problem

Form and Function

The massive Mastiff is heavy boned and with a powerful musculature, being slightly longer than tall. It combines great strength with endurance. Its power and strength are evident in its gait, which

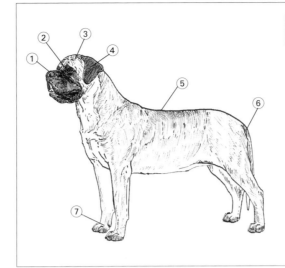

should have good reach and drive. The double coat consists of a dense undercoat and a straight, coarse, outer coat of moderately short length. The expression is alert but kindly. The overall impression should be one of grandeur and dignity.

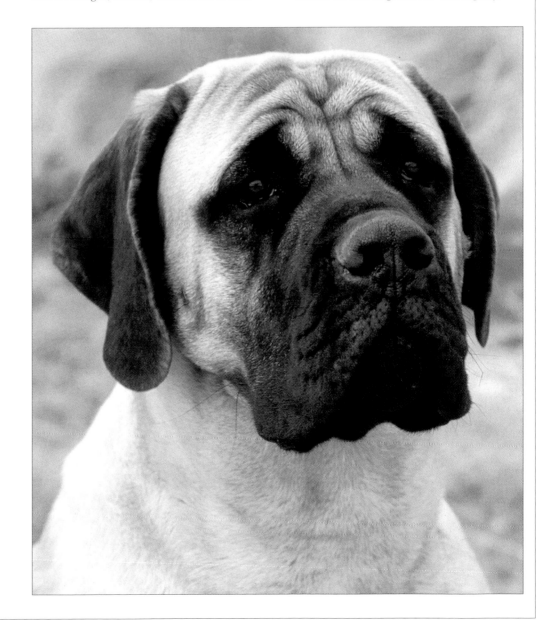

At a Glance

Energy level:	❏
Exercise requirements:	❏❏
Playfulness:	❏
Affection level:	❏❏❏
Friendliness toward dogs:	❏❏
Friendliness toward other pets:	❏❏❏
Friendliness toward strangers:	❏❏
Ease of training:	❏❏
Watchdog ability:	❏❏❏❏
Protection ability:	❏❏❏
Grooming requirements:	❏
Cold tolerance:	❏❏
Heat tolerance:	❏❏

Weight:	175–190 lb*
Height:	male: min. 30"; female: min. 27.5"

Newfoundland

History

As its name suggests, the Newfoundland was developed on the coast of Newfoundland. Here the agreement about its origin ceases. Although it ultimately traces back to the Tibetan Mastiff, no actual record exists of Tibetan Mastiffs being brought to Newfoundland. Some authorities believe that it descends from the Tibetan Mastiff by way of the Great Pyrenees. In 1662, the first permanent colony at Roougnoust was settled, complete with Great Pyrenees dogs. These dogs were crossed with black English retrievers belonging to English settlers. Some Husky blood may also have been introduced. Whatever the ingredients, the result was a massive water-loving, cold-resistant dog found in either solid black or black and white coloration. The latter "Landseer" Newfoundland was only identified in 1779. The Newfoundland name predates it only by a few years, named after an individual dog called Newfoundland. The Newfoundland distinguished itself as an all-purpose water dog, hauling heavy fishing

AKC Ranking: 49
Family: Livestock Dog, Sheepdog, Mastiff
Area of Origin: Canada
Date of Origin: 1700s
Original Function: All-purpose water dog and fishing aid, draft
Today's Function: Water rescue
Other Name: None

nets through the cold water and saving many people from watery graves. Its work didn't stop on dry land; here it served as a draft dog and pack animal. European visitors were so impressed that they returned to Europe with many specimens, and it is here that the breed first entered the show ring. The export of dogs from Newfoundland, along with laws forbidding ownership of more than one dog, drove the breed's numbers down in its place of origin. The breed's stronghold switched to England, and American fanciers resorted to replenishing their stock with English dogs. After World War II, the tables turned, and American Newfoundlands were responsible for reviving the decimated English stock. Recovery in both countries is now complete, and the Newfoundland is one of the more popular of the giant breeds of dogs. Although the solid black color is most identified with the breed, the black and white Newfoundlands (dubbed Landseers after the well-known artist who first portrayed them) are also popular.

At a Glance

Energy level:	☐☐
Exercise requirements:	☐☐
Playfulness:	☐☐☐
Affection level:	☐☐☐☐☐
Friendliness toward dogs:	☐☐☐☐
Friendliness toward other pets:	☐☐☐☐☐
Friendliness toward strangers:	☐☐☐☐☐
Ease of training:	☐☐☐
Watchdog ability:	☐☐☐
Protection ability:	☐☐☐☐
Grooming requirements:	☐☐☐
Cold tolerance:	☐☐☐☐☐
Heat tolerance:	☐

Weight: male: 130–150 lb; female: 100–120 lb

Height: male: 28" average; female: 26" average

Illustrated Standard

1. Broad skull
2. Eyes relatively small and deep set
3. Proud head carriage
4. Ears relatively small, triangular with rounded tips
5. Tail held down when relaxed; never carried over the back
6. Cat feet, webbed

❑ **Color:** solid black, brown, or gray, may have white on chin, chest, toes, and tail tip; or white base color with black markings ("Landseer")

❑ **DQ:** any colors not specified

Temperament

The most important single characteristic of the Newfoundland is sweetness of temperament. The Newfoundland is calm, patient, easygoing, gentle, and amiable—a friend to all. If its family is threatened, however, the Newfoundland can act protectively.

Upkeep

This easygoing dog needs daily exercise to stay fit, either in the form of a moderate walk or short romp. It loves to swim and pull, especially in cold weather. Some breeders contend that Landseers tend to be more active and need more exercise than solids. It does not do well in hot weather and should be kept outside only in temperate to cold weather. It is best when allowed access to both house and yard, but it needs lots of room inside to stretch out. Its coat needs combing twice weekly, more when shedding. Newfs do drool and also tend to be messy drinkers.

Health

- Major concerns: SAS, pulmonic stenosis, elbow dysplasia, CHD, gastric torsion
- Minor concerns: OCD, entropion, ectropion, vWD, cataract
- Occasionally seen: epilepsy
- Suggested tests: hip, elbow, cardiac, blood, (eye)
- Life span: 8–10 years
- Note: Newfoundlands do not tolerate heat well; some are sensitive to anesthesia.

Form and Function

The Newfoundland is a large, heavily boned, powerful dog, strong enough to pull a drowning man from rough seas and imposing enough to make an effective guard dog. It is slightly longer than it is tall. Its gait gives the impression of effortless power, with good reach and drive. Its double coat consists of a soft, dense undercoat and a coarse, moderately long and straight outer coat. Its soft expression reflects its benevolent and dignified temperament.

Portuguese Water Dog

History

The consummate water working dog, the Portuguese Water Dog probably shares some of its ancestry with the Poodle. Their ancestors were herding dogs from the central Asian steppes, either brought to Portugal by way of the Visigoths in the fifth century or by way of the Berbers and then Moors in the eighth century. Once in Portugal, it distinguished itself through its affinity for water, eventually herding fish into nets, retrieving lost nets or equipment, and serving as a boat-to-boat or boat-to-shore courier. Later the dogs were part of trawler crews fishing the waters from Portugal to Iceland. The breed is known in its native land as Cao de Agua (pronounced Kown-d'Ahgwa), which means dog of water. It comes in a long-haired variety known as the *Cao de Agua de Pelo Ondulado* and a curly-coated variety known as the *Cao de Agua de Pelo Encaradolado*. With the demise of traditional fishing methods, the Portuguese fishermen and their dogs began to disappear from the coast in the early twentieth century. The

AKC Ranking: 84
Family: Gundog, Water Dog
Area of Origin: Portugal
Date of Origin: Middle Ages
Original Function: Fishing aid
Today's Function: Water rescue
Other Name: Cao de Agua

breed was saved largely through the attempts of one man, Dr. Vasco Bensuade, a wealthy shipping magnate. He promoted the breed, and through his efforts, the breed club was reorganized, a standard was written, and the first dogs were exhibited in the show ring. After a brief appearance in England in the 1950s, the breed virtually died out there. Around this time, the first PWDs came to America, where they slowly gained a following. After they were officially AKC recognized in 1984, their popularity grew more rapidly, and the breed is now proving itself as a family companion.

Temperament

The gregarious Portuguese Water Dog is a fun-loving, family-loving, water-loving dog. It is good with children, other dogs, and pets. It is sensitive and responds well to direction. It is a good breed for an active person wanting an adventurous, affectionate, biddable partner.

Upkeep

This is an active breed needing daily physical and mental exercise, preferably involving swimming and retrieving. Otherwise, it needs a long walk or jog or a vigorous romp. The Portuguese Water Dog can live outdoors in temperate climates, but it is generally happier living close to its family and spending days in the yard. The coat needs combing every other day, plus monthly clipping or scissoring.

Health

- Major concerns: PRA, CHD
- Minor concerns: glycogen storage disease, distichiasis
- Occasionally seen: none
- Suggested tests: eye, hip
- Life span: 10–14 years

Form and Function

The Portuguese Water Dog is a robust dog of medium build, slightly longer than it is tall. It is strong and well muscled, able to work both in and out of the water for long periods. It has a profuse single coat, either wavy or curly. Two clips are acceptable: the lion clip, in which the muzzle and middle part, up to the tail tip, are clipped, and the retriever clip, in which the entire coat is scissored to about 1 inch in length, with tail tip again left full length. The Water Dog's expression is steady, penetrating, and attentive, reflecting its spirited disposition.

Illustrated Standard

1. Stop well defined
2. Eyes roundish, medium size
3. Large head
4. Ears set high, heart shaped
5. Topline level
6. When at attention, the tail is held in a ring, the front of which should not reach forward of the loin
7. Feet round and rather flat, with webbed toes; central pad very thick

❑ **Color:** black, white, brown, or combinations of black or brown with white
❑ **DQ:** none

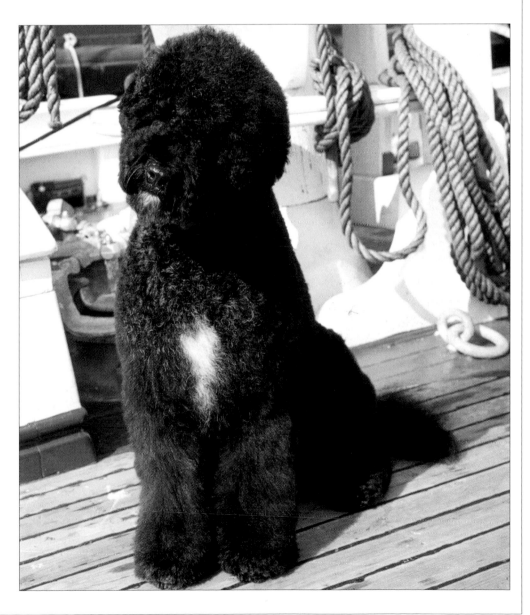

At a Glance

Energy level:	☐☐☐☐☐
Exercise requirements:	☐☐☐☐☐
Playfulness:	☐☐☐☐☐
Affection level:	☐☐☐☐☐
Friendliness toward dogs:	☐☐☐☐☐
Friendliness toward other pets:	☐☐☐☐☐
Friendliness toward strangers:	☐☐☐☐☐
Ease of training:	☐☐☐☐☐
Watchdog ability:	☐☐☐☐☐
Protection ability:	☐☐☐☐☐
Grooming requirements:	☐☐☐☐☐
Cold tolerance:	☐☐☐☐☐
Heat tolerance:	☐☐☐☐☐

Weight:	male: 42–60 lb; female: 35–50 lb
Height:	male: 20–23"; female: 17–21"

Rottweiler

History

The Rottweiler's ancestors were probably Roman drover dogs, responsible for driving and guarding herds of cattle as they accompanied Roman troops on long marches. At least one of these marches led to southern Germany, where some of the people and their dogs settled. Throughout the succeeding centuries, the dogs continued to play a vital role as cattle drovers around what was to become the town of Rottweil (which is derived from red tile, denoting the red tile roof of the Roman baths that had been unearthed there in the eighth century). Rottweil prospered and became a center of cattle commerce. Their dogs drove and guarded cattle, guarded the money earned by the cattle sales, and served as draft animals. So evolved the Rottweiler metzgerhund (butcher dog), an integral component in the town's industry until the mid nineteenth century. At that time, cattle driving was outlawed, and dog carting was

AKC Ranking: 2
Family: Livestock Dog, Sheepdog,
 Mastiff (draft/cattle)
Area of Origin: Germany
Date of Origin: Ancient times
Original Function: Cattle drover,
 guardian, draft
Today's Function: Security, herding
 trials, Schutzhund
Other Name: None

replaced by donkey carts and railroads. With little need for this once vital breed, the Rottweiler fell into such decline that it was nearly lost. With the realization that the breed was teetering near extinction, dog fanciers formed a club in 1901 and set about to revive it. Even though the 1901 club was short-lived, it did formulate a breed standard. Two subsequent clubs were formed in 1907, one of which promoted the breed as a police dog. The two clubs merged in 1921. The breed continued to grow, and by the 1930s it was competing in AKC competition. The Rottweiler has recovered from its brush with extinction to become the second most popular breed in America.

Temperament

Confident, bold, alert, and imposing, the Rottweiler is a popular choice for its protection abilities. As befitting its self-assured nature, it tends to be headstrong and stubborn and is often domineering. It is reserved, often wary, toward strangers. It may be overly protective if it perceives that its family is being threatened, and it may also attempt to "herd" children. This is a powerful breed that needs socialization, consistent training, and daily exercise to be the best it can be—a loyal family member and guardian.

Upkeep

The Rottweiler needs daily physical and mental activity, either in the form of long walks or jogs, or a vigorous game in a safe area, as well as obedience lessons. It enjoys cold weather and may become overheated in hot weather. It can live outdoors in temperate to cool climate, as long as plenty of shelter is available. It needs to spend significant time inside with its human family, however, so that proper bonding can occur. Coat care is minimal, consisting only of occasional brushing to remove dead hair.

Health

- Major concerns: CHD, elbow dysplasia, SAS, osteosarcoma, gastric torsion

Illustrated Standard

1. Head broad
2. Ears medium sized, triangular, pendant
3. Back level
4. Tail docked short, leaving one or two tail vertebrae; carried slightly above horizontal when dog is moving

❑ **Color:** black with tan markings
❑ **DQ:** entropion or ectropion; overshot or undershot; two or more missing teeth; long coat; any base color other than black, absence of all markings; a dog that attacks any person in the ring

- Minor concerns: OCD, entropion, ectropion, vWD, panosteitis
- Occasionally seen: PRA, cataract, epilepsy
- Suggested tests: hip, elbow, cardiac, blood, (eye)
- Life span: 8–11 years

Form and Function

The Rottweiler is a medium large breed, slightly longer than it is tall, and robust with a powerful, substantial build. It combines the abilities necessary to drive cattle for long distances as well as serve as a formidable guard dog, jobs that entail great strength, agility, and endurance. Its trot is sure and powerful, with strong reach and drive. Its coat is straight, coarse, and dense. Its expression reflects the Rottweiler at its best; noble, alert, and self-assured.

At a Glance

Energy level:	❑❑❑
Exercise requirements:	❑❑❑
Playfulness:	❑❑
Affection level:	❑❑
Friendliness toward dogs:	❑
Friendliness toward other pets:	❑❑
Friendliness toward strangers:	❑
Ease of training:	❑❑❑
Watchdog ability:	❑❑❑❑❑
Protection ability:	❑❑❑❑❑
Grooming requirements:	❑
Cold tolerance:	❑❑❑
Heat tolerance:	❑❑

Weight:	male: 85–135 lb; female: 80–100 lb*
Height:	male: 24–27"; female: 22–25"

Saint Bernard

History

The Saint Bernard probably has its roots in the Roman Molossian dogs, but it wasn't until between 1660 and 1670 that the breed developed into the magnificent dog responsible for saving so many lives. Around this time, the first of these large dogs arrived at the St. Bernard Hospice, a refuge for travelers crossing between Switzerland and Italy. The Saint Bernards originally came to help pull carts and turn spits and may have also functioned as watchdogs or companions, but the monks soon found them invaluable pathfinders through the deep snow. The dogs were adept at locating lost travelers. When a dog found a person, it would lick the person's face and lie beside him, thus reviving and warming the person. The dogs continued to serve in this invaluable role for three centuries, saving over 2000 lives. The most famous of all Saint Bernards was Barry, who was credited with saving 40 lives. Before Barry's death, the dogs were known by several names, including Hospice Dogs, but by the time he died he was of such fame that the dogs were called Barryhund in his honor. In the early 1800s many of the dogs were lost to severe weather,

AKC Ranking: 38
Family: Livestock Dog, Sheepdog, Mastiff
Area of Origin: Switzerland
Date of Origin: Middle Ages
Original Function: Draft, search and rescue
Today's Function: Companion
Other Name: St. Bernhardshund, Alpine Mastiff

disease, and inbreeding. Some of the remaining dogs were crossed with Newfoundlands in 1830. As a result, the first long-coated dogs of Saint Bernard type appeared. Although it seemed that long hair would help a dog in the cold snow, in fact it hindered them as the ice clung to the coat. Thus, these long-haired dogs were not kept for rescue work. The first Saints came to England around 1810, referred to by many different names, among them Sacred Dog. By 1865, the name Saint Bernard was in common use, and it became the official name in 1880. Around this time, the breed caught the eye of American fanciers. By 1900, the Saint Bernard was extremely popular. Although it has since vacillated in popularity, it is always one of the most popular of the giant breeds.

Temperament

The calm, easygoing Saint Bernard is gentle and patient around children, although it is not particularly playful. It is devoted to its family and is willing to please, although at its own pace. It can be stubborn.

Upkeep

The Saint Bernard needs daily exercise in order to stay fit. Its requirements can be met with moderate walks and short runs, however. It is best raised outdoors, away from slick surfaces. Overweight puppies raised indoors are more prone to hip problems. It enjoys cold weather and does not do well in heat. This breed can live outside in temperate to cold weather, but does best when allowed access to both house and yard. Its coat, whether long or short, needs weekly brushing, more so when shedding. All Saints drool.

Health

- Major concerns: CHD, gastric torsion, entropion, ectropion, distichiasis, elbow dysplasia, osteosarcoma
- Minor concerns: OCD, diabetes, heart conditions, cardiomyopathy, pyotraumatic dermatitis
- Occasionally seen: epilepsy
- Suggested tests: hip, elbow, cardiac, eye
- Life span: 8–10 years
- Note: The Saint Bernard does not tolerate heat well.

Illustrated Standard

1. Flews of upper jaw are well developed
2. Muzzle short and deep
3. Lower eyelids usually do not close completely but form an angular wrinkle
4. Skin wrinkled over eyes, but not excessively
5. Head powerful with massive skull
6. Ears rather high set, in shape of a rounded triangle
7. Straight back
8. Tail carried fairly low
9. Broad feet

❏ **Color:** white with red, red or brindle with white; white must appear on chest, feet, tail tip, noseband, and collar (or spot on nape); may have dark mask and ears
❏ **DQ:** none

Form and Function

The imposing Saint Bernard is powerful and proportionately tall. It is strong and well-muscled, necessary qualities in a dog that must trek through deep snow for miles. Its coat comes in two types: smooth, in which the short hair is very dense and tough, and long, in which the medium length hair is straight to slightly wavy. The expression should appear intelligent.

At a Glance

Energy level:	❏❏
Exercise requirements:	❏❏
Playfulness:	❏❏❏
Affection level:	❏❏❏❏
Friendliness toward dogs:	❏❏❏
Friendliness toward other pets:	❏❏❏❏
Friendliness toward strangers:	❏❏❏
Ease of training:	❏❏❏
Watchdog ability:	❏❏
Protection ability:	❏
Grooming requirements: (smooth)	❏❏
(long)	❏❏❏
Cold tolerance:	❏❏❏❏❏
Heat tolerance:	❏

Weight:	120–200 lb*
Height:	male: min. 27.5"; female: min. 25"

Samoyed

History

The nomadic Samoyed people, for whom the Samoyed dog is named, came to northwestern Siberia from central Asia. They depended upon herds of reindeer for food, and had to keep on the move in order that the reindeer could find sufficient food for themselves. They also depended upon strong hardy spitz dogs to herd the reindeer and to guard them against the fierce predators of the Arctic. They occasionally helped to hunt bears and tow boats and sledges. These dogs lived as part of the family in the hide tents of their people, where one of their "jobs" was to keep the children warm in bed. The first Samoyeds came to England in the late 1800s, but not all these early imports were the pure white the breed is known for today. One of these dogs was presented to Queen Alexandria, who did much to promote the breed. Descendants of the queen's dogs can still be found in modern pedigrees. In 1906, the

AKC Ranking: 48
Family: Spitz, Northern (herding)
Area of Origin: Russia (Siberia)
Date of Origin: Ancient times
Original Function: Herding reindeer, guardian, draft
Today's Function: Sled pulling, herding trials
Other Name: Samoyedskaya

first Samoyed came to America, originally a gift of Russia's Grand Duke Nicholas. Meanwhile, the breed was becoming a popular sled dog because it was more tractable than other sledding breeds. In the early 1900s, Samoyeds formed part of the sled teams on the expeditions to Antarctica and shared in the triumph of reaching the South Pole. The breed's exploits, combined with its glistening good looks, soon won the public's attention in America, and its popularity has grown tremendously since the Second World War. Although the once nomadic Samoyed people have long since settled in one place, the breed they created has journeyed around the world.

Temperament

Gentle and playful, the Samoyed makes a good companion for a child or person of any age. It is a closely bonded family dog.

It is amiable with strangers, other pets, and usually, other dogs. It is calm indoors, but this clever, sometimes mischievous breed needs daily physical and mental exercise. If allowed to become bored, it will dig and bark. It is independent and often stubborn, but it is willing to please and is responsive to its owner's wishes. It may tend to herd children.

Upkeep

The Samoyed is active and needs a good workout every day, either in the form of a long walk or jog or a vigorous play session. It likes to pull and herd, and it loves cold weather. It can live outdoors in temperate to cold climates, but it much prefers to live indoors with its human family. Its thick coat needs brushing and combing two to three times a week, daily when shedding.

Health

- Major concerns: CHD
- Minor concerns: gastric torsion
- Occasionally seen: PRA
- Suggested tests: hip, (eye)
- Life span: 10–12 years

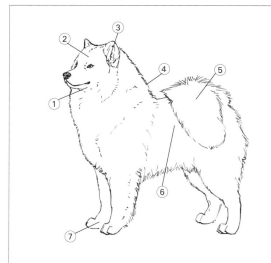

Illustrated Standard

1. Lips slightly curved up at corners of mouth
2. Skull wedge shaped, broad
3. Ears erect, triangular with slightly rounded tips, well covered inside with hair
4. Neck carried proudly erect
5. Tail profusely covered with hair and carried over the back or side when alert
6. Loins slightly arched
7. Large long hare feet, slightly spread with hair between toes

❑ **Color:** white, white and biscuit, cream, or all biscuit
❑ **DQ:** any color other than specified, blue eyes

Form and Function

The Samoyed combines strength, agility, dignity, and grace in a general spitz outline. Slightly longer than it is tall, it is nonetheless compact. It has a strong, muscular body that is able to combine power, speed, agility, and endurance. It has a quick, agile stride with good reach and drive. Its double coat is heavy and weather resistant. The undercoat is soft and thick, whereas the outer coat is straight and harsh, standing straight out from the body, and glistening with a silver sheen. The expression is animated, with the characteristic "Samoyed smile" created by the upcurved corners of the mouth.

At a Glance

Energy level:	☐☐☐
Exercise requirements:	☐☐☐
Playfulness:	☐☐☐☐
Affection level:	☐☐☐☐
Friendliness toward dogs:	☐☐☐
Friendliness toward other pets:	☐☐☐☐☐
Friendliness toward strangers:	☐☐☐☐
Ease of training:	☐☐
Watchdog ability:	☐☐☐☐☐
Protection ability:	☐
Grooming requirements:	☐☐☐
Cold tolerance:	☐☐☐☐☐
Heat tolerance:	☐

Weight:	male: 45–65 lb; female: 35–50 lb*
Height:	male: 21–23.5"; female: 19–21"

Siberian Husky

History

The Chukchi people of northeast Asia developed the breed now known as the Siberian Husky. Its ancestry is unknown, but it is of obvious spitz stock, evolved over hundreds of years as a sledge dog for these nomadic people. During the Alaskan gold rush, dogs became a vital part of life in the Arctic regions, and dog racing became a favorite source of entertainment. The All-Alaska sweepstakes race, covering 408 miles between Nome and Candle, was especially popular, and in 1909 the first team of these Chukchi huskies brought over from Siberia was entered. Smaller and more docile than most of the other competitors, they aroused little admiration, with the exception of one racer who was so impressed he imported seventy to train for the 1910 race. His three teams placed first, second, and fourth and so set the stage for the Siberian

AKC Ranking: 16
Family: Spitz, Northern (draft)
Area of Origin: Russia (Siberia)
Date of Origin: Ancient times
Original Function: Sled pulling
Today's Function: Sled racing
Other Name: Arctic Husky

Husky's unrivaled dominance in this race. Throughout the rest of the year, the dogs earned their keep as utilitarian sledders, but it was in 1925 that they gained their greatest acclaim. Teams of Huskies raced 340 miles with life-saving serum for diphtheria stricken Nome and were credited with saving the town. A statue in their honor stands in Central Park. The first Siberian Huskies came to Canada, and then the United States, at around this time. The AKC recognized the breed in 1930. During World War II, many Siberians served in the U.S. Army's Search and Rescue teams, further capturing the public's admiration. The breed's popularity continued to grow until it was cherished as much for a family pet as for a racing sled dog or show dog. It remains one of the most popular of the Arctic breeds.

Temperament

Fun-loving, adventurous, alert, independent, clever, stubborn, mischievous, and obstinate all describe the Siberian Husky. This breed loves to run and will roam if given the chance. It may be aggressive toward strange dogs, but it is generally good with other household dogs. In fact, it is a very social dog that must have human or canine companionship. It may chase strange cats or livestock. Some howl, dig, and chew.

Upkeep

This is an active dog, bred to run tirelessly for miles. It needs ample daily exercise, either in the form of a long jog or a long run off-leash in a safe area. It also loves to pull and enjoys cold weather. It can live outdoors in cool or cold climates, but ideally it can divide its time between indoors and out. Its coat needs brushing one or two times a week, daily during periods of heaviest shedding.

Health

- Major concerns: none
- Minor concerns: PRA, distichiasis, cataract, corneal opacities
- Occasionally seen: CHD, glaucoma
- Suggested tests: eye, (hip)
- Life span: 11–13 years

Form and Function

The Siberian Husky combines power, speed, and endurance, enabling it to carry a light load at moderate speed over a great distance. It is moderately compact, slightly longer than it is tall, and of definite Northern heritage. It is quick and light on its feet, with a smooth and effortless stride exhibiting both good reach and drive. It has a double coat of medium length, with a soft, dense undercoat and straight, somewhat flat-lying outer coat. Its expression is keen but friendly, interested, and even mischievous.

Illustrated Standard

① Eyes almond shaped; brown, blue, or any combination
② Ears erect, well furred, slightly rounded tips
③ Skull slightly rounded
④ Neck carried proudly erect and arched
⑤ Topline level
⑥ Well-furred tail of fox brush shape, carried in a sickle curve
⑦ Feet oval, medium sized, well furred between toes and pads

❏ **Color:** all colors from black to pure white
❏ **DQ:** males over 23.5″ or females over 22″

At a Glance

Energy level:	■■■□□
Exercise requirements:	■■■■□
Playfulness:	■■■■□
Affection level:	■■■■□
Friendliness toward dogs:	■■■□□
Friendliness toward other pets:	■■■□□
Friendliness toward strangers:	■■■■■
Ease of training:	■□□□□
Watchdog ability:	■■■□□
Protection ability:	■□□□□
Grooming requirements:	■■■□□
Cold tolerance:	■■■■■
Heat tolerance:	■□□□□

Weight:	male: 45–60 lb; female: 35–50 lb
Height:	male: 21–23.5″; female: 20–22″

Standard Schnauzer

History

The Standard Schnauzer is the prototypical Schnauzer, the oldest of the three breeds. Definite evidence of the breed exists as early as the fourteenth century; even then, it was appreciated as a household pet and hunting companion. The breed is a fortuitous blend of terrier, working, and hunting stock, most likely derived from crossing Wire-Haired Pinschers with black German Poodles and gray wolf spitz. The result was a hardy rat catcher that also functioned as a capable guard dog. By the beginning of the twentieth century, they were the most popular dogs for guarding farmers' carts at the marketplace while the farmers were elsewhere. The first Schnauzers entered the show ring as Wirehaired Pinschers at an 1879 German show. Their smart looks quickly enamored them to the dog fanciers, and they became very popular as show dogs by 1900. Although the first Schnauzers came to America by this time, they were slower to catch on with American dog fanciers. The breed was initially

AKC Ranking: 98
Family: Schnauzer, Livestock Guard, Terrier
Area of Origin: Germany
Date of Origin: Middle Ages
Original Function: Ratting, guardian
Today's Function: Companion
Other Name: Mittelschnauzer

classified as a terrier, but it was later reclassified as a working dog. Their alert and intelligent nature gained them a role as dispatch carrier and aide during World War I. Like the larger Giant Schnauzer, the Standard Schnauzer was also used in police work. Only after World War II did it gain more public attention; even so, it has not achieved the popularity of the other Schnauzers.

Temperament

Bold and lively, the Standard Schnauzer is a fun-loving companion and guardian. It is clever and headstrong, and unless given daily physical and mental exercise, it can be mischievous. It does best with a firm, patient owner. It is a devoted family dog and very reliable with children. It is good with family pets, but it can be aggressive toward strange dogs, animals, or rodents. It is reserved with strangers, sometimes acting suspicious and protective.

Upkeep

The Standard Schnauzer needs daily exertion, either a long walk on leash, a vigorous game, or an off-lead outing in a safe area. It can live outdoors in temperate climates, but it is better off dividing its time between house and yard. Its harsh coat needs combing twice weekly, plus professional scissoring and shaping four times yearly. Shaping is done by clipping for pets and stripping for show dogs.

Health

- Major concerns: none
- Minor concerns: CHD, follicular dermatitis
- Occasionally seen: none
- Suggested tests: hip
- Life span: 12–14 years

Form and Function

This is a robust, sturdily built, heavy-set dog of square proportion. It is both strong and agile, enabling it to perform as both a guard and ratter. Its stride is quick, powerful, and ground covering. Its coat is hard, wiry, and thick, with soft undercoat. Its hallmark whiskers, mustache, and eyebrows add to its alert, spirited expression.

Illustrated Standard

1. Expression alert and spirited
2. Eyes oval with long eyebrows, which should not impair vision
3. Head strong, rectangular, and long
4. Ears set high; carried erect if cropped; V-shaped and mobile so they break at skull level if uncropped
5. Topline slopes slightly down
6. Tail carried erect and docked from 1 to 2"
7. Feet small, round, compact

❏ **Color:** pepper and salt or pure black
❏ **DQ:** males under 18" or over 20"; females under 17" or over 19"

At a Glance

Energy level:	❏❏❏❏
Exercise requirements:	❏❏❏
Playfulness:	❏❏❏
Affection level:	❏❏
Friendliness toward dogs:	❏❏
Friendliness toward other pets:	❏❏❏
Friendliness toward strangers:	❏
Ease of training:	❏❏❏
Watchdog ability:	❏❏❏❏❏
Protection ability:	❏❏❏❏❏
Grooming requirements:	❏❏❏❏
Cold tolerance:	❏❏❏
Heat tolerance:	❏❏❏

Weight: male: 40–45 lb; female: 35–40 lb*

Height: male: 18.5–19.5"; female: 17.5–18.5"

The Terrier Group

Dogs of the Terrier Group have in common the proclivity to kill rodents and vermin, often by digging or going to ground after them. The word *terrier*, in fact, refers to earth or *terra*. Some terriers were developed in part to kill rats in pit contests, and later to fight against each other. The vermin-catching terriers are roughly divided into long-legged and short-legged breeds.

Airedale Terrier

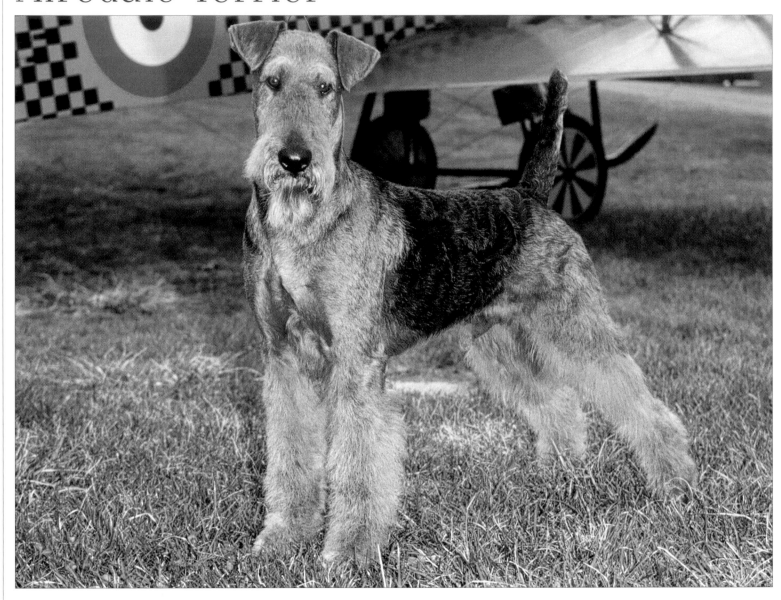

History

Known as the King of Terriers, the Airedale is the tallest terrier. Like many terriers, it counts the old English, or Black and Tan, Terrier as one of its primary progenitors. These medium-sized dogs were prized by Yorkshire hunters for hunting a variety of game from water rats to fox. Around the mid 1800s, some of these terriers around the River Aire in South Yorkshire were crossed with Otterhounds in order to improve their hunting ability around water, as well as their scenting ability. The result was a dog adept at otter hunting, originally called the Bingley or Waterside Terrier but recognized as the Airedale Terrier in 1878. As it entered the world of the show dog, crosses to the Irish and Bull Terriers were made in order to breed away from some of the remnants of the Otterhound cross that were now considered less than beautiful.

AKC Ranking: 47
Family: Terrier
Area of Origin: England
Date of Origin: 1800s
Original Function: Badger and otter hunting
Today's Function: Guardian, police dog
Other Name: Waterside Terrier, Bingley Terrier

By 1900, the patriarch of the breed, Champion Master Briar, was gaining renown, and his offspring carried on his influence in America. The Airedale's size and gameness continued to win it worldwide fame as a hunter, even proving itself as a big game hunter. Its smart looks and manners won it a place as a police dog and family pet, both roles it still enjoys. After World War I, however, its popularity declined, and today its reputation is greater than its numbers.

Temperament

Among the most versatile of terriers, the Airedale is bold, playful, and adventurous; it is a lively yet protective companion. It is intelligent, but often stubborn and headstrong. Some can be domineering, but most are biddable, reliable, and responsive to their owner's wishes. It makes a good housedog as long as it gets daily mental and physical exercise. It likes to be the head dog and may not do well when another dog challenges that position, although they usually get along well with smaller dogs.

Upkeep

This is an active breed that needs a chance to get vigorous exercise every day. Its needs can be met with a long walk, a strenuous game, or a chance to hunt and romp in a safe area. It can live outside in temperate climates, but it is better suited for indoor sleeping. Its wire coat needs combing twice weekly, plus scissoring and shaping (clipping for pets, and hand stripping for show dogs) every one to two months. Ears often need "glue-ing" as puppies in order to ensure proper shape as adults.

Health

- Major concerns: CHD
- Minor concerns: gastric torsion
- Occasionally seen: colonic disease
- Suggested tests: hip
- Life span: 10–13 years

Illustrated Standard

1. Skull long and flat
2. Eyes small
3. Stop hardly visible
4. V-shaped ears with fold above the level of the skull
5. Back short and level
6. Tail set and carried high, of fair length
7. Feet small and round

❏ **Color:** tan with black or grizzle saddle
❏ **DQ:** none

Form and Function

The Airedale Terrier is a neat, upstanding, long-legged terrier, not exaggerated in any way. It has strong round bone and combines strength and agility, enabling it to hunt tough game. Its jaws are strong and punishing. Its gait is free. The coat is hard, dense, and wiry; it lies straight and close, with some hair crinkling or waving.

At a Glance

Energy level:	❏❏❏❏
Exercise requirements:	❏❏❏
Playfulness:	❏❏❏❏
Affection level:	❏❏❏
Friendliness toward dogs:	❏
Friendliness toward other pets:	❏❏
Friendliness toward strangers:	❏❏❏
Ease of training:	❏❏❏
Watchdog ability:	❏❏❏❏
Protection ability:	❏❏❏❏
Grooming requirements:	❏❏❏❏
Cold tolerance:	❏❏❏
Heat tolerance:	❏❏❏

Weight:	about 45 lb*
Height:	male: 23"; female: slightly less

American Staffordshire Terrier

History

The American Staffordshire Terrier and the Staffordshire Bull Terrier descended from the same lines. The prototype originally sprang from crossing the old type of Bulldog with some old terrier types, probably the English Smooth Terrier. The result was aptly called the Bull and Terrier, later to be dubbed the Staffordshire Bull Terrier. The dogs gained fame among fanciers of dog fighting, a popular sport despite its having been declared illegal. Their fighting ability gained them passage to America in the late 1800s, where they dominated the fighting "pits." Here they became known as the Pit Bull Terrier, American Bull Terrier, and even Yankee Terrier. Americans favored a slightly bigger dog than the English preferred, and with time the two strains diverged. In 1936, the AKC recognized the breed as the Staffordshire Terrier (the name was changed in 1972 to American Staffordshire Terrier). Docility and tractability have always been vital traits in a powerful dog that must be handled even in the midst of a dog

AKC Ranking: 67
Family: Terrier, Mastiff (Bull)
Area of Origin: United States
Date of Origin: 1800s
Original Function: Bullbaiting, dog fighting
Today's Function: Companion
Other Name: None

fight; therefore, the Am Staff evolved to have a sweet and trustworthy disposition around people. Unfortunately, this game dog has too often appealed to people seeking it for its fighting rather than its loving abilities. Often in the midst of controversy, beginning in the 1980s, it sometimes found itself the target of breed-specific laws aimed at banning or controlling certain types of dogs. Despite this, the Am Staff is currently enjoying one of its most popular periods among people wanting a people- and fun-loving dog.

Temperament

Typically docile and playful with its family, the American Staffordshire Terrier is also generally friendly toward strangers as long as its owners are present. It is generally very good with children. It is a protective breed and can be aggressive toward other dogs—especially those that challenge it. It is stubborn, tenacious, and fearless. For all of its tough persona, the most important thing in life to this breed is its owner's fond attention.

Upkeep

The Staff needs a daily outlet for its energy, preferably in the form of a long walk on leash or a vigorous game in the yard. Though it can live outdoors in temperate climates, this breed is far better suited temperamentally to sharing its family's home. Coat care is minimal. As one of the breeds popularly considered a "pit bull," public acceptance may sometimes be low.

Health

- Major concerns: CHD
- Minor concerns: none
- Occasionally seen: PDA
- Suggested tests: OFA, (cardiac)
- Life span: 12–14 years
- Note: The high pain threshold may mask problems

Form and Function

This stocky dog should be muscular, giving the impression not only of great strength for its size but also of grace and agility. Its gait is springy. Its low center of gravity helped it stay on its feet in a fight, and its nimbleness helped it avoid its opponent's teeth. Its own jaws are strong with great power. Its coat is short, close, and glossy.

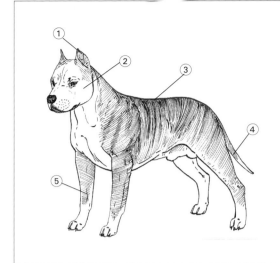

Illustrated Standard

1. Ears set high, cropped or uncropped (preferred); uncropped ears short and held half rose or prick
2. Head broad, pronounced cheek muscles, distinct stop
3. Back fairly short, sloping slightly to rear
4. Tail short but not docked
5. Forelegs set wide, straight

❏ **Color:** any solid or partial color, but more than 80 percent white, black and tan, or liver are less preferred
❏ **DQ:** none

At a Glance

Energy level:	❏❏❏
Exercise requirements:	❏❏❏
Playfulness:	❏❏❏
Affection level:	❏❏❏
Friendliness toward dogs:	❏
Friendliness toward other pets:	❏
Friendliness toward strangers:	❏❏❏
Ease of training:	❏
Watchdog ability:	❏❏❏❏❏
Protection ability:	❏❏❏❏❏
Grooming requirements:	❏
Cold tolerance:	❏❏❏
Heat tolerance:	❏❏❏

Weight:	57–67 lb*
Height:	male: 18–19"; female: 17–18"

Australian Terrier

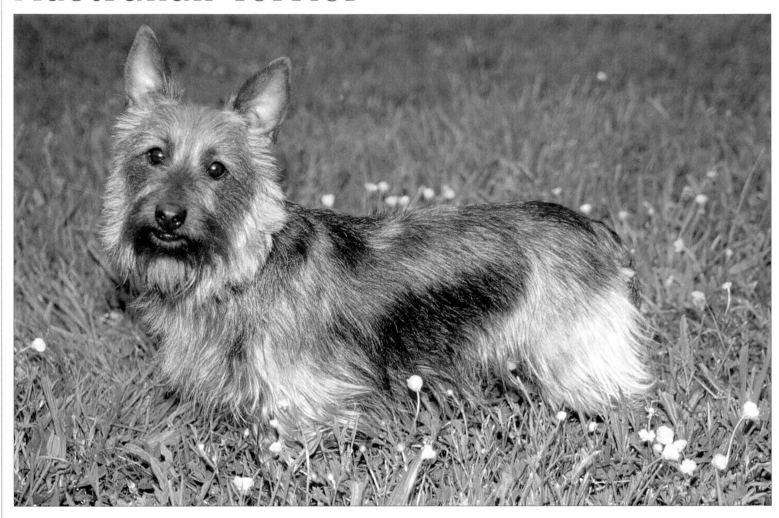

History

The national terrier of Australia, this is one of the smallest of the working terriers. It was born in Tasmania, from various European breeds, and shares much of its background with the Silky Terrier. In Tasmania, the Rough Coated Terrier was an all-purpose companion, killing vermin and snakes, controlling livestock, and sounding the alarm at intruders. A cornucopia of breeds was crossed with this root stock, among them the precursors of the Skye, Dandie Dinmont, Scotch, Yorkshire, and Manchester Terriers. The result was a dog that was both useful and striking in appearance. The first of the breed was shown in the late 1800s as a "broken-coated terrier of blackish blue sheen." The name was soon changed to the Blue and Tan, the Toy, then the Blue, Terrier, then in 1900 the Rough-Coated Terrier, Blue and Tan. Although mainly known for its blue and tan coloration, a red or sandy color was also found among the early representatives of the breed. Soon after the breed had made its way to British show rings and homes, and by 1925 it had come to America. It received AKC recognition in 1960.

AKC Ranking: 99
Family: Terrier
Area of Origin: Australia
Date of Origin: 1900s
Original Function: Killing small vermin
Today's Function: Earthdog trials
Other Name: None

Temperament

One of the quieter terriers, the Aussie is nonetheless a plucky, tough character, ready to go after a rodent when the chance arises. It is fun loving and adventurous, and needs daily exercise to keep it from becoming frustrated. It is clever and generally eager to please, making it one of the more obedient terriers. It gets along fairly well with other dogs and household pets. It is reserved with strangers. Reflecting its earth dog heritage, it does like to dig.

Upkeep

This is an active breed that needs a good outing every day, either a moderate walk, a rollicking game, or an off-lead run in a safe area. It was created to withstand harsh Australian conditions and is physically able to stay outdoors in temperate to warm climates. It is also a good housedog and needs to spend time with its family. Its wire coat needs weekly combing plus twice yearly stripping of dead hairs (regular plucking of dead hairs will keep the coat in optimal condition year round). Some trimming around the feet will add to a tidy look.

At a Glance

Energy level:	▢▢▢
Exercise requirements:	▢▢▢
Playfulness:	▢▢▢
Affection level:	▢▢▢
Friendliness toward dogs:	▢▢▢
Friendliness toward other pets:	▢▢▢
Friendliness toward strangers:	▢▢
Ease of training:	▢▢
Watchdog ability:	▢▢▢▢▢
Protection ability:	▢
Grooming requirements:	▢▢▢
Cold tolerance:	▢▢▢
Heat tolerance:	▢▢▢

Weight:	12–14 lb*
Height:	10–11″

Illustrated Standard

① Eyes small and oval
② Head long and strong
③ Ears small, erect, and pointed
④ Topline level
⑤ Tail set high and carried at twelve or one o'clock, docked leaving just less than one half*
⑥ Small cat feet

❏ **Color:** blue and tan, solid sandy, and solid red
❏ **DQ:** none

*Docking is optional.

Health
- Major concerns: none
- Minor concerns: none
- Occasionally seen: Legg–Perthes, patellar luxation, diabetes
- Suggested tests: none
- Life span: 12–14 years

Form and Function
The Australian Terrier is small, sturdy, and medium boned; it is long in proportion to height. This is a working terrier that should exhibit a ground-covering gait and hard condition. Its weatherproof coat is made up of a short, soft undercoat and a harsh, straight, outer coat, about 2.5 inches long, shorter on the tail and lower legs. It sports a ruff around the neck and a topknot of longer hair adds to its keen, intelligent expression.

Bedlington Terrier

History

One of the most unusual members of the terrier group is the Bedlington Terrier. It is an English product, hailing from the Hanny Hills of Northumberland. Its exact origin is obscure, but in the late eighteenth century a strain of game terriers was developed that became known as Rothbury Terriers. In 1825, Joseph Ainsley of the town of Bedlington bred two of his Rothbury Terriers and christened their offspring a Bedlington Terrier. Occasional crosses to other breeds arguably included the Whippet (for speed) and Dandie Dinmont Terrier (for coat), but no documented evidence of such crosses exist, and some breed historians assert that such crosses were never made. Whatever the process, the result was an agile game terrier that was effective on badger, fox, otter, rats, and even rabbits. By the late 1800s, the breed had stepped into the show ring as well as into the homes of the more elite. At one time the liver color was more popular, although the blue has since passed it in popularity. The Bedlington's lamb-like appearance draws many admirers, but the emphasis on show trimming eventually dampened the breed's popularity as a show dog. With more

AKC Ranking: 120
Family: Terrier
Area of Origin: England
Date of Origin: 1800s
Original Function: Killing rat, badger, and other vermin
Today's Function: Earthdog trials
Other Name: Rothbury Terrier

easily available grooming tools and instructions, the Bedlington has regained much of its popularity with the public.

Temperament

The Bedlington is among the softer terriers, not only in looks and feel but in temperament. It is companionable, demonstrative, and loyal. It enjoys its creature comforts and is a fairly quiet housedog. Even though it will seldom initiate a fight, it will not allow itself to be intimidated by other dogs and can be a scrappy fighter when pushed. It will give chase to small animals outdoors, but it can usually coexist with them indoors.

Upkeep

The Bedlington needs daily exercise in a safe place; it loves to run and chase. Its needs can be met with a good long walk or vigorous romp. This is not a breed that should live outside. Its coat needs combing once or twice weekly, plus scissoring to shape the coat every other month. Hair that is shed tends to cling to the other hair rather than shedding.

At a Glance

Energy level:	▢▢▢
Exercise requirements:	▢▢▢
Playfulness:	▢▢▢
Affection level:	▢▢▢
Friendliness toward dogs:	▢▢▢
Friendliness toward other pets:	▢▢
Friendliness toward strangers:	▢▢▢▢
Ease of training:	▢▢
Watchdog ability:	▢▢▢▢▢
Protection ability:	▢
Grooming requirements:	▢▢▢▢▢
Cold tolerance:	▢▢▢
Heat tolerance:	▢▢▢

Weight:	17–23 lb
Height:	male: 16.5"; female: 15.5"

Health

- Major concerns: copper toxicosis
- Minor concerns: retinal dysplasia, renal cortical hypoplasia, distichiasis
- Occasionally seen: patellar luxation
- Suggested tests: DNA for copper toxicosis, eye
- Life span: 12–14 years

Form and Function

This graceful, lithe dog has a distinctive silhouette. Its arched loin and racy outline give it great speed and agility. A wolf in lamb's clothing, the Bedlington is unrivaled in its ability to chase and fight agile but tough quarry. Its gait is light and springy. Its coat is a mixture of hard and soft hair standing off the skin, affording good protection as well as outstanding appearance.

Border Terrier

History

Perhaps the oldest of Britain's terriers, the Border Terrier originated around the Cheviot Hills forming the border country between Scotland and England. The dog originated to chase and dispatch the fox that were considered a nuisance to farmers. The smallest of the long-legged terriers, the Border Terrier had to be fast enough to keep up with a horse yet small enough to go in after the fox once it had gone to ground. The first evidence of these dogs dates from the eighteenth century. Its progenitors are unknown, although it is probably related to the Dandie Dinmont. The breed was once known as the Coquetdale Terrier (among other names), but the name Border Terrier, taken from the Border Hunt, was adopted in 1870. By this time, the breed had risen from its utilitarian roots to take a valued place alongside the Foxhounds in the gentry's elegant foxhunts. The Border Hunt had a long association with these game yet amiable terriers whose job it was to dispatch

AKC Ranking: 87
Family: Terrier
Area of Origin: Border of Scotland and England
Date of Origin: 1700s
Original Function: Fox bolting, ratting
Today's Function: Earthdog trials
Other Name: None

the fox. The first Border Terrier was shown in the 1870s. The breed was recognized by the AKC in 1930. Less flashy than many other terriers, the Border continued to be better appreciated by patrons of the hunt than of the show ring. In recent years, it has experienced a rise in popularity and is fast becoming a fairly popular pet and successful show dog.

Temperament

One of the few terriers bred to run with the pack, the Border is one of the most amiable and tractable of the group. It is inquisitive, busy, friendly, and biddable. It does like to hunt and can be independent, ingredients that make for a dog that may tend to roam if given the chance. It is generally good with other dogs and cats, but not with rodents. It is very good with children and makes a good companion for people of all ages. It digs, and some bark. Some are talented escape artists.

Upkeep

The Border likes activity and needs either a good walk on leash, a vigorous game session, or an off-lead expedition in a safe area every day. It can live outdoors in temperate climates, but it does much better when allowed to divide its time between house and yard. Its harsh coat needs brushing weekly, plus stripping of dead hairs about four times yearly to maintain its clean outline.

Health

- Major concerns: none
- Minor concerns: none
- Occasionally seen: CHD, heart defects
- Suggested tests: hip, cardiac
- Life span: 12–15 years

Form and Function

The Border Terrier is of medium bone, slightly taller than long. Its long legs impart the speed, agility, and endurance necessary to follow a horse over all sorts of terrain, whereas its fairly narrow body allows it to squeeze through narrow passages in pursuit of a fox. Its gait displays good length of stride. Its coat consists of a short, dense undercoat covered by a very wiry, straight, somewhat broken outer coat, which should conform to the body. Its hide is very thick and loose fitting, affording protection from the bites of its quarry. The Border is known for its distinctive otter head, and its alert expression matches its alert demeanor.

Illustrated Standard

1. Muzzle short, darker colored and with a few short whiskers
2. Eyes medium sized
3. Head similar to an otter
4. Small, V-shaped ears, dropping forward
5. Tail moderately short, carried gaily when alert
6. Feet small

❑ **Color:** red, grizzle and tan, blue and tan, or wheaten
❑ **DQ:** none

At a Glance

Energy level:	▢▢▢
Exercise requirements:	▢▢▢
Playfulness:	▢▢▢
Affection level:	▢▢▢
Friendliness toward dogs:	▢▢▢
Friendliness toward other pets:	▢▢
Friendliness toward strangers:	▢▢▢
Ease of training:	▢▢▢▢
Watchdog ability:	▢▢▢▢
Protection ability:	▢
Grooming requirements:	▢▢▢
Cold tolerance:	▢▢▢
Heat tolerance:	▢▢▢

Weight:	male: 13–15.5 lb; female: 11.5–14 lb
Height:	10–11"*

Bull Terrier

History

Bull baiting and dog fighting were long considered great entertainment by many Europeans, and patrons were constantly trying crosses to achieve the ultimate fighting dog. Around 1835, a cross between a Bulldog and the old English Terrier produced a particularly adept pit dog known as the Bull and Terrier. A later cross to the Spanish Pointer added needed size, and the result was a tenacious, strong, yet agile dog that came to dominate the pits. As interest in the exhibition of dogs grew in England, little attention was paid to these dogs so long associated with the lower echelons

AKC Ranking: 82
Family: Terrier, Mastiff (Bull)
Area of Origin: England
Date of Origin: 1800s
Original Function: Dog fighting
Today's Function: Companion
Other Name: English Bull Terrier

of society. With the abolition of dog fighting, however, some Bull Terrier patrons turned to this new venue to compete with their dogs, and they began to breed for appearance. Around 1860 James Hinks crossed the Bull and Terrier with the White English Terrier and the Dalmatian, producing an all-white strain he called Bull Terriers. The new all-white strain immediately succeeded in the ring and captured the attention of the public; they became a fashionable companion for young gentlemen who wanted a good-looking masculine dog at their sides. The dogs gained the reputation for defending themselves, but not

At a Glance

Energy level:	☐☐☐☐
Exercise requirements:	☐☐☐
Playfulness:	☐☐☐☐☐
Affection level:	☐☐☐
Friendliness toward dogs:	☐
Friendliness toward other pets:	☐☐☐
Friendliness toward strangers:	☐☐☐
Ease of training:	☐
Watchdog ability:	☐☐☐☐☐
Protection ability:	☐☐☐☐
Grooming requirements:	☐
Cold tolerance:	☐☐☐
Heat tolerance:	☐☐☐

Weight:	male: 55–65 lb; female: 45–55 lb*
Height:	21–22″*

Illustrated Standard

① Head long, strong and deep, curving from skull to nose; oval outline viewed face on
② Eyes small, triangular, deep set, and placed close together
③ Ears small, erect, close set
④ Short strong back
⑤ Tail short, carried horizontally
⑥ Cat feet
⑦ Big boned but not coarse

❏ **Color:** white variety: white, with markings on head permissible; colored variety: any color other than white, or any color with white markings; brindle preferred
❏ **DQ:** blue eyes; in colored variety, any dog predominantly white

provoking a fight, and were thus dubbed "the white cavalier." The dogs gradually became more streamlined, and the Bull Terrier's distinctive head evolved. Around 1900, crosses with Staffordshire Bull Terriers reintroduced color into the breed. It was not well accepted at first, but it finally gained equal status as a separate AKC variety in 1936. The white variety still continues as the more popular variety, but both colors have enjoyed great popularity as show dogs and pets. Their comical nature and expression wins them many friends, and they have proven to be very successful in movies and advertising.

Temperament

Exuberant, comical, playful, assertive, and very mischievous describes the Bull Terrier. It is an imaginative breed that often sees things its own way and is stubborn to the end. It needs daily physical and mental exercise lest it exercise its powerful jaws on your home. For all its tough bravado, this is an extremely sweet-natured, affectionate, and devoted breed. It can be aggressive with other dogs and small animals.

Upkeep

The Bull Terrier needs to be entertained, either with a good exercise session or mental stimulation every day—preferably both. This is an active breed that enjoys a good run, but it is best to run it only in a safe area. It should not stay outdoors except in temperate weather, but it should live primarily as a housedog with access to a yard. Coat care is minimal.

Health

- Major concerns: deafness (whites), kidney problems
- Minor concerns: heart problems, patellar luxation
- Occasionally seen: lens luxation
- Suggested tests: hearing (whites), UP:UC ratio for kidney function, cardiac, (eye)
- Life span: 11–14 years

Form and Function

The Bull Terrier is the cavalier gladiator—a good looking tough character. It is strongly built and muscular, longer than it is tall. Its muscle mass combined with its relatively low center of gravity make it difficult for opponents to knock it off its feet. Its distinctive head not only

shows off its keen and determined expression, but also its great jaw strength. Its gait is smooth and easy. Its skin is tight, and its coat short, flat, and harsh.

Cairn Terrier

History

One of a family of short-legged terriers developed on the Scottish Isle of Skye, the Cairn Terrier probably still resembles the ancestral form to a greater degree than others descended from the same stock. These dogs seem to have existed since the fifteenth century and were used to hunt fox, badger, and otter. The dogs were adept at bolting otters from the cairns (piles of stone that served as landmarks or memorials). The dogs came in a variety of colors, ranging from white to gray to red, and were all considered Scotch Terriers when they began to enter the show ring. In 1873, they were divided into Dandie Dinmont and Skye Terriers, with the Cairn in the latter group. This group was later again divided into Skye and Hard-haired Terriers in 1881, and the Hard-haired Terriers eventually separated into Scotch, West Highland White, and the breed eventually known as the Cairn. At one time, the Cairn was called the Short-haired Skye, then the Cairn Terrier or Skye, and finally, around 1912, the Cairn Terrier. Some of the most influential early Cairns were all white, but

AKC Ranking: 45
Family: Terrier
Area of Origin: Scotland
Date of Origin: Middle Ages
Original Function: Killing vermin
Today's Function: Earthdog trials
Other Name: None

white, as well as crossing to West Highland Whites, was banned by the 1920s. The breed became quite popular in England, and fairly popular in America, gaining its greatest fame as the dog playing Toto in the *Wizard of Oz*. As one of the more natural and less sculpted terriers, the breed is highly regarded by those who appreciate a working terrier. Perhaps the motto of the British breed club sums it up best: "The best little pal in the world."

Temperament

The Cairn is the essence of terrier; plucky, spirited, bold, inquisitive, hardy, clever, stubborn, and scrappy. It is responsive to its owner's wishes, however, and tries to please; in fact, it is surprisingly sensitive. This breed can be a good house pet as long as it is given daily physical and mental exercise in a safe area. It enjoys playing with children and is tough enough to withstand some rough-housing. It can be aggressive with other dogs and chases small animals; it loves to sniff, explore, and hunt. It digs; some bark.

Upkeep

Despite its small size, the Cairn needs outdoor exercise every day, either a moderate walk on leash, a fun game in the yard, or an excursion in a safe area. It can live outdoors in temperate climates, but it does better sleeping indoors. Its wire coat needs combing once weekly, plus stripping of dead hair at least twice yearly.

Health

- Major concerns: none
- Minor concerns: globoid cell leukodystrophy
- Occasionally seen: vWD, Legg–Perthes, patellar luxation
- Suggested tests: none
- Life span: 12–15 years

Form and Function

This is a working terrier, and it should be hardy, game, and active. It is short-legged, and longer than it is tall, but not as low to the ground as the Sealyham or Scottish Terriers. Its build enables it to fit into close quarters in pursuit of its quarry. Its head is shorter and wider than any other terrier, giving it good jaw strength. Its

Illustrated Standard

1. Eyes sunken, with shaggy eyebrows
2. Skull broad, well-defined stop
3. Ears small, pointed, erect, set wide
4. Level back of medium length
5. Tail carried gaily but not curled over back

❏ **Color:** any color but white; dark ears, muzzle, tail tip desired
❏ **DQ:** none

weather-resistant coat consists of a soft, close undercoat and a profuse, harsh outer coat. Furnishing around the face adds to its somewhat foxy expression.

At a Glance

Energy level:	❑❑❑❑
Exercise requirements:	❑❑❑
Playfulness:	❑❑❑
Affection level:	❑❑❑
Friendliness toward dogs:	❑❑❑
Friendliness toward other pets:	❑
Friendliness toward strangers:	❑
Ease of training:	❑
Watchdog ability:	❑❑❑❑❑
Protection ability:	❑
Grooming requirements:	❑❑❑
Cold tolerance:	❑❑❑
Heat tolerance:	❑❑❑

Weight:	male: 14 lb; female: 13 lb
Height:	male: 10"; female: 9.5"

Dandie Dinmont Terrier

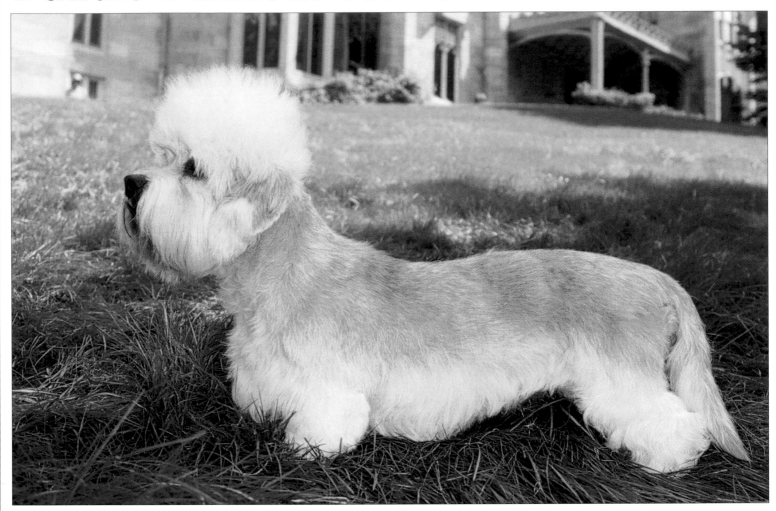

History

The Dandie Dinmont Terrier stands out as a most unusual terrier in appearance, yet its roots are as quintessentially terrier as any. It first appeared as a distinct type of terrier in the eighteenth century around the border country of Scotland and England. Here they were owned by farmers and gypsies and valued for drawing and killing otters, badgers, and foxes. At one time, they were known as Catcleugh, Hindlee, or Pepper and Mustard terriers. The most well known of these dogs were owned by James Davidson, who named almost all his dogs either Pepper or Mustard along with some identifying adjective. Davidson and his dogs are believed by some to have been the models for Sir Walter Scott's characters of Dandie Dinmont and his dogs in *Guy Mannering*, published in 1814. The dogs became known as Dandie Dinmont's Terriers. A letter written by James Davidson proclaimed that all Dandies descended from two of his dogs named Tarr and Pepper. At one time the breed was included in the general family of Scotch Terriers, which encompassed several short-legged terri-

AKC Ranking: 137
Family: Terrier
Area of Origin: Border of Scotland and England
Date of Origin: 1700s
Original Function: Otter and badger hunting
Today's Function: Earthdog trials
Other Name: None

ers now recognized as distinct breeds. The Dandie was recognized separately from this group in 1873. The Dandie Dinmont has never been extremely popular, and remains one of the lesser-known terriers. An old Scottish saying says, "A Dandie looks at you as though he's forgotten more than you will ever know."

Temperament

The Dandie Dinmont is no "dandified" dog; it is rough and tumble and ready for the hunt. Yet it functions well as a dignified house pet, affectionate but not doting. It is a loyal companion suitable for people of all ages, but it does need daily exercise to keep it from becoming frustrated. It is intelligent and very independent. It tends to be reserved with strangers and aggressive toward strange dogs. Some dig.

Upkeep

The Dandie enjoys the chance to hunt around and explore in a safe area and needs a moderate walk to stay in condition. It does

At a Glance

Energy level:	❑❑❑
Exercise requirements:	❑❑❑
Playfulness:	❑❑❑
Affection level:	❑❑❑
Friendliness toward dogs:	❑❑❑
Friendliness toward other pets:	❑❑❑
Friendliness toward strangers:	❑
Ease of training:	❑❑
Watchdog ability:	❑❑❑❑
Protection ability:	❑
Grooming requirements:	❑❑❑
Cold tolerance:	❑❑❑
Heat tolerance:	❑❑❑

Weight:	18–24 lb
Height:	8–11″

Illustrated Standard

① Large, round eyes
② Head is covered with soft silky hair
③ Ears set low, hanging
④ Topline is low at withers, arching over the loin
⑤ Tail is long, carried a little above the level of the body, with a curve
⑥ Hindlegs slightly longer than forelegs
⑦ Round feet

❑ **Color:** pepper (all shades of gray and silver) or mustard (all shades of brown and fawn). Dandie Dinmont puppies are much darker than adults.
❑ **DQ:** none

best as an indoor/outdoor dog, and should sleep inside. Its coat needs combing twice weekly, plus regular scissoring and shaping. Shaping for show dogs is done on an almost continual (but light) basis; that for pets can be done by stripping or clipping about four times a year.

Health

• Major concerns: intervertebral disc disease
• Minor concerns: shoulder and elbow luxation
• Occasionally seen: patellar luxation, otitis externa
• Suggested tests: (elbow)
• Life span: 11–13 years

Form and Function

Unlike the prototypical terrier, the Dandie is made up of a series of curves, topped off with a long, scimitar-shaped tail. It is almost twice as long as tall, constructed to go to ground after tough quarry. Its hind legs are definitely longer than its front legs. Its gait is free and easy. It has a distinctive coat made up of about two-thirds hardish (not wiry) hair and one-third soft hair, about 2 inches in length. The head is covered with soft, silky hair, lending to the appearance of a large head. The topknot also enhances the expression, which is determined, dignified, soft, and wise.

Fox Terrier (Smooth)

History

The Smooth Fox Terrier's ancestors are not documented, but the breed was certainly known by 1800 and was already popular before the advent of dog shows. It accompanied Foxhound packs and dislodged foxes that had taken cover. Predominantly white dogs were preferred because they could be more easily distinguished from the quarry in dim lighting. Some speculation exists that the Smooth and Wire Fox Terriers arose from distinct backgrounds, with the Smooth descending from the smooth-coated Black and Tan, the Bull Terrier, and even the Greyhound and Beagle. The Smooth Fox Terriers were among the first breeds to enter the show ring, classified initially with the Sporting breeds. The two varieties were interbred extensively at one time, but the practice gradually declined. Because the two breeds had long since ceased to be crossed by the latter part of the 1900s, the AKC divided them into separate breeds in 1985.

AKC Ranking: 85
Family: Terrier
Area of Origin: England
Date of Origin: 1700s
Original Function: Vermin hunting, fox bolting
Today's Function: Earthdog trials
Other Name: None

Temperament

Energetic, inquisitive, bold, feisty, playful, mischievous, independent, and adventurous describe the Fox Terrier. This breed lives to run, chase, and explore. It is usually fairly reserved with strangers. It tends to bark and dig.

Upkeep

The Smooth Fox Terrier is energetic and cannot be ignored. As an active dog, it will do much to exercise itself given the room. It enjoys a vigorous game or walk, as well as an off-lead outing in a safe area. Even though this breed can live outdoors in a warm climate, it does better living in the house and playing in the yard. Smooth coat care consists of weekly brushing to remove shedding hair. In fact, the Smooths shed more than the Wires. Some training of the ears may be necessary as puppies for proper adult shape to develop.

At a Glance

Energy level:	☐☐☐☐☐
Exercise requirements:	☐☐☐
Playfulness:	☐☐☐☐
Affection level:	☐☐☐☐
Friendliness toward dogs:	☐☐☐
Friendliness toward other pets:	☐☐
Friendliness toward strangers:	☐☐☐☐
Ease of training:	☐☐☐☐
Watchdog ability:	☐☐☐☐☐
Protection ability:	☐
Grooming requirements:	☐
Cold tolerance:	☐☐☐
Heat tolerance:	☐☐☐

Weight:	male: 17–19 lb; female: 15–17 lb
Height:	male: should not exceed 15.5"; female: smaller

Illustrated Standard

① Skull flat and moderately narrow, head 7–7.25" long
② Rather small, deep-set, round eyes
③ Small, V-shaped ears, dropping forward with fold above skull level
④ Tail set high and carried gaily, but not over back or curled; about one fourth docked off
⑤ Feet round and compact

❑ **Color:** white should predominate (brindle, red, or liver markings are objectionable)
❑ **DQ:** ears prick, tulip, or rose; nose white, cherry or considerably spotted with white or cherry; much undershot or overshot

Health

- Major concerns: none
- Minor concerns: lens luxation, distichiasis, cataract, Legg–Perthes, shoulder dislocation
- Occasionally seen: deafness, patellar luxation
- Suggested tests: eye
- Life span: 10–13 years

Form and Function

The Smooth Fox Terrier is square proportioned, standing over a lot of ground but with a short back. Its conformation combines speed, endurance, and power, enabling it to gallop and stay with the horses and hounds during the hunt and to follow a fox up a narrow passage. The gait while trotting gets most of its propulsion from the rear quarters. The expression, like the attitude, is keen; the carriage is alert and expectant. The coat is flat, hard, and dense, also with a short, fine undercoat.

Fox Terrier (Wire)

History

The ultimate show dog, the Wire Fox Terrier has its roots as an effective hunting dog. Its forebears were adept at bolting and perhaps dispatching game, especially fox, that had gone to ground. Some speculation exists that the Smooth and Wire Fox Terriers arose from distinct backgrounds, with the Wire descending from the rough-coated Black and Tan Terrier of Wales. The Wire entered the show ring about 15 to 20 years after the Smooth made its debut. The two varieties were interbred extensively at one time, mainly with the objective of improving the Wire variety by decreasing its size, increasing the amount of white on its coat, and imparting a sleeker outline. This objective was met quite early. Wire Fox Terriers became extremely popular in the years following World War II. In 1985, 100 years after the establishment of the American Fox Terrier Club, the AKC divided the Fox Terrier into two separate breeds. That century had seen many triumphs for the breed both as a show dog and a pet; the split into two varieties seemed a logical step because they were no longer interbred.

AKC Ranking: 61
Family: Terrier
Area of Origin: England
Date of Origin: 1800s
Original Function: Vermin hunting, fox bolting
Today's Function: Earthdog trials
Other Name: None

Temperament

A true "live-wire," the Wire Fox Terrier is always up for adventure. This breed lives to play, explore, run, hunt, and chase. It can be mischievous and independent and may dig and bark. It is usually fairly reserved with strangers. The Wire has a reputation for being somewhat scrappier with other dogs when compared to the Smooth.

Upkeep

The Fox Terrier must have daily exercise. It will do much to exercise itself given the room, but it profits from a good walk on leash, a vigorous play session, or an off-lead outing in a safe area. This breed can live outdoors in a temperate to warm climate, but it does better as an indoor dog with access to a secure yard. The Wire's coat needs combing two or three times weekly, plus shaping every three months. Shaping for pets is by clipping, and for show dogs, by stripping. Some training of the ears may be necessary as puppies for proper adult shape to develop.

At a Glance

Energy level:	☐☐☐☐
Exercise requirements:	☐☐☐
Playfulness:	☐☐☐☐
Affection level:	☐☐☐☐
Friendliness toward dogs:	☐
Friendliness toward other pets:	☐☐
Friendliness toward strangers:	☐☐☐☐
Ease of training:	☐☐☐☐
Watchdog ability:	☐☐☐☐☐
Protection ability:	☐
Grooming requirements:	☐☐☐☐
Cold tolerance:	☐☐☐
Heat tolerance:	☐☐☐

Weight:	male: 17–19 lb; female: 15–17 lb
Height:	male: should not exceed 15.5"; female: smaller

Health

- Major concerns: none
- Minor concerns: lens luxation, distichiasis, cataract, Legg–Perthes, shoulder dislocation
- Occasionally seen: deafness, patellar luxation
- Suggested tests: eye
- Life span: 10–13 years

Form and Function

The Wire Fox Terrier is short backed and square proportioned, but at the same time standing over a lot of ground. Its conformation combines speed, endurance, and power, enabling it to gallop and stay with the horses and hounds during the hunt and to follow a fox up a narrow passage. The gait while trotting gets most of its propulsion from the rear quarters. The expression, like the attitude, is keen; the carriage is alert and expectant. The coat is dense, wiry, broken, and twisted, almost appearing like coconut matting, with a short, fine undercoat. The outer coat may be crinkled, but it should not be curly.

Illustrated Standard

1. Rather small, deep-set, and round eyes
2. Skull flat and moderately narrow, head 7–7.25" long
3. Small, V-shaped ears, dropping forward with fold above skull level
4. Tail set high and carried gaily, but not over back or curled; about one fourth docked off
5. Feet round and compact

❏ **Color:** white should predominate (brindle, red, or liver markings are objectionable)
❏ **DQ:** ears prick, tulip, or rose; nose white, cherry or considerably spotted with white or cherry; much undershot or overshot

Irish Terrier

History

The quintessential long-legged terrier, the Irish Terrier is also one of the oldest terrier breeds. Its creation is not documented, but it may have descended from the old Black and Tan Terrier and a larger but racier solid wheaten-colored terrier, both of which were found in Ireland and used for hunting fox, otter, and vermin. Its similarity to the Irish Wolfhound has led to conjecture that it may have descended at least in part from that breed. The Irish Terrier is the raciest member of the Terrier Group, with a longer body and longer legs than the other terriers. Early Irish Terriers came in a variety of colors, including black and tan, gray, and brindle; only near the end of the nineteenth century did the solid red color become a fixture of the breed. The first Irish Terrier was shown in 1875. By the 1880s, the breed was the fourth most popular in England. At that time, it was fashionable to crop the ears of many terriers, but in 1889 the Irish Terrier Club of England banned ear cropping in the breed. The ruling was to have

AKC Ranking: 111
Family: Terrier
Area of Origin: Ireland
Date of Origin: 1700s
Original Function: Hunting fox, otter, and other vermin
Today's Function: Vermin hunting
Other Name: Irish Red Terrier

far-reaching implications for all dogs because it instigated the debate about ear cropping and eventually led to the abolition of cropped ears in all breeds shown in England. The breed also became quite popular in America, ranking thirteenth of all breeds in the late 1920s. It was a dominant force in the show rings of the day. In World War I, the breed proved its mettle by serving as a messenger and sentinel. With such an auspicious beginning, the Irish Terrier seemed certain to remain one of the most popular terriers, but it didn't. Today the Irish is one of the rarer terriers, an uncommon sight in either the show ring or home.

Temperament

Called the daredevil of dogdom, the Irish Terrier is brash, bold, assertive, playful, inquisitive, independent, strong-willed, and ever ready for action and adventure. It is usually aggressive toward other dogs and small animals and tends to be reserved with strangers. It likes to chase and run and hunt and explore; it needs daily physical and mental exercise in a safe area. Given sufficient exercise, it is surprisingly well-mannered and dignified indoors. It is a loyal and entertaining companion.

Upkeep

This is a dog with an active mind and body. It needs daily entertainment and exercise. It makes a good walking and jogging companion, as well as hiking or hunting partner. Its needs can also be met with a rigorous play session. Its wire coat needs combing one or two times weekly, plus scissoring and shaping (clipping for pets and stripping for show dogs) two to four times yearly. Some training of the ears is necessary to ensure proper adult shape.

Health

- Major concerns: none
- Minor concerns: urolithiasis
- Occasionally seen: none
- Suggested tests: none
- Life span: 12–15 years

Illustrated Standard

1. Head long and fairly narrow
2. Eyes small, with intense expression
3. Small, V-shaped ears, dropping forward with fold above skull level
4. Body moderately long
5. Tail set high but not curled; about one fourth docked off
6. Feet rounded

❑ **Color:** red, golden red, red wheaten, or wheaten
❑ **DQ:** none

Form and Function

The Irish Terrier has a graceful, racy outline, with a moderately long body. It should not have the short back characteristic of so many of the long legged terriers. It is sturdy and strong in substance, but it is also active and lithe in move-ment. This is an all-round terrier that must combine speed, endurance, agility, and power to perform a great variety of jobs. Its broken coat is dense and wiry, never so long as to obscure the body shape. Its expression, like its nature, is intense.

At a Glance

Energy level:	❑❑❑
Exercise requirements:	❑❑❑
Playfulness:	❑❑❑❑❑
Affection level:	❑❑
Friendliness toward dogs:	❑
Friendliness toward other pets:	❑
Friendliness toward strangers:	❑❑
Ease of training:	❑
Watchdog ability:	❑❑❑❑❑
Protection ability:	❑❑❑❑
Grooming requirements:	❑❑❑❑
Cold tolerance:	❑❑❑
Heat tolerance:	❑❑❑

Weight: male: ideally 27 lb; female: ideally 25 lb
Height: about 18"

Jack Russell Terrier

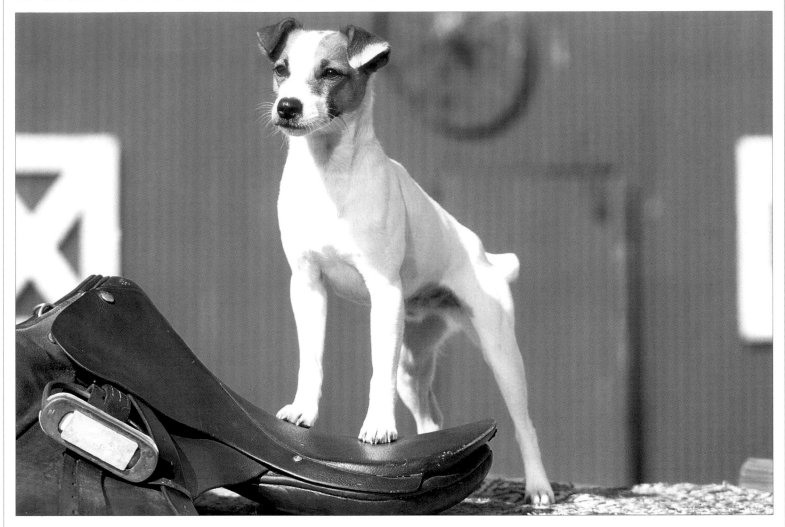

History

Jack Russell Terriers descend in most part from a dog named Trump, which was obtained by the Parson John Russell of Devonshire, England, in the mid 1800s. John Russell was a fox-hunting enthusiast, and he sought to develop a line of terriers that could keep up with the horses and bolt and dispatch fox. His line was so successful that it eventually carried his name: Jack Russell Terrier. Although John Russell eventually became extremely active in the English Kennel Club, for some reason he declined to show his own breed in conformation shows. Jack Russell Terrier aficionados followed his example, proving their dogs' mettle in the field rather than the show ring. This tradition holds true even today, although some JRTs have now entered the show ring. After heated debates in which most JRT fanciers objected to AKC recognition, the breed was nonetheless admitted into the Miscellaneous class in 1998. In England, it was admitted into conformation classes as the Parson Jack Russell Terrier in 1991. Jack Russells have long been popular with horse owners and are frequently seen around stables, but the type of terrier

AKC Ranking: 115
Family: Terrier
Area of Origin: England
Date of Origin: 1800s
Original Function: Fox bolting
Today's Function: Earthdog trials
Other Name: Parson Jack Russell
  Terrier

more often seen there has short legs and a long body. The term Parson was added to distinguish the traditional long-legged JRT. In the 1990s, the JRT became a popular media dog, and its exposure caused great interest in the breed from pet owners. As a result, its numbers are growing at an alarming rate. As irresistibly cute as this irascible scamp may be, it is definitely not a breed for everyone.

Temperament

This is a dog that thrives on action and adventure. In the process, it often finds itself in the middle of trouble. It is a true hunter at heart and will explore, wander, chase, and dig when it gets a chance. It is very playful and intelligent. It gets along well with children and strangers. It can be scrappy with strange dogs, but is better than many terriers. It does well with horses, but it may chase cats and is not good with rodents. It may tend to bark and dig. It makes an ideal companion for an active person with a good sense of humor who wants a lot of entertainment—and mischief—in one dog.

At a Glance

Energy level:	▢▢▢▢▢
Exercise requirements:	▢▢▢▢
Playfulness:	▢▢▢▢▢
Affection level:	▢▢▢
Friendliness toward dogs:	▢▢
Friendliness toward other pets:	▢
Friendliness toward strangers:	▢▢▢
Ease of training:	▢▢▢
Watchdog ability:	▢▢▢▢▢
Protection ability:	▢▢
Grooming requirements: smooth:	▢
broken:	▢▢▢
Cold tolerance:	▢▢▢
Heat tolerance:	▢▢▢

Weight:	13–17 lb
Height:	12–14"

Upkeep

The Jack Russell needs a lot of mental and physical stimulation every day. It is not a dog that can sit around inside. It needs a long walk or strenuous game every day, plus a short training session. It enjoys the chance to explore on its own, but it must do so only in a safe area because it tends to go off in search of trouble, and some go down holes and must be dug out! It can live outdoors in temperate climates. It does best when allowed access to a house and yard, and it is not a good apartment dog. Coat care for the smooth type consists only of weekly brushing to remove dead hair; for the broken coat it also consists of occasional hand stripping.

Health

• Major concerns: none
• Minor concerns: lens luxation, patellar luxation
• Occasionally seen: glaucoma, ataxia, Legg–Calvés, deafness
• Suggested tests: eye, knee
• Life span: 13–15 years

Illustrated Standard

① Almond-shaped eyes
② Skull flat
③ Button ears; small V-shaped drop ear carried forward with the tip pointing toward the eye
④ Topline straight, with loin slightly arched
⑤ Tail set high and carried gaily; docked so tip is about level with skull
⑥ Cat feet

❑ **Color:** predominantly white with tan, black, or brown markings
❑ **DQ:** under 12" or over 15" tall; prick ears; liver nose; four or more missing teeth; overshot, undershot, or wry mouth; brindle markings; overt aggression toward dogs or humans

Form and Function

The JRT is slightly taller than it is long, of medium bone. Its long legs enable it to keep up with the horses and hounds during a long fox hunt. Its slender build allows it to fit into small passageways in pursuit of its quarry. Spanning is a critical part of judging the JRT. The chest behind the elbows must be easily spanned by average-size hands, such that the thumbs should meet at the spine and the fingers under the chest. Its gait is free and lively, with good reach and drive. Its coat can be either smooth or broken, both coarse and weatherproof with short, dense undercoat. The outer coat of the smooth is flat and hard; that of the broken is harsh, straight, tight, and close lying, with no sculpted furnishings. The JRT's expression is keen and full of life.

Kerry Blue Terrier

History

The Kerry Blue originated in the south and west of Ireland, first gaining notice in the Ring of Kerry. Here the dog had been known for at least a century as a versatile hunter of vermin, small game, and even birds, as well as a land and water retriever and even a sheep and cattle herder. How such a talented and attractive dog should have remained unknown outside of Ireland for so long is a mystery, but it only came on the English and American show scenes around the 1920s. It received AKC recognition in 1924. Early specimens were somewhat disheveled, but as more grooming became accepted, the breed caught on and became a popular show dog. Once groomed, the Kerry Blue is one of the most striking of all dogs. It has the peculiarity of being born black, the blue coloration not appearing until between 9 months and 2 years of age. It remains a versatile dog, adding police work and trailing to its list of talents. Despite this, it enjoys only modest popularity as a pet.

AKC Ranking: 105
Family: Terrier
Area of Origin: Ireland
Date of Origin: 1700s
Original Function: Ratting, badger and
  fox hunting
Today's Function: Ratting
Other Name: Irish Blue Terrier

Temperament

A versatile terrier, the Kerry Blue's personality is many faceted. It can guard, hunt, herd, or just be a fun-loving companion. It needs daily mental and physical activity in a safe area. It loves to run, chase, hunt, explore, play, and dig. Indoors, it is well mannered. It can be protective toward strangers yet greet verified friends with great enthusiasm. It is apt to be aggressive toward other dogs and small animals. It is clever and independent, often stubborn. Some tend to bark.

Upkeep

The Kerry Blue needs a good amount of exercise, but its needs can be met with either a long walk on leash, a vigorous play session, or a chance to explore off-leash in a safe area. It can live outdoors in temperate climates, but it does better with access to the house. Its coat needs combing about twice a week, plus scissoring and coat shaping every month. Its ears need to be taped when developing to ensure proper shape.

Health

- Major concerns: PNA, cerebellar abiotrophy
- Minor concerns: cataract, spiculosis, hair follicle tumors, entropion, KCS, narrow palpebral fissure distichiasis, CHD
- Occasionally seen: retinal folds
- Suggested tests: eye, (hip)
- Life span: 12–15 years

Form and Function

This versatile breed has the build of a dog able to perform a variety of tasks, all requiring athletic ability. It can run, herd, trail, retrieve, swim, and dispatch vermin—the ideal all around farm companion. In keeping with this, it is not exaggerated in build. It is an upstanding, long-legged terrier with a short back, displaying strong bones and muscle. Its coat is soft, dense, and wavy, and of a distinctive blue-gray color.

Illustrated Standard

1. Head long
2. Eyes small, keen expression
3. Small, V-shaped ears, dropping forward with fold above skull level
4. Back short and straight
5. Tail set high, carried gaily erect and straight
6. Feet fairly round and moderately small

❏ **Color:** any shade of blue-gray in mature (over 18 months) dog; immature dogs may be very dark blue or have tinges of brown
❏ **DQ:** solid black, dewclaws on hind legs

At a Glance

Energy level:	☐☐☐
Exercise requirements:	☐☐☐
Playfulness:	☐☐☐☐
Affection level:	☐☐☐
Friendliness toward dogs:	☐
Friendliness toward other pets:	☐
Friendliness toward strangers:	☐
Ease of training:	☐
Watchdog ability:	☐☐☐☐☐
Protection ability:	☐☐☐
Grooming requirements:	☐☐☐☐☐
Cold tolerance:	☐☐☐
Heat tolerance:	☐☐☐

Weight:	male: 33–40 lb; female: less
Height:	male: 18–19.5"; female: 17.5–19" (optimal)

Lakeland Terrier

History

The first Lakeland Terriers were kept by farmers who took them along with small packs of hounds in order to kill the foxes that were a problem in the area. The dogs were extremely game and were also used on otter and vermin with great success. Although its background is not documented, it shares common ancestors with the Border Terrier, Bedlington Terrier, and Fox Terrier. As fox hunting became valued more for its sporting aspect, the terriers became more fashionable as a part of the fox hunt. Those dogs from the English Lake region gained a reputation as particularly game dogs, although at that time they were identified as Patterdale, Fell, and Elterwater Terriers, all of which came from the Lakeland region. Only in 1921 were they recognized as Lakeland Terriers, although Cumberland is considered the exact birthplace of the breed. The breed was accepted for AKC registration in 1934. Since then, the Lakeland Terrier has been a prominent contender in the show ring, combining dapper good looks with unsurpassed showmanship. Its popularity as a pet, however, has remained moderate.

AKC Ranking: 125
Family: Terrier
Area of Origin: England
Date of Origin: 1700s
Original Function: Vermin hunting
Today's Function: Earthdog trials
Other Name: None

Temperament

The spunky Lakeland makes the most of every day, always busy investigating, playing, and, if it really gets its wish, hunting, running, and chasing. Given daily exercise in a safe area, it settles down in the home and makes an entertaining and endearing house pet. It is reserved with strangers and usually aggressive toward other dogs and small animals. Clever, independent, and stubborn, it can be mischievous. It is nonetheless sensitive and must be trained with patience as well as a sense of humor.

Upkeep

This is an active breed that needs daily entertainment or it will make it for itself. A moderate walk on leash or a hardy game in the yard can usually satisfy its needs, but it also enjoys the chance to explore off-leash in a safe area. It enjoys spending the day in a secure yard, but it should optimally sleep in the house. Its wire coat needs combing one or two times weekly, plus scissoring and shaping (clipping for pets and stripping for show dogs) four times yearly.

At a Glance

Energy level:	☐☐☐☐
Exercise requirements:	☐☐☐
Playfulness:	☐☐☐☐☐
Affection level:	☐☐☐
Friendliness toward dogs:	☐
Friendliness toward other pets:	☐
Friendliness toward strangers:	☐
Ease of training:	☐
Watchdog ability:	☐☐☐☐☐
Protection ability:	☐
Grooming requirements:	☐☐☐
Cold tolerance:	☐☐☐
Heat tolerance:	☐☐☐

Weight:	male: about 17 lb
Height:	male: 14.5"; female: 13.5"

Health
- Major concerns: none
- Minor concerns: lens luxation, distichiasis
- Occasionally seen: Legg–Perthes, vWD
- Suggested tests: eye
- Life span: 12–16 years

Form and Function
The Lakeland Terrier is a rather small dog of short-backed, square proportion with a sturdy, workmanlike build. Its legs are fairly long, enabling it to run at good speed and traverse the rugged shale terrain of its native mountain countryside. Its gait is smooth and ground covering, with good reach and drive. Its body is deep and narrow, allowing it to squeeze through small passages after its quarry. Its expression reflects its mood, ranging from intense to gay or impish. Its double coat consists of a soft undercoat and a hard, wiry outer coat.

Manchester Terrier

History

One of the most popular and accomplished terriers of early England was the Black and Tan Terrier, mentioned as early as the sixteenth century. The Black and Tan was a skilled dispatcher of rats, either along the watercourses or in the pits. With the advent of industrialization, sport of the working class in England's towns centered around rat killing with Black and Tans and dog racing with Whippets. It was only a matter of time before the two breeds were crossed, and this was done by John Hulme of Manchester, with the goal of creating a dog that could excel in both arenas. The result was a refined black and tan terrier with a slightly arched back. Similar crosses had almost certainly been made in other regions because other dogs resembling this new strain were not uncommon, but the breed's popularity centered around Manchester. In 1860, the breed was formally dubbed the Manchester Terrier. The name did not catch on, however, and it

AKC Ranking: 96
Family: Terrier
Area of Origin: England
Date of Origin: 1500s
Original Function: Ratting, rabbit
  hunting
Today's Function: Earthdog trials
Other Name: Black and Tan Terrier

was dropped in favor of Black and Tan Terrier, only to be revived in 1923. The breed has always had a large size range, and until 1959 Standard and Toy Manchesters were shown as two separate breeds, although interbreeding was allowed. In 1959, they were reclassified as one breed with two varieties, legitimizing the practice of interbreeding. Besides size, the only difference in the two varieties is in whether cropping is allowed (it is allowed in the Standard variety only).

Temperament

The Manchester Terrier has been described as "catlike," being impeccably clean, independent, reserved with strangers, yet sensitive. It is more responsive than many terriers and is generally a well-mannered housedog. It is devoted to its family, and enjoys napping at its special person's side. Otherwise, it is busy, ever nosing around for adventure or a game. Some tend to dig.

Upkeep

This alert and active breed can have its exercise needs met with a moderate walk on leash, good romp in the yard, or off-lead foray in a safe area. This is not a breed that should live outdoors, although it appreciates access to a yard during the day. It likes a warm, soft bed. Coat care is minimal.

Health

- Major concerns: lens luxation
- Minor concerns: none
- Occasionally seen: epilepsy, skin fragility
- Suggested tests: eye
- Life span: 15–16 years

Form and Function

The Manchester Terrier is perhaps the sleekest and raciest of all terriers, with a smooth, compact, muscular body, slightly longer than tall, and a slightly arched topline. The combination of power and agility enables the breed to course and kill small game and vermin. Its gait is free and effortless, not hackney. Its expression is keen and alert, and its coat is smooth and glossy.

Illustrated Standard

1. Head resembles a blunted wedge in profile and from front
2. Small, almond-shaped eyes
3. Naturally erect, button, or cropped ear
4. Slight arch over loin
5. Tapered tail carried in a slight upward curve
6. Tucked up abdomen

❏ **Color:** black and tan, with a black "thumbprint" patch on the front of each foreleg and "pencil marks" on the top of each toe

❏ **DQ:** patch of white over 1/2 inch at its longest dimension, any color other than black and tan, weight over 22 lb, (in Toy variety only: cropped or cut ears)

At a Glance

Energy level:	❑❑❑❑
Exercise requirements:	❑❑❑
Playfulness:	❑❑❑❑
Affection level:	❑❑❑
Friendliness toward dogs:	❑❑❑
Friendliness toward other pets:	❑
Friendliness toward strangers:	❑
Ease of training:	❑❑
Watchdog ability:	❑❑❑❑❑
Protection ability:	❑
Grooming requirements:	❑
Cold tolerance:	❑
Heat tolerance:	❑❑❑❑

Weight:	Standard: over 12 lb to 22 lb (Toy: under 12 lb)
Height:	15–16"*

Miniature Bull Terrier

History

The Miniature Bull Terrier comes directly from the Bull Terrier and so shares the breed's early history. In the early days of the Bull Terrier, the standards allowed for a great range of weights, reflecting the great range in size of the Bull Terrier's ancestors: the Bulldog, White English Terrier, and Black and Tan Terrier. Smaller Bull Terriers have long been a part of the breed, with specimens weighing as little as 4 pounds being recorded early on. These smallest white Bull Terriers were at one time called Coverwood Terriers after the kennel that produced them. These tiny toys tended to have poor type and interest waned in them. Better type was found in slightly larger specimens, the miniatures rather than toys. By 1939, the Miniature Bull Terrier was recognized by the English Kennel Club, yet this recognition as a separate breed proved to be a problem. As a separate breed, the Miniature could no longer be interbred with standard-sized Bull Terriers, and there were so few Miniatures that considerable inbreeding resulted. The breed never gained popular attention and grew only slowly. In 1991 it was rec-

AKC Ranking: 131
Family: Terrier, Mastiff (Bull)
Area of Origin: England
Date of Origin: 1800s
Original Function: Ratting, dog fighting
Today's Function: Earthdog trials
Other Name: None

ognized by the AKC. Still an uncommon breed, it is bound to increase in popularity as a true miniature version of the popular Bull Terrier.

Temperament

Very much like the larger Bull Terrier, the Mini is comical, lively, playful, and mischievous. Despite its smaller size, it is not a lap dog. It is every bit as tough as the larger version and apt to want to prove itself even more. It is a sweet clown, devoted but not fawning. It is stubborn and independent and needs to be trained with a firm yet gentle hand—and a good sense of humor. It likes to play and investigate. It likes to dig, and it needs ample exercise.

Upkeep

The Mini's exercise needs are daily, but not excessive. It needs either a moderate walk or a romp in a safe area. It is not a breed that should live outdoors, but it does do well with access to a yard. It can, however, do well as an apartment or city dog. Coat care is minimal.

At a Glance

Energy level:	☐☐☐☐
Exercise requirements:	☐☐☐
Playfulness:	☐☐☐☐☐
Affection level:	☐☐
Friendliness toward dogs:	☐☐
Friendliness toward other pets:	☐☐☐
Friendliness toward strangers:	☐☐☐
Ease of training:	☐
Watchdog ability:	☐☐☐☐☐
Protection ability:	☐☐☐
Grooming requirements:	☐
Cold tolerance:	☐☐☐
Heat tolerance:	☐☐☐

Weight:	25–33 lb*
Height:	10–14"

Illustrated Standard

① Long, strong, deep head, curving from skull to nose; oval outline viewed face on
② Eyes small, triangular, deep set, and placed close together
③ Ears small, erect, close set
④ Short strong back, slight arch over loin
⑤ Tail short, carried horizontally
⑥ Cat feet

❏ **Color:** for white: pure white; for colored: any color to predominate
❏ **DQ:** none

Health

- Major concerns: deafness (whites)
- Minor concerns: none
- Occasionally seen: patellar luxation, lens luxation
- Suggested tests: hearing (whites), (eye), (knee)
- Life span: 11–14 years

Form and Function

This is a strongly built, square-proportioned dog, big boned but not coarse. It should reflect those attributes that made the standard-sized Bull Terrier a formidable foe in the fighting ring with its sturdy bone and muscle and strong jaws. Its gait is free and easy. Its skin is tight and its coat is short, flat, and harsh. It wears a keen and determined expression on its characteristic clown face.

Miniature Schnauzer

History

The smallest and most popular of the Schnauzers, the Miniature Schnauzer was developed in the late 1800s as a small farm dog and ratter in Germany. In fact, the Miniature Schnauzer is the only terrier not originating from European Isle stock. It was derived from crossing the Standard Schnauzer with the Affenpinscher (and possibly Poodle). All the Schnauzers get their name from one individual dog named Schnauzer who was exhibited around 1879—an apt name, since Schnauzer means small beard. The Miniature Schnauzer was exhibited as a breed distinct from the Standard Schnauzer by 1899 in Germany, although it wasn't until 1933 that the AKC divided the Standard and Miniature into separate breeds. The Miniature is the only Schnauzer to remain in the Terrier Group in America. In England it joins the other Schnauzers in the Utility Group. The Miniature Schnauzer came to America long after its Standard and Giant counterparts, but in the years after World War II, it far outpaced them in popularity, eventually rising to become the third most

AKC Ranking: 14
Family: Terrier
Area of Origin: Germany
Date of Origin: 1800s
Original Function: Ratting
Today's Function: Earthdog trials
Other Name: Zwergschnauzer

popular breed in America at one time. It remains as a perennial favorite, a smart looking and acting alert family pet and competitive show dog.

Temperament

The Miniature Schnauzer deserves its place as one of the most popular terrier pets. It is playful, inquisitive, alert, spunky, and companionable. It is a well-mannered housedog that also enjoys being in the middle of activities. It is less domineering than the larger Schnauzers and less dog-aggressive than most terriers. It is also better with other animals than most terriers, although it will gladly give chase. It is clever and can be stubborn, but it is generally biddable. It enjoys children. Some may bark a lot.

Upkeep

This energetic breed can have its exercise requirements met with a moderate walk on leash or a good game in the yard. Even though it can physically survive living outdoors in warm to temperate climates, it emotionally needs to share its life with its family inside the home. Its wire coat needs combing once or twice weekly, plus scissoring and shaping (clipping for pets and stripping for show dogs) every couple of months.

Health

- Major concerns: urolithiasis, PRA
- Minor concerns: follicular dermatitis, esophageal achalasia, vWD
- Occasionally seen: pulmonic stenosis, Legg–Perthes, cataract
- Suggested tests: eye, DNA test for vWD, (cardiac)
- Life span: 12–14 years

Form and Function

The Miniature Schnauzer is a robust, sturdily built terrier of nearly square proportion. It was developed as a ratter and is quick and tough. Its gait displays good reach and drive. Its coat is double, with a close undercoat, and hard, wiry, outer coat which is longer on the legs, muzzle, and eyebrows. Its facial furnishings add to its keen expression.

Illustrated Standard

① Head strong, rectangular, and long
② Eyes small, oval, and deep set
③ Ears set high; carried erect and pointed if cropped; if uncropped, small and V-shaped, folding close to the skull
④ Topline straight, slopes slightly down
⑤ Tail set high and carried erect, docked just long enough to be visible over backline
⑥ Cat feet

❏ **Color:** salt and pepper, black and silver, or black
❏ **DQ:** under 12" or over 14", white except for small white spot permitted on chest of black dogs (white not to be confused with silver white under throat and chest)

At a Glance

Energy level:	❏❏❏
Exercise requirements:	❏❏❏
Playfulness:	❏❏❏❏
Affection level:	❏❏❏❏
Friendliness toward dogs:	❏❏❏
Friendliness toward other pets:	❏❏❏
Friendliness toward strangers:	❏❏❏
Ease of training:	❏❏❏
Watchdog ability:	❏❏❏❏❏
Protection ability:	❏
Grooming requirements:	❏❏❏
Cold tolerance:	❏❏❏
Heat tolerance:	❏❏❏

Weight:	13–15 lb*
Height:	12–14"

Norfolk Terrier

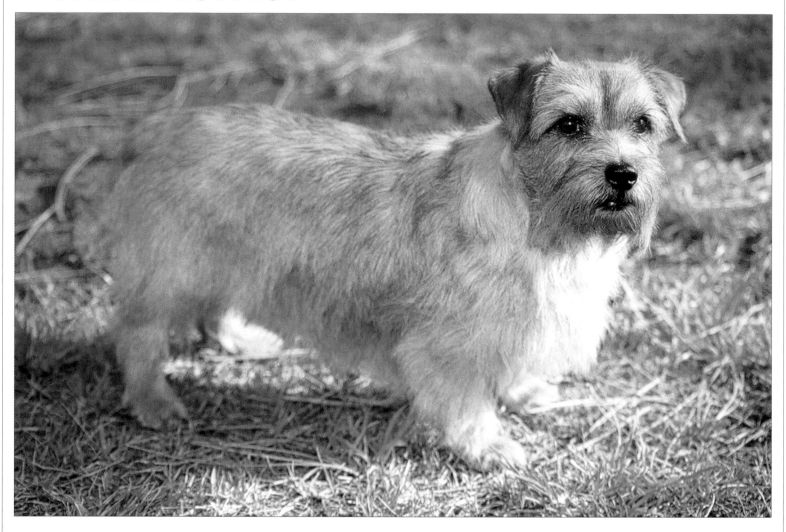

History

The Norfolk Terrier shares an identical early history with the Norwich Terrier. During the development of these breeds, both prick and drop ears were seen, and neither could lay claim to being more authentic or original than the other.

In the 1930s, soon after their entry into the show rings, breeders found that crossing the two types of ear carriage resulted in uncertain ear carriage in the offspring, so they began avoiding crossing the two ear types. The prick-eared type were more numerous; in fact, the drop-eared type almost vanished during World War II. The drop-eared strain owes its existence to the single-handed and determined efforts of Miss Macfie of the Colansays. In the 1940s, breeders came to her to renew breeding the drop-eared type of Norwich, and they soon caught up with the prick-eared type in popularity, although not in show awards.

Eventually, amid some controversy, the breed was officially changed from one breed with two varieties to two separate breeds.

AKC Ranking: 113
Family: Terrier
Area of Origin: England
Date of Origin: 1800s
Original Function: Ratting, fox bolting
Today's Function: Earthdog trials
Other Name: None

This happened in 1964 in England and in 1979 in the United States.

Temperament

Feisty, bold, inquisitive, game, scrappy, stubborn, and independent, the Norfolk is all terrier. It has been called a "demon" in the field, and it loves to hunt, dig, and investigate. It must be exercised in a safe area. It is clever and amiable but strong willed.

Upkeep

The Norfolk Terrier needs an exercise outing every day, either a short to moderate walk or a lively and boisterous play session. It especially likes to hunt and investigate, but it must do so in a safe area. Even though it could live outside in temperate to warm climates, it is such a family-oriented dog that it is emotionally unsuited for outdoor living. It does best as a housedog with access to a yard. Its wire coat needs combing once or twice weekly, plus stripping of dead hairs three to four times yearly.

At a Glance

Energy level:	▢▢▢□
Exercise requirements:	▢▢□
Playfulness:	▢▢□
Affection level:	▢
Friendliness toward dogs:	▢▢□
Friendliness toward other pets:	▢▢□
Friendliness toward strangers:	▢▢□
Ease of training:	▢□
Watchdog ability:	▢▢▢▢□
Protection ability:	▢
Grooming requirements:	▢▢□
Cold tolerance:	▢▢□
Heat tolerance:	▢▢□

Weight:	11–12 lb
Height:	9–10"

Health
- Major concerns: none
- Minor concerns: none
- Occasionally seen: cardiomyopathy, patellar luxation
- Suggested tests: (cardiac), (knee)
- Life span: 13–15 years

Form and Function
Unlike the Norwich Terrier, the Norfolk is slightly longer than it is tall. Like the Norwich, it is a formidable adversary to vermin and fox and can bolt and dispatch its quarry working along or with a pack. It is small, short-legged, and compact, with good bone and substance. Its gait is low and driving. Its double coat is weather resistant, with the outer coat consisting of hard, wiry, straight hair about 1.5 to 2 inches long, with a longer ruff. It wears a keen, intelligent expression.

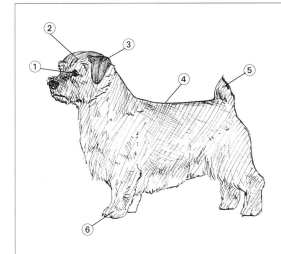

Illustrated Standard
1. Small, oval eyes
2. Skull wide, slightly rounded
3. V-shaped ears, tips slightly rounded, dropped with a break at skull level
4. Topline level
5. Tail medium docked, set on high
6. Feet round

❏ **Color:** all shades of red, wheaten, black and tan, or grizzle
❏ **DQ:** none

Norwich Terrier

History

Short-legged ratting terriers have long been valued in England, but only in the 1880s did the breed that would eventually become both the Norwich and Norfolk Terriers emerge from obscurity. At that time, owning one of these small ratters became a fad among Cambridge University students. The little terriers became known as CanTab, and later Trumpington, Terriers. Around 1900, a Trumpington Terrier named Rags came to a stable near Norwich and gained notoriety as a ratter as well as sire. He sired countless offspring and is the patriarch of the modern Norwich. One of his sons came to America and proved to be an amiable ambassador for the breed. To this day, many people still refer to the Norwich as the "Jones" Terrier, after this dog's owner. The "Jones" Terrier was incorporated into various fox-hound hunt packs. The AKC recognized the breed in 1936.

AKC Ranking: 109
Family: Terrier
Area of Origin: England
Date of Origin: 1800s
Original Function: Ratting, fox bolting
Today's Function: Earthdog trials
Other Name: None

At that time the breed had both prick and drop ears, but in 1979 the dropped-eared variety was recognized as a separate breed, the Norfolk Terrier. Although lacking the flash of its long-legged competitors in the Terrier group, the Norwich has proven itself as formidable a competitor in the show ring as it ever was in the field. Despite its show ring success, however, it enjoys only moderate popularity as a pet.

Temperament

The Norwich Terrier, like the Norfolk, is a true terrier at heart, always ready for adventure and excitement. It is a hunter and may chase small animals. It is a pert, independent, amusing—but sometimes challenging—companion, best suited for people with a sense of adventure and humor.

Upkeep

The Norwich needs to stretch its legs with a good walk or short run every day. It especially likes combining a run with a chance to explore, but any such off-leash expeditions must be done only in a safe area. It is better suited as a housedog with yard access, but it can stay outdoors during the day if need be in temperate to warm climates. Its wiry coat needs combing one to two times weekly, plus stripping of dead hairs three to four times a year.

Health

• Major concerns: none
• Minor concerns: none
• Occasionally seen: cardiomyopathy, patellar luxation
• Suggested tests: (cardiac), (knee)
• Life span: 13–15 years

Form and Function

This spirited dog, one of the smallest of the working terriers, is sturdy and stocky, of square proportion. Its small size is an asset when following vermin or fox down tight passageways. Its teeth are large, to aid in dispatching its quarry. It shows

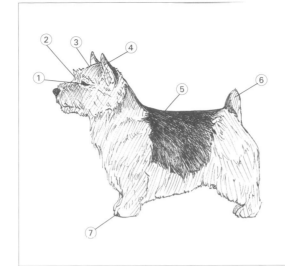

Illustrated Standard

① Small, oval eyes
② Well-defined stop
③ Skull broad and slightly rounded
④ Medium-sized ears, erect with pointed tips
⑤ Topline level
⑥ Tail medium docked, carried erect
⑦ Feet round

❏ **Color:** all shades of red, wheaten, black and tan, or grizzle
❏ **DQ:** none

great power in its movement. The tail should be long enough to grasp firmly, so that the dog can be pulled from a hole. The double coat has a hard, wiry, and straight outer coat that lies close to the body and is thicker around the mane for protection. The dog bears a slightly foxy expression.

At a Glance

Energy level:	❏❏❏❏
Exercise requirements:	❏❏❏
Playfulness:	❏❏❏
Affection level:	❏❏❏❏
Friendliness toward dogs:	❏❏❏
Friendliness toward other pets:	❏❏❏
Friendliness toward strangers:	❏❏❏
Ease of training:	❏❏❏
Watchdog ability:	❏❏❏❏❏
Protection ability:	❏
Grooming requirements:	❏❏❏
Cold tolerance:	❏❏❏
Heat tolerance:	❏❏❏

Weight:	approx. 12 lb
Height:	ideally 10"

Scottish Terrier

History

Great confusion exists about the background of the Scottish Terrier, stemming from the early custom of calling all terriers from Scotland Scottish or Scotch Terriers. To further confuse matters, the present Scottish Terrier was once grouped with Skye Terriers, in reference not to the modern Skye Terrier but of a large group of terriers from the Isle of Skye. Whatever the origin, the early Scottish Terriers were definitely a hardy lot of Highlanders, used for going to ground in pursuit of their prey. Only in the late 1800s can the Scottish Terrier's history be confidently documented. Of the several short-legged harsh-coated terriers, the dog now known as the Scottish Terrier was most favored in the Aberdeen area, and so for a time it was called the Aberdeen Terrier. By the 1870s, the situation had become so confusing that a series of protests were made, ultimately leading to a detailed description of how the true Scottish Terrier should appear. Around 1880, the first breed standard was put forth. The first Scotty came to America in 1883. It gradually gained popularity until World War II, after which its popularity soared. The most well-known Scotty in America was Fala,

AKC Ranking:	43
Family:	Terrier
Area of Origin:	Scotland
Date of Origin:	1800s
Original Function:	Vermin hunting
Today's Function:	Earthdog trials
Other Name:	Aberdeen Terrier

Franklin Roosevelt's dog, who was his constant companion in life and buried at his side in death. The Scottish Terrier remains a fixture of the Terrier Group, always a contender in the show ring and a favorite in the home.

Temperament

Nicknamed The Diehard in reference to its rugged character, the Scottish Terrier is a tough, determined character, ready for action. It is fearless and feisty and may be aggressive toward other dogs and animals. It is reserved, but friendly, with strangers, and devoted to its family. Although independent and stubborn, it is sensitive. It tends to dig and bark.

Upkeep

This is a dog on the lookout for adventure, and it needs some excitement and exercise in its life every day. This can take the form of a moderate walk on leash, a boisterous game, or an off-leash exploration in a safe area. Although it could live outdoors in a temperate to warm climate, it is far better suited as a housedog with access to a yard. Its wire coat needs combing two to three

At a Glance

Energy level:	☐☐☐
Exercise requirements:	☐☐☐
Playfulness:	☐☐☐
Affection level:	☐☐☐
Friendliness toward dogs:	☐☐☐
Friendliness toward other pets:	☐☐☐
Friendliness toward strangers:	☐☐☐
Ease of training:	☐
Watchdog ability:	☐☐☐☐☐
Protection ability:	☐☐
Grooming requirements:	☐☐☐
Cold tolerance:	☐☐☐
Heat tolerance:	☐

Weight:	male: 19–22 lb; female: 18–21 lb
Height:	about 10"

times weekly, plus shaping every three months. Shaping for pets is by clipping, and for show dogs by stripping.

Health

• Major concerns: vWD, CMO
• Minor concerns: Scotty cramp, intervertebral disc disease
• Occasionally seen: none
• Suggested tests: DNA for vWD
• Life span: 11–13 years

Form and Function

The Scottish Terrier is a short-legged, compact, relatively heavy boned dog, giving the impression of great power in a small package. This combination is essential in a dog that must meet tough adversaries in tight spaces. Its coat is a combination of dense undercoat and extremely hardy and wiry outer coat, about 2 inches in length. The distinctive eyebrows and beard add to its expression, which is keen and sharp.

Sealyham Terrier

History

Although some evidence exists of a small, white, long-backed terrier imported into Wales in the fifteenth century, the documented history of the Sealyham begins only in the mid 1800s. The only reason the earlier observation receives some credence is that the originator of the breed, Captain John Edwardes of Sealyham, was a descendant of the family said to have imported the particular dog centuries earlier. Regardless, Captain Edwardes worked from 1850 to 1891 to develop the breed now known as the Sealyham Terrier. The breeds that went into its makeup are a mystery; some suggest that the Dandie Dinmont Terrier may have played a role. Whatever the ingredients, the result was a plucky terrier that soon gained notoriety for its ability to face badgers, otters, and foxes. Its smart appearance made it a dog show natural, and it first entered the show ring in 1903. The AKC recognized the Sealyham in 1911. Demand for these terriers quickly grew, especially because they were still exceptional hunting dogs as well as extremely competitive show dogs. Today the breed's popularity has waned somewhat, but the Sealyham

AKC Ranking: 139
Family: Terrier
Area of Origin: Wales
Date of Origin: 1800s
Original Function: Badger, otter, and
  fox hunting
Today's Function: Earthdog trials
Other Name: None

still retains its dual abilities to excel in both ring and field.

Temperament

One of the calmer terriers, the Sealyham is nonetheless ready for action, always happy to investigate, dig, or give chase. It is often aggressive toward other dogs or pets. It is a well-mannered housedog but needs some daily exercise. It is reserved with strangers, but devoted to its family. It is stubborn and independent. It digs and barks.

Upkeep

The Sealyham's exercise needs are not too demanding, consisting of a short to moderate walk or game session every day. If allowed off leash, it should be in a safe area because it may tend to follow its nose. This breed is suited for indoor life, preferably with yard access, although it can live in an apartment. Its wire coat needs combing two to three times weekly, plus shaping every three months. Shaping for pets is by clipping, and for show dogs by stripping.

At a Glance

Energy level:	☐☐
Exercise requirements:	☐☐
Playfulness:	☐☐
Affection level:	☐☐☐
Friendliness toward dogs:	☐☐☐
Friendliness toward other pets:	☐☐☐
Friendliness toward strangers:	☐☐☐
Ease of training:	☐
Watchdog ability:	☐☐☐☐
Protection ability:	☐
Grooming requirements:	☐☐☐
Cold tolerance:	☐☐☐
Heat tolerance:	☐☐☐

Weight:	male: 23–24 lb; (female: 18–22 lb*)
Height:	approx. 10.5″

Health
• Major concerns: none
• Minor concerns: retinal dysplasia, lens luxation
• Occasionally seen: deafness
• Suggested tests: eye
• Life span: 11–13 years

Form and Function
The Sealyham Terrier is a short-legged terrier, slightly longer than it is tall. Its body is strong, short-coupled, and substantial, allowing for plenty of flexibility. This combination of short legs with a strong and flexible body allows the Sealyham to maneuver in tight quarters. Its weather-resistant coat consists of a soft, dense undercoat and a hard, wiry outer coat. This is a keen, alert, and determined breed and should look the part.

Skye Terrier

History

Scotland has long been a stronghold of small plucky terriers, and the Skye Terrier is among the oldest of them. They developed along the west coastal area, where they hunted fox and otter from among the rocky cairns. The purest of these dogs were found on the Isle of Skye, and the dogs were thus dubbed Skye Terriers. It was first described in the sixteenth century, when it was already noteworthy for its long coat. Some confusion exists in tracing its history because, for a time, several different breeds were grouped under the name Skye Terrier. The true Skye Terrier became prominent in 1840 when Queen Victoria fancied the breed, keeping both drop- and prick-eared dogs. This enhanced its popularity both in high society and among commoners, and the Skye soon came to America. The AKC recognized the breed in 1887, and it quickly rose to the top of the show scene. Despite this strong start and the breed's distinctive appearance, its popularity has waned, and it is now among the least known terriers. The most famous Skye of all time was Greyfriar's Bobby, who slept on his master's grave for 14 years until his own death;

AKC Ranking: 130
Family: Terrier
Area of Origin: Scotland
Date of Origin: 1500s
Original Function: Fox and otter hunting
Today's Function: Earthdog trials
Other Name: None

he continues his vigil still, being buried where he waited next to his master. A statue commemorates this most loyal of dogs.

Temperament

The Skye Terrier's soft look belies its tough nature. It is a fearless and a deadly rodent hunter. It is also a mild-mannered house pet, one of the few terriers calm enough to live in the city. It still needs daily exercise in a safe area or on leash, however. It is sensitive yet stubborn. The Skye is affectionate with its family but cautious with strangers. It gets along fairly well with other dogs in the same household but may not mingle well with strange dogs. It is extremely courageous and game and makes a good watchdog.

Upkeep

This is a hunting dog at heart and enjoys a daily outing, exploring in a safe area. It also needs a short to moderate walk to stay in shape. The Skye enjoys life as a housedog, and prefers not to live outdoors. Regular combing (about twice a week) is all that is

At a Glance

Energy level:	❑❑
Exercise requirements:	❑❑
Playfulness:	❑❑❑
Affection level:	❑❑❑❑
Friendliness toward dogs:	❑
Friendliness toward other pets:	❑
Friendliness toward strangers:	❑
Ease of training:	❑❑❑
Watchdog ability:	❑❑❑❑❑
Protection ability:	❑
Grooming requirements:	❑❑❑
Cold tolerance:	❑❑❑❑
Heat tolerance:	❑❑

Weight:	18–20 lb*
Height:	male: 10"; female: 9.5"

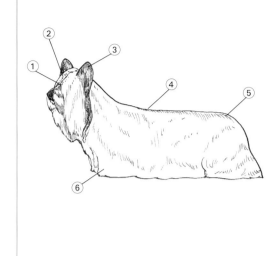

Illustrated Standard

① Medium-sized, close-set eyes
② Head long and powerful
③ Ears, if prick: placed high, held erect; if drop: larger and set lower
④ Topline level
⑤ Tail long, well-feathered, preferably carried no higher than backline
⑥ Large hare feet

❑ **Color:** black, blue, gray, silver, fawn, or cream, preferably with black ears, muzzle, and tail tip. Adult color may not be present until 18 months.
❑ **DQ:** dudley, flesh colored, or brown nose

Health

- Major concerns: none
- Minor concerns: premature closure of distal radius
- Occasionally seen: none
- Suggested tests: none
- Life span: 12–14 years

Form and Function

The Skye Terrier is a stylish and elegant dog that is, first of all, a working terrier. It is solidly built, with substantial bone, and twice as long as it is tall. The Skye's short legs enable it to go to ground in pursuit of fox and badger, and the long back imparts flexibility within a confined space. Its strong jaws further aid it in dispatching its prey. Its movement is free and effortless. The hard outer coat and close undercoat afford protection from the teeth of its quarry as well as harsh weather. The outer coat lies straight and flat, 5.5 inches or more in length.

needed to keep the Skye looking good. An occasional bath will not soften the coat too much, as is often the case with other terriers. The hair around the eyes and mouth may need extra cleaning.

Soft Coated Wheaten Terrier

History

One of only three large terriers of Ireland, the Soft Coated Wheaten Terrier originated as an all-around farm dog, perhaps serving in this function for hundreds of years. Besides the ever-essential terrier function of extinguishing vermin, it also helped round up stock and guard the homestead. It was later even known to be trained as a gundog. Its early history is largely undocumented; however, it is mentioned as a progenitor of the Kerry Blue Terrier. The Wheaten was a comparative latecomer to the show scene. Only in 1937 was it granted breed status in Ireland. For many years, an Irish Championship required that a dog not only prove itself in the ring but also in the field over badger, rat, and rabbit. The English Kennel Club recognized the breed in 1943, and in 1946 the first Wheaten came to America. The breed did not instantly catch the public's attention, but instead it took its time building a firm basis of support. In 1973 the AKC granted recognition. The Soft Coated Wheaten Terrier has remained a breed of only moderate popularity.

AKC Ranking: 63
Family: Terrier
Area of Origin: Ireland
Date of Origin: 1700s
Original Function: Vermin hunting, herding, guardian
Today's Function: Companion
Other Name: None

Temperament

The Wheaten makes a playful companion at home and a fun-loving partner in the field. It is affectionate, congenial, and much gentler than most terriers. It is generally responsive to its owner's wishes but can be headstrong at times. It is good with children (although some may be overly boisterous with small children) and usually good with other household dogs and pets. It may dig or jump.

Upkeep

This is an athletic dog that needs a good daily workout, either in the form of a moderate to long walk or an invigorating game in the yard. It should be allowed loose only in a safe area because it still loves to hunt and chase. The Wheaten can live outdoors in temperate climates, but it is far better suited as an indoor dog. Its long coat needs brushing or combing every two days. As a nonshedding dog, loose hair becomes entangled in the coat and will mat if not combed out. Bathing and trimming every other month is necessary to maintain the desirable coat and silhouette; pets can be better managed if their coats are clipped to about 3 inches, but then they lose the breed's typical outline.

Health

- Major concerns: protein wasting diseases (PLE and PLN)
- Minor concerns: renal dysplasia, allergies
- Occasionally seen: PRA, CHD, vWD, heart problems
- Suggested tests: blood and urine protein screens, eye, (hip), (cardiac)
- Life span: 12–14 years

Form and Function

The Soft Coated Wheaten Terrier is an all-around dog, square-proportioned, graceful, and strong, not exaggerated in any way. It is large enough to function as a general farm worker yet agile enough to perform its job as vermin exterminator. Its gait is free and lively with good reach and drive; the tail held erect. Its abundant, soft, single coat distinguishes it from all other terriers. It is long and silky with a gentle wave. The overall appearance is one of grace and strength in an alert and happy dog.

Illustrated Standard

1. Medium-sized, slightly almond-shaped eyes
2. Head appears rectangular, powerful
3. Ears fairly small, breaking level with skull
4. Back strong and level
5. Tail docked, carried gaily but not over back
6. Feet round

❏ **Color:** any shade of wheaten
❏ **DQ:** none

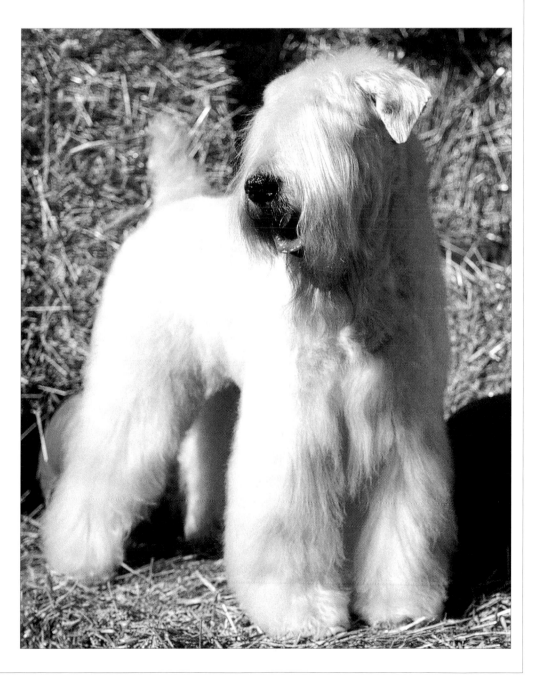

At a Glance

Energy level:	▣▣☐
Exercise requirements:	▣▣☐
Playfulness:	▣▣▣☐
Affection level:	▣▣▣▣▣
Friendliness toward dogs:	▣▣☐
Friendliness toward other pets:	▣▣☐
Friendliness toward strangers:	▣▣▣☐
Ease of training:	▣▣☐
Watchdog ability:	▣▣▣☐
Protection ability:	▣▣
Grooming requirements:	▣▣▣☐
Cold tolerance:	▣▣☐
Heat tolerance:	▣

Weight:	male: 35–40 lb; female: 30–35 lb
Height:	male: 18–19"; female: 17–18"

Staffordshire Bull Terrier

History

In the early 1800s, the sport of rat killing had become quite popular among the working classes. Bull baiting, which had been popular in earlier times, did not lend itself to the cities, and fanciers of the rat pit became increasingly enamored of dog fighting as a more exciting alternative to rat killing. In their efforts to produce a fearless, quick, strong contender for the dog pit, they crossed the Bulldog of the time with the Black and Tan Terrier, thus producing the Bull and Terrier. Selective breeding resulted in a small nimble dog with incredibly strong jaws. It also produced a dog that was specifically not aggressive toward people because it had to be handled safely when it was at its most aroused state. By the time dog fighting was banned in England, these dogs had so endeared themselves to their fans that they continued to have a loyal following. Although some fanciers continued to fight them in clandestine gatherings, true aficionados sought a legal venue of competition and found their answer in the show ring. Concerted

AKC Ranking: 100
Family: Terrier, Mastiff (Bull)
Area of Origin: England
Date of Origin: 1800s
Original Function: Ratting, dog fighting
Today's Function: Companion
Other Name: None

efforts to produce a dog more amenable to the ring and attractive as a pet finally resulted in the breed's recognition by the English Kennel Club in 1935, but it was not until 1974 that the AKC confirmed similar status. Although the breed's reputation as a combatant may have dogged it into the present, those who live with one know it as a lover, not a fighter.

Temperament

The Staffordshire Bull Terrier is a fun-loving character that loves playing with its family and friends. It is typically playful, companionable, amiable, docile, and generally responsive to its owner's wishes. Its love of a good game is rivaled only by its need for human companionship. It is also characteristically friendly toward strangers. Some can be strong willed. Although it doesn't usually look for a fight, it is fearless and tenacious. It may not do well around strange dogs or sometimes even household dogs that challenge it. It is generally very good with children; although usually gentle, some can be rambunctious. In the United Kingdom the Stafford is known as the Nanny Dog, in reference to its eagerness and ability to assume the role of a child's nursemaid.

Upkeep

This is an athletic breed that needs a good walk on leash every day. It also enjoys a good game in the yard or a run in a safe area. Although the Stafford is capable of living outdoors in mild weather, it can be affected by cold and, more importantly, it is a dog that craves human contact; thus, it is far better suited as a housedog. Coat care is minimal.

Health

- Major concerns: none
- Minor concerns: none
- Occasionally seen: cataract, CHD
- Suggested tests: (CERF), (OFA)
- Life span: 12–14 years
- Note: The high pain threshold may mask problems.

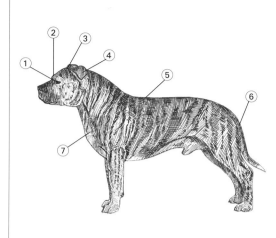

Form and Function

The Stafford is slightly longer than it is tall, and relatively wide, giving it a low center of gravity and firm stance. Its small size imparts a surprising agility, while its heavy musculature provides great strength. The wide head provides ample room for attachment of jaw muscles. Its gait should be powerful and agile. Its coat is smooth, short, and close.

At a Glance

Energy level:	☐☐☐
Exercise requirements:	☐☐☐
Playfulness:	☐☐☐☐☐
Affection level:	☐☐☐☐
Friendliness toward dogs:	☐☐
Friendliness toward other pets:	☐☐☐
Friendliness toward strangers:	☐☐☐
Ease of training:	☐☐☐
Watchdog ability:	☐☐☐
Protection ability:	☐☐☐
Grooming requirements:	☐
Cold tolerance:	☐☐
Heat tolerance:	☐☐

Weight:	male: 35–40 lb; female: 30–35 lb
Height:	male: 18–19"; female: 17–18"

Welsh Terrier

History

One of only two terriers native to Wales, the Welsh Terrier probably descended from the old Black and Tan Rough Terrier that was popular in Britain in the eighteenth and nineteenth centuries. By the late 1700s, a distinctive strain—known as Ynysfor—was running with Otterhounds in North Wales. At the same time, a similar dog, the "Old English Broken Haired" Terrier, was being bred in northern England. The two strains were so similar that when they began to be shown, the same dog could compete successfully as either breed, and they were classified together. Eventually, they all became known as Welsh Terriers, regardless of their origin. After all, both strains had shared similar backgrounds and were used to hunt otter, fox, and badger. In 1886, the English Kennel Club recognized the breed. The early dogs were too rough to be competitive in the show ring, and breeders sought to improve the Welsh's lines not only by selective breeding but also with crosses to the racier Wire Fox Terrier. The result was a dog that in some ways resembles a miniature Airedale

AKC Ranking: 93
Family: Terrier
Area of Origin: Wales
Date of Origin: 1700s
Original Function: Otter, fox, badger, and rat hunting
Today's Function: Earthdog trials
Other Name: None

Terrier. It became a competitive show dog, but for some reason it has never attained the heights of show ring success that similar small, long-legged terriers have achieved.

Temperament

The Welsh, although more mild-mannered than many terriers, is still playful and mischievous enough to provide plenty of entertainment and challenges, yet it is calm enough to be a reliable house pet. It is independent, inquisitive, and sensitive, reserved with strangers, and possibly scrappy with other dogs and pets. It needs daily exercise in a safe area. It tends to dig and bark.

Upkeep

The Welsh Terrier needs a moderate walk on leash every day or an invigorating play session. If allowed to run off leash, it should be in a safe area because it tends to hunt. The Welsh can live happily outdoors during nice weather, but it should sleep inside in cold weather. It does best when allowed access to house and

At a Glance

Energy level:	▢▢▢
Exercise requirements:	▢▢▢
Playfulness:	▢▢▢
Affection level:	▢▢▢
Friendliness toward dogs:	▢▢▢
Friendliness toward other pets:	▢
Friendliness toward strangers:	▢
Ease of training:	▢
Watchdog ability:	▢▢▢▢▢
Protection ability:	▢
Grooming requirements:	▢▢▢▢
Cold tolerance:	▢▢▢
Heat tolerance:	▢▢▢

Weight:	male: 35–40 lb; female: 30–35 lb
Height:	male: 18–19"; female: 17–18"

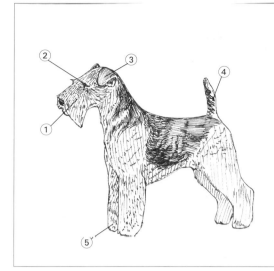

Illustrated Standard

1. Head rectangular
2. Small, almond-shaped eyes
3. Small, V-shaped ears, folding just above level of skull
4. Tail carried upright, docked to level of occiput
5. Small cat feet

❏ **Color:** deep tan with black or grizzle jacket
❏ **DQ:** none

yard. Its wiry jacket needs combing two to three times weekly, plus shaping every three months. Shaping for pets is by clipping, and for show dogs is by stripping. The ears of puppies may need to be trained in order to ensure proper adult shape.

Health

- Major concerns: none
- Minor concerns: lens luxation
- Occasionally seen: cataracts, patellar luxation, distichiasis
- Suggested tests: eye, (knee)
- Life span: 12–14 years

Form and Function

This is a square-proportioned, compact, sturdy dog of medium size, capable of running at good speed for long distances and then bolting or dispatching its quarry. Its gait is free and effortless, with good reach and drive. Its coat is double, with a short, soft undercoat and a hard, dense, wiry outer coat. The expression and demeanor are confident and alert.

West Highland White Terrier

History

The West Highland White Terrier shares its roots with the other terriers of Scotland, proving itself on fox, badger, and various vermin. At one time the Westie, Dandie Dinmont, Skye, Cairn, and Scottish Terriers were all considered one breed with considerable diversity. Selective breeding based on such qualities as coat type or color could have produced distinctive strains that would have been easily maintained in the relative isolation of the various islands in the country. The Westie first gained attention in 1907 as the Poltalloch Terrier, named for the home of Col. E.D. Malcolm, who had been breeding the short-legged white terriers for the previous 60 years. The breed has gone under several different names, including Roseneath, Poltalloch, White Scottish, Little Skye, and Cairn. In fact, the AKC first registered it as the Roseneath Terrier in 1908, but the name was changed to West Highland White Terrier in 1909. Since that date it has made quite a name for itself, establishing itself as one of the most competitive terriers in the show ring and one of the most popular terriers in the home.

AKC Ranking: 36
Family: Terrier
Area of Origin: Scotland
Date of Origin: 1800s
Original Function: Fox, badger, and vermin hunting
Today's Function: Earthdog trials
Other Name: Poltalloch Terrier

Temperament

The busy Westie is happy, curious, and always in the thick of things. It is affectionate and demanding, one of the friendliest terriers. It is not friendly, however, toward small animals. It enjoys a daily romp in a safe area or a walk on lead, as well as playtime at home. It is independent and somewhat stubborn. It barks and digs.

Upkeep

The Westie enjoys the outdoors, but it can also function as an indoor dog if taken for regular exercise. It needs either a short to

At a Glance

Energy level:	☐☐☐☐
Exercise requirements:	☐☐☐
Playfulness:	☐☐☐
Affection level:	☐☐☐☐☐
Friendliness toward dogs:	☐☐☐
Friendliness toward other pets:	☐☐☐
Friendliness toward strangers:	☐☐☐☐
Ease of training:	☐☐☐☐
Watchdog ability:	☐☐☐☐
Protection ability:	☐
Grooming requirements:	☐☐☐☐
Cold tolerance:	☐☐☐
Heat tolerance:	☐☐☐

Weight:	15–21 lb*
Height:	male: 11"; female: 10"

Illustrated Standard

1. Muzzle blunt
2. Medium-sized, almond-shaped eyes
3. Stop defined
4. Head appears round
5. Small, erect, pointed ears
6. Relatively short, carrot-shaped tail, carried gaily but not over back
7. Feet round

☐ **Color:** white
☐ **DQ:** none

fox in closed quarters. The harsh double coat, especially the hard, straight outer coat, provided protection from the fox's teeth, especially around the head, as well as from the elements. The tail needed to be sufficiently long to provide a handhold by which the dog could be pulled from shallow holes.

moderate walk on leash or a good game in the yard every day. It should sleep inside in all but the mildest climates. Its wire coat needs combing two or three times weekly, plus shaping every three months. Shaping for pets is by clipping, and for show dogs is by stripping. In some areas, it may be difficult to keep the coat white.

Health
- Major concerns: globoid cell leukodystrophy, Legg–Perthes, CMO
- Minor concerns: copper toxicosis, cataract, patellar luxation
- Occasionally seen: deafness
- Suggested tests: hip, knee
- Life span: 12–14 years

Form and Function
The Westie is compact and short coupled. It must be small enough to fit between rocks in a narrow passageway that was the typical fox den in its area of origin. These passages were often so narrow that the dog could not turn around. Short legs aided in maneuverability in the cramped passages. It had to have formidable teeth and jaws in order to face a

The Toy Group

Dogs of the Toy Group are the miniature versions of the dog world. Many of these breeds are quite ancient, attesting to the value people have long placed in dogs for the sake of companionship and adornment. It is difficult to ascribe behavioral characteristics to the entire group because many of these dogs are basically miniaturized versions of dogs from other groups, although several others are of such ancient origin that they cannot be traced to their larger ancestors.

Affenpinscher

History

The Affenpinscher's name describes it well: *Affen* meaning monkey and *Pinscher* meaning terrier. In France the Affenpinscher is known as the "diablotin moustachu"—moustached little devil, which also aptly describes it! As one of the oldest toy breeds, the Affenpinscher's origins are obscure. Paintings by the old Dutch Masters from the fifteenth century often included dogs resembling Affenpinschers, but more definite evidence of the breed is absent. Small terriers adept at dispatching rats were abundant in central Europe by the seventeenth century. In Germany, they were used to rid stables and kitchens of rodents. Even smaller versions of these dogs were preferred for lady's lap dogs, able to kill mice in the home, warm their mistress' lap, and amuse the entire household with their antics. This small version eventually became the Affenpinscher, which was later refined by occasional

AKC Ranking: 127
Family: Terrier, Pinscher
Area of Origin: Germany
Date of Origin: 1600s
Original Function: Small vermin hunting, lapdog
Today's Function: Companion
Other Name: None

crosses with the Pug, German Pinscher, and German Silky Pinscher. The Affenpinscher in turn became the progenitor of other wire-coated toys, most notably the Brussels Griffon. The breed was most popular in Germany, which can lay claim as its homeland. In 1936 the AKC recognized the Affenpinscher, but World War II slowed any momentum in popularity the breed had gained. Since then, the breed has remained extremely rare even in America and Germany, its comparative strongholds.

Temperament

The Affenpinscher lives up to its name monkey terrier in both looks and actions. It is a terrier at heart, busy, inquisitive, bold, and stubborn, but it also loves to monkey around, being playful and mischievous. It tends to bark and even climb. Unlike most terriers, it is fairly good with other dogs and pets. This little dog is best with a family that likes entertainment and has a very good sense of humor.

Upkeep

Although an energetic and active dog, the exercise needs of the Affenpinscher can be met with vigorous indoor games or romps in the yard, or with short walks on leash. It enjoys playing outside, but it cannot live outdoors. Its harsh coat needs combing two or three times weekly, plus shaping every three months. Shaping for pets is by clipping, whereas show dogs require stripping.

Health

- Major concerns: none
- Minor concerns: patellar luxation, Legg–Perthes
- Occasionally seen: PDA, open fontanel
- Suggested tests: knee, (cardiac)
- Life span: 12–14 years

Form and Function

The Affenpinscher is square-proportioned, compact and sturdy, with medium bone. It is a smaller version of a working

At a Glance

Energy level:	☐☐☐☐
Exercise requirements:	☐☐☐
Playfulness:	☐☐☐☐
Affection level:	☐☐☐☐
Friendliness toward dogs:	☐☐☐
Friendliness toward other pets:	☐☐☐
Friendliness toward strangers:	☐☐☐
Ease of training:	☐☐
Watchdog ability:	☐☐☐☐☐
Protection ability:	☐
Grooming requirements:	☐☐☐☐
Cold tolerance:	☐☐
Heat tolerance:	☐☐☐

Weight:	7–9 lb*
Height:	9–11.5"

Illustrated Standard

① Undershot bite
② Short muzzle
③ Domed skull, well-defined stop
④ Ears either cropped to a point and erect, or uncropped and erect, semi-erect, or drop
⑤ Tail natural or docked 1–3" long, carried erect
⑥ Small round feet

❏ **Color:** black, gray, silver, or black and tan
❏ **DQ:** none

terrier, and as such is not a delicate dog. This is an active, tough dog that is agile enough to catch and dispatch rats and mice. The gait is light, sound, and confident. The Affenpinscher has a monkey-like facial expression with long eyebrows and beard, which lends it an air of comic seriousness. Its rough coat is about 1 inch long on the body, somewhat longer on the head, neck, chest, stomach and legs. This coat type provided protection from vermin and harsh conditions.

Brussels Griffon

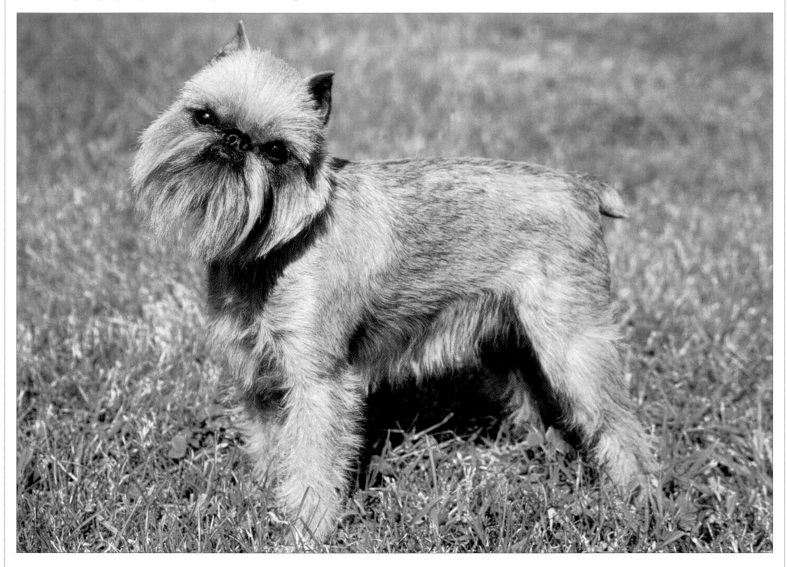

History

A product of Belgium, the Brussels Griffon's forebears were probably the Affenpinscher and a Belgian street dog, the Griffon d'Ecurie (Stable Griffon). The breed gained favor as a guard of cabs in Brussels, where its cocky but comic demeanor was probably more effective at attracting riders than dissuading robbers. In the late 1800s, this mixture was then crossed with the Pug, at that time extremely popular in neighboring Holland. The Pug crosses account for the brachycephalic head type and for the smooth-coated individuals of the breed, known then (and still in some countries) as the Petit Brabancon. Although the smooths were initially destroyed (after all, griffon means wiry), they were soon after accepted. By 1880, the breed was sufficiently established to be recognized at Belgian dog shows. Around this same time there is some suggestion that additional crosses were made with the Yorkshire Terrier and English Toy Spaniel, the latter further con-

AKC Ranking: 91
Family: Terrier, Companion
Area of Origin: Belgium
Date of Origin: 1800s
Original Function: Small vermin hunting, companion
Today's Function: Companion
Other Name: Griffon Belge, Griffon Bruxellois, Belgian Griffon

tributing to the Brussels Griffon's head configuration. By the early 1900s, the little street urchin had risen to the heights of popularity in Belgium and found itself in great demand by nobility. Although its numbers were decimated by World War I, the breed recovered and has since gained ardent admirers around the world. In some countries, only the red longer-coated dogs are classified as the Brussels Griffon; black longer-coated dogs are known as the Belgian Griffon; and smooth-coated dogs are known as the Petit Brabancon.

Temperament

The spunky Brussels Griffon is full of itself, brimming with self-confidence and gusto. It is bold, playful, stubborn, and mischievous. It is usually good with other dogs and pets. It tends to bark and climb, and some can be escape artists. It makes a saucy companion for a family wanting an entertaining, sensitive pet.

At a Glance

Energy level:	☐☐☐☐
Exercise requirements:	☐☐
Playfulness:	☐☐☐☐
Affection level:	☐☐☐☐
Friendliness toward dogs:	☐☐☐
Friendliness toward other pets:	☐☐☐
Friendliness toward strangers:	☐☐☐
Ease of training:	☐☐☐
Watchdog ability:	☐☐☐☐☐
Protection ability:	☐
Grooming requirements: Smooth:	☐
Rough:	☐☐☐☐
Cold tolerance:	☐☐
Heat tolerance:	☐☐

Weight:	8–10 lb
Height:	7–8″*

poseful trot, with moderate reach and drive. In temperament it is full of self-importance, and its carriage reflects this attitude. Its almost human expression attracts attention and admirers. Its coat can be rough, with hard wiry hair, which is longer around the head; or smooth, with a short glossy coat.

Upkeep

The Brussels Griffon is an active breed, always on the lookout for action. It needs daily mental and physical stimulation, but its small size makes such stimulation possible with a robust indoor game. It also enjoys a short walk on leash. This breed cannot live outside, although it appreciates the opportunity to spend time in the yard. The rough coat needs combing two or three times weekly, plus shaping by stripping every three months. Grooming for the smooth coat is minimal, consisting only of occasional brushing to remove dead hair.

Health

- Major concerns: none
- Minor concerns: none
- Occasionally seen: weak bladder, patellar luxation, distichiasis
- Suggested tests: none
- Life span: 12–15 years

Form and Function

The Brussels Griffon is square-proportioned, thickset, and compact. It has good bone for its size. Its movement is a pur-

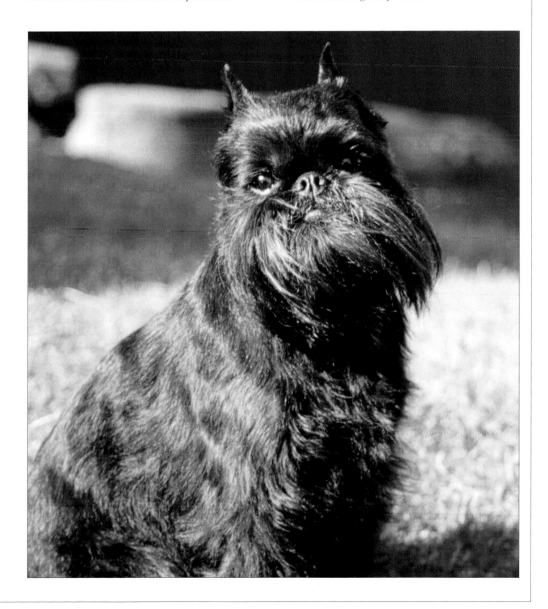

Cavalier King Charles Spaniel

History

As its name implies, the Cavalier King Charles Spaniel is derived from spaniel roots. The European toy dogs were probably the result of breeding small spaniels to Oriental toy breeds such as the Japanese Chin and perhaps the Tibetan Spaniel. These Tudor lapdogs, known as "comforter spaniels," served as lap and foot warmers, and even surrogate hot water bottles. In addition, they served the vital function of attracting fleas from their owners' bodies! The toy spaniels became especially popular because they appealed to all members of the family. In the 1700s, King Charles II was so enamored with his toy spaniels that he was accused of ignoring matters of state in favor of his dogs. The dogs were so closely associated with him that they became known as King Charles Spaniels. After his death, the Duke of Marlborough took over as the major advocate of the breed; the red and white "Blenheim" color, which was his favorite, is named after his estate. The King Charles Spaniel continued to grace the homes of the wealthy for generations, but with time a shorter-nosed dog was preferred. By the early 1900s, the few dogs that resembled

AKC Ranking: 70
Family: Spaniel, Companion
Area of Origin: England
Date of Origin: 1600s
Original Function: Flushing small birds, lapdog
Today's Function: Companion
Other Name: None

the early members of the breed were considered to be inferior. A twist of fate occurred when a wealthy American, Roswell Eldridge, came to England and offered outlandish prize money for the best "pointed-nosed" spaniels, most resembling the old type. Breeders bred their old-type dogs together in an effort to gain the prize, and in so doing, many came to appreciate the old type. Ironically, these dogs, named Cavalier King Charles Spaniels in honor of the Cavalier King, eventually outstripped their short-nosed counterparts in popularity, becoming one of the most popular breeds in England. They were slower to catch on in America, and many Cavalier owners fought AKC recognition in an effort to control the problems that so often accompany popularity. In 1996, the AKC recognized the Cavalier; it is too early to tell whether its popularity will soar as a result.

Temperament

The Cavalier in many ways fits the bill as an ideal house pet. It is sweet, gentle, playful, willing to please, affectionate, and quiet. It is amiable toward other dogs, pets, and strangers. Outdoors, its spaniel heritage kicks in, and it loves to explore, sniff, and chase.

Upkeep
The Cavalier needs a fair amount of exercise every day, either in the form of a moderate walk on leash or a romp in a safe area. This is not a breed that should live outdoors. Its long coat needs brushing every other day.

Health
- Major concerns: MVI, CHD
- Minor concerns: patellar luxation, entropion
- Occasionally seen: retinal dysplasia
- Suggested tests: cardiac, hip, knee, eye
- Life span: 9–14 years
- Note: Cavaliers should not be bred until the age of 5 years, and only after being checked at that age for MVD.

Form and Function
The Cav is an elegant, royal, toy spaniel, slightly longer than tall, with moderate bones. It retains the build of a working spaniel, yet in a smaller version. Its gait

Illustrated Standard
1. Full muzzle
2. Large, round eyes, with cushioning beneath
3. Ears high set and long
4. Level topline
5. Compact seat with long hair
6. Tail carried happily and in motion when the dog is moving; may be docked with no more than one third removed
7. Long feathering on feet

❏ **Color:** ruby (solid red), Blenheim (red and white), black and tan, tricolor
❏ **DQ:** none

is free and elegant, with good reach and drive. Its silky coat is of moderate length, with a slight wave permissible. Long feathering on the feet is a breed characteristic. A hallmark of the breed is its gentle, sweet, melting expression.

At a Glance

Energy level:	❏❏❏
Exercise requirements:	❏❏❏
Playfulness:	❏❏❏❏
Affection level:	❏❏❏❏❏
Friendliness toward dogs:	❏
Friendliness toward other pets:	❏❏❏❏
Friendliness toward strangers:	❏❏❏❏❏
Ease of training:	❏❏❏❏
Watchdog ability:	❏❏❏
Protection ability:	❏
Grooming requirements:	❏❏❏
Cold tolerance:	❏❏❏
Heat tolerance:	❏❏

Weight:	13–18 lb
Height:	12–13"

Chihuahua

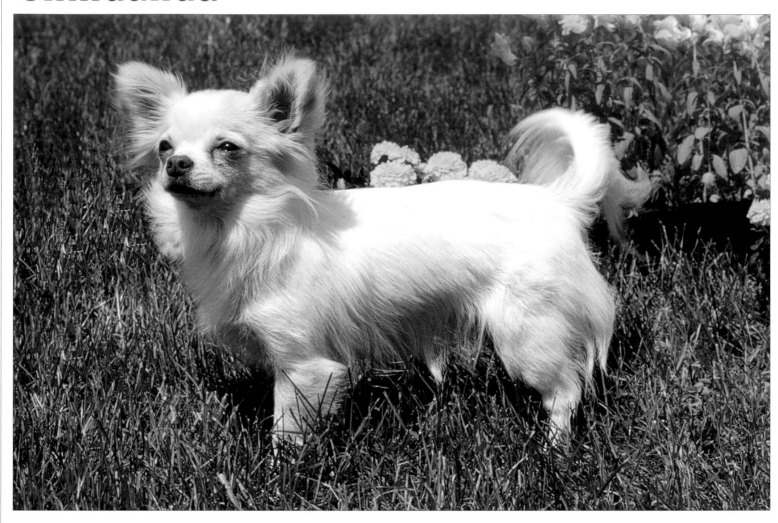

History

The smallest breed of dog, the Chihuahua has a controversial history. One theory holds that it originated in China and was brought to the New World by Spanish traders, where it was then crossed with small native dogs. The other theory contends that it originated entirely in Central and South America, descending from the native Techichi, a small mute dog that was sometimes sacrificed in Toltec religious rituals. A small red dog was believed to guide the soul to the underworld, and every Aztec family kept such a dog that was sacrificed and buried with any deceased family member. To make matters worse for the Techichi, the Toltecs and their conquerors, the Aztecs, often ate dogs and the Techichi may have sometimes been on the menu. Despite what may have been short lives, the Techichis apparently were well cared for during life by the priests or their families. In fact, the most likely origin of the Chihuahua is a combination of these theories: the native Techichi was probably crossed with tiny hairless Chinese dogs, but again the date when this occurred is controversial. The Chinese dogs may have been brought over when a land bridge spanned the

AKC Ranking: 12
Family: Companion, Southern (Pariah)
Area of Origin: Mexico
Date of Origin: 1500s
Original Function: Ceremonial
Today's Function: Companion
Other Name: None

Bering Strait, or they may have been brought later by Spanish traders. When Cortes conquered the Aztecs in the sixteenth century, the little dogs were abandoned and left to fend for themselves. About 300 years later, in 1850, three tiny dogs were found in Chihuahua, Mexico. A few were brought to the United States, but they aroused only moderate attention. Only when Xavier Cugat ("the rhumba king") appeared in public with a Chihuahua as his constant companion did the breed capture the public's hearts. It experienced a meteoric rise in popularity and has continued as one of America's most popular breeds.

Temperament

The saucy Chihuahua has earned its place as a favored toy dog because of its intense devotion to a single person. It is reserved with strangers but good with other household dogs and pets. Some try to be protective, but they are not very effective. Some may be quite bold; others may be timid. It is often temperamental. Some bark.

At a Glance

Energy level:	☐☐☐☐☐
Exercise requirements:	☐
Playfulness:	☐☐
Affection level:	☐☐
Friendliness toward dogs:	☐
Friendliness toward other pets:	☐☐☐
Friendliness toward strangers:	☐
Ease of training:	☐☐
Watchdog ability:	☐☐☐☐☐
Protection ability:	☐
Grooming requirements: Smooth	☐
Long:	☐☐
Cold tolerance:	☐
Heat tolerance:	☐☐☐

Weight:	not to exceed 6 lb
Height:	6–9"*

Upkeep

The Chihuahua is a lively dog that none-theless can get its exercise running from room to room indoors. It enjoys exploring the yard or going for a short walk on leash and especially enjoys accompanying its owner on outings. The Chihuahua is not an outdoor dog; it hates the cold and seeks out warmth. Coat care for the smooth is minimal. Care of the long coat entails brushing two to three times a week.

Health

- Major concerns: none
- Minor concerns: pulmonic stenosis, hydrocephalus, patellar luxation, KCS, hypoglycemia
- Occasionally seen: none
- Suggested tests: cardiac, knee
- Life span: 14–18 years
- Note: A soft spot (molera) in the skull (due to incomplete fontanel closure) is a common breed trait.

Form and Function

The Chihuahua is graceful, small, and compact, slightly longer than it is tall.

Illustrated Standard

1. Moderately short, slightly pointed muzzle
2. Apple dome skull
3. Large erect ears
4. Tail carried either up, out, or over the back
5. Dainty feet

☐ **Color:** any
☐ **DQ:** over 6 lb in weight; broken down or cropped ears; cropped tail, bobtail; in long coats, too thin coat that resembles bareness

It has a saucy expression and alert, terrier-like attitude. It should move out at a swift pace with good reach and drive.

Its coat can be smooth, with soft, glossy hair, or long, with soft straight or wavy coats and fringed ears.

Chinese Crested Dog

History

The origins of the Chinese Crested are difficult to trace. Hairless dogs seem to arise by mutation all over the world, but they have been principally perpetuated in Central and South America. The Chinese Crested is the exception, apparently existing in China as early as the thirteenth century. Chinese seafarers are said to have kept the dogs on ship as ratters and curios and to trade them with local merchants wherever they called. Thus, the breed was distributed to Turkey, Egypt, South Africa, and possibly Central and South America. Only in the 1800s were they recorded in Europe, with paintings and later, photographs, including dogs of Chinese Crested type. In the late 1800s, the breed found a proponent in the American Ida Garrett, who popularized several types of hairless dogs. With the help of a

AKC Ranking: 68
Family: Companion, Southern (hairless)
Area of Origin: China
Date of Origin: 1200s
Original Function: Ratter, lapdog, curio
Today's Function: Companion
Other Name: None

handful of committed breeders (including the famed Gypsy Rose Lee), the Chinese Crested gradually gained admirers in both America and Europe. In 1991—after a century of effort—the breed was recognized by the AKC. The Chinese Crested quickly became popular with dog showing enthusiasts, but the breed has been slower to attract average pet owners. As the breed gets more exposure, this situation is almost certain to change.

Temperament

The Chinese Crested is a combination of playful pixie, gentle lapdog, and sensitive companion. It is devoted to its family and willing to please; it is also good with other dogs, pets, and strangers. Its demeanor should be gay and alert.

Upkeep

The Crested enjoys a romp outside, but it hates the cold. It is small enough that it can get sufficient exercise with vigorous inside games. Hairless varieties will need a sweater for cold weather outings. This is not a breed for outdoor living. The Chinese Crested is a gifted jumper and some climb. Powderpuff coat care entails brushing every day or two. The muzzle is usually shaved every two weeks in Puffs. The Hairless needs regular skin care such as application of moisturizer, sun block, or bathing to combat blackheads. Most Hairless need some stray hairs that appear on the body to be removed prior to showing.

Health

- Major concerns: none
- Minor concerns: none
- Occasionally seen: Legg–Perthes
- Suggested tests: none
- Life span: 13–15 years
- Note: The Hairless is susceptible to blackheads, sunburn, wool allergy, and tooth loss. The Hairless has irregular dentition and thinner enamel.

Illustrated Standard

1. Almond-shaped eyes
2. Wedge-shaped head
3. Ears large and erect
4. Level topline with slightly sloping croup
5. Tail carried gaily
6. Hare feet

❏ **Color:** any
❏ **DQ:** none

Form and Function

The Chinese Crested is fine boned and slender, among the most elegant and graceful of breeds. It is slightly longer than tall. Its gait is lively and agile. It has an alert, intense expression. In the Hairless variety, soft silky hair is found only on the head (crest), tail (plume), and feet and lower legs. The skin of the hairless areas is smooth and soft. In the Powderpuff the entire dog is covered with soft silky coat of moderate density and length.

At a Glance

Energy level:	❏❏❏
Exercise requirements:	❏
Playfulness:	❏❏❏❏
Affection level:	❏❏❏❏
Friendliness toward dogs:	❏❏❏
Friendliness toward other pets:	❏❏❏❏❏
Friendliness toward strangers:	❏❏❏❏❏
Ease of training:	❏❏❏
Watchdog ability:	❏❏❏❏
Protection ability:	❏
Grooming requirements: Hairless:	❏❏❏
Powderpuff:	❏❏❏
Cold tolerance:	❏
Heat tolerance:	❏❏❏❏

Weight:	5–12 lb*
Height:	11–13"

English Toy Spaniel

History

The English Toy Spaniel and the Cavalier King Charles Spaniel share identical early histories. They began as one breed, probably resulting from crosses of small spaniels with Oriental toy breeds. Some evidence supports the theory that Mary, Queen of Scots, brought the first toy spaniels to Scotland with her from France. These "comforter spaniels" became very popular with the wealthy classes, and served as foot and lap warmers as well as delightful companions. They reached their height of early popularity during the seventeenth century reign of King Charles II, who so doted on his dogs that the breed was soon being called King Charles Spaniels—the name by which the breed is still known in England. These early dogs were all black and tan; other colors were developed later, with the first Duke of Marlborough credited with developing the red and white "Blenheims," named after his estate. The red and white coloration may have come from crosses with Chinese Cocker Spaniels. The duke's spaniels were said to be good hunting dogs for woodcock. Most proponents of the breed were more interested in having an eye-catching lapdog than a hunting

AKC Ranking: 116
Family: Spaniel, Companion
Area of Origin: England
Date of Origin: 1600s
Original Function: Flushing small
  birds, lapdog
Today's Function: Companion
Other Name: King Charles Spaniel

dog, and in the ensuing centuries the King Charles Spaniel was bred down in size and selected for a rounder head and flatter nose. In America, the name was changed to English Toy Spaniel and is shown as two varieties: the red particolored Blenheim and black and tan particolored Prince Charles, and the red solid-colored Ruby and black and tan solid-colored King Charles. The breed has continued to find favor with owners desiring an aristocratic but fun-loving lapdog.

Temperament

The haughty English Toy Spaniel enjoys a life of leisure, punctuated with rollicking romps. It is a lapdog par excellence, gentle, amiable, calm, and quiet, yet it is playful and attentive. It is utterly devoted to its family and reserved with strangers. It is somewhat stubborn.

Upkeep

Although it enjoys a nice walk on leash or a fun game in the house or yard, the English Toy Spaniel is not overly active and its exercise needs can be met with minimal effort. It does not do well in heat and is temperamentally totally unsuited for living outside away from its family. Its long coat needs combing twice weekly.

Health
- Major concerns: patellar luxation
- Minor concerns: early tooth loss, "lazy" tongue (never fully extracts into mouth)
- Occasionally seen: PDA
- Suggested tests: knee
- Life span: 10–12 years
- Note: A soft spot in the skull (due to incomplete fontanel closure) sometimes occurs. The breed is sensitive to anesthesia.

Form and Function
Square-proportioned, compact and cobby, the English Toy Spaniel is profusely coated with a silky, flowing coat. The coat can be straight or slightly wavy. It has heavy fringing, including feathering on the feet. The hallmark of the breed, however, is its head and expression. The head should be domed, with lustrous dark eyes and well-cushioned face, creating a soft appealing expression.

Illustrated Standard
1. Slightly undershot
2. Broad, square jaw
3. Large eyes
4. Domed skull with deep stop
5. Large head with a plush, chubby look
6. Low-set long ears, fringed with heavy - feathering
7. Tail docked 2–4" in length, carried at or slightly above horizontal, with long silky hair

❏ **Color:** solid red, black and tan, or either of these colors on a white background
❏ **DQ:** none

At a Glance

Energy level:	❏
Exercise requirements:	❏
Playfulness:	❏ ❏ ❏
Affection level:	❏ ❏
Friendliness toward dogs:	❏ ❏ ❏ ❏
Friendliness toward other pets:	❏ ❏ ❏ ❏
Friendliness toward strangers:	❏ ❏
Ease of training:	❏ ❏ ❏
Watchdog ability:	❏ ❏ ❏ ❏
Protection ability:	❏
Grooming requirements:	❏ ❏ ❏
Cold tolerance:	❏ ❏ ❏
Heat tolerance:	❏

Weight:	8–14 lb
Height:	10–11"*

Havanese

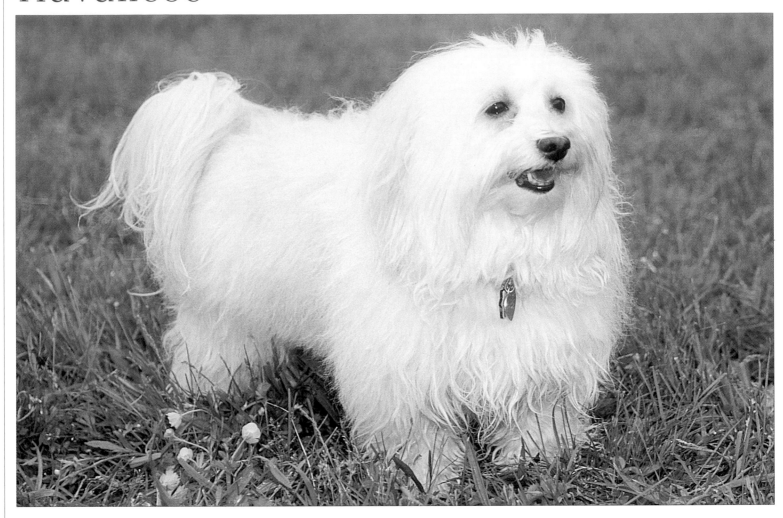

History

The Havanese is one of the Barbichon (later shortened to Bichon) family of small dogs originating in the Mediterranean in ancient times. Spanish traders brought some of these dogs with them as gifts for Cuban women, allowing them to establish trading relationships. In Cuba, the little dogs were pampered as the special pets of the wealthy. They became known as Habeneros, and eventually some found their way back to Europe, where they were called the White Cuban. They became quite popular, not only as pets of the elite but also as performing dogs. Their popularity as pets waned, however, and their stronghold remained in the circus, where they performed throughout Europe as trick dogs. Eventually the breed declined in numbers to such an extent that it was almost extinct not only in Europe but also in its native Cuba. A few remained in Cuba, however, and three families with their Havanese left Cuba for the United States during the 1950s and 1960s. Most present-day Havanese descend from these dogs. It has gradually aroused attention from dog fanciers and pet owners,

AKC Ranking: 104
Family: Bichon, Companion, Water Dog
Area of Origin: Cuba
Date of Origin: Ancient times
Original Function: Lapdog, performer
Today's Function: Companion
Other Name: Bichon Havanais

and in 1996 the first Havanese entered an AKC show ring, and was accepted for regular recognition as a member of the Toy Group as of the first day of 1999. The Havanese is also known as the Havana Silk Dog.

Temperament

This is a busy, curious dog; it is happiest when it is the center of attention. It loves to play and clown and is affectionate to its family, children, strangers, other dogs, and pets—basically everyone! The Havanese is willing to please and learn easily, but it tends to be vocal.

Upkeep

Although energetic, the Havanese can have its exercise needs met with a short walk or a good play session. It is not a dog that can live outside. Coat care entails brushing two to four times a week. This is a non-shedding dog, which means that loose hairs are caught in the outer hairs, tending to tangle, unless they are combed out.

At a Glance

Energy level:	☐☐☐☐
Exercise requirements:	☐☐☐
Playfulness:	☐☐☐☐☐
Affection level:	☐☐☐☐☐
Friendliness toward dogs:	☐☐☐☐
Friendliness toward other pets:	☐☐☐☐
Friendliness toward strangers:	☐☐☐☐☐
Ease of training:	☐☐☐☐
Watchdog ability:	☐☐☐☐
Protection ability:	☐
Grooming requirements:	☐☐☐
Cold tolerance:	☐☐
Heat tolerance:	☐☐☐

Weight:	7–13 lb
Height:	8.5–11.5"

Illustrated Standard

① Large, almond-shaped eyes
② Drop ears form a gentle fold and are slightly raised and moderately pointed
③ Topline straight with slight rise over croup
④ Tail set high and carried over the back; plumed
⑤ Compact feet

❑ **Color:** all colors or combination of colors, including white
❑ **DQ:** under 8.5" or over 11.5"; total absence of pigment on one or both eye rims; dudley nose; nose and lips other than black, except for solid brown on true chocolate dog; coat trimmed in any way except for neatening of feet

Health

- Major concerns: none
- Minor concerns: patellar luxation
- Occasionally seen: PRA, otitis externa, cataract
- Suggested tests: knee, eye
- Life span: 12–14 years

Form and Function

The Havanese is a small, sturdy, short-legged dog. Its unique gait is exceptionally lively and springy, accentuating the dog's happy nature. The coat is double, with both under and outer coat soft. The profuse outer coat is very long, reaching 6 to 8 inches in length, and ranges from straight to curly, with wavy preferred. The curly coat is allowed to cord. The expression is gentle.

Italian Greyhound

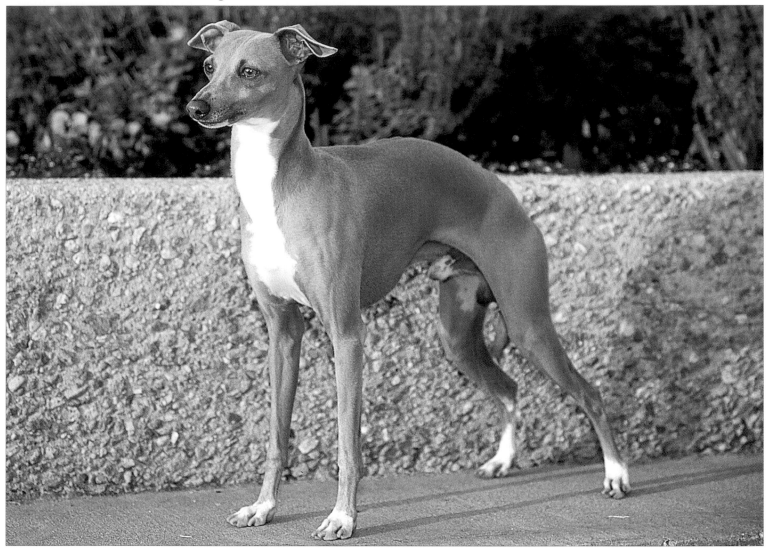

History

The Italian Greyhound has been around for
many centuries, but exactly how and when this
miniaturized Greyhound was developed has
been lost in time. Evidence of dogs resembling
the Italian Greyhound can be found in art dating
nearly 2000 years ago from Turkey, Greece, and
other areas around the Mediterranean. By the
Middle Ages, miniaturized Greyhounds could be found throughout
southern Europe, but they found special favor with Italian
courtiers. The breed came to England in the seventeenth century,
quickly becoming as popular with nobility there as they had been
in their Italian homeland. In 1820, the Italian Greyhound was one
of only two toy breeds mentioned in a book about dogs. The Italian
Greyhound continued to find favor, reaching its peak during the
reign of Queen Victoria. After that time, its numbers declined,
however, and the breed had dwindled to such an extent that it had
almost disappeared in England after World War II. One possible

AKC Ranking: 54
Family: Sighthound, Southern
 (sighthound)
Area of Origin: Italy
Date of Origin: Ancient times
Original Function: Lapdog
Today's Function: Companion
Other Name: Piccolo Levrieve Italiani

reason for its decline was a degradation in
quality because dogs were bred for tiny size,
often without regard to soundness and health.
Fortunately, Italian Greyhounds had come to
America in the late 1800s, and even though
their numbers were small, they were of high
quality. These dogs, along with other imports,
helped revive the breed in Europe. Since then,
the breed has risen gradually in popularity and is now enjoying a
second renaissance.

Temperament

A sighthound in a small package, the Italian Greyhound shares
its larger relatives' characteristics. It loves to run and chase.
It is extremely gentle and sensitive. Reserved, often timid, with
strangers, it is devoted to its family and is good with children,
other dogs, and pets. However, it can be easily injured by boisterous children and larger dogs.

Upkeep

The Italian Greyhound likes a daily romp outdoors, but it hates the cold. Its exercise needs are best met with a good walk on leash or even a rollicking game indoors. It also likes to stretch out and sprint in a fenced area. This breed cannot live outdoors. Care of the fine short hair is minimal, consisting only of occasional brushing to remove dead hair. Regular brushing of the teeth is important in this breed.

Health

- Major concerns: peridontal disease
- Minor concerns: epilepsy, leg fractures, patellar luxation, PRA
- Occasionally seen: none
- Suggested tests: knee, eye
- Life span: 12–15 years
- Note: The breed is susceptible to leg and tail fractures. It shares the sighthound sensitivity to anesthesia and barbituates.

Form and Function

Essentially a slender miniature Greyhound, the Italian Greyhound is exceptionally elegant and graceful. It embodies the same qualities that enable the full-sized Greyhound to run at top speed using the double-suspension gallop: a curvaceous outline with a slight arch over the loin and good rear angulation. Its gait is high stepping and free. The coat is short and glossy like satin.

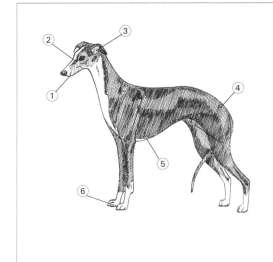

Illustrated Standard

1. Long, narrow head
2. Slight stop
3. Small folded ears
4. Back curved and drooping at hindquarters
5. Deep narrow chest
6. Hare feet

❑ **Color:** any color but brindle or black and tan
❑ **DQ:** brindle markings, tan markings in the areas normally found on black and tan dogs of other breeds

At a Glance

Energy level:	❑❑❑❑
Exercise requirements:	❑❑
Playfulness:	❑❑❑
Affection level:	❑❑❑❑❑
Friendliness toward dogs:	❑❑❑❑
Friendliness toward other pets:	❑❑❑❑
Friendliness toward strangers:	❑❑
Ease of training:	❑❑❑
Watchdog ability:	❑❑❑
Protection ability:	❑
Grooming requirements:	❑
Cold tolerance:	❑
Heat tolerance:	❑❑❑❑

Weight:	7–14 lb*
Height:	13–15″

Japanese Chin

History

Despite its name, the Japanese Chin is actually of ancient Chinese origin, probably sharing a close relationship with the Pekingese. Like the Pekingese, the Chin was kept by Chinese aristocracy, and some-times presented as a gift to visiting nobility. Different stories exist about how it arrived in Japan: Zen Buddhist teachers may have brought them some time after A.D. 520, a Korean prince may have taken some to Japan in A.D. 732, or a Chinese emperor may have presented a pair to a Japanese emperor about a thousand years ago. However it got there, it gained great favor with the Japanese Imperial family and was kept as a lapdog and ornament; some particularly small Chins were reportedly kept in hanging "bird" cages. Portuguese sailors first traded with Japan in the sixteenth century and may have been the first to bring Chins to Europe. The first official record of Chins coming to Europe was in 1853, however, when

AKC Ranking: 78
Family: Companion
Area of Origin: Japan
Date of Origin: Ancient times
Original Function: Lapdog
Today's Function: Companion
Other Name: Japanese Spaniel

Commodore Perry presented a pair from his trip to Japan to Queen Victoria. In the succeeding years, traders brought back many more Chins, selling them in Europe and America. The breed was recognized by the AKC in the late 1800s as the Japanese Spaniel. These early imports were larger than modern Chins, and it is possible that some crossing with English Toy Spaniels may have occurred to reduce size. World War I ended the steady supply of importations, but the breed had already gained a strong foothold. It maintains a modest popularity in America, but still enjoys its greatest popularity in Japan.

Temperament

The Japanese Chin is a devoted companion, relishing a warm lap as much as a boisterous game. It is sensitive and willing to please, tending to shadow its owner. It is a friend to all: strangers, dogs, and pets. Its playfulness and gentleness make it a good child's companion for equally gentle children. The breed has been described as almost cat-like, some even climb.

Upkeep

The Japanese Chin is lively but small enough that its exercise needs can be met with a short walk, romp, or game. This is not a breed that can live outside. It does not do well in hot humid weather. Some Chins tend to wheeze. The long coat needs combing twice weekly.

Health

- Major concerns: none
- Minor concerns: patellar luxation, KCS, entropion
- Occasionally seen: achondroplasia, epilepsy
- Suggested tests: knee, (eye)
- Life span: 12–14 years
- Note: The breed is sensitive to anesthesia and does not tolerate heat well. It is also prone to corneal abrasions.

Form and Function

Small, lively, and aristocratic, the Japanese Chin is a square-proportioned small dog. It has a bright inquisitive

expression, distinctly Oriental. A small amount of white shows in the inner corners of the eyes, imparting a look of astonishment. Its gait is stylish, lively, and light. The single coat is abundant, straight, and silky, tending to stand out from the body. The overall appearance is one of Oriental aristocracy.

At a Glance

Energy level:	❑❑❑
Exercise requirements:	❑
Playfulness:	❑❑❑❑
Affection level:	❑❑❑❑❑
Friendliness toward dogs:	❑❑❑❑
Friendliness toward other pets:	❑❑❑
Friendliness toward strangers:	❑❑❑❑❑
Ease of training:	❑❑❑
Watchdog ability:	❑❑❑❑❑
Protection ability:	❑
Grooming requirements:	❑❑❑
Cold tolerance:	❑❑
Heat tolerance:	❑❑

Weight:	4–7 lb*
Height:	8–11″

Maltese

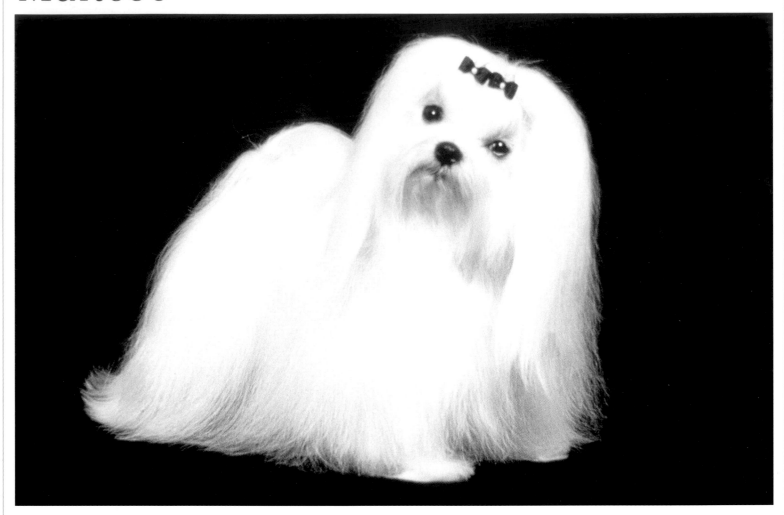

History

The Maltese is the most ancient of the
European toy breeds, and among the oldest of
all breeds. The island of Malta was an early
trading port, visited by Phoenician sailors by
1500 B.C. Maltese dogs are specifically mentioned in writings as early as 300 B.C. Greek
art includes dogs of Maltese type from the fifth
century on; there is evidence that they even
erected tombs to favored Maltese. Although the dogs were often
exported and subsequently widely distributed throughout Europe
and the Orient, the core population on Malta remained relatively
isolated from other dogs, resulting in this distinctive pure-breeding dog that bred true for centuries. Though the Maltese's hallmark is its long, silky, dazzling white hair, early Maltese came in
colors other than white. By the early fourteenth century, Maltese
had been brought to England, where they became the darlings of
upper-class ladies. Writers of the succeeding centuries continual-
ly commented upon their diminutive size. Still these little dogs
were never commonplace, and an 1830 painting entitled "The
Lion Dog from Malta—Last of His Race" suggests that the breed

AKC Ranking: 21
Family: Bichon, Companion, Terrier,
  Water Dog
Area of Origin: Malta
Date of Origin: Ancient times
Original Function: Lapdog
Today's Function: Companion
Other Name: Bichon Maltiase

may have been in danger of extinction. Soon
after, two Maltese were brought to England
from Manila. Although originally intended as
a gift for Queen Victoria, they passed into other
hands, and their offspring became the first
Maltese exhibited in England. At this time,
they were called Maltese Terriers, despite the
lack of terrier ancestry or characteristics.

In America, the first Maltese were shown
as Maltese Lion Dogs around 1877. The name lion dog probably
arose from the habit of dog fanciers, particularly those in
the Orient, of clipping the dogs to look like lions. The AKC recognized the breed as the Maltese in 1888. The Maltese slowly
increased in popularity, and now it ranks as one of the more
popular toys.

Temperament

Long a favorite lapdog, the gentle Maltese fills this role
admirably. It also has a wild side, and it loves to run and play.
Despite its innocent look, it is bold and feisty and may challenge
larger dogs. It is reserved with strangers. Some bark a lot.

Upkeep

The exercise requirements of the Maltese are easily met with indoor games, a romp in the yard, or a short walk on leash. Despite its coat, the Maltese is not an outdoor dog. The coat needs combing every one or two days; show coats may be "wrapped" for protection. The white coat may be difficult to keep clean in some areas. Pets may be clipped for easier care, but then an essential trait of the breed is lost.

Health

- Major concerns: none
- Minor concerns: patellar luxation, open fontanel, hypoglycemia, hydrocephalus, distichiasis, entropion
- Occasionally seen: deafness, white shaker-dog syndrome
- Suggested tests: knee, (eye)
- Life span: 12–14 years

Form and Function

Even though the breed is known for its coat, its body structure, facial expression, and overall carriage are essential components of the type. The Maltese is a diminutive dog with a compact, square body, covered all over with long, flat,

silky, white hair hanging almost to the ground. The expression is gentle yet alert. It is a vigorous dog, with a jaunty, smooth, flowing gait. The well-built Maltese seems to float over the ground when trotting.

At a Glance

Energy level:	❏❏❏
Exercise requirements:	❏
Playfulness:	❏❏❏
Affection level:	❏❏
Friendliness toward dogs:	❏❏
Friendliness toward other pets:	❏❏
Friendliness toward strangers:	❏
Ease of training:	❏❏
Watchdog ability:	❏❏❏❏
Protection ability:	❏
Grooming requirements:	❏❏
Cold tolerance:	❏❏
Heat tolerance:	❏

Weight:	under 7 lb, preferably 4–6 lb
Height:	9–10"

Toy Manchester Terrier

History

One of the preeminent dogs of England was the Black and Tan Terrier, a breed valued for its rat-killing prowess since the sixteenth century. Rat-killing dogs were valuable not only for ridding homes of vermin but also for the entertainment value of betting upon how many rats a dog could kill in an allotted time. Manchester, England, was populated by workers who looked to their rat-killing contests and dog-racing contests for entertainment. It was only natural that eventually a cross between the Black and Tan Terrier ratter and the Whippet racer would be made, and the result was the dog known since about 1860 as the Manchester Terrier. At times the Manchester Terrier was considered no different from its Black and Tan Terrier forebears, and it was not until 1923 that the name was officially changed back to Manchester Terrier. Other breeds have probably been intermin-

> AKC Ranking: 96
> Family: Terrier
> Area of Origin: England
> Date of Origin: about 1860
> Original Function: Hunting small
>   rodents
> Today's Function: Companion
> Other Name: English Toy Terrier,
>   Black and Tan Toy Terrier

gled with the Manchester during its development, most notably the Italian Greyhound. This may account for the breed's wide size range. An early standard of 1881 described the existence of a toy variety even then. The smaller dogs were in high demand, and breeders resorted to inbreeding to achieve even smaller specimens, which eventually led to exceedingly small frail dogs. Upon realizing the state of these dogs, breeders endeavored to breed a miniature, but not tiny, version. The result is the Toy Manchester Terrier. The AKC initially considered the Manchester and Toy Manchester separate but interbreeding breeds. In 1959, they were changed to be two interbreeding varieties of one breed. Besides size, the Toy Manchester differs from its larger counterpart in that cropped ears are not allowed. The Toy Manchester Terrier is also known as the English Toy Terrier.

At a Glance

Energy level:	☐☐☐☐
Exercise requirements:	☐
Playfulness:	☐☐☐☐
Affection level:	☐☐
Friendliness toward dogs:	☐
Friendliness toward other pets:	☐☐
Friendliness toward strangers:	☐
Ease of training:	☐
Watchdog ability:	☐☐☐☐☐
Protection ability:	☐
Grooming requirements:	☐
Cold tolerance:	☐
Heat tolerance:	☐☐☐

Weight:	under 12 lb (usually 6–8 lb)
Height:	10–12"

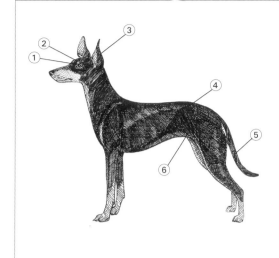

Illustrated Standard

① Small, almond-shaped eyes
② Head resembles a blunted wedge in profile and from front
③ Naturally erect ear
④ Slight arch over loin
⑤ Tapered tail carried in a slight upward curve
⑥ Tucked up abdomen

❏ **Color:** black and tan, with a black "thumbprint" patch on the front of each foreleg and "pencil marks" on the top of each toe
❏ **DQ:** cropped or cut ears, patch of white over ½" at its longest dimension, any color other than black and tan

Temperament

Although true to its terrier heritage when it comes to scrappiness and hunting instincts, the Toy Manchester is among the gentlest and most sensitive of breeds. It is playful with its family, yet reserved, sometimes even timid, with strangers. The Toy Manchester Terrier is inquisitive and may chase small pets.

Upkeep

This is not an outdoor breed. It enjoys a romp outdoors, but it hates the cold. Indoors, it appreciates a soft, warm bed. Coat care is minimal, consisting of occasional brushing to remove dead hair.

Health

- Major concerns: none
- Minor concerns: lens luxation, Legg–Perthes, vWD
- Occasionally seen: epilepsy
- Suggested tests: eye, DNA for vWD
- Life span: 14–16 years

Form and Function

The Toy Manchester Terrier is a miniature version of the standard Manchester. As such it is sleek, racy, and compact. It is slightly longer than it is tall, with a slightly arched topline. Its gait is free and effortless, not hackney. Its expression is keen and alert, and its coat is smooth and glossy.

Miniature Pinscher

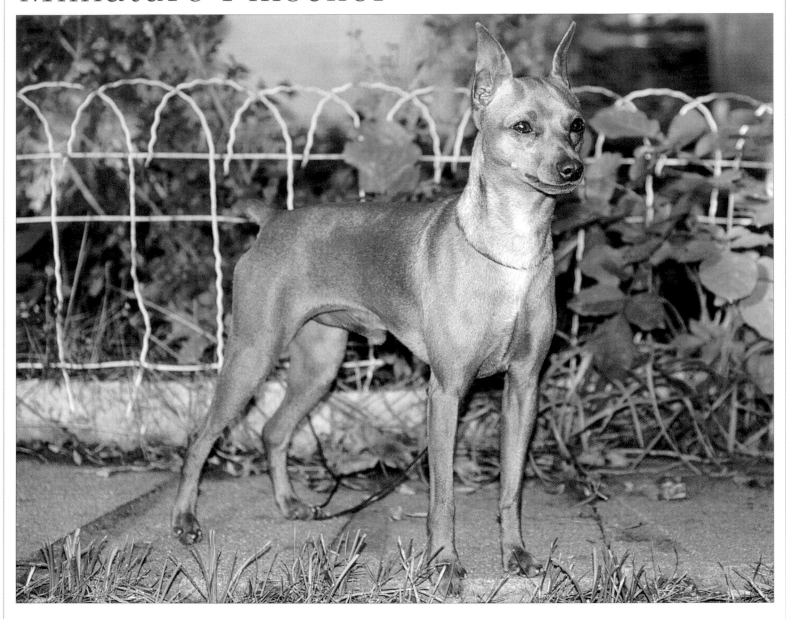

History

The Miniature Pinscher is not a miniature version of the Doberman Pinscher. In fact, the Min Pin is the older of the two breeds. Clues about the Miniature Pinscher's origin are scarce, but it is noteworthy that a cat-sized red dog resembling a Min Pin is depicted in a seventeenth century painting. By the nineteenth century, several paintings include dogs of distinct Min Pin type. These dogs probably resulted from crossing a small short-haired terrier (German Pinscher) with the Dachshund and Italian Greyhound. Many of the traits from these breeds can be seen in today's Min Pins: the strong body structure, feistiness, and black and tan coloration of the German Pinscher; the fearlessness and red coloration of the Dachshund; and the elegance,

AKC Ranking: 18
Family: Terrier, Pinscher
Area of Origin: Germany
Date of Origin: 1600s
Original Function: Small vermin
    hunting
Today's Function: Companion
Other Name: Reh Pinscher,
    Zwergpinscher

playfulness, and lithe movement of the Italian Greyhound. Yet the Min Pin is more than the sum of its parts; it is perhaps the world's most energetic breed! These little German spitfires were developed into a distinct breed, the "reh pinscher" in the early 1800s, so named because of their resemblance to the small red German roe (reh) deer. Pinscher simply means terrier. The emphasis in the late 1800s was on breeding the tiniest specimens, resulting in crippled ugly dogs. Fortunately, the trend was reversed, and by 1900, the emphasis had returned to elegance and soundness. The breed quickly became one of the most competitive and popular show dogs in pre-World War I Germany, but after the war, the breed experienced a plunge in numbers. Its future was left to those dogs that had been exported before the war. Its popularity continued to grow in America, and it received AKC recognition in 1929. Dubbed the king of toys, the Min Pin slowly accumulated admirers and is presently one of the more popular toy breeds in the United States.

Temperament

Among the most energetic of all breeds, the Min Pin is a perpetual motion machine. It is busy, inquisitive, playful, bold, and brash. It retains terrier-like traits and tends to be stubborn and independent. It can be scrappy with other dogs and may chase small animals. It is reserved with strangers.

Upkeep

The Min Pin needs lots of activity. Because of its small size, its exercise needs can be met indoors or out; regardless, it needs several play sessions every day. It enjoys a romp outdoors in a safe area, but it hates the cold. This is not a breed to live outdoors. Its coat is virtually carefree, requiring only occasional brushing to remove dead hair.

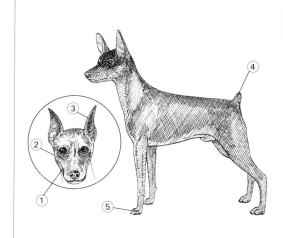

Illustrated Standard

① Narrow tapering head
② Strong muzzle
③ Erect ears, cropped or natural
④ Tail held erect and docked
⑤ Small cat feet

❑ **Color:** clear red, stag red, black and tan
❑ **DQ:** under 10" or over 12.5" in height, any color other than listed, thumbmark (patch of dark hair on the front of the foreleg between the foot and wrist), white anywhere exceeding ½" in its longest dimension

Health

- Major concerns: none
- Minor concerns: Legg–Perthes, patellar luxation
- Occasionally seen: PRA
- Suggested tests: knee, (eye)
- Life span: 12–14 years

Form and Function

The square-proportioned Min Pin has a compact, sturdy body with moderate tuck up and sort coupling. Its hallmark traits are its spirited animation, complete self-possession, and high-stepping hackney gait. It is upstanding and alert. The coat is smooth, hard, and short. It is among the most athletic of toy breeds.

At a Glance

Energy level:	☐☐☐☐☐
Exercise requirements:	☐☐
Playfulness:	☐☐☐☐☐
Affection level:	☐☐
Friendliness toward dogs:	☐☐
Friendliness toward other pets:	☐
Friendliness toward strangers:	☐
Ease of training:	☐
Watchdog ability:	☐☐☐☐☐
Protection ability:	☐
Grooming requirements:	☐
Cold tolerance:	☐
Heat tolerance:	☐☐☐

Weight:	8–10 lb*
Height:	10–12.5", with 11–11.5" preferred

Papillon

History

The name Papillon is French for butterfly, which the face and ears of this spritely little dog should resemble. The Papillon has its roots in the dwarf spaniels so popular throughout Europe from at least the sixteenth century. These little dogs were extremely popular with the nobility; as time went on, Spain and Italy became the centers of dwarf spaniel breeding and trading. The court of Louis XIV of France was particularly fond of these little dogs and imported many of them. At one time the Papillon was known as the Squirrel Spaniel because it carried its plumed tail over its back in the same way a squirrel does. These early dogs had drooping ears, but through some unknown event, some dogs sported erect ears. Both drop- and erect-eared Papillons could be found in the same litter. Even today both ear types are equally correct, although the erect-eared dog is much more popular. In America, the drop-eared Pap is known as the Phalene, which is French for moth, whereas in Europe it is called the Epagneul Nain or

AKC Ranking: 52
Family: Spitz, Spaniel, Companion
Area of Origin: France
Date of Origin: 1500s
Original Function: Lapdog
Today's Function: Companion
Other Name: Epagneul Nain (Phalene is also known as Continental Toy Spaniel)

Continental Toy Spaniel. By 1900, the Papillon was well represented at French dog shows and soon afterward was being shown in England and America. These earlier exhibits tended to be larger than those seen today, and were mostly solid colored, usually of some shade of red. Selective breeding has resulted in a smaller dog that is distinguished by its striking colors broken by patches of white. A symmetrically marked face with white blaze adds to the butterfly appearance. The Papillon has become one of the more popular toy dogs, functioning equally well as a loving pet, beautiful show dog, and adept obedience competitor.

Temperament

One of the most obedient and responsive of the toy breeds, the vivacious Papillon is also gentle, amiable, and playful. It is friendly toward strangers, other dogs, and pets and is very good with children. Some can be timid.

At a Glance

Energy level:	☐☐☐☐
Exercise requirements:	☐
Playfulness:	☐☐☐☐☐
Affection level:	☐☐☐☐☐
Friendliness toward dogs:	☐☐☐☐
Friendliness toward other pets:	☐☐☐☐
Friendliness toward strangers:	☐☐☐☐
Ease of training:	☐☐☐☐☐
Watchdog ability:	☐☐☐☐☐
Protection ability:	☐
Grooming requirements:	☐☐☐
Cold tolerance:	☐
Heat tolerance:	☐☐☐

Weight:	9–10 lb*
Height:	8–11″

Illustrated Standard

① Round eyes
② Small rounded head with fine muzzle
③ Ears erect or dropped
④ Long tail carried arched over body and covered with a long plume

❑ **Color:** white with patches of any color
❑ **DQ:** over 12″ in height, all white dog or dog with no white

Upkeep

The lively Papillon thrives on mental stimulation, and it enjoys a daily walk on leash as well as challenging games indoors or out. This is not a breed that can live outdoors. Its coat needs brushing twice weekly.

Health

• Major concerns: none
• Minor concerns: PRA, patellar luxation
• Occasionally seen: none
• Suggested tests: knee, eye
• Life span: 12–15 years

Form and Function

The Papillon is a small, dainty, elegant dog of fine-boned structure, slightly longer than it is tall. Its gait is quick, easy, and graceful. Its abundant coat is long, silky, straight, and flowing. Its hallmark characteristic, besides its friendly temperament and alert expression, is its butterfly ears.

Pekingese

History

The Pekingese owes its existence to the Lamaist form of Buddhism in China, in which the lion was an exalted symbol of Buddha, sometimes appearing in miniaturized form. The Foo dogs then in existence bore some resemblance to a lion and were carefully bred to accentuate this similarity. In fact, these dogs eventually came to be known as lion dogs. Extensive breeding programs fell under the auspices of palace eunuches, with no expense spared. At the height of their favor (during the T'ang dynasty from A.D. 700 to A.D. 1000) many of these lion dogs were literally treated as royalty, pampered by personal servants. Smaller Pekingese were called sleeve dogs because they could be carried in the large sleeves of their Chinese masters. In 1860, the imperial summer palace was looted by the British. Among their loot were five royal lion dogs, which were taken back to England. One was presented to Queen Victoria, and it, along with the other four, caused such interest among dog fanciers that there arose great demand for more of these dogs. Still, their numbers rose slowly, remaining for decades a dog only for the wealthiest of

AKC Ranking: 27
Family: Companion
Area of Origin: China
Date of Origin: Ancient times
Original Function: Lapdog
Today's Function: Companion
Other Name: Lion Dog, Peking
  Palasthund

owners. With time, the breed became more readily available and has since suffered from overpopularity. Today its main role is as a companion and show dog.

Temperament

The Pekingese is decidedly not a sissy lapdog. It is a courageous character that will not start a fight but will not back down from one. It tends to be aloof around strangers. It is extremely devoted to its family, but it is independent and not overly demonstrative. Its stubbornness is legendary. Although playful around family members, it may not be athletic or playful enough to satisfy many children.

Upkeep

The Pekingese enjoys a leisurely walk outdoors, but it is equally happy to romp inside. It can easily die of heat prostration. It must be kept in air conditioning in warm weather. It can spend time outside in cool weather, but it should sleep inside. It is an ideal apartment dog. The coat will mat unless combed at the very least weekly, preferably more often. The overnose wrinkle should be cleaned daily to avoid infection. The coat around the anus must be inspected daily for soiling. Pekingese tend to snore!

Health
- Major concerns: none
- Minor concerns: elongated soft palate, stenotic nares, KCS, patellar luxation, disticiasis, trichiasis, skin fold dermatitis
- Occasionally seen: urolithiasis
- Suggested tests: knee, (eye)
- Life span: 13–15 years
- Note: The breed is sensitive to anesthesia and does not tolerate heat well. It is also prone to corneal abrasions. Puppies must often be delivered by Caesarian.

Form and Function
The Pekingese is a compact dog with a pear shaped body, heavy forequarters and lighter hindquarters. It is slightly longer than it is tall, with a stocky, heavy build. Its image is lionlike. It should imply courage, boldness, and self-esteem rather than prettiness, daintiness, or delicacy. Its gait is dignified and unhurried, with a slight roll resulting from its wider,

Illustrated Standard
① Slightly undershot
② Nose positioned at a height between the eyes
③ Large, round eyes
④ Flat profile
⑤ Wrinkle extends over the bridge of the nose in an inverted V
⑥ Massive, broad, flat skull
⑦ Heart-shaped ears
⑧ Tail carried over back
⑨ Front feet large, flat, and turned slightly out

❏ **Color:** All colors and patterns are allowable
❏ **DQ:** weight over 14 lb

heavier forequarters. It has a thick undercoat, and its outer coat is long, coarse, straight, and stands off. It forms a mane around the shoulders.

The Pekingese must suggest its Chinese origins in its lionlike appearance, bold and direct character, and distinctive expression.

At a Glance

Energy level:	❏
Exercise requirements:	❏
Playfulness:	❏
Affection level:	❏
Friendliness toward dogs:	❏❏❏
Friendliness toward other pets:	❏❏❏❏
Friendliness toward strangers:	❏
Ease of training:	❏
Watchdog ability:	❏❏❏❏❏
Protection ability:	❏
Grooming requirements:	❏❏❏❏❏
Cold tolerance:	❏❏❏
Heat tolerance:	❏

Weight:	not to exceed 14 lb
Height:	6–9"*

Pomeranian

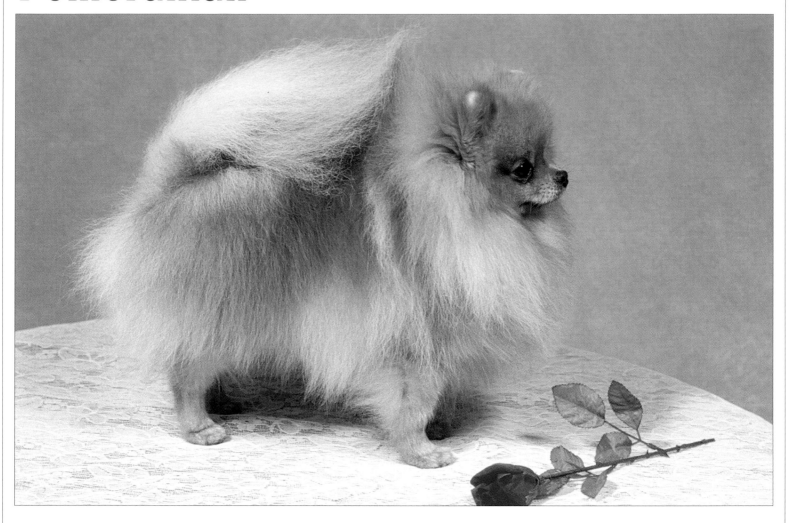

History

The smallest member of the spitz family, the
Pomeranian boasts tough sledding dog ancestors.
Exactly when it began to be bred down in size
is not known; nor is it known exactly where this
miniaturization took place, although Germany,
and specifically, Pomerania, is the most likely
locale. The breed's likely ancestor was the Deutscher Spitz.
Only when the breed was taken to England was it dubbed the
Pomeranian, but these early dogs were not the "Poms" known
today. They weighed as much as 30 pounds and were often
white. In fact, the Japanese Spitz closely resembles these early
Pomeranians and very likely descends from them. Although the
Pomeranian was recognized by the English Kennel Club in 1870,
it was not until Queen Victoria brought a Pomeranian from Italy
that its popularity grew. The queen's Pomeranians were rather
large gray dogs, and even then most fanciers preferred smaller,
more colorful specimens. By 1900, Poms had been recognized by
the AKC, and dogs were being shown in both England and America

AKC Ranking: 10
Family: Spitz, Northern (companion)
Area of Origin: Germany
Date of Origin: 1800s
Original Function: Companion
Today's Function: Companion
Other Name: None

in an array of colors. The Pomeranian has continued to be bred down in size; at the same time,
an emphasis on coat has led to its unsurpassed
"puff-ball" appearance. This miniature sled dog
always attracts admirers and is a very popular
pet and show dog.

Temperament

Bouncy, bold, and busy, the Pomeranian makes the most of every
day. It is curious, playful, self-confident (even cocky), and attentive,
ever ready for a game or adventure. It is reserved toward strangers.
Some can be aggressive toward other dogs. Some bark a lot.

Upkeep

The Pomeranian is active but diminutive, needing daily exercise
but able to meet its needs with indoor games or short walks.
Although it has a warm coat, it is too small and too family oriented to live as an outdoor dog. Its double coat needs brushing twice
weekly, more when shedding.

At a Glance

Energy level:	☐☐☐☐
Exercise requirements:	☐
Playfulness:	☐☐☐☐
Affection level:	☐
Friendliness toward dogs:	☐
Friendliness toward other pets:	☐☐☐
Friendliness toward strangers:	☐
Ease of training:	☐
Watchdog ability:	☐☐☐☐☐
Protection ability:	☐
Grooming requirements:	☐☐☐
Cold tolerance:	☐☐☐
Heat tolerance:	☐☐☐

Weight:	3–7 lb, preferably 4–5 lb
Height:	8–11"*

Illustrated Standard

① Short neck
② Almond-shaped eyes
③ Wedge-shaped head
④ Small, high-set, erect ears
⑤ Tail arched over back and carried flat
⑥ Compact feet

❏ **Color:** all colors and patterns allowed
❏ **DQ:** none

Health

• Major concerns: patellar luxation
• Minor concerns: open fontanel, hypoglycemia, shoulder luxation, PRA, entropion
• Occasionally seen: tracheal collapse, PDA
• Suggested tests: knee, eye, (cardiac)
• Life span: 12–16 years

Form and Function

The Pomeranian is a small, square-proportioned, miniature spitz with a cobby, rounded body. It shares the spitz characteristics of small ears, double coat, and curled tail. It has an alert, foxlike expression. Its gait is smooth and free with good reach and drive. The soft thick undercoat combined with the longer harsh outer coat, standing off from the body, combine to give the dog a unique puffy appearance. This look is further accentuated by the thick ruff and a head carriage that is naturally upgazing.

Toy Poodle

History

The Toy Poodle's history is described with Standard and Miniature Poodles in the Non-Sporting Group section.

Temperament

The pert and peppy Toy Poodle is one of the brightest and easiest breeds to train. It is alert, responsive, playful, lively, sensitive, and eager to please. It is devoted to its family. Some can be reserved with strangers, some may bark a lot.

Upkeep

Poodles need a lot of interaction with people. They also need mental and physical exercise. The Toy Poodle's exercise needs can be met with a short walk or even indoor games. This is not a breed that should ever live outside, although it enjoys access to a yard.

AKC Ranking: 5
Family: Water Dog, Companion
Area of Origin: Central Europe
Date of Origin: 1500s
Original Function: Lapdog
Today's Function: Companion
Other Name: Caniche

Its coat should be brushed every day or two. Poodle hair, when shed, does not fall out but becomes caught in the surrounding hair, which can cause matting if not removed. Clipping should be done at least four times a year, with the face and feet clipped monthly. Although most Poodles are professionally groomed, owners can learn to groom their own dog.

Health

- Major concerns: PRA, patellar luxation, Legg–Perthes, epilepsy
- Minor concerns: trichiasis, entropion, lacrimal duct atresia, cataract
- Occasionally seen: urolithiasis, intervertebral disc degeneration
- Suggested tests: eye, knee, hip
- Life span: 12–14 years

At a Glance

Energy level:	☐☐☐☐
Exercise requirements:	☐☐
Playfulness:	☐☐☐☐☐
Affection level:	☐☐☐☐
Friendliness toward dogs:	☐☐☐
Friendliness toward other pets:	☐☐☐
Friendliness toward strangers:	☐☐☐☐
Ease of training:	☐☐☐☐☐
Watchdog ability:	☐☐☐☐☐
Protection ability:	☐
Grooming requirements:	☐☐☐☐☐
Cold tolerance:	☐☐
Heat tolerance:	☐☐☐

Weight:	4–8 lb*
Height:	not to exceed 10"

Illustrated Standard

① Long, fine, chiseled muzzle
② Slight but definite stop
③ Oval eyes
④ Tail straight and carried up; docked
⑤ Level topline
⑥ Small oval feet

❏ **Color:** any solid color
❏ **DQ:** over 10" in height, a dog in any but one of the specified clips, a dog not a solid color

Form and Function

The Poodle is a square, proportioned dog with proud carriage and elegant appearance. It should move with a light, springy, effortless stride. The Poodle stems from working retriever stock, and its conformation should reflect its athletic background. The coat is curly, harsh, and dense. The traditional clips stem from the function of the coat in protecting and insulating the dog's joints and chest.

Pug

History

The Pug has been known by many names: Mopshond in Holland (which refers to its grumbling tendencies); Mops in Germany, and Dutch or Chinese Pug in England. The word *Pug* is derived either from the Latin *pugnus* meaning fist, as the head may have resembled a clenched fist, or from the marmoset "Pug" monkeys that were popular pets in the eighteenth century and that the Pug dogs somewhat resemble. Whatever the name, one thing is true: the Pug's official motto "Multum in Parvo" (a lot in a little) fits it exactly. The Pug is somewhat of an exception in the Toy Group because it is perhaps the only one to be descended from mastiff forebears. Although its exact ancestry has been lost in antiquity, the Pug retains many mastiff characteristics. This is an ancient breed, one of several miniaturized in the Orient, where it was a favorite pet of Buddhist monasteries in Tibet many centuries ago. In China, the facial wrinkles were an essential breed feature, most notably the "prince mark," or vertical wrinkle on the forehead, which bore a resemblance to the Chinese character for "prince." Pugs probably came to Holland by way of the Dutch East India

AKC Ranking: 19
Family: Companion, Mastiff (Bulldog)
Area of Origin: China
Date of Origin: Ancient times
Original Function: Lapdog
Today's Function: Companion
Other Name: Mops, Carlin

Trading Company. Here they became quite popular and were recognized as the official dog of the House of Orange after one saved the life of Prince William by sounding an alarm at the approach of Spanish soldiers in 1572. By 1790, the Pug could be found in France; Napoleon's wife Josephine used her Pug to carry messages to Napoleon when she was imprisoned. Pugs were first brought to England during Victorian times and became incredibly popular with the wealthy, displacing the King Charles Spaniel as the favored royal breed. Pugs of Victorian England usually had cropped ears, further accentuating their wrinkled faces. Several Pugs were brought to England from China in 1886. A year earlier, the breed had been recognized by the AKC. Since that time, it has remained popular as both a pet and show dog.

Temperament

A delightful blend of dignity and comedy, the Pug is an amiable, playful, and confident companion. It can be stubborn and headstrong, but it is pleasant and generally willing to please. It loves to cavort and show off.

Upkeep

The Pug needs daily exercise, either in the form of a lively game or a moderate walk on leash. It does not do well in heat and humidity and should not be kept outdoors. It needs minimal coat care but daily cleaning of facial wrinkles. Its smooth coat needs only occasional brushing to remove dead hairs; however, the wrinkles need regular cleaning and drying to prevent skin infections. The Pug wheezes and snores.

Health

- Major concerns: none
- Minor concerns: elongated palette, stenotic nares, patellar luxation, Legg–Perthes, entropion
- Occasionally seen: epilepsy
- Suggested tests: (eye)
- Life span: 12–15 years
- Note: Skin fold dermatitis occurs if wrinkles are not regularly cleaned. The Pug cannot tolerate heat and is sensitive to anesthesia. It is prone to corneal abrasion and obesity.

Illustrated Standard

1. Slightly undershot
2. Short, square muzzle
3. Large, prominent eyes
4. Massive, round head
5. Thin, small ears, either rose or button
6. Tail curled as tightly as possible over hip; double curl preferred

❏ **Color:** silver, apricot-fawn, or black, with black muzzle or mask, ears, cheek moles, and trace down back
❏ **DQ:** none

Form and Function

Square-proportioned, compact and of a cobby build, the Pug is a large dog in a little space. The gait is strong and jaunty, but with a slight roll of the hindquarters. The distinctive expression is soft and solicitous. The forehead has large, deep wrinkles. The coat is fine, smooth, and short.

At a Glance

Energy level:	❏❏❏
Exercise requirements:	❏❏
Playfulness:	❏❏❏❏
Affection level:	❏❏❏❏
Friendliness toward dogs:	❏❏❏
Friendliness toward other pets:	❏❏❏
Friendliness toward strangers:	❏❏
Ease of training:	❏❏❏
Watchdog ability:	❏❏❏❏❏
Protection ability:	❏
Grooming requirements:	❏❏
Cold tolerance:	❏❏❏
Heat tolerance:	❏

Weight:	14–18 lb
Height:	10–11"*

Shih Tzu

History

The Shih Tzu (or more properly, Shih Tzu Kou) means Lion Dog, designating the breed as one of the most esteemed animals in China because of its association with Buddhism. Even though the Shih Tzu is most often associated with China, it probably originated in Tibet as early as the seventeenth century, where it enjoyed status as a holy dog. The Shih Tzu as it is known today developed most distinctively in China during the reign of the Dowager Empress Cixi (Tz'u-shi, 1861–1908). The Shih Tzu and Pekingese share similar histories; however, the Shih Tzu can usually be differentiated from the Pekingese in Chinese art by the presence of bumps on the tops of the head, denoting a topknot, or pien-ji. The Shih Tzu was a favored house pet during the Ming dynasty and was highly prized by the royal family. When the British looted the Imperial Palace,

AKC Ranking: 11
Family: Companion, Herding
Area of Origin: China
Date of Origin: 1800s
Original Function: Lapdog
Today's Function: Companion
Other Name: Chrysanthemum Dog

most of the dogs were lost, and the breed suffered a great setback. The Shih Tzu was first exhibited in China as the Lhassa Terrier or Tibetan Poodle. In 1935, it was exhibited as the Lhassa Lion Dog; by that time, it was becoming very popular. A similar state of confusion existed in England, where the Lhasa Apso and Shih Tzu were both lumped together as the Apso (meaning shaggy). In 1934, soon after the Apso was first shown, it was divided into two separate breeds, with the smaller, wider-skulled, shorter-nosed dogs from Peking dubbed Shih Tzu, their colloquial Chinese name. In 1952 a single Pekingese cross was authorized to improve certain points, but such crosses have never again been permitted. In the United States, the breed began to become extremely popular in the 1960s, leading to AKC recognition in 1969. Its popularity has continued to grow, and it is one of the most popular toys.

Temperament

The spunky but sweet Shih Tzu is both a gentle lapdog and a vivacious companion. It has an upbeat attitude and loves to play and romp. It is affectionate to its family and good with children. It is surprisingly tough and does have a stubborn streak.

Upkeep

Despite its small size, the Shih Tzu needs daily exercise. Because of its small size, it can meet its requirements with vigorous indoor games or short frolics outside or with short walks on leash. It does not do well in hot humid weather, and it should never be expected to live outdoors. Its luxurious coat needs brushing or combing every other day; puppies should be taught to accept grooming from a young age. Pets may be clipped.

Health

- Major concerns: none
- Minor concerns: renal cortical hypoplasia, entropion, trichiasis, PRA, KCS, CHD, otitis externa, portacaval shunt, inguinal hernias

- Occasionally seen: vWD
- Suggested tests: eye
- Life span: 11–14 years

Form and Function

Compact, yet slightly longer than it is tall, the Shih Tzu hides a sturdy body beneath its mantle of luxurious hair. It has a smooth, effortless stride with good reach and drive. Even though its function is that of companion, it should nonetheless be structurally sound. Its expression is warm, sweet, and wide-eyed, imparting the impression of trust and friendliness. The long, dense coat is double and fairly straight.

At a Glance

Energy level:	❏❏❏
Exercise requirements:	❏
Playfulness:	❏❏❏❏
Affection level:	❏❏❏❏
Friendliness toward dogs:	❏❏❏❏
Friendliness toward other pets:	❏❏❏❏
Friendliness toward strangers:	❏❏❏❏
Ease of training:	❏❏
Watchdog ability:	❏❏❏
Protection ability:	❏
Grooming requirements:	❏❏❏❏
Cold tolerance:	❏❏
Heat tolerance:	❏

Weight:	9–16 lb
Height:	8–11" (ideally, 9–10.5")

Silky Terrier

History

In the late 1800s, Yorkshire Terriers were brought to Australia from England. These dogs had striking steel blue and tan coat coloration and were bred with the native blue and tan Australian Terriers in an effort to improve the latter's coat color while retaining its more robust conformation. Both the Yorkshire Terrier and the Australian Terrier were rather recent developments from crosses of a number of other terrier breeds. Some of the descendents from these crosses were shown as Yorkshire Terriers and some as Australian Terriers. A few, however, were exhibited under a new name, Silky Terriers, because it was felt that they were the beginning of a separate breed, intermediate in size and coat length between its parental stock. Interbreeding these Silkies did, in fact, produce a true breeding strain within a short time. Because the breed was

AKC Ranking: 64
Family: Terrier
Area of Origin: Australia
Date of Origin: Late 1800s
Original Function: Companion, small
    vermin hunting
Today's Function: Earthdog trials
Other Name: Sydney Silky, Australian
    Silky Terrier

developed in two separate areas of Australia, separate breed standards were drawn up from each area in 1906 and 1910, with weight being the major disagreement. In 1926, a revised standard encompassing all areas was accepted, with accepted weights being somewhat of a compromise. The breed was popularly known as the Sydney Silky Terrier in Australia until it was changed to Australian Silky Terrier in 1955. In America, the name was changed to Silky Terrier in 1955, just prior to its recognition by the AKC. Although not a rare breed, the Silky Terrier has been somewhat slow to attract admirers and is only moderately popular.

Temperament

The Silky Terrier is no mellow lapdog. It is bold, feisty, inquisitive, and playful, ever ready for action—a terrier at heart. It can be aggressive toward other dogs or pets. It is clever, but tends to be stubborn, and can be mischievous. It tends to bark a lot.

Upkeep

This is an active breed requiring slightly more exercise than most toys. It enjoys a moderate walk on leash, but it especially likes the chance to nose around on its own in a safe area. Much of its exercise requirements can be met with vigorous games in the yard, or even house. Despite its hardiness, it is not a breed for outdoor living. Its coat needs brushing or combing every other day.

Health

- Major concerns: none
- Minor concerns: intervertebral disc disease, elbow dysplasia, patellar luxation, Legg–Perthes
- Occasionally seen: diabetes, epilepsy, tracheal collapse
- Suggested tests: elbow, knee
- Life span: 11–14 years

Form and Function

The Silky Terrier is a miniature version of a working terrier, and as such retains the

Illustrated Standard

① Small, almond-shaped eyes
② Flat skull with shallow stop
③ Small, V-shaped, erect ears
④ Docked tail carried high
⑤ Small cat feet

❏ **Color:** blue and tan
❏ **DQ:** none

essential features of a vermin hunter. It is somewhat longer than tall, and though of refined bone, it should nonetheless have sufficient strength and substance to suggest that it could kill small rodents.

The gait is free and light-footed; the expression is piercingly keen. The straight, single coat is silky and glossy, following the body outline rather than falling to the floor.

At a Glance

Energy level:	❏❏❏◻
Exercise requirements:	❏❏
Playfulness:	❏❏❏◻
Affection level:	❏❏❏
Friendliness toward dogs:	❏❏❏
Friendliness toward other pets:	❏❏❏
Friendliness toward strangers:	❏❏❏
Ease of training:	❏❏❏
Watchdog ability:	❏❏❏❏❏
Protection ability:	❏
Grooming requirements:	❏❏❏
Cold tolerance:	❏❏❏
Heat tolerance:	❏❏❏

Weight:	8–11 lb*
Height:	9–10"

Yorkshire Terrier

History

The Yorkshire Terrier doesn't look like a product of the working class, nor does it look like a ratter, but it is both. In fact, the Yorkshire area of England is known for producing fine animals, and it is thought that the Yorkie was no accident but rather the result of purposeful crosses between a variety of terriers, probably including the Waterside Terrier, Clydesdale Terrier, Paisley Terrier, rough-coated English Black and Tan Terrier, and perhaps even the Skye Terrier, Dandie Dinmont Terrier, and Maltese. The Waterside Terrier was one of its major progenitors; these were small blue-gray dogs with fairly long hair, usually weighing around 10 pounds, brought from Scotland by weavers. Because of its modest roots, the Yorkshire Terrier was initially looked down upon by the wealthier

AKC Ranking: 9
Family: Terrier
Area of Origin: England
Date of Origin: 1800s
Original Function: Small vermin
  hunting
Today's Function: Companion
Other Name: None

dog fanciers. Even the most snobbish could not deny the breed's obvious beauty, however, and in short order, Yorkies were gracing show rings and the laps of wealthy mistresses. By 1880, Yorkies had come to America, but the breed varied so much in size that there was great confusion concerning how big a Yorkshire Terrier should be. Many of these early Yorkies weighed between 12 and 14 pounds. By 1900, fanciers on both sides of the Atlantic had decided that the small size was preferable and made a concerted effort to breed a smaller Yorkie with even longer coat. They were successful, and the modern Yorkshire Terrier is one of the smaller and most luxuriously coated dogs in existence. These traits, along with its terrier heritage, have placed it as a consistent favorite with pet owners and show fanciers alike.

Temperament

The Yorkshire Terrier seems oblivious of its small size, ever eager for adventure and trouble. It is busy, inquisitive, bold, stubborn, and can be aggressive to strange dogs and small animals—in other words, it is true to its terrier heritage. Although some tend to bark a lot, it can easily be taught not to do so.

Upkeep

Yorkies tend to exercise themselves within the home, but they also need to have interaction in the form of games. They appreciate a short walk outdoors on leash and enjoy the chance to explore a safe area. This is definitely not a dog that can live outdoors. The long coat needs brushing or combing every day or two.

Health

- Major concerns: portacaval shunt, tracheal collapse, Leggs–Perthes
- Minor concerns. patellar luxation
- Occasionally seen: PRA
- Suggested tests: liver ultrasound, (knee), (eye)
- Life span: 14–16 years

Illustrated Standard

1. Medium-sized eyes
2. Small, V-shaped ears, carried erect
3. Small head, rather flat on top
4. Level topline
5. Tail docked to a medium length and carried slightly higher than the level of back
6. Round feet

❏ **Color:** blue and tan. Yorkshire Terriers are born black, gradually attaining their blue and tan coloration as they mature.
❏ **DQ:** none

Form and Function

The Yorkie's terrier heritage can be seen in its sharp, intelligent expression, confident carriage, and compact body. It is a diminutive breed, however, now more noted for its long, silky hair, which should be fine, glossy, and perfectly straight. Color is a hallmark of this breed, with the blue a dark steel blue and the tan a clear tan.

At a Glance

Energy level:	❏❏❏
Exercise requirements:	❏
Playfulness:	❏❏❏
Affection level:	❏❏
Friendliness toward dogs:	❏❏
Friendliness toward other pets:	❏❏
Friendliness toward strangers:	❏❏❏
Ease of training:	❏❏
Watchdog ability:	❏❏❏❏❏
Protection ability:	❏
Grooming requirements:	❏❏❏
Cold tolerance:	❏❏
Heat tolerance:	❏❏❏

Weight:	not to exceed 7 lb
Height:	8–9″*

The Non-Sporting Group

The Non-Sporting Group is the most diverse of all groups, sometimes considered a catch-all for breeds that defy categorization elsewhere or that no longer have a tenable function. Some prefer to call it the Companion Group because these dogs tend to have in common at least a recent background of being bred solely for companionship purposes. The background of these dogs is so varied, however, that it would be unrealistic to classify them as generally better companions than any other group. Each breed must be evaluated on its own merits in this group.

American Eskimo Dog

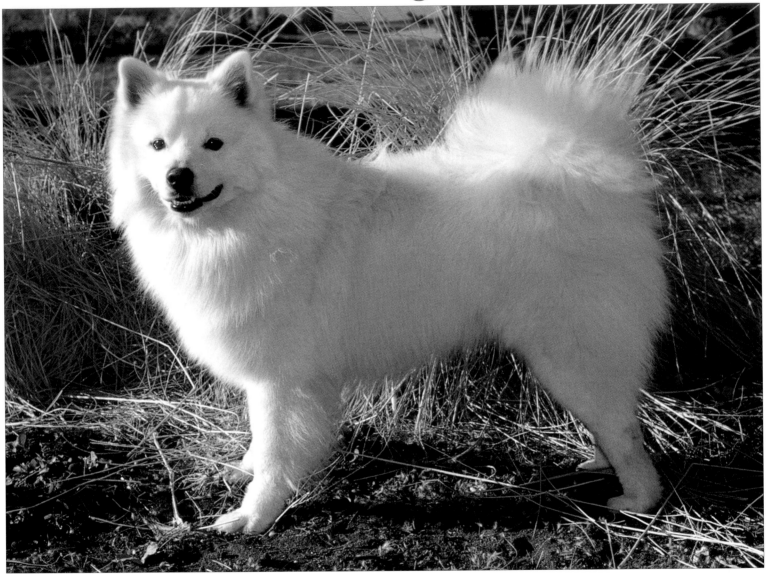

History

As the prototypical spitz, the Eskie (as it is often called) is just as often simply called spitz by pet owners. In fact, the American Eskimo Dog descended from one of the varieties of spitz developed in Germany, with influences from other spitz breeds such as the Keeshond, Pomeranian, and Volpino Italiano. Ironically, it was the success of these other breeds that held the Eskie back. Although the Keeshond originally came in several colors, when it was decided to accept only gray specimens, the white Keeshonden were suddenly excluded. When the Pomeranian standard was drawn up to exclude dogs over 8 pounds, larger dogs were excluded as Pomeranians. Thus, by the early 1900s, there was two groups of medium-sized white dogs that, although pure-breds, were excluded from their breeds. Their fate is unknown, but it is likely that they became pets of the working

AKC Ranking: 94
Family: Spitz, Northern (companion)
Area of Origin: United States
Date of Origin: early 1900s
Original Function: Companion, performer
Today's Function: Companion
Other Name: None

people. When European workers came to America, they brought these dogs with them. The turning point came in the 1920s, when the American Spitz (as it had come to be called) became a favorite of circus performers. Spectators often left the circus with a new purchase and family member—an offspring of one of the dazzling performers. Many present-day Eskies can be traced back to their circus ancestors. After World War I, the breed's name was changed to American Eskimos, to remove any Germanic sound from the name. Most Eskies were kept as pets and farm dogs. A few families registered their dogs with the United Kennel Club, but it wasn't until 1994 that the AKC recognized the breed. Despite its acceptance into the AKC world of show dogs, the Eskie remains a dog of the people, far more popular as a pet than as a competitor.

Temperament

The American Eskimo is bright, eager to please, lively, and fun loving—in short, an enjoyable and generally obedient companion. True to its spitz heritage, it is independent and tenacious and loves to run, especially in cold weather. But it is among the most biddable of spitz breeds, and it is calm and well-mannered inside. It is good with children, other dogs, and pets and is generally outgoing to everyone.

Upkeep

The Eskie is energetic and needs a good workout every day. The extent of the workout depends on the size of the dog, with the larger Eskies needing a good jog or long walk and the smaller Eskies needing only a vigorous game in the yard or short walk. The larger Eskies can live outdoors in temperate or cool climates, but this breed is so attuned to its family that it does better indoors. The double coat needs brushing and combing twice weekly, more often when shedding.

Illustrated Standard

1. Black lips, nose, and eye rims
2. Softly wedge-shaped head
3. Erect, triangular ears
4. Lionlike ruff
5. Compact body
6. Oval feet

❑ **Color:** white, or white with biscuit cream
❑ **DQ:** any color other than white or biscuit cream, blue eyes, height under 9" or over 19"

Health

- Major concerns: none
- Minor concerns: patellar luxation
- Occasionally seen: none
- Suggested tests: (knee)
- Life span: 12–14 years

Form and Function

The Eskie is built along classic Nordic lines, a form that has proved effective at pulling heavy loads through snow and ice. It is compactly built, slightly longer than tall. The stand-off, double coat resists soaking and provides insulation against the cold. The small thick ears are also cold resistant. The breed's smaller size has moved it from the realm of sled dog, but it remains a sled dog in miniature. Its trot is agile and bold. The expression is keen and alert.

At a Glance

Energy level:	▢▢▢
Exercise requirements:	▢▢▢
Playfulness:	▢▢▢▢
Affection level:	▢▢▢
Friendliness toward dogs:	▢▢▢
Friendliness toward other pets:	▢▢▢▢
Friendliness toward strangers:	▢▢▢
Ease of training:	▢▢▢▢
Watchdog ability:	▢▢▢▢▢
Protection ability:	▢
Grooming requirements:	▢▢▢
Cold tolerance:	▢▢▢▢
Heat tolerance:	▢

Weight:	Standard: 20–40 lb*
	Miniature: 11–20 lb*
	Toy: 6–10 lb*
Height:	Standard: 15–19"
	Miniature: 12–15"
	Toy: 9–12"

Bichon Frise

History

The Bichon Frise has its roots in the Mediterranean, originally produced by crossing the Barbet (a large water dog) with small white lapdogs. This cross eventually produced a family of dogs known as barbichons, which was later shortened to bichons. The bichons were divided into four types: the Bichon Maltaise, Bolognese, Havanese, and Teneriffe. The Teneriffe, which was to later become the Bichon Frise, developed on the Canary Island of Teneriffe, probably having been taken there by Spanish seafarers in ancient times. In the fourteenth century, Italian sailors brought specimens back from the island to the continent, where they quickly became favored pets of the upper class. Following a series of French invasions of Italy in the 1500s, the little dogs were adopted by the French. They were special pets of Francis I and his successor, Henry III. They also enjoyed popularity in Spain, but for some reason, the breed's popularity waned throughout Europe. It did experience a brief resurgence during the reign of Napoleon III in the early

AKC Ranking: 28
Family: Bichon, Companion, Water Dog
Area of Origin: France
Date of Origin: Ancient times
Original Function: Companion, performer
Today's Function: Companion
Other Name: Tenerife Dog, Bichon Tenerife, Bichon a poil Frise

nineteenth century, but once again it quickly faded from favor. This began a new chapter in the Bichon's history, as it sank from court favorite to common street dog. The Bichon survived, however, because of its propensity for performing tricks, and it teamed with peddlers and organ grinders to entertain passerby or fair-goers for money. With the advent of World War I, the little dogs were nearly lost. A few dogs were brought back home by soldiers, but no real effort to save the breed was made until a few French breeders began an earnest effort to establish the breed. In 1933, the name officially became Bichon a poil Frise (Bichon of the curly coat). The breed was once again threatened by World War II, and it was not until it came to America in the 1950s that its future became more secure. Even then, the Bichon Frise did not catch on until it received a new hair cut and greater publicity in the 1960s. The breed suddenly caught the attention of fanciers and was recognized by the AKC in 1971.

Temperament

Perky, bouncy, and playful, the Bichon Frise's happy-go-lucky outlook endears it to all. It is friendly toward strangers and other dogs and pets, and it is very good with children. It is sensitive, responsive, and affectionate, as eager to cuddle as it is to play. It can bark a lot.

Upkeep

Although small, the Bichon is an active dog and needs daily exercise. Its needs can be met with a vigorous indoor game or, better, a romp in the yard or a short walk on leash. The white powderpuff coat needs brushing and combing every other day, plus scissoring and trimming every two months. It doesn't shed, but the loose hairs become entangled in the coat and can mat. It may be difficult to keep white in some areas. This is not a dog that should live outdoors.

Health

- Major concerns: patellar luxation
- Minor concerns: tooth loss, cataract
- Occasionally seen: none
- Suggested tests: knee, eye
- Life span: 12–15 years

At a Glance

Energy level:	☐☐☐☐
Exercise requirements:	☐☐
Playfulness:	☐☐☐☐☐
Affection level:	☐☐☐☐☐
Friendliness toward dogs:	☐☐☐☐
Friendliness toward other pets:	☐☐☐☐
Friendliness toward strangers:	☐☐☐☐☐
Ease of training:	☐☐☐☐
Watchdog ability:	☐☐☐☐
Protection ability:	☐
Grooming requirements:	☐☐☐☐☐
Cold tolerance:	☐☐☐
Heat tolerance:	☐☐☐

Weight:	7–12 lb*
Height:	9.5–11.5″

Illustrated Standard

1. Round, dark eyes
2. Drop ears
3. Plumed tail curved over back
4. Moderate tuck-up
5. Round feet

❏ **Color:** white, may have cream shadings
❏ **DQ:** none

Form and Function

The striking powder-puff appearance of the Bichon derives from its double coat, with a soft dense undercoat and coarser, curly outercoat, causing the coat to stand off the body and even spring back when patted. It is a merry, agile breed, longer than it is tall, with an effortless trot. Its looks combined with its fitness enabled it to earn its living as a street performer. Its soft, inquisitive expression enabled it to worm its way into many hearts and laps.

Boston Terrier

History

Unlike most breeds, the origin of the Boston Terrier is well documented. Around 1865, the coachmen employed by the wealthy people of Boston began to interbreed some of their employers' fine dogs. One of these crosses, between an English Terrier and a Bulldog, resulted in a dog named Hooper's Judge. Although Judge weighed over 30 pounds, he was bred to a smaller female, and their son was in turn bred to another smaller female. Their progeny, probably interbred with one or more French Bulldogs, provided the foundation for the Boston Terrier. By 1889, the breed had become sufficiently popular in Boston that fanciers formed the American Bull Terrier Club, but this proposed name for the breed was not well received by Bull Terrier fanciers. The breed's nickname, roundheads, was similarly inappropriate. Shortly after, the breed was named the Boston Terrier, after its birthplace. The Boston's rise from nonexistence to AKC recognition was meteoric by modern standards, as the breed was recognized by the AKC in 1893, less than 20 years after the breed was born. Breeders continued to seek greater consistency. In early years, color and markings were not particularly important, but by the early 1900s,

AKC Ranking: 20
Family: Terrier, Companion, Mastiff (Bulldog)
Area of Origin: United States
Date of Origin: 1800s
Original Function: Ratting, companion
Today's Function: Companion
Other Name: None

the breed's distinctive markings had become an essential breed feature. The handsome little Boston Terrier quickly gained favor throughout America, ranking as one of the most popular breeds in the early to middle 1900s and retaining great popularity today.

Temperament

The Boston is devoted and sensitive to its owner's wishes and moods. It is well-mannered indoors but saucy and playful (especially enjoying ball chasing) whenever the chance arises. Somewhat stubborn, it is nonetheless clever and learns readily. It is reserved with strangers, and some may be aggressive toward strange dogs. Some bark a lot.

Upkeep

This is a lively dog that needs daily exercise and interaction with its people. It loves games, and most of its exercise requirements can be met with a romp in the yard or a short walk on leash. It cannot live outdoors. Some Bostons wheeze and snore, and many don't tolerate heat well. The coat requires only minimal care, an occasional brushing to remove dead hairs.

At a Glance

Energy level:	▢▢▢
Exercise requirements:	▢
Playfulness:	▢▢▢
Affection level:	▢▢▢
Friendliness toward dogs:	▢▢▢
Friendliness toward other pets:	▢▢▢▢
Friendliness toward strangers:	▢▢▢
Ease of training:	▢▢▢
Watchdog ability:	▢▢▢▢▢
Protection ability:	▢
Grooming requirements:	▢
Cold tolerance:	▢
Heat tolerance:	▢

Weight:	10–25 lb* (25 lb maximum)
Height:	15–17″*

Health

- Major concerns: none
- Minor concerns: cataract, PDA, patellar luxation, stenotic nares
- Occasionally seen: deafness, hydrocephalus, esophageal achalasia, distichiasis, persistent right aortic arch
- Suggested tests: none
- Life span: 10–14 years
- Note: This breed does not tolerate the heat and is sensitive to anesthesia. It is prone to corneal abrasions. Caesarian deliveries are commonly needed.

Form and Function

The Boston Terrier is a compactly built, square-proportioned, short-backed, clean-cut dog. It should convey the impression of determination, strength, sturdiness, liveliness, and style, with a graceful carriage. It retains many of the attributes of its Bulldog ancestors, but in a clean-cut package that makes a handy house companion. Its short fine coat, with distinctive markings, adds to its dapper appearance.

Illustrated Standard

1. Alert kind expression
2. Large, round eyes
3. Abrupt brow
4. Square, wrinkle-free skull
5. Small, erect ears, natural or cropped
6. Short straight or screw tail carried below level of back
7. Small round feet

- **Color:** brindle, seal, or black with white markings on muzzle, between eyes, and forechest, and possibly white collar and lower legs
- **DQ:** blue eyes, dudley nose, docked tail, liver or gray, lack of required white areas

Bulldog

History

With the most distinctive mug in dogdom, the Bulldog has an equally distinctive history. The Bulldog's origin lies in the cruel sport of bull baiting, which originated in England around the thirteenth century. The dog's purpose was to attack and madden the bull by grabbing it, usually by the nose, and not releasing its grip. Not only was this considered entertainment, but it also was believed that a bull's meat was tastier if the bull was baited before being butchered. Some Bulldogs were also set against bears for bear baiting, purely for entertainment. Bulldog owners set great store by their dog's ferocity and, especially, fortitude in the face of pain—so much so that horrifying stories exist of owners proving their dog's toughness by demonstrating that it would hang onto the bull despite being tortured or mutilated by the owner. In 1835, bull baiting was outlawed, and a new phase began for the Bulldog. Some efforts were made to have the dogs fight one another, but this was clearly not the Bulldog's forte. Now a dog without a cause, the breed's popularity plummeted. By all rights,

AKC Ranking: 26
Family: Livestock Dog, Mountain Dog, Mastiff (Bulldog)
Area of Origin: England
Date of Origin: 1200s
Original Function: Bull baiting
Today's Function: Companion
Other Name: English Bulldog

the breed should have become extinct, except that it had gained so many ardent admirers that they set out to rescue the Bulldog by selecting against ferocity while still maintaining—and often accentuating—its distinctive physical characteristics. So successful were they that the Bulldog became an extremely amiable character, with a personality not at all like its "sourmug" might suggest. Its tough steadfast persona led it to be identified as a national symbol of England. It's amiable clownish personality belies its appearance, and the Bulldog is a popular pet.

Temperament

Despite its "sourmug," the Bulldog is jovial, comical, and amiable, among the most docile and mellow of dogs. It is willing to please, although it retains a stubborn streak. It is very good with children. Most are moderately friendly toward strangers. Although some can be aggressive with strange dogs, the breed is quite good with other pets.

Upkeep

The Bulldog appreciates a daily outing but cannot tolerate hot humid weather. It should not be expected to jog or walk great distances, or to jump from any heights. Most Bulldogs cannot swim. Most Bulldogs wheeze and snore, and some drool. Coat care is minimal, but facial wrinkles (and any folds around the tail) should be cleaned daily.

Health

- Major concerns: CHD, KCS, stenotic nares, elongated soft palate, shoulder luxation, internalized tail
- Minor concerns: entropion, ectropion, distichiasis, CHD, elbow dysplasia, cherry eye, patellar luxation
- Occasionally seen: urethral prolapse, vaginal hyperplasia
- Suggested tests: hip, elbow, knee, (eye)
- Life span: 8–10 years
- Note: It is prone to skin fold dermatitis unless the wrinkles are kept clean and dry. It cannot tolerate heat. Special precautions must be taken when anesthetizing a Bulldog. Caesarian deliveries are commonly needed. Hip radiographs

show most Bulldogs to be dysplastic but few show overt symptoms.

Form and Function

The Bulldog's heavy, thick-set, low-slung body with wide shoulders gives it a low center of gravity, a vital asset when fighting a large animal. The massive head, of which the circumference should equal at least the height of the dog at the shoulder, gives ample room for muscular attachment for the strong, wide jaws. The undershot bite allows a tight grip, at the same time giving breathing room through the nose. The limbs are sturdy, the gait loose-jointed, shuffling, and rolling—this is not a breed that needs to run! The coat is fine and glossy.

Illustrated Standard

1. Head and face covered with wrinkles; dewlap present
2. Undershot
3. Pendent flews completely overhanging massive jaws
4. Short broad muzzle turned upward, tip of nose set between the eyes
5. Broad head
6. Wheel back
7. Short straight or screwed tail, carried low
8. Hind legs longer than forelegs
9. Rounded ribs

❑ **Color:** brindle, solid white, red, or fawn, or any of these on a white background
❑ **DQ:** brown or liver-colored nose

At a Glance

Energy level:	❑
Exercise requirements:	❑
Playfulness:	❑❑❑❑
Affection level:	❑❑❑❑❑
Friendliness toward dogs:	❑
Friendliness toward other pets:	❑❑❑❑
Friendliness toward strangers:	❑❑❑❑
Ease of training:	❑❑
Watchdog ability:	❑
Protection ability:	❑❑
Grooming requirements:	❑❑
Cold tolerance:	❑
Heat tolerance:	❑

Weight:	male: 50 lb; female: 40 lb
Height:	12–15"

Chinese Shar-Pei

History

The Chinese Shar-Pei may have existed in the southern provinces of China since the Han dynasty (around 200 B.C.). Certainly by the thirteenth century strong evidence in the form of writings describing a wrinkled dog point to the breed's existence. Its origins are unknown, but because only it and the Chow Chow have blue-black tongues, and both come from China, it is likely that they share some common ancestry. The Shar-Pei's history is difficult to trace because most records relating to its past were lost when China became communist. At this time Shar-Peis were the working breed of peasant farmers, fulfilling roles of guard dog, wild boar hunter, and dog fighter. After the nation became communist, most of China's dogs were eliminated, with only a few remaining outside of the cities. A few Shar-Peis were bred in British Hong Kong and Taiwan, and the Hong Kong Kennel Club recognized the breed in 1968. Around this same time, a few specimens came to America, but the turning point occurred with a 1973 article alerting American fanciers to the breed's perilously low numbers. Touted as the world's rarest dog, fanciers vied to

AKC Ranking: 32
Family: Livestock Dog. Mountain Dog. Northern (companion)
Area of Origin: China
Date of Origin: 1200s
Original Function: Dog fighting, herding, hunting, guardian
Today's Function: Companion
Other Name: Chinese Fighting Dog

obtain the few available Shar-Peis. The breed has since been brought from the brink of extinction to the height of popularity, and it is one of the most recognizable breeds in America. Though known for its loose skin and profuse wrinkles, which are superabundant in puppies, the wrinkles of adults may be limited only to the head, neck, and shoulders.

Temperament

The Shar-Pei is self-assured, serious, independent, stubborn, and very much self-possessed. Although not particularly demonstrative, it is devoted and very protective of its family. It is reserved, even suspicious, toward strangers. It can be aggressive toward other dogs and may chase livestock and other animals, although it is generally good with other family pets.

Upkeep

The Shar-Pei needs daily mental and physical stimulation, but its needs can be met with lively games throughout the day or a good long walk. It is not generally amenable to exclusive outdoor living, but it can divide its time between house and yard. The coat needs only weekly brushing, but wrinkles need regular attention to ensure that no irritations develop within the skin folds.

Other Considerations

The name Shar-Pei means sandy coat, referring to the gritty sandpaper texture of the coat. When rubbed backward, the prickly coat can be uncomfortable, and even cause welts on the skin of an occasional sensitive person.

Health

- Major concerns: entropion, CHD
- Minor concerns: patellar luxation, elbow dysplasia, demodectic mange
- Occasionally seen: ciliary dyskinesia, renal amoidosis
- Suggested tests: hip, knee, elbow, (eye)
- Life span: 8–10 years
- Note: The breed is susceptible to fevers of unknown origin, often occurring with swollen hocks.

Form and Function

The Shar-Pei is compact and square, with a head slightly large for its body.

Illustrated Standard

① Abundant dewlap and folds of loose skin around neck
② Broad full "hippopotamus" muzzle
③ Blue-black tongue and mouth (lavender in dilute colors)
④ Small, sunken, almond-shaped eyes
⑤ Large head framed with profuse wrinkles
⑥ Small, high-set, triangular ears lying flat
⑦ High-set, thick, tapering tail curled over to side of back

❏ **Color:** any solid color including sable
❏ **DQ:** pricked ears, solid pink tongue, absence of a complete tail, not a solid color, albino

Its signature wrinkles enabled it to twist away when grabbed by a dog when in a fight. Its stiff bristly coat further afforded protection against bites. The coat can be of either brush (not to exceed 1 inch) or horse (very short) types, both it should be extremely harsh, straight, and stand off the body. The small, close ears and small, sunken eyes afford further protection. The gait is free, with good reach and drive. The wide, powerful jaws, scowling expression, and hippopotamus muzzle create a look unique to the breed.

At a Glance

Energy level:	❏❏❏
Exercise requirements:	❏❏❏
Playfulness:	❏
Affection level:	❏
Friendliness toward dogs:	❏
Friendliness toward other pets:	❏❏❏
Friendliness toward strangers:	❏
Ease of training:	❏
Watchdog ability:	❏❏❏❏❏
Protection ability:	❏❏❏❏
Grooming requirements:	❏❏
Cold tolerance:	❏❏❏
Heat tolerance:	❏❏

Weight:	45–60 lb
Height:	18–20"

Chow Chow

History

The Chow Chow has some spitz characteristics. Because of this, it has been proposed that the Chow Chow either descends from spitz forebears or is itself an ancestor of some of the spitz breeds. Unfortunately, the origin of the breed has been lost in time, but it has been known in China for hundreds, if not thousands, of years. Its original purpose may have been as a hunting dog, sniffing out and even pointing birds for the nobility. The breed declined in quality and numbers after the Imperial hunts were ended, but a few pure descendents were kept in isolated monasteries and wealthy households. Other accounts contend that the breed was a source of fur pelts and food in Manchuria and Mongolia. One of the most distinctive features of the breed is its black tongue, which was also the basis for its more common names in China. Only when dogs were brought to England along with other Chinese importations in the late 1700s was the name Chow Chow adopted. The name is probably derived from a term simply meaning Oriental knick knack and assorted curios, and may

AKC Ranking: 35
Family: Spitz, Northern (companion)
Area of Origin: China
Date of Origin: Ancient times
Original Function: Guardian, cart
 puller, food source
Today's Function: Companion
Other Name: None

have come to be applied to the dogs because they were lumped into a ship's log of cargo. These early imports were, in fact, looked upon as curios. Not until the late 1800s was the breed imported to England and then America in earnest. Queen Victoria's interest in these dogs helped draw attention to the breed. AKC recognized the Chow Chow in 1903. The breed's distinctive noble look has always attracted fanciers, but in the 1980s the breed soared in popularity among pet owners, as well, ultimately peaking as the sixth most popular breed in America.

Temperament

Dignified, even lordly, the Chow Chow conducts itself with reserve. It is not very demonstrative, even with its family, and is somewhat suspicious of strangers. It is independent and stubborn. It can be aggressive toward other dogs but is generally good with other household pets. It is serious and protective, devoted to its family.

Upkeep

This is an alert breed that needs regular, but not strenuous, outdoor activity. It does not do well in hot humid weather. Its needs are best met with casual morning or evening walks in warm weather or several short play sessions throughout the day. It can live outdoors in temperate or cool weather, but it is best allowed to stay inside during warm weather. The smooth type needs brushing once weekly; the rough type needs brushing every other day, and daily when shedding.

Health

- Major concerns: CHD, entropion
- Minor concerns: elbow dysplasia, cataract, distichiasis, PPM, gastric torsion, stenotic nares, patellar luxation, elongated palate
- Occasionally seen: renal cortical hypoplasia
- Suggested tests: hip, elbow, eye
- Life span: 8–12 years

Form and Function

The Chow is an Arctic-type dog, powerful, squarely built, and sturdy with heavy

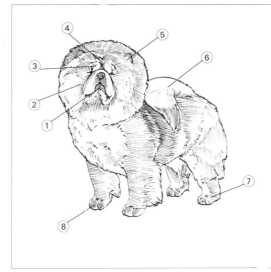

bone and strong muscular development. It is a breed suited for a number of tasks, rather than specializing in one, and its build reflects its ability to hunt, herd, pull, and protect. It can have either a rough coat, which is straight and off-standing or a smooth coat, which is hard and smooth; both coat types have wooly undercoats, providing ample insulation from the cold. The characteristic straight angulation of the hind legs produces a short, stilted gait unique to the breed. The scowling expression and black tongue are essential components of breed type.

At a Glance

Energy level:	❑
Exercise requirements:	❑❑
Playfulness:	❑
Affection level:	❑❑
Friendliness toward dogs:	❑
Friendliness toward other pets:	❑❑❑
Friendliness toward strangers:	❑
Ease of training:	❑
Watchdog ability:	❑❑❑❑❑
Protection ability:	❑❑❑❑
Grooming requirements: Smooth:	❑❑
Rough:	❑❑❑❑
Cold tolerance:	❑❑❑❑❑
Heat tolerance:	❑

Weight:	45–70 lb*
Height:	17–20"

Dalmatian

History

The spotted Dalmatian is the most distinctly patterned breed of any dog, but the origin of its coat pattern is unknown. In fact, although art evidence points to an ancient origin, the time and place of the breed's birth is also unknown. It gets it name from Dalmatia, a region in western Yugoslavia, but it probably did not originate there. Their ancestors may have included a small version of the spotted Great Dane or pointers, though this, too, is conjectural. Even the breed's original function is unclear, but that is more likely because of its use in so many roles rather than any lack of employment. These roles included war dog, sentinel, shepherd, draft dog, ratter, retriever, bird dog, trailer, and even circus dog. It was as a coach dog in Victorian England, however, that the Dalmatian found its niche. The coach dog served both a practical

AKC Ranking: 17
Family: Scenthound, Pointer
Area of Origin: Yugoslavia
Date of Origin: Ancient times
Original Function: Carriage dog
Today's Function: Companion
Other Name: None

and esthetic role; it protected the horses from marauding dogs and added a touch of style to the procession. The dogs would trot alongside, in front, or beneath the axle (considered the most elegant position) of the coach; interestingly, some evidence exists that coaching position may have a hereditary component. Some of these early dogs apparently had cropped ears. With the advent of the automobile, the Dalmatian lost its place in high society, and its popularity declined. It continued as a coach dog for horse-drawn fire engines, and this association led to its adoption as the modern "fire-dog." Its flashy coloration has always ensured that it has been popular as a pet and show dog; however, its feature in popular children's movies has catapulted the breed to one of the most popular breeds in America in the years following the movies' releases.

At a Glance

Energy level:	☐☐☐☐
Exercise requirements:	☐☐☐
Playfulness:	☐☐☐
Affection level:	☐☐☐☐☐
Friendliness toward dogs:	☐☐☐
Friendliness toward other pets:	☐☐☐
Friendliness toward strangers:	☐☐☐
Ease of training:	☐☐☐
Watchdog ability:	☐☐☐☐
Protection ability:	☐☐☐
Grooming requirements:	☐☐
Cold tolerance:	☐☐
Heat tolerance:	☐☐☐

Weight:	40–60 lb*
Height:	19–23″

Temperament

Bred to run for miles, the Dalmatian retains this tireless enthusiasm. It is a playful, eager companion that must get daily hard exercise in a safe area if it is expected to behave at home. It loves to run and may roam. It may be aggressive toward strange dogs, but it is generally good with other pets and is especially good with horses. It may be too energetic for young children. It tends to be reserved toward strangers. It can be stubborn.

Note: Deaf Dalmatians present special training and behavioral problems. They are easily startled and may snap. They are not advised for families with children.

Upkeep

The Dalmatian needs a lot of regular exercise and attention. It needs more than a short walk on leash; it makes a good jogging companion. It can also have its needs met with vigorous games and runs. Although the Dal can live outside in temperate or warm climates, it needs shelter, soft bedding, and most of all, companionship. Thus, it is best allowed to live in the house and play in the yard. The coat needs only minimal care, but more frequent brushing will help remove dead hair.

Health

- Major concerns: deafness, urolithiasis
- Minor concerns: allergies, epilepsy
- Occasionally seen: CHD, vWD
- Suggested tests: hearing
- Life span: 12–14 years
- Note: A unique defect of the Dalmatian is its inability to metabolize uric acid into allantoin, which leads to the tendency to form urinary calculi (stones).

Form and Function

The Dalmatian is a square-proportioned, athletic dog of good substance and sturdy bone. It is built for efficiency at the trot and great endurance, and its movement should be steady and effortless. The expression is alert and intelligent; the coat short and sleek. The distinctive spots are an essential point of type; solid patches (distinguished from masses of spots by the patch's sharply defined, smooth edges) are a disqualification.

Finnish Spitz

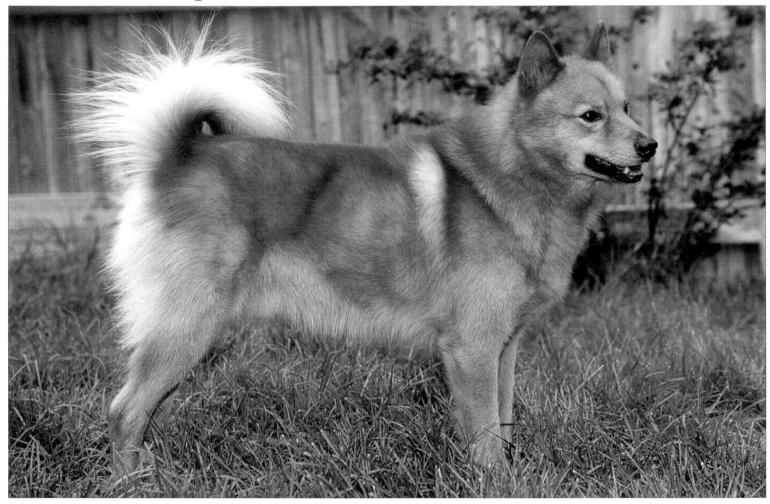

History

The Finnish Spitz originated from ancestral northern spitz dogs that accompanied early Finno-Ugrian tribes as they journeyed across Eurasia to Finland. These dogs probably originated as camp followers and watchdogs, later developing into hunting dogs. The breed remained pure, not by design but by isolation until the early 1800s. When other groups of people brought their dogs to the region in the 1800s, interbreeding almost obliterated the pure Finnish Spitz. In the late 1800s, two Finnish sportsmen spotted some dogs that had apparently not been interbred, and they were so impressed that they determined to rescue the imperiled breed. Early names for the breed included Suomenpystykorva (Finnish Cock-Eared Dog) and Finnish Barking Bird Dog. When it first came to England it was called the Finsk Spets (derived from its Swedish name), but in 1891, the name was officially changed to Finnish Spitz. The breed gained its nickname of Finkie after its arrival in England in the 1920s. It wasn't until the 1960s that Finkies began to be bred in the United States. The breed was officially admitted into the

AKC Ranking: 138
Family: Spitz, Northern (hunting)
Area of Origin: Finland
Date of Origin: Ancient times
Original Function: Hunting birds and
   small mammals
Today's Function: Hunting
Other Name: Suomenpystykorva,
   Finsk Spets

Non-Sporting Group in 1988. Although prized primarily as a pet in America, it is still used for hunting in Finland. There they hunt the capercaille (a turkeylike bird) and black grouse, although they will hunt virtually anything from insects to elk if given the chance. The dogs work by ranging out from the hunter, locating the bird, and barking loudly. If the bird moves, they follow it until it lands and then resume barking. Some claim that the barking mesmerizes the game. Conformation champions in Finland must first prove themselves in the field; their barking talents are so valued that they select a King Barker each year. The Finnish Spitz is the national dog of Finland.

Temperament

Like most spitz breeds, the Finkie is independent and somewhat stubborn, although it is more hunting oriented than other spitz breeds. It is alert, inquisitive, and playful, but it is also sensitive, tending to be devoted to one person. It is a breed conscious of its place in the dominance hierarchy, and some males can try to be domineering. It is good with children, and generally good with other pets, but it can be aggressive to strange dogs. It is reserved, even aloof or suspicious, with strangers. In keeping with its barking heritage, the Finkie is proud of its barking ability and likes to show it off—loudly!

Upkeep

This is an active and lively breed and needs daily exercise, either a long walk on leash or a run in a fenced area. As a hunting breed, care must be taken that they do not go off on a hunt by themselves. The Finkie can live outdoors in temperate and cool climates, but it enjoys living indoors. Its double coat needs brushing one or two times weekly, more often when shedding. It is not oily so that the Finkie has little doggy odor; in fact, the Finkie is a particularly clean breed.

Health

- Major concerns: none
- Minor concerns: none
- Occasionally seen: CHD, patellar luxation, epilepsy
- Suggested tests: none
- Life span: 12–14 years

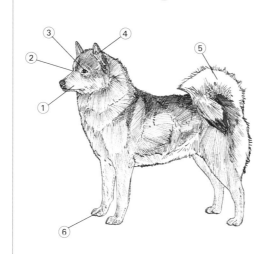

Illustrated Standard

1. Foxlike head and expression
2. Pronounced stop
3. Almond-shaped eyes
4. Small, high-set, erect ears
5. Plumed tail curving forward and round to lie against either thigh
6. Round feet

❏ **Color:** shades of golden-red (Puppies are born with a black overlay that disappears by around 8 weeks of age.)
❏ **DQ:** none

Form and Function

The Finnish Spitz has a foxlike appearance, incorporating the typical traits of a northern breed: small erect ears, dense double coat, and curled tail. It is square-proportioned, and without exaggeration, quick and light on its feet. It has the conformation and temperament to hunt actively and tirelessly under the coldest of conditions. Its double coat, consisting of a short soft undercoat and harsh straight outer coat about 1 to 2 inches long, provides insulation from the snow and cold, allowing it to hunt tirelessly under the coldest of conditions.

At a Glance

Energy level:	❑❑❑
Exercise requirements:	❑❑❑
Playfulness:	❑❑❑
Affection level:	❑❑❑
Friendliness toward dogs:	❑❑❑
Friendliness toward other pets:	❑❑❑
Friendliness toward strangers:	❑
Ease of training:	❑❑❑
Watchdog ability:	❑❑❑❑
Protection ability:	❑❑❑
Grooming requirements:	❑❑❑
Cold tolerance:	❑❑❑❑
Heat tolerance:	❑❑

Weight:	male: 31–36 lb; female: 23–29 lb*
Height:	male: 17.5–20"; female: 15.5–18"

French Bulldog

History

In the nineteenth century, the Bulldog was fairly popular in England, especially around Nottingham. Some of these Bulldogs were quite small, weighing less than 25 pounds. When many of the lace workers of the region went to France for work in the mid 1800s, they took their "Toy" Bulldogs with them. The French women, especially, were attracted to these little Bulldogs, especially those with erect ears (a common but disliked feature in England). Dog dealers brought more of the clownish little dogs to France, where they soon became the rage of Paris. The dogs were dubbed Bouledogue Francais. French breeders sought to consistently produce the erect "bat ears," much to the chagrin of English breeders. By the late 1800s, the breed had caught the attention of the upper class and had moved into some of the finer homes in France. Around this same time, American visitors to France brought several back to America and began to breed the dogs in earnest. Amid continued controversy over which ear type was correct, an American club was formed

AKC Ranking: 76
Family: Companion, Mastiff (Bulldog)
Area of Origin: France
Date of Origin: 1800s
Original Function: Lapdog
Today's Function: Companion
Other Name: Bouledogue Francais

and, in 1898, sponsored one of the most elegant dog shows (just for French Bulldogs) ever held. The gracious setting attracted wealthy spectators, and the Frenchie had soon conquered America. Their popularity among high society soared, and by 1913 they were among the most popular show dogs in America. The breed has since been passed by many others in popularity, but it still boasts some of the most elite and ardent fans in dogdom.

Temperament

The French Bulldog is a clown in a lapdog. It enjoys playing and entertaining its family, as well as cuddling and snoozing with its favorite person. It is amiable, sweet, companionable, and willing to please.

Upkeep

The Frenchie has minimal exercise requirements, although it is a fun-loving dog. It enjoys a romp outdoors, but it doesn't do well in

hot, humid weather. Most cannot swim.
A short walk on lead is sufficient to meet
most of its physical needs. This breed
should not live outdoors. The Frenchie
snores and may wheeze and drool. It
requires minimal coat care, but its facial
wrinkles should be regularly cleaned.

Health
- Major concerns: stenotic nares, elongated soft palate, intervertebral disc degeneration, hemivertebrae
- Minor concerns: CHD, patellar luxation, entropion
- Occasionally seen: distichiasis, cataract, deafness
- Suggested tests: hip, spine, knee, eye
- Life span: 9–11 years
- Note: This breed does not tolerate heat well and may be sensitive to anesthesia.

Form and Function
The Frenchie shares many of the traits
that made its Bulldog ancestors so
successful in the bull baiting arena: low
center of gravity, wide body, heavy bone,
muscular build, and large, square head. It
has soft loose skin forming wrinkles about
the head and shoulders. Unlike the

Illustrated Standard
1. Broad, hanging flews
2. Large, square head
3. Round eyes
4. Bat ears
5. Roach back
6. Short straight or screwed tail carried low
7. Hind legs longer than forelegs

❏ **Color:** brindle, fawn, white, brindle and white, and any color not specifically mentioned as a disqualification
❏ **DQ:** any alteration other than removal of dewclaws; weight over 28 lb; other than bat ears; nose other than black, except in the case of lighter-colored dogs; solid black, mouse, liver, black and tan, black and white, and white with black

Bulldog, it has an alert, curious expression, which is aided by its bar ears. Also, unlike the Bulldog, its movement is unrestrained and free, with reach and drive. It is a hardy, entertaining home companion and a solid lapdog.

At a Glance

Energy level:	❏❏❏
Exercise requirements:	❏
Playfulness:	❏❏❏
Affection level:	❏❏❏
Friendliness toward dogs:	❏❏❏
Friendliness toward other pets:	❏❏❏❏
Friendliness toward strangers:	❏
Ease of training:	❏❏
Watchdog ability:	❏❏❏
Protection ability:	❏
Grooming requirements:	❏
Cold tolerance:	❏❏❏
Heat tolerance:	❏

Weight:	not to exceed 28 lb
Height:	11–13"*

Keeshond

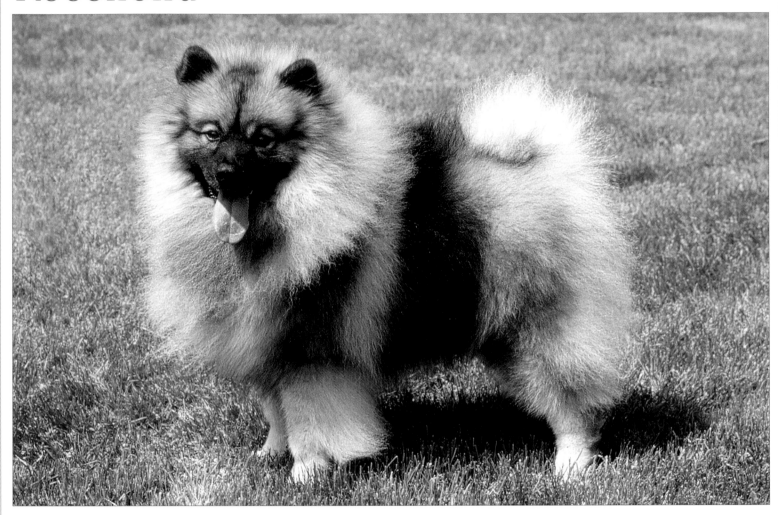

History

The Keeshond (plural: Keeshonden) is one of the family of spitz dogs, although its exact origin is undocumented. It seems to have been well established in Holland at least since the eighteenth century as a companion and watchdog. The breed later became known as the barge dog because it was often kept as a watchdog on the small vessels navigating the Rhine River. By a stroke of fate, the breed became entangled in the political events of Holland in the years preceding the French Revolution. The leader of the Patriot faction was a man named Kees de Gyselaer, who in turn owned a barge dog named Kees. The dog Kees appeared in so many political cartoons that he and his breed—a dog of the people—became the symbol of the Patriots. Unfortunately for the Keeshond, the Patriots did not prevail, and many Keeshond owners disposed of their dogs lest they be identified with the losing party. To make things worse for the Keeshond, the barges that floated the Rhine became larger, and the small Keeshond became less favored as a barge dog. Nonetheless, the breed did survive, although with a low profile, through the efforts of a few loyal river boatmen and

AKC Ranking: 57
Family: Spitz, Northern (companion)
Area of Origin: The Netherlands
Date of Origin: 1700s
Original Function: Barge watchdog
Today's Function: Companion
Other Name: Wolf Spitz

farmers. In 1920, the Baroness van Hardenbroek began an effort to rescue the surviving members. She was so successful at winning friends for the breed that the Keeshond was in England by 1925. AKC recognition soon followed in 1930. So much did the Keeshond recover in its native land that it is now the national dog of Holland.

Temperament

The Keeshond combines many traits of the best housedogs: fairly energetic and playful, very attentive and loving, and ready for adventure yet content to take it easy. It is sensitive and learns readily. It makes a good companion for a child or adult. It is friendly to all but, nonetheless, an alert watchdog.

Upkeep

This is a lively breed that can have its exercise needs met with moderate exercise. A good walk on leash, combined with a vigorous game, can satisfy its needs. It can live outside in temperate or cool climates, but it is such a sociable dog that it prefers to share its life with its family. The double coat needs brushing once or twice weekly, and more when shedding.

Health

- Major concerns: none
- Minor concerns: CHD, epilepsy, skin problems
- Occasionally seen: renal cortical hypoplasia, tetralogy of Fallot, mitral valve insufficiency
- Suggested tests: hip, (cardiac)
- Life span: 12–14 years

Form and Function

The Keeshond is a square-proportioned, sturdy dog of Northern type. It is an all-purpose dog, a generalist rather than a specialist, and its build reflects this. The gait of the Keeshond is distinctive: clean, bold, and brisk, with only slight to moderate reach and drive. It has a long straight harsh outer coat standing off from its body, a good mane, and a thick downy undercoat—all imparting superb insulation from cold and damp.

Illustrated Standard

1. Almond-shaped eyes
2. Distinctive "spectacles" add to alert expression
3. Wedge-shaped skull when viewed from above
4. Small, high-set, triangular ears carried erect
5. Tail tightly curled over back, lying flat and close to body
6. Round feet

❏ **Color:** mixture of gray, black, and cream. Undercoat is pale, and tips of the outercoat hairs are black. Black muzzle, ears, tail tip, and spectacle lines reaching from the outer eyes corners to the ears. Lighter ruff, shoulders, trousers, legs, feet, and tail plume.

❏ **DQ:** none

At a Glance

Energy level:	▢▢▢
Exercise requirements:	▢▢▢
Playfulness:	▢▢▢
Affection level:	▢▢▢▢▢
Friendliness toward dogs:	▢▢▢
Friendliness toward other pets:	▢▢▢▢
Friendliness toward strangers:	▢▢▢
Ease of training:	▢▢▢
Watchdog ability:	▢▢▢▢▢
Protection ability:	▢
Grooming requirements:	▢▢▢
Cold tolerance:	▢▢▢▢
Heat tolerance:	▢

Weight:	male: about 45 lb; female: about 35 lb*
Height:	male: 18" (17–19" acceptable); female: 17" (16–18" acceptable)

Lhasa Apso

History

The origin of the Lhasa Apso has been long lost; it is an ancient breed bred and revered in the villages and monasteries of Tibet. Its history is intertwined with Buddhist beliefs, including a belief in reincarnation. The souls of lamas were said to enter the sacred dog's bodies upon death, thus imparting an added reverence for these dogs. The dogs also performed the role of monastery watchdog, sounding the alert to visitors, thus giving rise to their native name of Abso Seng Kye (Bark Lion Sentinel Dog). It is likely that the breed's western name of Lhasa Apso is derived from its native name, although some contend that it is a corruption of the Tibetan word *rapso*, meaning goat (in reference to its goatlike coat). In fact, when the breed first came to England, it was known as the Lhassa Terrier, although it is in no way a terrier. The first Lhasa Apsos were seen in the Western world around 1930, with some of the first dogs arriving as gifts of the thirteenth Dalai Lama. The breed was admitted into the AKC Terrier Group in

AKC Ranking: 31
Family: Companion, Herding
Area of Origin: Tibet
Date of Origin: Ancient times
Original Function: Companion, watchdog
Today's Function: Companion
Other Name: None

1935, but it was reassigned to the Non-Sporting Group in 1959. After a slow start, the Lhasa quickly outpaced its fellow Tibetan breeds to become a popular pet and show dog.

Temperament

Despite its lapdog appearance, the Lhasa is a tough character. It is independent, stubborn, and bold. Although it is eager for a romp or game, it will be happy as long as it is given exercise. It will also happily snooze beside its owner. These characteristics make it an excellent small companion in adventure. It is somewhat reserved with strangers.

Upkeep

The Lhasa is an active dog, but its relatively small size makes it possible to meet its energy needs either with short walks or vigorous play sessions in the yard, or even home. It makes a fine apartment dog. It is not suited for outdoor living. The long coat needs brushing and combing every other day.

At a Glance

Energy level:	▢▢▢
Exercise requirements:	▢
Playfulness:	▢▢▢
Affection level:	▢▢▢
Friendliness toward dogs:	▢▢▢
Friendliness toward other pets:	▢▢▢
Friendliness toward strangers:	▢
Ease of training:	▢
Watchdog ability:	▢▢▢▢▢
Protection ability:	▢
Grooming requirements:	▢▢▢▢
Cold tolerance:	▢▢▢
Heat tolerance:	▢▢

Weight:	13–15 lb*
Height:	10–11″ (females may be smaller)

Illustrated Standard

1. Fairly narrow head covered with heavy furnishings, especially whiskers and beard
2. Level or slightly undershot bite
3. Medium-sized eyes
4. Narrow skull, not quite flat
5. Pendant, heavily feathered ears
6. Tail carried over back in a screw
7. Round feet

❏ **Color:** any
❏ **DQ:** none

Health

- Major concerns: none
- Minor concerns: patellar luxation, entropion, distichiasis, PRA, renal cortical hypoplasia
- Occasionally seen: CHD, urolithiasis, vWD
- Suggested tests: knee, eye
- Life span: 12–14 years

Form and Function

The Lhasa Apso is longer than it is tall, with a strong loin. Although the breed has never been used for purposes requiring great athleticism, it should nonetheless have a strong loin and well-developed quarters and thighs. The head is well covered with a good fall over the eyes and good whiskers and beard, imparting a dignified, almost lionlike look. The bite should be either level or slightly undershot. The coat is heavy, straight, long, and hard.

Löwchen

History

Löwchen (pronounced Lerv-chun) means Little Lion Dog, and in France the breed is known as Le Petit Chien Lion. The Löwchen shares common roots with other members of the Bichon family, which also includes the Bichon Frise and Havanese, among others. Germany, Russia, and France have all laid claim to the breed. The exact time and place of its origin is obscure, but dogs resembling the Löwchen, sporting the distinctive lion trim, can be found in sixteenth-century German art. In the traditional lion trim, the coat is clipped short from the last rib to and including the hindquarters down to the hock joint. The front legs are clipped from elbow to just above the pastern. The feet are clipped, and about half the tail is clipped, leaving a plume at the tip. Any long hair is to be left unshaped. In the 1960s, the breed's numbers had dwindled to perilous numbers; through the efforts of two breeders, several related dogs from Germany were brought to Britain. Because of their small numbers, these dogs were interbred extensively and formed the basis of the breed in Britain as well as America.

AKC Ranking: 141
Family: Companion, Water Dog
Area of Origin: France, Germany
Date of Origin: 1500s
Original Function: Companion
Today's Function: Companion
Other Name: Little Lion Dog

The Löwchen entered the AKC Miscellaneous class in 1996 and was admitted as a member of the Non-Sporting Group as of the first day of 1999.

Temperament

This is a lively, inquisitive, affectionate dog. It is a mixture of playful spirit and calm soul mate, a good companion for a quiet family. It is willing to please and responsive to commands, and it is devoted to its family. Some may bark or dig a lot.

Upkeep

The Löwchen can receive ample exercise with a short walk or active game every day. It enjoys a mental challenge. It is not a breed that should live outside, although it appreciates access to a yard during the day. Its coat needs brushing or combing about every other day. Clipping to maintain the traditional lion trim must be done every month or two. Many pet owners prefer to keep their dogs in a puppy clip.

At a Glance

Energy level:	☐☐☐
Exercise requirements:	☐
Playfulness:	☐☐☐
Affection level:	☐☐☐
Friendliness toward dogs:	☐☐☐☐
Friendliness toward other pets:	☐☐☐☐
Friendliness toward strangers:	☐☐☐
Ease of training:	☐☐☐
Watchdog ability:	☐☐☐☐
Protection ability:	☐
Grooming requirements:	☐☐☐☐
Cold tolerance:	☐☐☐
Heat tolerance:	☐☐☐

Weight:	8–18 lb*
Height:	12–14"

Illustrated Standard

① Eyes round and forward looking
② Topline level
③ Tail set high and carried in a cup-handle fashion when the dog is moving
④ Pendant ears

❑ **Color:** any colors or combinations
❑ **DQ:** any trim other than specified, shaping or scissoring of the long coat

Health

- Major concerns: none
- Minor concerns: patellar luxation
- Occasionally seen: none
- Suggested tests: none
- Life span: 13–15 years

Form and Function

The Löwchen is a compact small dog, very slightly longer than it is tall, with strong, sturdy—but never coarse—bone. Its gait is effortless with good reach and drive, and it proudly carries its head and tail. Its coat is dense and long, moderately soft with a slight to moderate wave. It is traditionally clipped in a lion trim. The Löwchen has a relatively short, broad topskull and muzzle, and its expression is alert, bright, and lively.

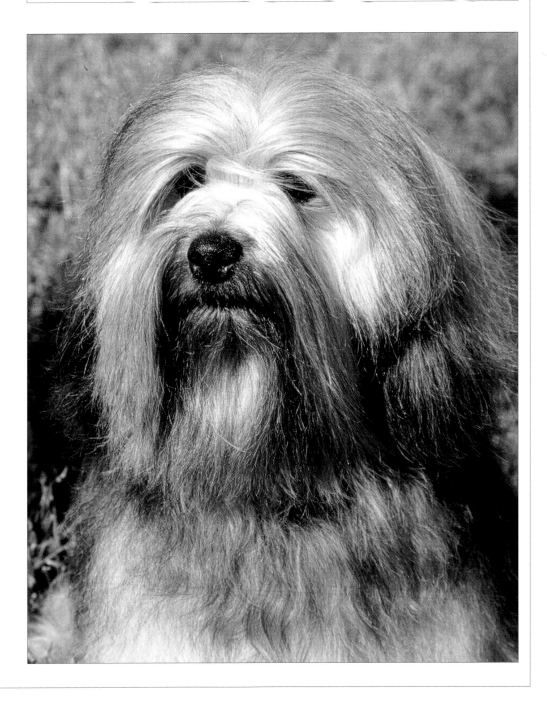

Poodle (Standard and Miniature)

History

Although the Poodle is most often identified with France, its earliest ancestors were probably curly-coated dogs from central Asia that assisted with herding and followed many routes into various parts of Europe. Interwoven in their ancestry are also several rough-coated water dogs. Perhaps the earliest incarnation of the Poodle was the Barbet, a curly-coated dog distributed in France, Russia, Hungary, and elsewhere. It is the German version, however, that exerted most influence on the modern Poodle. In fact, the word *poodle* comes from the German word *pfudel*, meaning puddle or "to splash," probably reflecting the dog's water abilities. In France, it was known as *caniche* or *chien canard*, both referring to its duck-hunting abilities. Thus, from herding and water roots the Poodle became a talented water-hunting companion. The Poodle was also drawn into service as a military dog, guide dog, guard dog, wagon

AKC Ranking: 5
Family: Gun Dog, Companion, Water Dog
Area of Origin: Germany and Central Europe
Date of Origin: 1500s
Original Function: Water retrieving, performer
Today's Function: Companion
Other Name: Barbone, Caniche

puller for performers, and eventually, a circus performer. Its coat was shorn close to facilitate swimming, but left slightly longer on the chest for warmth in cold water. Although some believe the puffs of hair around the leg joints and tail tip were for protection when hunting, compelling evidence suggests that they arose as decoration during the Poodle's performing days. The Poodle found favor as an elegant companion for fashionable ladies. It became favored by French aristocracy and eventually became the national dog of France. Its characteristic clip was accentuated, and a successful effort was made to perfect the smaller specimens. Poodles entered the show ring in the late 1800s. Some of the early show Poodles were shown in corded coats, in which the hair is allowed to mat in long thin tresses rather than be brushed out. While eye-catching, the upkeep was difficult and the trend died out by the early 1900s, being replaced by the bouffant styles still in vogue.

At the same time Poodle popularity in America waned, so that, by the late 1920s, Poodles had almost died out in North America. In the 1930s, the breed staged a comeback that eventually placed it as the all-time most popular dog in America.

Temperament

Miniature: The Miniature Poodle is lively, amiable, playful, eager to please, responsive, smart, and obedient—small wonder that it has remained one of the most popular varieties of dog for so long. It is sensitive, tending to be devoted to one person, and initially reserved with strangers. It is good with children, other pets, and dogs. Some tend to bark a lot.

Standard: Among the very smartest and most obedient of dogs, the Standard Poodle combines playful exuberance with a zest for life's adventures. It retains its hunting heritage, and loves to run, swim, and retrieve. It gets along well with everyone, although it is somewhat reserved with strangers. It is excellent with children.

Upkeep

All Poodles need a lot of interaction with

people. They also need mental and physical exercise. A brief but challenging obedience or play session, combined with a walk, should be part of every Poodle's day. Standard Poodles will need more exercise and may especially enjoy swimming. No Poodle should live outdoors. The show Poodle should preferably be brushed every day or weekly for shorter coats. Poodle hair, when shed, does not fall out but becomes caught in the surrounding hair, which can cause matting if not removed. The pet clips are easier to maintain and can be done every four to six weeks.

Health

Miniature
- Major concerns: PRA, Legg–Perthes, patellar luxation, epilepsy
- Minor concerns: trichiasis, entropion, lacrimal duct atresia, cataract, glaucoma, distichiasis
- Occasionally seen: urolithiasis, intervertebral disc degeneration
- Suggested tests: eye, knee, hip
- Life span: 13–15 years

Standard
- Major concerns: sebaceous adenitis, gastric torsion, Addison's
- Minor concerns: distichiasis, entropion, cataract, CHD, epilepsy
- Occasionally seen: PDA, vWD
- Suggested tests: skinpunch for SA, eye, (hip)
- Life span: 10–13 years

Form and Function

The Poodle is a square-proportioned dog with proud carriage and elegant appearance. It should move with a light, springy, effortless stride. The Poodle stems from working retriever stock, and its conformation should reflect its athletic background. The coat is curly, harsh, and dense; if corded, it should hang in tight even cords. The traditional clips stem from functional and decorative tradition; acceptable clips for show purposes are the puppy (for puppies only), English saddle, Continental, and (for some nonregular classes only) sporting.

Miniature at a Glance

Energy level:	▢▢▢▢
Exercise requirements:	▢▢▢
Playfulness:	▢▢▢▢▢
Affection level:	▢▢▢
Friendliness toward dogs:	▢▢▢▢
Friendliness toward other pets:	▢▢
Friendliness toward strangers:	▢▢▢▢
Ease of training:	▢▢▢▢▢
Watchdog ability:	▢▢▢▢▢
Protection ability:	▢
Grooming requirements:	▢▢▢▢▢
Cold tolerance:	▢▢▢
Heat tolerance:	▢▢▢

Weight:	12–18 lb*
Height:	10–15"

Standard at a Glance

Energy level:	▢▢▢
Exercise requirements:	▢▢▢▢
Playfulness:	▢▢▢▢
Affection level:	▢▢▢
Friendliness toward dogs:	▢▢▢
Friendliness toward other pets:	▢▢▢▢
Friendliness toward strangers:	▢▢▢
Ease of training:	▢▢▢▢▢
Watchdog ability:	▢▢▢▢▢
Protection ability:	▢▢▢
Grooming requirements:	▢▢▢▢▢
Cold tolerance:	▢▢▢
Heat tolerance:	▢▢▢

Weight:	45–65 lb*
Height:	over 15" (usually over 21"*)

Schipperke

History

The origin of the Schipperke is controversial. One plausible theory is that it originated as a dog of the boatmen who traveled between Brussels and Antwerp. The Flemish word for boat is *schip*, and Schipperke is thus thought to mean little boatman. The breed was less commonly called Schipperke by Belgian townspeople, however, who more often referred to it as spitz. The other plausible theory of origin is that it was a dog of tradesmen guilds and middle-class households, who wanted a small watchdog and ratter. The breed resembles a miniature Belgian Sheepdog, and it is possible that Schipperke derives from the word for shepherd, *scheper*. In fact, a breed of dog intermediate in size was one known in the region. Although small black tailless dogs are mentioned in Belgian writings of the fifteenth and sixteenth centuries, definite evidence of Schipperkes is not found until 1690. A group of Brussels shoemakers organized regular Schipperke competitions, taking special pride in adorning their companions with ornate brass collars. By the nineteenth century the breed was so popular in central Belgium that it was virtually

AKC Ranking: 51
Family: Sheepdog, Spitz, Northern (companion)
Area of Origin: Belgium
Date of Origin: 1600s
Original Function: Barge dog, watchdog, ratter
Today's Function: Companion
Other Name: None

the only housedog found there, and it was acknowledged as the national dog. In 1885 Queen Marie Henriette acquired a Schipperke she saw at a dog show. After people saw the little dog with her, it sparked great interest in the breed from people of all classes, and the workman's companion thus became companion to the elite. At the same time, the breed's numbers were depleted by exports to England, where they had become extremely fashionable. Most people in Belgium considered the breed common and preferred more exotic breeds. In the late 1880s, a group of Belgian Schipperke fanciers grouped to try to save the breed, setting forth the breed's desirable points. Soon after, the first Schipperke came to America. It aroused little interest at first, but it has since amassed a modest but loyal following.

Temperament

The Schipperke is a bold companion, even though it can be an independent and headstrong one. This little dynamo is happiest when busy, poking its nose into every cranny and ever on the lookout for adventure. It is reserved with strangers and an alert watchdog. It can make an amiable and pleasant housedog but needs daily exercise.

Upkeep

The active nature of this breed makes exercise—both mental and physical—imperative. Its small stature makes getting that exercise fairly easy, however. Either a vigorous game in the yard or a moderate walk on leash will usually suffice to meets its needs. The Schipperke should not live outdoors, even though it enjoys spending the day in the yard. Its double coat needs weekly brushing, more when shedding.

Health

- Major concerns: none
- Minor concerns: Legg–Perthes
- Occasionally seen: entropion, distichiasis, PRA
- Suggested tests: none
- Life span: 13–15 years

Form and Function

The Schipperke is a small, cobby dog, square-proportioned, appearing to slope

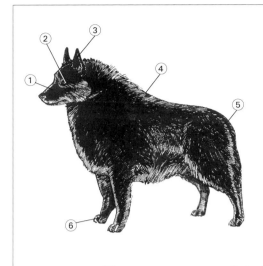

Illustrated Standard

① Foxlike face
② Small eyes
③ Small, triangular, high-set, erect ears
④ Appearance of being slightly higher at shoulders than rump
⑤ Docked tail so that tail is not visible
⑥ Small round feet

❏ **Color:** black
❏ **DQ:** drop ear, any color other than black

from shoulders to croup. This appearance is helped by its double coat, which forms a stand-out ruff, cape, and culottes. The foxlike face is questioning and mischievous, even impudent. The trot is smooth and graceful. This is an agile, active dog developed as a watchdog and vermin hunter.

At a Glance

Energy level:	❏❏❏❏
Exercise requirements:	❏❏❏
Playfulness:	❏❏❏
Affection level:	❏❏
Friendliness toward dogs:	❏❏❏
Friendliness toward other pets:	❏❏❏
Friendliness toward strangers:	❏
Ease of training:	❏
Watchdog ability:	❏❏❏❏❏
Protection ability:	❏❏❏❏
Grooming requirements:	❏❏
Cold tolerance:	❏❏❏
Heat tolerance:	❏❏

Weight:	12–16 lb*
Height:	male: 11–13"; female: 10–12"

Shiba Inu

History

Native Japanese dogs are divided into six breeds. Of these, the smallest and probably most ancient is the Shiba Inu. In fact, one theory about the name *shiba* is that it simply denotes small; however, it may also mean brushwood in reference to the brilliant red brushwood trees that so closely matched the breed's red coat and through which they hunted. These theories have resulted in the Shiba's being nicknamed the little brushwood dog. The origin of the Shiba is unclear; but it is clearly of spitz heritage and may have been used as early as 300 B.C. as a hunting dog in central Japan. Although they were used mostly to flush birds and small game, they were occasionally used to hunt wild boar. Three main types existed and each was named for its area of origin: the Shinshu Shiba (from the Nagano Prefecture), the Mino Shiba (from the Gifu Prefecture), and the Sanin Shiba (from the northeast mainland). After World War II, the breed was nearly lost, and it was further decimated by distemper in 1952. In an attempt to save the Shiba Inu, the different types were interbred, crossing the heavier-boned dogs from

AKC Ranking: 58
Family: Spitz, Northern (companion)
Area of Origin: Japan
Date of Origin: Ancient times
Original Function: Hunting and
    flushing small game
Today's Function: Companion
Other Name: Brushwood Dog,
    Japanese Small-size Dog

mountainous regions with the lighter-boned dogs from other regions. As a result, the Shiba survived as one breed with some variation in bone substance. The first Shiba came to America in 1954 and was officially recognized by the AKC in 1993. Since then, Shibas have achieved a staunch following, and their popularity continues to grow.

Temperament

Bold, independent, and headstrong, the Shiba is brimming with self-confidence. It is lively outdoors, yet calm indoors, as long as it gets daily exercise. It may be aggressive with strange dogs of the same sex and may chase small animals. It is a hardy breed, ready for adventure. Some tend to be headstrong and domineering. It is territorial, alert, and reserved with strangers—ingredients making for an excellent watchdog. It is quite vocal; some bark a lot.

Upkeep

The Shiba needs a daily workout, either in the form of a vigorous game in the yard, a long walk, or a good run in a safe area. It can

At a Glance

Energy level:	☐☐☐
Exercise requirements:	☐☐☐
Playfulness:	☐☐☐
Affection level:	☐☐☐
Friendliness toward dogs:	☐☐
Friendliness toward other pets:	☐☐
Friendliness toward strangers:	☐☐☐
Ease of training:	☐☐
Watchdog ability:	☐☐☐☐☐
Protection ability:	☐☐
Grooming requirements:	☐☐☐
Cold tolerance:	☐☐☐
Heat tolerance:	☐☐

Weight:	20–30 lb*
Height: male: 14.5–16.5"; female: 13.5–15.5"	

live outdoors in temperate or cool climates, given warm shelter, but it does best when allowed to divide its time between inside and out. Its double coat needs brushing one or two times weekly, more when shedding.

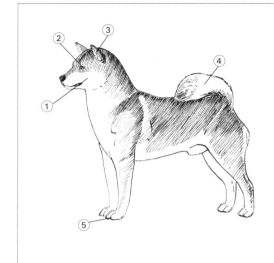

Health

- Major concerns: none
- Minor concerns: patellar luxation
- Occasionally seen: none
- Suggested tests: knee
- Life span: 12–15 years

Form and Function

The Shiba Inu is moderately compact, being slightly longer than it is tall. It has typical traits of dogs from northern heritage: small erect ears, thick fur, powerful body, and curled tail. Its expression is bold, spirited, and good natured. The gait is light, quick, and agile, with an effortless, smooth stride. The double coat consists of a strong straight outer coat with a soft undercoat, imparting great insulation. These traits enabled the Shiba to hunt small game through dense cover.

Tibetan Spaniel

History

The Tibetan Spaniel's history is interwoven with the Buddhist beliefs of Tibet. The Lamaist form of Buddhism regarded the lion as an important symbol, as it was said to follow Buddha like a dog. The little lionlike dogs that followed their Lama masters were regarded as symbols of the sacred lion and were thus highly valued. The Chinese also cultivated a lion dog, the Pekingese, and dogs from each country were often presented between countries, encouraging some interbreeding between the Tibetan and Chinese dogs. Although breeding occurred in the villages, the best breedings were products of the monasteries, which usually bred only the smallest specimens. The little dogs served more than a decorative purpose; they perched on the monastery walls and sounded the alarm when strangers or wolves approached. They also served as prayer dogs, turning the prayer wheels by means of small treadmills. Although the first Tibby came to England in the late 1800s, no concerted breeding program was attempted until the 1920s,

AKC Ranking: 106
Family: Companion, Herding
Area of Origin: Tibet
Date of Origin: Ancient times
Original Function: Watchdog, companion
Today's Function: Companion
Other Name: None

when the Griegs (known for promoting the Tibetan Spaniel) obtained several specimens. Only one of their dogs, Skyid, survived World War II, but its descendents can be found in modern pedigrees. The start of most Western Tibbies dates from around 1940, when several dogs came to England by way of an English couple living in Sikkim. It wasn't until the 1960s that the breed came to America, and only in 1984 did it receive AKC recognition. This sacred dog has been slow to garner fanciers, but it is worshiped by those who have adopted it.

Temperament

The Tibetan Spaniel is independent, bold, and stubborn, but it is also sensitive and biddable. It has a happy attitude, enjoying games and outings with its family. It also enjoys snoozes next to its special person. It is an exceptionally enjoyable and fastidious housedog. It is amiable with other dogs and animals, but reserved with strangers.

At a Glance

Energy level:	▢▢▢
Exercise requirements:	▢▢
Playfulness:	▢▢▢
Affection level:	▢▢▢
Friendliness toward dogs:	▢▢▢▢
Friendliness toward other pets:	▢▢▢▢
Friendliness toward strangers:	▢
Ease of training:	▢▢▢
Watchdog ability:	▢▢▢▢▢
Protection ability:	▢
Grooming requirements:	▢▢▢
Cold tolerance:	▢▢▢
Heat tolerance:	▢▢

Weight:	9–15 lb
Height:	about 10"

Illustrated Standard

1. Slightly undershot
2. Blunt muzzle
3. Small head
4. Slightly domed skull
5. Oval eyes
6. Pendant ears
7. Tail carried in a gay curl over back, richly plumed
8. Hare foot with long feathering

❏ **Color:** all colors and mixtures; white allowed on feet
❏ **DQ:** none

Upkeep

The Tibbie's exercise needs are minimal, but daily. Its needs can be met by games inside the house or yard, or with a short walk on leash. This breed is suited for apartment life and should not live outside. Its coat needs brushing and combing twice weekly.

Health

- Major concerns: none
- Minor concerns: patellar luxation
- Occasionally seen: PRA
- Suggested tests: knee, eye
- Life span: 12–15 years

Form and Function

The Tibbie is slightly longer than it is tall. Its head is small in proportion to its body; its wide eye set gives it an "apelike" expression. The mouth is undershot. The gait is quick moving, straight, and free. The coat is double, with a flat-lying, silky outer coat of moderate length and a longer mane. The tail is plumed, and long feathering grows from between the toes.

Tibetan Terrier

History

The history of the Tibetan Terrier is as shrouded in mystery as the mountains and valleys from whence it comes. The Tibetan Terrier was bred in Lamaist monasteries nearly 2000 years ago. The dogs were kept not as workers, but as family companions that might occasionally help out with the herding or other farm chores. They were known as "luck bringers" or "holy dogs." Much of the breed's history is speculation or myth; one story claims that a major access route to their valley was obliterated by an earthquake in the fourteenth century. Few visitors hazarded the treacherous journey to the "Lost Valley" after that; the few that did were often given a luck-bringer dog to help them on their return trip. As befitting any bringer of luck, these dogs were never sold, but they were often presented as special gifts of gratitude. So it was that in 1920 Dr. A. Grieg, an Indian physician, was given one of the special dogs in return for medical treatment. Dr. Grieg became interested in the breed, obtained additional dogs, and began to breed and promote them. The Tibetan Terrier first became recognized in India, and by

AKC Ranking: 90
Family: Companion, Herding
Area of Origin: Tibet
Date of Origin: Ancient times
Original Function: Herder, good luck, companion
Today's Function: Companion
Other Name: Dhokhi Apso

1937 it had made its way into English dog shows. From there it came to America in the 1950s and was admitted to AKC registration in 1973. Incidentally, the Tibetan Terrier is in no way a terrier, having only been given that name because it was of terrier size.

Temperament

Gentle and amiable, the Tibetan Terrier makes a charming, dependable companion both indoors and out. It is equally up for an adventure in the field, a game in the yard, or a snooze in the house. It is sensitive, very companionable, and willing to please.

Upkeep

The Tibetan Terrier likes to run and explore, and needs daily exercise in a safe area. Its needs can also be met by a vigorous game in the yard or a moderately long walk on leash. Although capable of living outdoors in temperate or modestly cool climates, it is better as an indoor, or indoor/outdoor, dog. Its long coat needs thorough brushing or combing once or twice a week.

At a Glance

Energy level:	☐☐☐
Exercise requirements:	☐☐☐
Playfulness:	☐☐☐
Affection level:	☐☐☐☐
Friendliness toward dogs:	☐☐☐
Friendliness toward other pets:	☐☐☐
Friendliness toward strangers:	☐☐
Ease of training:	☐☐☐
Watchdog ability:	☐☐☐☐
Protection ability:	☐
Grooming requirements:	☐☐☐☐
Cold tolerance:	☐☐☐
Heat tolerance:	☐☐☐

Weight: average 20–24 lb, but may be 18–30 lb

Height: male: 15–16", females slightly smaller

Illustrated Standard

① Small amount of beard
② Profusely coated with a fall of hair covering the eyes and foreface
③ Pendant, heavily feathered ears
④ Tail falls forward over the back
⑤ Large, flat, round feet

❏ **Color:** any
❏ **DQ:** none

Health

- Major concerns: lens luxation, PRA, ceroid lipofuscinosis
- Minor concerns: patellar luxation, cataract, CHD
- Occasionally seen: distichiasis
- Suggested tests: eye, hip
- Life span: 12–15 years

Form and Function

The Tibetan Terrier evolved as an all-purpose dog, able to accompany its owner on any job. It is square-proportioned, compact, and powerfully built. Its double coat, consisting of a profuse fine, long (straight or slightly wavy) outer coat and a soft wooly undercoat, provided protection from the harsh Tibetan climate. Long hair falls forward over the eyes and foreface. The feet are large, flat, and round, producing a snowshoe effect for maximum traction in difficult terrain. The stride is free and effortless.

The Herding Group

Dogs of the Herding Group have in common the desire and ability to control the movements of other animals, most often sheep and cattle. In some species, this is accomplished by stalking and staring, in others by barking, and in others by nipping. Some herders have gathering tendencies, whereas others have driving tendencies. All have in common the ability to work using both their owner's commands and their own judgment. Herding breeds make intelligent and devoted partners.

Australian Cattle Dog

History

In the early 1800s, vast land areas in Australia became available for grazing cattle. The cattle raised on these lands became so wild and intractable that the traditional European herding breeds that had proved satisfactory on tamer cattle were no longer suited for the job. A dog was needed that could withstand traveling long distances over rough terrain in hot weather and that could control cattle without barking (which only served to make wild cattle wilder). In 1840, a man named Hall bred some smooth blue merle Highland Collies to Dingos, producing a strain known as Hall's Heelers. One particularly influential stud was a dog named Bentley's Dog, who is credited with stamping the white blaze found on the head of Australian Cattle Dogs

AKC Ranking: 65
Family: Livestock, Herding
Area of Origin: Australia
Date of Origin: 1800s
Original function: Cattle herding
Today's function: Cattle herding, herding trials
Other Name: Queensland Heeler, Blue Heeler, Hall's Heeler

today. Other breeders crossed their Hall's Heelers with other breeds, including the Bull Terrier, Dalmatian, and, later, Black and Tan Kelpie, a sheepherding breed. The result was a dog with the herding instincts of the Collie and Kelpie, the endurance, ruggedness, and quiet style of the Dingo, and the horse sense and protectiveness of the Dalmatian, all with a distinctively patterned coat. As the dogs became increasingly vital to the cattle industry of Queensland, they gained the name Queensland Blue Heeler. They later became known as Australian Heeler, and then Australian Cattle Dog. A standard for the breed, emphasizing its Dingo characteristics, was drawn up in 1897. The Australian Cattle Dog was slow to catch on in America, however, perhaps because it bore little resemblance to established herding breeds. When given a chance, it proved its merits and was welcomed as a herder and pet. The AKC recognized the breed in 1980, and it has since become a capable show dog, without sacrificing its functional makeup.

Temperament

Smart, hardy, independent, stubborn, tenacious, energetic, and untiring—these are all traits essential to a driver of headstrong cattle, and all traits of the Australian Cattle Dog. This dog must have a job to do or it will expend its efforts on unacceptable jobs of its own. Given challenging mental and hard physical exercise daily, it is among the most responsive and obedient of dogs, an exemplary partner in adventure. It tends to nip at heels of running children.

Upkeep

The Australian Cattle Dog was bred to be active and tireless. This dog needs a lot of physical and mental activity, more than a simple walk on leash can provide. A good jog or long workout, coupled with obedience lessons or other intellectual challenges, is essential every day. It is happiest when it has a job to perform,

Illustrated Standard

1. Medium-sized, oval eyes
2. Broad skull
3. Rather small pricked ears
4. Tail set low, hanging in slight curve
5. Round feet

❏ **Color:** blue or blue-mottled with or without other markings; red speckled. Puppies are born white but get their color within a few weeks.
❏ **DQ:** none

and especially when that job is herding. The Australian Cattle Dog can live outdoors in temperate to cool climates. It is unsuited for apartment life. Its coat needs brushing or combing weekly to remove dead hairs.

Health

- Major concerns: CHD, OCD, deafness, PRA
- Minor concerns: none
- Occasionally seen: cataract, lens luxation, PPM, vWD
- Suggested tests: hip, hearing, eye
- Life span: 10–13 years

Form and Function

The Australian Cattle Dog is of moderate build, enabling it to combine great endurance with bursts of speed and extreme agility necessary in controlling unruly cattle. It is sturdy and compact, slightly longer than it is tall. Its gait is supple and tireless, and it must be capable of quick and sudden movement. Its ability to stop quickly is aided by the rudderlike action of its tail (which is never docked). Its weather-resistant coat consists of a short, dense undercoat and moderately short, straight outer coat of medium texture.

At a Glance

Energy level:	▢▢▢▢▢
Exercise requirements:	▢▢▢▢▢
Playfulness:	▢▢▢▢
Affection level:	▢▢▢
Friendliness toward dogs:	▢▢▢
Friendliness toward other pets:	▢▢
Friendliness toward strangers:	▢▢
Ease of training:	▢▢▢▢▢
Watchdog ability:	▢▢▢▢▢
Protection ability:	▢▢▢▢
Grooming requirements:	▢▢
Cold tolerance:	▢▢▢
Heat tolerance:	▢▢▢

Weight:	35–45 lb*
Height:	male: 18–20"; female: 17–19"

Australian Shepherd

History

The Australian Shepherd is not really an Australian breed, but it came to America by way of Australia. One popular theory of the breed's origin begins during the 1800s when the Basque people of Europe settled in Australia, bringing with them their sheep and sheepdogs. Shortly thereafter, many of these shepherds relocated to the western United States, with their dogs and sheep. American shepherds naturally dubbed these dogs Australian Shepherds because that was their immediate past residence. The rugged area of Australia and western America placed demands on the herding dogs that they had not faced in Europe, but through various crosses and rigorous selection for working ability, the Basque dog soon adapted and excelled under these harsh conditions. The breed kept a low profile until the 1950s, when they were featured in a popular trick-dog act that performed in rodeos and was featured in film. Many of these dogs, owned by Jay Sisler, can be found in the pedigrees of today's Aussies. The first Aussie was registered with the International English Shepherd Registry, now known as the National Stock Dog Registry. In 1957 the Australian Shepherd Club of America (ASCA) was formed and subsequently became the largest Aussie

> AKC Ranking: 40
> Family: Livestock, Herding
> Area of Origin: United States
> Date of Origin: 1800s
> Original Function: Sheep herding
> Today's Function: Sheep herding, herding trials
> Other Name: None

registry in America. Because many ASCA members felt that AKC recognition was not desirable for their breed, proponents of AKC recognition formed the United States Australian Shepherd Association. The AKC recognized the Australian Shepherd in 1993. Its popularity according to AKC statistics underestimates the popularity of this breed as a pet because a large proportion of this working breed remains unregistered with the AKC. It is among the most versatile of breeds, excelling at conformation, obedience, herding, and agility competition. The Aussie is also adept at working cattle; in fact, some believe its close working style is more suited to cattle than to sheep.

Temperament

The Australian Shepherd has a great deal of stamina and is loving, bold, alert, confident, independent, smart, and responsive. If it doesn't get a chance to exercise and challenge its strongly developed mental and physical activities, it is apt to become frustrated and difficult to live with. With proper exercise and training, it is a loyal, utterly devoted, and obedient companion. It is reserved with strangers, and has a protective nature. It may try to herd children and small animals by nipping.

Upkeep

This breed needs a good workout every day, preferably combining both physical and mental challenges. Even though it is physically able to live outside in temperate climates, it is a breed for which human contact is so vital that it is emotionally unsuited for a life in the yard. Its coat needs brushing or combing one to two times weekly.

Health

- Major concerns: cataract, CEA
- Minor concerns: CHD, nasal solar dermatitis, Pelger-Huet syndrome, iris coloboma
- Occasionally seen: lumbar sacral syndrome, epilepsy, PRA, vWD, distichiasis, PDA, PPM
- Suggested tests: hip, eye
- Life span: 12–15 years
- Note: This breed is often sensitive to ivermectin; however, the dosage for heartworm preventive is considered safe. Merle-to-merle breedings result in some offspring that are homozygous merle, which is detrimental to health, commonly resulting in deafness and blindness. Natural bobtail-to-natural

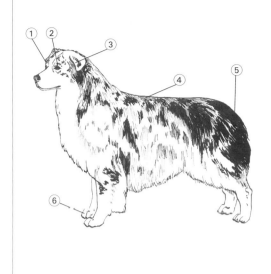

Illustrated Standard

① Moderate well-defined stop
② Eye color is brown, blue, amber, in any combination or with flecks
③ Triangular, high-set ears; at attention they break forward and over or to the side
④ Straight, strong, level back
⑤ Tail docked close or naturally bobbed
⑥ Feet oval

❏ **Color:** blue merle, black, red merle, or red, all with or without white markings and/or tan points
❏ **DQ:** undershot, overshot more than ⅛", white body splashes (white on body between withers and tail or on sides between elbows and back of hindquarters)
❏ **Note:** The Australian Shepherd Club of America standard contains more disqualifications; they are not included here.

bobtail breedings can result in some offspring with serious spinal defects.

Form and Function

This is an athletic dog of medium size and bone; it is lithe, agile, and slightly longer than it is tall. It is muscular and powerful enough to work all day, without sacrificing the speed and agility necessary to cope with bolting livestock. Its gait is free and easy, and it must be able to change direction or speed instantly. Its double coat is weather resistant, with the outer coat of medium texture and length, straight to wavy. The expression is keen, intelligent, and eager.

At a Glance

Energy level:	▢▢▢▢
Exercise requirements:	▢▢▢▢▢
Playfulness:	▢▢▢▢▢
Affection level:	▢▢▢▢
Friendliness toward dogs:	▢▢▢
Friendliness toward other pets:	▢▢▢
Friendliness toward strangers:	▢▢
Ease of training:	▢▢▢▢▢
Watchdog ability:	▢▢▢▢▢
Protection ability:	▢▢▢
Grooming requirements:	▢▢▢
Cold tolerance:	▢▢▢
Heat tolerance:	▢▢▢

Weight:	male: 50–65 lb; female: 40–55 lb*
Height:	male: 20–23"; female: 18–21"

Bearded Collie

History

The Bearded Collie probably originated from the central European Magyar Komondor or Lowland Polish Sheepdog. In fact, records show that in 1514 two Lowland Polish Sheepdogs were brought to Scotland by Polish traders. Although dogs strongly resembling Bearded Collies are depicted in art dating from the eighteenth century, hard evidence of the breed cannot be found until the early nineteenth century, when the first breed description was published. These dogs were tireless herders of sheep and drovers of cattle over rough terrain in the cold Scottish mists. Long popular as a

AKC Ranking: 89
Family: Livestock, Herding
Area of Origin: Scotland
Date of Origin: 1800s
Original Function: Sheep herding
Today's Function: Herding trials
Other Name: None

herding dog in Scotland, after the Victorian era the breed also gained favor as a show dog. Two strains, the Border strain, which was brown and white with a slightly wavy coat, and the Highland strain, which had a gray and white coat, have since been interbred and merged into one breed. After World War I, the Beardie was once again bred solely for work. Their value as stock dogs made it difficult for outsiders to acquire one from their shepherd owners. Eventually, however, a few breeders interested in showing Beardies were able to bring some dogs to England and then to America. The AKC recognized the breed in 1977. It has since become a prominent show dog and continues as a capable herder, although it is more popular as a competitor in herding trials than as an actual working dog.

Temperament

The boisterous Beardie is lively and playful, full of enthusiasm and energy. It is smart and obedient, but it is an independent thinker with a clownish sense of humor. It likes children, but it may be too rambunctious for small children and may try to herd them when playing.

Upkeep

This active dog needs either a good jog, a very long walk, or a vigorous play session every day. It especially enjoys herding. The Beardie can live outside in cool climates, but it is happier when allowed access to the house with its family. Its long coat needs brushing or combing every other day.

Health

- Major concerns: none
- Minor concerns: CHD, epilepsy, colonic disease, pemphigus

- Occasionally seen: CHD, aortic stenosis, PRA, PPM, cataract, vWD
- Suggested tests: hip, (eye), (cardiac)
- Life span: 12–14 years

Form and Function

The Beardie is a medium-sized dog with a long, lean, strongly made body, which gives the impression of both strength and agility. Its gait is supple and powerful, with good reach and drive. The ability to make sharp turns, quick starts, and sudden stops is essential in a sheep herding breed, and the Beardie must be able to keep this activity up for a long period of time under all conditions. Its coat is double with a soft, furry undercoat. The outer coat is flat, harsh, and fairly straight; it is sufficient to protect the dog but not so much as to obscure the dog's lines. The Beardie's expression is bright and inquiring.

At a Glance

Energy level:	▫▫▫▫
Exercise requirements:	▫▫▫▫
Playfulness:	▫▫▫▫
Affection level:	▫▫▫▫
Friendliness toward dogs:	▫▫▫
Friendliness toward other pets:	▫▫▫
Friendliness toward strangers:	▫▫▫
Ease of training:	▫▫▫
Watchdog ability:	▫▫▫▫
Protection ability:	▫▫
Grooming requirements:	▫▫▫▫
Cold tolerance:	▫▫▫▫
Heat tolerance:	▫▫▫

Weight:	45–55 lb*
Height:	male: 21–22"; female: 20–21"

Belgian Malinois

History

The Belgian sheepherding breeds, collectively known as Chiens de Berger Belge, shared their early history as general-purpose shepherds and guard dogs of Belgium. As working dogs, they were bred for ability rather than esthetics, and no careful records were kept. Thus, when dog shows became popular in the late 1800s, it was not clear if Belgium had any recognizable breeds with which they could tout their national pride. In 1891, Professor Reul was asked to study the native dogs to see if they could be sorted into distinct breeds. He found a group of similar dogs that differed only in coat type and color, all of which were grouped as Belgian Shepherds. The short-haired variety was developed in the area around Malines, and so became known as the Belgian Malinois. It remains the most popular of the Belgian shepherd breeds in its native land, but has had a rockier road in

AKC Ranking: 95
Family: Livestock, Herding
Area of Origin: Belgium
Date of Origin: 1800s
Original Function: Stock herding
Today's Function: Security, police, contraband detection, assistance, herding trials, Shutzhund
Other Name: Malinois, Chien de Berger Belge

America. Between 1911 and World War II, the Malinois enjoyed a good deal of popularity in America. After the war, registrations plummeted, and it was rare to find a Malinois entered in competition. When the breeds were separated in 1959, Malinois registrations began to grow once again, but they still fell far behind the other Belgian breeds. More recently, the Malinois is becoming popular because of its reputation as one of the preeminent police dogs in the world, surpassing even the German Shepherd in demand. Thus, even though it may not be seen in many homes or show rings, it is making its presence known as a keeper of the peace throughout the world.

Temperament

Intense best describes the Belgian Malinois. This is a high-energy breed with a need for regular mental and physical stimulation.

At a Glance

Energy level:	▢▢▢◻
Exercise requirements:	▢▢▢▢◻
Playfulness:	▢▢▢◻
Affection level:	▢
Friendliness toward dogs:	▢▢◻
Friendliness toward other pets:	▢▢◻
Friendliness toward strangers:	▢
Ease of training:	▢▢▢▢◻
Watchdog ability:	▢▢▢▢◻
Protection ability:	▢▢▢▢◻
Grooming requirements:	▢
Cold tolerance:	▢▢◻
Heat tolerance:	▢▢◻

Weight:	60–65 lb*
Height:	male: 24–26"; female: 22–24"

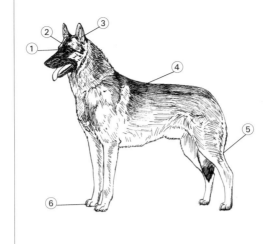

Illustrated Standard

1. Almond-shaped eyes
2. Flat skull
3. Ears stiff, erect, and in the shape of an equilateral triangle
4. Level topline
5. Tail raised with slight curve when dog is moving
6. Cat footed

❑ **Color:** rich fawn to mahogany, with black-tipped hairs; black mask and ears
❑ **DQ:** males under 23" or over 27", females under 21" or over 25"; ears hanging or semi-pricked; undershot bite in which two or more incisors fail to make contact with incisors of other jaw; cropped or stumped tail

Form and Function

The Belgian Malinois is a sturdy dog of square proportion with moderately heavy, but oval, bone. It is elegant, with very proud head carriage. The overall impression is of power without bulkiness. The gait is smooth and easy, seemingly effortless rather than hard driving. Such a gait gives the impression of tirelessness. The Malinois has a tendency to run in a wide circle rather than a straight line. Its coat is fairly short, straight, and hard, with a dense undercoat. Its expression is intelligent and questioning.

It is alert, smart, and serious, an ideal watchdog and guard dog. It is aloof with strangers and can be aggressive toward other dogs and animals. Some can be domineering. When confined, it often runs in sweeping circles in an effort to stay on the move. It is protective of its home and family.

Upkeep

The Malinois is a high-energy dog that needs a lot of exercise. Its needs cannot be met with a leisurely walk on leash. It instead needs a good jog or a vigorous play session. It especially enjoys herding. This breed can live outside in temperate to cool weather, but it would prefer to divide its time between house and yard. Its coat needs weekly brushing, more when shedding.

Health

- Major concerns: none
- Minor concerns: CHD, epilepsy, skin allergies
- Occasionally seen: none
- Suggested tests: hip
- Life span: 10–12 years

Belgian Sheepdog

History

The Belgian Sheepdog, Belgian Tervuren, and Belgian Malinois began as three local variations of one breed, which was known as the Belgian Shepherd or Continental Shepherd. The dog that was heir to the name Belgian Sheepdog was originally known as the Groenendael variation of the breed. Like all the Belgian shepherds, it was a working farm dog expected to both herd and guard. It differed from the others because it had a rather long, black coat. In 1910 these dogs were officially dubbed Groenendael after the kennel that had selectively bred the black dogs since 1893 (just after the Belgian Shepherds were recognized as a breed). By this time, the breed had gained some repute as a police dog and was already employed in this capacity in America. In World War I, they continued to shine as sentry dogs, messengers, and even draft dogs. It was here that they captured the attention

AKC Ranking: 101
Family: Livestock, Herding
Area of Origin: Belgium
Date of Origin: 1800s
Original Function: Stock herding
Today's Function: Herding trials, Schutzhund
Other Name: Groenendael, Chien de Berger Belge

of the public, and they soon enjoyed a fair amount of popularity after the war. In 1959, the three Belgian Shepherd breeds were divided into separate breeds, with the Groenendael subsequently known as the Belgian Sheepdog. With its shimmering black coat, it is the most striking of the Belgian breeds, and that fact, along with its versatile abilities, has won it many faithful supporters.

Temperament

Ever watchful and on the move, the Belgian Sheepdog glides in large circles. It is playful, alert, watchful, and protective, a tough, independent, and intense dog. It is aloof with strangers and can be aggressive toward other dogs and animals. Some can be domineering. It is intelligent and biddable, but independent. It is protective of its home and family.

Upkeep

The Belgian Sheepdog needs a good deal of exercise, either a good long jog or a long, strenuous play session. It needs room to move during the day and does best with access to a yard. Although it can live outdoors in temperate to cool climates, it is family oriented and happier if it can share time in the house with its family. Its double coat needs brushing and combing twice weekly, more when shedding.

IIealth

• Major concerns: none
• Minor concerns: epilepsy, skin allergies
• Occasionally seen: CHD
• Suggested tests: none
• Life span: 10–12 years

Form and Function

The Belgian Sheepdog is an elegant, square-proportioned dog that is alert and agile with proud carriage. Its bone is moderately heavy. As a dog expected to herd for long hours, its gait is smooth, tireless, and effortless rather than driving. It has a tendency to move in a circle rather than a straight line.

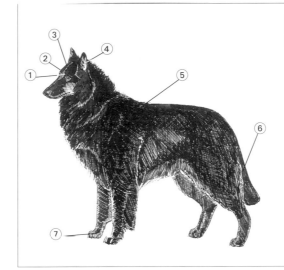

Illustrated Standard

① Almond-shaped eyes
② Moderate stop
③ Flat skull
④ Stiff, erect ears in the shape of a triangle
⑤ Level topline
⑥ Tail raised with slight curve when dog is moving, held low when at rest
⑦ Cat footed

❑ **Color:** black
❑ **DQ:** males under 22.5" or over 27.5", females under 20.5" or over 25.5"; ears hanging; cropped or stumped tail; any color other than black; viciousness

It has an extremely dense undercoat along with an outer coat of abundant guard hairs that are long, well-fitting, and straight. Its expression is intelligent and questioning; its black coloration is striking.

At a Glance

Energy level:	☐☐☐☐
Exercise requirements:	☐☐☐☐☐
Playfulness:	☐☐☐☐
Affection level:	☐
Friendliness toward dogs:	☐☐☐
Friendliness toward other pets:	☐☐☐
Friendliness toward strangers:	☐
Ease of training:	☐☐☐☐☐
Watchdog ability:	☐☐☐☐☐
Protection ability:	☐☐☐☐☐
Grooming requirements:	☐☐☐
Cold tolerance:	☐☐☐
Heat tolerance:	☐☐☐

Weight:	60–65 lb*
Height:	male: 24–26"; female: 22–24"

Belgian Tervuren

History

The Belgian Tervuren is one of four Belgian shepherd breeds, all sharing the same origins but distinguished by different coat types and colors. They are the wire-haired Laekenois, the shorthaired Malinois, the long black-haired Groenendael, and the long anything-but-black-haired Tervuren. All these herding–guard breeds were interbred before and after their recognition as one breed (the Belgian, or Continental, Shepherd) in 1891. The Tervuren was named after the village of Tervuren, where one of the breed's earliest proponents lived. The Tervuren lagged behind the other shepherd breeds in popularity, perhaps hindered by its less flashy color and disagreements over exactly what colors were desirable. The first Terv was registered in America in 1918, but the breed's numbers remained so low that they died out by the Depression. The Tervuren had to be almost recreated after World War II from long-haired offspring of Malinois parents. In 1959 the Belgian Shepherd was divided into three breeds, and the Tervuren was on its own. The Tervuren has

AKC Ranking: 97
Family: Livestock, Herding
Area of Origin: Belgium
Date of Origin: 1800s
Original Function: Stock herding
Today's Function: Herding trials, Schutzhund
Other Name: Tervuren, Chien de Berger Belge

since captured the eye of many fanciers because it is the most elegant of the three breeds. It now enjoys moderate popularity. The Belgian Tervuren is a versatile dog and is used less in guard work, but more in herding, than are its Belgian Shepherd counterparts.

Temperament

Alert, watchful, and energetic, the Tervuren is an active and dependable companion that functions best when given daily mental and physical exercise. It enjoys playing and running outside, and can be a well-mannered companion inside as long as it is given sufficient exercise. It is smart and obedient, but independent. It is aloof with strangers and can be aggressive toward other dogs and animals. It may nip at the heels of children in an attempt to herd them.

Upkeep

The Terv needs strenuous activity, either a long walk or jog or an invigorating play or work session every day. It especially enjoys herding, which is the ideal exercise. It can live outside in temperate to cool climates, but it does best when allowed access to both a house and yard. Its double coat needs brushing and combing twice weekly, more often when shedding.

Health

- Major concerns: none
- Minor concerns: epilepsy, skin allergies
- Occasionally seen: CHD
- Suggested tests: none
- Life span: 10–12 years

Form and Function

This breed combines elegance and strength. It is square-proportioned and of medium bone. It is noteworthy for its exceedingly proud carriage. Its movement is lively, graceful, and seemingly tireless, exhibiting an easy, effortless gait rather than a hard-driving action. It has a natural tendency to move in a circle rather than a straight line. It combines a dense undercoat with an outer coat consisting of abundant guard hairs that are long, well-fitting, straight and of medium harshness. Its expression is intelligent and questioning.

Illustrated Standard

① Almond-shaped eyes
② Moderate stop
③ Flat skull
④ Stiff, erect, triangular ears
⑤ Level topline
⑥ Tail raised with slight curve when dog is moving, held low when at rest
⑦ Cat footed

❏ **Color:** rich fawn to russet mahogany with black overlay (becoming darker with maturity); black mask and ears
❏ **DQ:** males under 23" or over 26.5", females under 21" or over 24.5"; ears hanging; undershot bite in which two or more incisors fail to make contact with incisors of other jaw; cropped or stumped tail; solid black, solid liver, or any area of white except for a small white patch on the chest, tips of toes, chin, and muzzle

At a Glance

Energy level:	■■■☐
Exercise requirements:	■■■■■
Playfulness:	■■■☐
Affection level:	■
Friendliness toward dogs:	■■☐
Friendliness toward other pets:	■■☐
Friendliness toward strangers:	■
Ease of training:	■■■■■
Watchdog ability:	■■■■■
Protection ability:	■■■■■
Grooming requirements:	■■☐
Cold tolerance:	■■☐
Heat tolerance:	■■☐

Weight:	60–65 lb*
Height:	male: 24–26"; female: 22–24"

Border Collie

History

The consummate sheepdog, the Border Collie is the result of over a century of breeding for function above all other criteria. In the 1800s, a variety of sheep herding dogs with differing herding styles existed in Great Britain. Some were "fetching" dogs, dogs having an innate tendency to circle stock and bring them back toward the shepherd. Most of these were noisy dogs, tending to nip and bark as they performed their job. Boasts of the superiority of certain dogs were only natural; in 1873 the first actual sheepdog trial was held in order to settle some of these boasts. This contest would indirectly lead to the first Border Collies, by way of a dog named Hemp, who so distinguished himself in trials that he sired a great number of offspring. He herded not by barking and nipping, but by calmly staring at the sheep ("giving eye") intimidating them into moving. Hemp is considered to be the father of the Border Collie. In 1906, the first standard was drawn up, but unlike the physical standards of most breeds, this was a description of working ability, with no regard to physical appearance. This emphasis has shaped the breed ever since. In fact, the

AKC Ranking: 74
Family: Livestock, Herding
Area of Origin: Great Britain
Date of Origin: 1800s
Original Function: Sheep herder
Today's Function: Sheep herder, herding trials, obedience
Other Name: None

dogs were still referred to simply as sheepdogs; only in 1915 was the name Border Collie first recorded, in reference to the dog's origin around the English and Scottish borders. The Border Collie came to America and instantly dazzled serious shepherds with its quick herding and obedience capabilities. In fact, the latter opened a new door for the breed as one of the top competitive breeds in obedience trials. Having worked hard to gain the reputation of one of the smartest breeds of dogs, a breed unspoiled by cosmetic emphasis, many Border Collie fanciers actively fought AKC recognition as a show dog. In 1995, however, the AKC recognized the breed and herded it into the show ring.

Temperament

The Border Collie is a bundle of mental and physical energy awaiting its chance to be unleashed on the world. Among the most intelligent and obedient of breeds, it is nonetheless a disastrous housedog if it is not given a challenging job every day. Given sufficient exercise, it is a dependable and loyal companion. It is intent on whatever it does and tends to stare, which can be unnerving to other animals. It also likes to chase other animals. It is reserved, even protective, toward strangers.

Upkeep

Few dogs are as work oriented as the Border Collie. This is a dog that needs a job. It needs a lot of physical and mental activity every day to satisfy its quest for work. It can live outdoors in temperate to cool climates, but it enjoys being with its family inside as well. This is a dog that cannot live in an apartment and that should preferably have ready access to a yard. Its coat needs brushing or combing twice weekly.

Health

- Major concerns: CHD
- Minor concerns: PRA, lens luxation, CEA, PDA, OCD, PPM
- Occasionally seen: cerebellar abiotrophy, ceroid lipofuscinosis, deafness
- Suggested tests: hip, eye
- Life span: 10–14 years

Illustrated Standard

① Blue eyes allowed in merles only
② Ears carried erect or semierect
③ Topline level with slight arch over loins
④ Tail set and carried low
⑤ Feet oval

❏ **Color:** solid, bicolor, tricolor, merle, and sable, of various colors; solid white not allowed
❏ **DQ:** none

Form and Function

This is a medium dog of strong bone, slightly longer than it is tall, combining grace, agility, substance, and stamina. Its trot is smooth, ground covering, and tireless, moving with stealth and strength. It is able to change speed and direction suddenly. The Border Collie must be able to display incredible agility even after working for long periods. The coat can be either smooth or rough. The smooth coat is short all over the body; the rough coat is medium to long in length and flat to slightly wavy in texture. Its expression is intelligent, alert, eager, and full of interest, a reflection of its temperament.

At a Glance

Energy level:	▢▢▢▢▢
Exercise requirements:	▢▢▢▢▢
Playfulness:	▢▢▢▢
Affection level:	▢▢▢
Friendliness toward dogs:	▢▢▢
Friendliness toward other pets:	▢
Friendliness toward strangers:	▢▢
Ease of training:	▢▢▢▢▢
Watchdog ability:	▢▢▢▢
Protection ability:	▢▢▢
Grooming requirements:	▢▢▢
Cold tolerance:	▢▢▢
Heat tolerance:	▢▢▢

Weight:	30–45 lb*
Height:	male: 20–23"; female: 18–21"

Bouvier des Flandres

History

The Bouvier des Flandres served farmers and cattle merchants in controlling cattle in the great farmlands of southwest Flanders and on the French northern plain. In fact, *bouvier* means cowherd or oxherd in French, although the dogs were formerly more often called *Vuilbaard* (dirty beard) or koe hond *(cow dog).* Besides its main duty as a cattle drover, the Bouvier was an all-around farm dog, functioning also as a livestock and farm guard and draft dog. As expected from a dog selected to perform a variety of tasks, these working dogs were of a variety of types, colors, and even sizes. This wide variety also reflected the fact that this was a working dog, and breeding stock was chosen by ability, not pedigree or esthetics. The derivation of the breed is not documented but may have included mastiff, sheepdog, and possibly even spaniel breeds.

AKC Ranking: 71
Family: Livestock, Herding
Area of Origin: Belgium
Date of Origin: 1600s
Original Function: Cattle herding
Today's Function: Security, herding trials
Other Name: Belgian Cattle Dog

The first breed standard, drawn up in 1912, reflected this diversity of types and signaled a growing interest in the breed from dog fanciers. In the midst of its rising popularity, most of the Bouviers were lost in World War I—although some Bouviers served as ambulance and messenger dogs during the war. One of the few survivors was of such superior quality that the breed was successfully revived through his progeny. This dog, Ch. Nic de Sottegem, can be found in virtually every modern Bouvier pedigree. In 1922, a revised standard further defined the desirable Bouvier type, and helped pave the way to a more homogeneous breed. When the first Bouviers entered American show rings in the 1930s, they aroused much attention among dog fanciers. The breed has never become extremely popular, but it is well known at dog shows and herding trials.

Temperament

The Bouvier is a steady, stalwart companion that is loyal, devoted, fearless, and protective. Given daily exercise, it is calm and well-mannered indoors, but ready for an adventure in the great outdoors. It is independent and confident of its own judgment, yet biddable and willing to please. It can be domineering. It is reserved, even protective, toward strangers and can be aggressive with strange dogs. It is very good with children, although it may nip at heels in play.

Upkeep

The Bouvier des Flandres is not a breed that can be put aside until the mood strikes to play with it. It needs daily exercise and daily interaction, and a lot of both. It loves the chance to herd, but its requirements can also be met with a good jog, a very long walk, or a vigorous play session. It can live outdoors in temperate to cool climates. It makes a good housedog, however, and would prefer access to both house and yard. Its harsh coat needs combing once or twice weekly, plus scissoring and shaping (clipping for pets and stripping for show dogs) every three months.

Illustrated Standard

1. Thick beard, mustache, and eyebrows
2. Oval eyes
3. Flat skull
4. High-set, rough-coated ears; if cropped, triangular
5. Tail docked to two or three vertebrae, carried upright when in motion
6. Rounded feet

❑ **Color:** from fawn to black, including salt and pepper, gray, and brindle
❑ **DQ:** none

Health

- Major concerns: CHD
- Minor concerns: gastric torsion
- Occasionally seen: entropion
- Suggested tests: hip
- Life span: 10–12 years

Form and Function

This is a versatile breed able to perform a variety of functions, including cattle herder, draft dog, and guard. As such, it combines great strength with agility and endurance. The Bouvier is a compact, short-coupled dog, of square proportion and rugged appearance. Its gait is free, bold, and proud. Its weatherproof coat is tousled and double, with a fine undercoat and a harsh, dry outer coat. It is trimmed (if necessary) to a length of about 2.5". The head is accentuated by a beard and moustache, which adds to the dog's bold and alert expression.

At a Glance

Energy level:	☐☐☐
Exercise requirements:	☐☐☐☐
Playfulness:	☐☐
Affection level:	☐☐☐
Friendliness toward dogs:	☐☐☐
Friendliness toward other pets:	☐☐☐
Friendliness toward strangers:	☐☐☐
Ease of training:	☐☐☐
Watchdog ability:	☐☐☐☐☐
Protection ability:	☐☐☐☐☐
Grooming requirements:	☐☐☐☐
Cold tolerance:	☐☐☐☐
Heat tolerance:	☐☐

Weight:	69–90 lb*
Height: male: 24.5–27.5"; female: 23.5–26.5"	

Briard

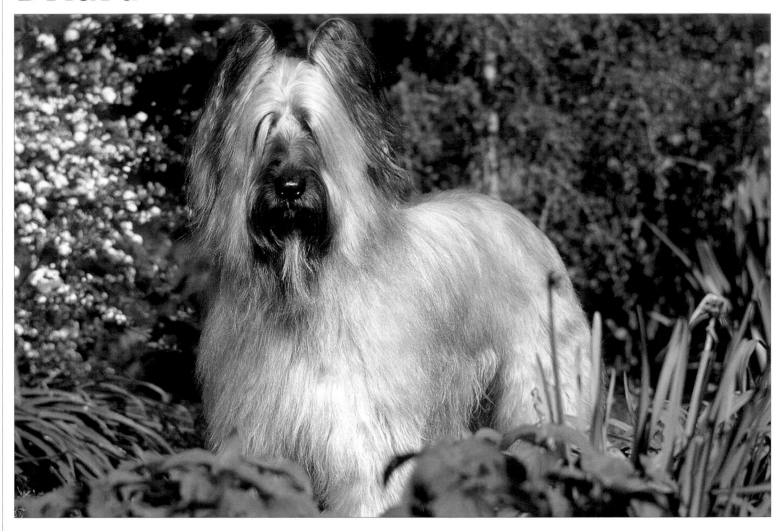

History

The Briard is one of four French sheepdog breeds, the others being the Beauceron, Picardy, and Pyrenean. It is the oldest of the four breeds, with dogs resembling Briards depicted in art from as long ago as the eighth century, and more definitive evidence by the fourteenth century. These early dogs were known as Chien Berger de Brie (Shepherd Dog of Brie), giving rise to the belief that the breed originated in the province of Brie; however, it may also be a corruption of Chien d'Aubry, referring to the dog of Aubry de Montdidier that saved his son's life (according to fourteenth-century legend). The name Briard was not used until 1809. Originally employed as a herd protector, the Briard was expected to tackle wolves if the need arose. After the French Revolution, which resulted in the land being divided into smaller sectors, it was important that the flocks be kept close to home, and the Briard turned its talents to herding, rather than guarding sheep. Only around 1900 did it become a show dog. The first breed standard was written in 1897, but it was replaced by another in 1909. Briards came to America very early, with evidence that both

AKC Ranking: 108
Family: Livestock, Herding
Area of Origin: France
Date of Origin: 1300s
Original Function: Herding and guarding sheep
Today's Function: Herding trials
Other Name: Berger de Brie

Lafayette and Thomas Jefferson brought some of the first specimens to the New World. These dogs did not have a lasting influence, however. After World War I, American soldiers brought some Briards to America, and this was the beginning of the modern American Briard. Popularity of the breed has been modest in America, but it remains the most popular sheepherder in its native France.

Temperament

Devoted and faithful, the Briard is a loving and protective companion. It is independent, intelligent, and self-assured, but it is also willing to please and eager to serve as a partner in adventure. It is reserved with strangers. It can be aggressive with other dogs and may nip at people's heels when playing. It tends to stay at home and may attempt to keep the family's children home as well!

Upkeep

This is a dog that needs a good amount of activity and interaction every day. Its favorite exercise is the chance to herd, but it can also

At a Glance

Energy level:	☐☐☐
Exercise requirements:	☐☐☐☐
Playfulness:	☐☐☐
Affection level:	☐☐☐
Friendliness toward dogs:	☐
Friendliness toward other pets:	☐☐☐
Friendliness toward strangers:	☐
Ease of training:	☐
Watchdog ability:	☐☐☐☐☐
Protection ability:	☐☐☐☐☐
Grooming requirements:	☐☐☐☐
Cold tolerance:	☐☐☐
Heat tolerance:	☐☐

Weight:	75–100 lb*
Height:	male: 23–27"; female: 22–25.5"

Illustrated Standard

1. Wide muzzle with mustache and beard
2. Large, calm eyes
3. High-set ears; natural ear is straight, lying away from the head and covered with hair, cropped ear is long with rounded tip.
4. Tail carried low and ending in curve (called a crochet)
5. Two dewclaws on each hindleg
6. Rear toes turn out slightly

❏ **Color:** all uniform colors except white (includes black, tawny, and gray shades)
❏ **DQ:** under minimum size limits; yellow or spotted eyes; nose any color other than black; non-existent or cut tail; spotted or white coat, or white spots exceeding 1" in diameter

Health

- Major concerns: gastric torsion, CHD
- Minor concerns: nightblindness
- Occasionally seen: PRA, heart problems
- Suggested tests: hip, eye, (cardiac)
- Life span: 10–12 years

Form and Function

The Briard is square or slightly longer than it is tall and powerful without being course; the overall appearance is one of handsome form. Like all good herding dogs, it combines strength, flexibility, agility, and endurance with the ability to make abrupt turns, springing starts, and sudden stops. Its movement has been described as "quicksilver," with supple, light strides that give the impression of gliding. Its undercoat is fine and tight, and its outer coat is coarse and dry, lying flat in long, slightly wavy locks. On the shoulders, the coat's length is 6 inches or more. The questioning confident expression is enhanced by the longer eyebrows, as well as the long-appearing head.

be satisfied with a long walk or jog, or a long play session coupled with a little training. The Briard can live outside in temperate to cool climates, but is happiest if allowed access to both house and yard. Its long coat needs brushing or combing every other day or mats can form.

Canaan Dog

History

Canaan Dogs have evolved through hundreds, and perhaps thousands, of years of hardship. It is thought that the breed originated in the biblical land of Canaan and were known as Kelev Kanani (Dog of Canaan). When the Israelites were dispersed from their homeland by the Romans 2000 years ago, most of the Israeli dogs were left to fend for themselves in the Sebulon Coastal Plain and Negev Desert. Bedouins captured male puppies from the wild to raise as guard and livestock dogs. When the Israeli Defense Force tried to develop service dogs in the 1930s, the traditional European service breeds weren't able to adapt to the harsh climate. The Canaan Dog owes its existence primarily to the efforts of one woman, Dr. Rudolphina Menzel. Her search for a more suitable dog led her to the native feral dogs. Several dogs were captured, and a breeding and training program was begun. The dogs quickly proved their worth, serving as sentry dogs, messengers, mine detectors, Red Cross helpers, and even locators of wounded soldiers during the Second World War and as guide dogs for the blind after the war. Perhaps no other breed of dog has ever risen from feral roots to become such a useful and dedicated companion in so short a time. The first Canaan Dog came to America in 1965. Not the flashiest of breeds, the Canaan's understated good looks may have made many people overlook it, despite its companionship credentials. Nonetheless, it slowly attracted admirers, and the AKC finally admitted it into the Herding Group in 1997. Now beginning a new era as a show dog, the increased exposure is sure to attract many more people looking for a loyal and hardy pet.

AKC Ranking: 103
Family: Livestock, Herding, Primitive, Southern (Pariah)
Area of Origin: Israel
Date of Origin: Ancient times
Original Function: Sentry, messenger, and assistance
Today's Function: Herding trials
Other Name: Kalef K'naani

Temperament

Not only does the Canaan Dog excel as a herder, but it has also proven itself in a variety of tasks involving dependability and obedience. This is an intelligent, devoted, docile dog that is quite tractable and willing to please. It is aloof toward strangers and protective of its family. The Canaan Dog is generally good with other household pets and dogs, but it may be aggressive toward strange dogs. It is a natural guardian and tends to bark a lot.

Upkeep

Few breeds can claim as pure a working heritage as the Canaan Dog. This dog will not be happy just sitting around. It needs lots of exercise and mental and physical challenges. These needs can be met with herding exercise, a long jog, a strenuous game session along with a challenging training session. It can live outdoors in warm to cool climates, but it also makes an excellent housedog. Its coat needs brushing about once a week to remove dead hairs.

Health

- Major concerns: none
- Minor concerns: none
- Occasionally seen: none
- Suggested tests: none
- Life span: 12–13 years

Form and Function

The Canaan Dog resembles none of the other herding breeds, arising from a completely different background. Nonetheless, it shares similar traits needed in any dog that must herd for hours. It is a medium-sized, square-proportioned dog of moderate substance that combines strength, agility, and endurance. It is not exagger-

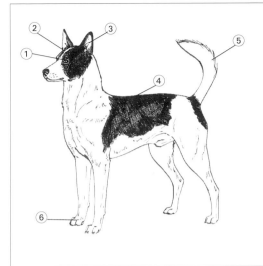

Illustrated Standard

1. Almond-shaped eyes
2. Elongated head, wedge-shaped from above
3. Ears erect and set low, slightly rounded tip
4. Topline level with slight arch over loin
5. Tail set moderately high, may be carried over back when excited
6. Cat feet

❏ **Color:** may be either predominantly white with mask with or without additional color patches, or solid color with or without white trim. The mask should be symmetrical and must completely cover both eyes and ears.
❏ **DQ:** males under 20" or over 25"; females under 18" or over 23"; gray or brindle; all white

ated in any way. Its movement is athletic and graceful, with a brisk, ground-covering trot. It is able to change directions instantly. It has a double coat, with a short, soft undercoat that varies in density according to climate, and a straight, flat-lying, harsh outer coat, with a slight ruff. This breed must adapt to great extremes in weather ranging from hot days to cold nights.

At a Glance

Energy level:	❑❑❑
Exercise requirements:	❑❑❑❑
Playfulness:	❑❑❑
Affection level:	❑❑❑
Friendliness toward dogs:	❑❑❑
Friendliness toward other pets:	❑❑❑❑
Friendliness toward strangers:	❑❑
Ease of training:	❑❑❑❑
Watchdog ability:	❑❑❑❑❑
Protection ability:	❑❑❑
Grooming requirements:	❑
Cold tolerance:	❑❑❑
Heat tolerance:	❑❑❑

Weight:	male: 45–55 lb; female: 35–45 lb
Height:	male: 20–24"; female: 19–23"

Collie

History

The derivation of the Collie is as obscure as the derivation of its name. One theory of the breed's origins is that it was derived from the same root stock as the Border Collie. One theory of the name's origin is that it was derived from a Gaelic word meaning useful, which certainly described the useful farm or stock dogs valued by the Celts who first settled on the British Isles. Although sheepherding and guarding are some of the most ancient of canine services, evidence of the Collie dates only from about 1800. Both rough- and smooth-coated "Scotch" collies existed by that time, but they apparently were derived from different crosses. The rough-coated dogs were characteristically smaller and broader headed, and usually black or black and white. As the breed caught the interest of dog fanciers, both rough- and smooth-coated Collies became taller and more refined. The rough-coated Collie was especially influenced by the progeny of a dog named Old Cockie, born in 1867 and thought to be responsible not only for setting type but also for introducing the sable color.

AKC Ranking: 30
Family: Livestock, Herding
Area of Origin: Scotland
Date of Origin: 1800s
Original Function: Sheep herder
Today's Function: Herding trials
Other Name: Scottish Collie

Around this same time, Queen Victoria became enthusiastic about the breed; under her sponsorship, its popularity grew not only with shepherds appreciative of its working value, but also with the upper class who were enamored of its beauty. By 1886 a standard was drawn up that still describes the breed as it is today.

Meanwhile, as sheepherding became more important in America, settlers brought Collies with them to the New World. In 1878, Queen Victoria once again put the breed in the limelight by entering two Collies in the Westminster Dog Show. This provided the impetus for America's social elite to join the Collie clan, and soon the Collie could be found in some of the most prestigious estates in America. Later the Collie found a champion in Albert Payson Terhune, whose stories about Collies heightened their popularity with people from all walks of life. The most famous Collie of all, the television star Lassie, further popularized the breed, helping to make the Rough Collie one of the all-time favorite breeds in America. The Smooth Collie has never shared the same popularity.

At a Glance

Energy level:	☐☐☐
Exercise requirements:	☐☐☐
Playfulness:	☐☐☐
Affection level:	☐☐☐
Friendliness toward dogs:	☐☐☐
Friendliness toward other pets:	☐☐☐☐
Friendliness toward strangers:	☐☐☐
Ease of training:	☐☐☐
Watchdog ability:	☐☐☐☐☐
Protection ability:	☐☐☐
Grooming requirements: Smooth:	☐
Rough:	☐☐☐☐
Cold tolerance: Smooth:	☐☐☐
Rough:	☐☐☐☐
Heat tolerance: Smooth:	☐☐☐
Rough:	☐☐

Weight:	male: 60–75 lb; female: 50–65 lb
Height:	male: 24–26"; female: 22–24"

Temperament

The Collie is gentle and devoted, a mild-mannered friend to all. It is a dog with a working heritage, and it needs daily mental and physical exercise or it can become frustrated. It is sensitive, intelligent, and willing to please, although it is sometimes a bit stubborn. It can nip at heels in play. Some may bark a lot.

Upkeep

A good walk or jog on leash or a fun play session is needed every day. Herding is an excellent exercise. The Collie can live outdoors in temperate to cool climates, but it is such a family-oriented dog that it is far happier indoors. The coat of the Smooth variety needs minimal care; the coat of the Rough variety needs brushing or combing every other day, more when shedding.

Health

- Major concerns: CEA
- Minor concerns: distichiasis, pyotraumatic dermatitis

Illustrated Standard

1. Head resembles a blunt lean wedge from profile and front views
2. Slight stop
3. Flat skull
4. Small ears, carried semierect when alert with the top quarter tipping forward
5. Medium-sized, almond-shaped eyes
6. Strong level back
7. Tail carried low
8. Small oval feet
9. Heavily frilled neck

❑ **Color:** sable and white; tricolor, blue merle; white (predominantly white, preferably with markings)
❑ **DQ:** none

- Occasionally seen: PDA, deafness, cerebellar abiotrophy (Rough)
- Suggested tests: eye, (cardiac), (hearing)
- Life span: 8–12 years
- Note: Often sensitive to ivermectin. Merles should not be bred to merles because homozygous merle is lethal or detrimental to health.

Form and Function

The Collie is an active, lithe, strong dog that combines strength, speed, and grace. Its gait suggests effortless speed as well as the ability to change speed and direction instantly, as required in herding dogs. The coat can be of two types, both with a soft, abundant undercoat. The outer coat of the Smooth variety is short, hard, and flat; that of the Rough variety is straight, harsh, abundant, and long, particularly on the mane and ruff. The Collie's expression is an important hallmark of the breed, and depends upon the shape and balance of the skull and muzzle, as well as the characteristics of the eyes and ears. It should be bright, alert, and intelligent, traits accentuated by a fairly refined head.

German Shepherd Dog

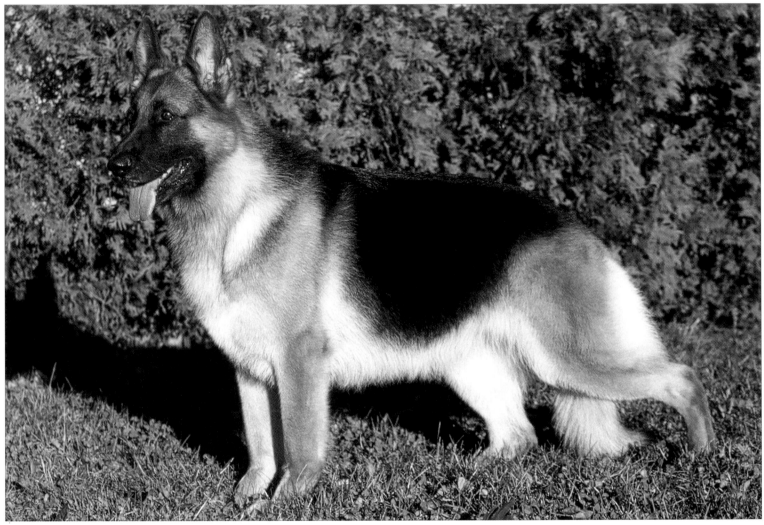

History

Despite an outward appearance slightly resembling a wolf, the German Shepherd Dog is a fairly recently developed breed and, contrary
to naíve beliefs, it is no more closely related to
the wolf than any other breed of dog. The breed
is the result of a conscious effort to produce the
ideal shepherd, capable of herding and guarding
its flocks. Perhaps never in the history of any
breed has such concerted effort been put into
improving a dog, mostly due to the formation in
1899 of the Verein fur Deutsche Scharferhunde SV, an organization
devoted to overseeing the breeding of the German Shepherd.
Breeders sought to develop not only a herding dog but also one that
could excel at jobs requiring courage, athleticism, and intelligence.
In short order, the German Shepherd had proved itself a more than
capable police dog, and subsequent breeding strove to perfect its
abilities as an intelligent and fearless companion and guardian.
During World War I, it was the obvious choice for a war sentry. At
the same time, the AKC changed the breed's name from German

AKC Ranking: 3
Family: Livestock, Herding
Area of Origin: Germany
Date of Origin: 1800s
Original Function: Sheep herder,
  guardian, police dog
Today's Function: Police, contraband
  detection, assistance, herding trials,
  Schutzhund
Other Name: Alsatian, Deutscher
  Schaferhund

Sheepdog to Shepherd Dog, and Britain changed
it to Alsatian Wolfdog, both attempts to dissoci-
ate the dog from its unpopular German roots.
The Wolfdog was later dropped as it caused
many people to fear the dogs. In 1931, the AKC
restored the breed's name to German Shepherd
Dog. The greatest boon to the Shepherd's popularity came in the form of two dogs, both movie
stars: Strongheart and Rin Tin Tin. The German
Shepherd held the number one spot in American
popularity for many years. Although presently it
has dropped from the top spot, the German Shepherd remains as
one of the most versatile dogs ever created, serving as a police dog,
war dog, guide dog, search-and-rescue dog, narcotics- or explo-
sives-detecting dog, show dog, guard dog, pet—and even shepherd.

Temperament

Among the most intelligent of breeds, the German Shepherd Dog
is so intent on its mission—whatever that may be—that it is
virtually unsurpassed in working versatility. It is utterly devoted

and faithful. Aloof and suspicious toward strangers, it is protective of its home and family. It can be domineering. It can be aggressive toward other dogs, but it is usually good with other pets.

Upkeep

This breed needs daily mental and physical challenges. It enjoys a good exercise session as well as learning session. It can live outside in temperate to cool climates, but it is family oriented and does equally well as a housedog. Its coat needs brushing one or two times weekly.

Health

- Major concerns: CHD, elbow dysplasia
- Minor concerns: panosteitis, vWD, progressive posterior paresis, cauda equina, pyotraumatic dermatitis, skin allergies, malignant neoplasms, pannus, cataract, gastric torsion, perianal fistulas, cardiomyopathy
- Occasionally seen: pancreatic insufficiency
- Suggested tests: hip, elbow, eye (blood)
- Life span: 10–12 years
- Note: GSDs are especially susceptible to a potentially fatal systemic fungal infection from *Aspergillus*.

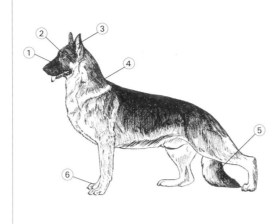

Form and Function

The German Shepherd Dog has an outline of smooth curves on a body that is longer than it is tall. It is strong, agile, and substantial. Its gait is exceptionally outreaching and elastic, covering the ground in great strides. It has a double coat, with the outer coat consisting of dense, straight or slightly wavy, harsh, close lying hair of medium length.

At a Glance

Energy level:	▢▢▢
Exercise requirements:	▢▢▢▢
Playfulness:	▢▢
Affection level:	▢▢▢
Friendliness toward dogs:	▢
Friendliness toward other pets:	▢▢▢
Friendliness toward strangers:	▢▢
Ease of training:	▢▢▢▢▢
Watchdog ability:	▢▢▢▢▢
Protection ability:	▢▢▢▢▢
Grooming requirements:	▢▢
Cold tolerance:	▢▢▢
Heat tolerance:	▢▢▢

Weight:	75–95 lb*
Height:	male: 24–26"; female: 22–24"

Old English Sheepdog

History

The Old English Sheepdog originated in the west of England, possibly from the Bearded Collie or Russian Owtcharka. The breed was the answer to the need for a strong dog capable of defending the flocks and herds from the wolves that existed at one time in England. By the middle of the nineteenth century, these dogs were used mainly to drive cattle and sheep to market. As working dogs, they were exempt from dog taxes, but their tails had to be docked as proof of their occupation. This custom continues in modern times and has led to their nickname Bobtail. The breed was first exhibited in the late 1800s, and by the early 1900s the breed was a popular show exhibit. The Old English was recognized by the AKC in 1905. Early Old English Sheepdogs could be brown, but were later restricted to shades of gray with white. Although the modern Bobtail is very similar to the early specimens, it has a

| AKC Ranking: 60 |
| Family: Livestock, Herding |
| Area of Origin: England |
| Date of Origin: 1800s |
| Original Function: Sheep herding |
| Today's Function: Herding trials |
| Other Name: None |

more profuse coat and compact body. Popularity as a pet was slower to grow, until the 1970s when the breed became a favorite media animal. Its popularity exploded with pet owners wanting an exotic but lovable mop. Since that time, its numbers have gradually declined, but the OES still remains a well-known breed. It is now more often seen as a pet or show dog than a working dog.

Temperament

The amiable Old English is jolly but gentle. At home, it is a well-mannered house pet that often amuses its family with comical antics. It thrives on human companionship and is very much a homebody. It is extremely devoted to its family and protective of family members, tending children as flock members. It is friendly toward strangers. Some can be headstrong.

At a Glance

Energy level:	▣▣▢
Exercise requirements:	▣▣▢
Playfulness:	▣▣▢
Affection level:	▣▣▣▣▣
Friendliness toward dogs:	▣▣▢
Friendliness toward other pets:	▣▣▣▣▣
Friendliness toward strangers:	▣▣▣▢
Ease of training:	▣
Watchdog ability:	▣▣▢
Protection ability:	▣▣▢
Grooming requirements:	▣▣▣▢
Cold tolerance:	▣▣▣▢
Heat tolerance:	▣▢

Weight: male: 70–90 lb; female: 60–80 lb*

Height: male: 22″ and up; female: 21″ and up

Upkeep

The Old English Sheepdog needs daily exercise, either a moderate to long walk or a vigorous romp. It particularly enjoys herding. It can live outside only in temperate to cool climates, but it is strongly advised that this breed have access to the house or indoor quarters because it thrives on togetherness. Its coat needs brushing or combing every other day, or it may form mats. It may tend to track in debris.

Health

- Major concerns: CHD
- Minor concerns: gastric torsion, otitis externa, retinal detachment, cataract, deafness
- Occasionally seen: none
- Suggested tests: hip, eye, (hearing)
- Life span: 10–12 years

Form and Function

This is a square-proportioned, thick-set dog, combining agility with strength. Its compact body is broader at the rump than shoulders. A distinguishing characteristic is the topline, which is lower at the withers than the loin. Its gait is free and powerful, ground covering, yet gives

Illustrated Standard

1. Eyes brown or blue (or one of each)
2. Well-defined stop
3. Skull capacious and rather broad
4. Medium-sized ears, carried flat to head
5. Lower at withers than at loin
6. Round hindquarters
7. Tail naturally bobtailed or (more often) docked close to body
8. Small round feet

❑ **Color:** any shade of gray, grizzle, blue, blue merles with or without white markings
❑ **DQ:** none

the appearance of being effortless. It may pace or amble at slower speeds. Its ambling gait is sometimes described as a "bearlike" roll or shuffle. The coat is profuse, but not excessive. It consists of a waterproof undercoat and a hard, shaggy outer coat that is neither straight nor curly. The expression is intelligent. The Bobtail's bark should be loud, with a "pot-casse" ring to it.

Puli

History

Around the ninth century the Magyar tribes came from the eastern Urals to occupy the central Danube area, intermingling with Turkish people along the way. They brought with them various sheepdogs, including the forebear of the modern Puli. The Puli's resemblance in body structure to the Tibetan Spaniel has led some to surmise that the latter may have played a role in the Puli's development. Whatever the origin, the small dogs were agile sheepherders, able even to turn a sheep by jumping on its back. The black color was important so that it could be easily spotted by the shepherd among the sheep. Thus, the Magyar's larger dogs were probably used as nighttime guards, and the small black dogs as daytime herders. After the decimation of Hungary by invaders in the sixteenth century, the country was repopulated by people, sheep, and dogs from western Europe. These dogs interbred with the native Pulik to produce the Pumi, and then the Puli and Pumi were interbred to such an extent that the original Puli breed was nearly lost. In the early 1900s, an effort began to resurrect the Puli; the first standard was written in 1925. Around that time,

AKC Ranking: 126
Family: Livestock, Herding, Gundog
Area of Origin: Hungary
Date of Origin: Middle Ages
Original Function: Sheep herding
Today's Function: Herding trials
Other Name: Hungarian Puli,
   Hungarian Water Dog

Pulik in Hungary varied greatly in height from large "police" through medium "working" to small "dwarf" sizes. The medium-sized dogs were most representative of the traditional herding Puli and were established as the desired size. In 1935, the United States Department of Agriculture imported several Pulik in an effort to improve herding dogs in America. This effort was thwarted by war, but the breed's working ability became known in America, and by 1936 the AKC recognized the Puli. The breed's fame spread farther throughout Europe as a result of Hungarians fleeing the war, bringing with them their dogs. The modern Puli remains an adept herder, but it enjoys only modest popularity as a pet or show dog.

Temperament

A mop on springs, the Puli is full of bouncing energy. It is busy and curious and needs daily exercise. This smart dog is also headstrong and tough. It can be aggressive toward other dogs. Alert and watchful, it is also protective of its family. It barks a lot.

Upkeep

This is an energetic breed on the lookout for a job, preferably something to herd. It can be satisfied with a good walk or jog, or a lively game and training session, however. It can live outdoors in temperate to cool climates, but it also makes an excellent housedog. Its coat can hold debris. Its nonshedding coat can be brushed or corded; if brushed, it needs brushing every one to two days. If corded, the cords must be regularly separated because the coat tends to hold dirt; bathing is time consuming and drying takes as much as one day. Pets can be clipped, but then part of the breed's unique appeal is lost.

Health

- Major concerns: CHD
- Minor concerns: none
- Occasionally seen: PRA
- Suggested tests: hip, eye
- Life span: 12–16 years

Form and Function

The Puli is a compact dog of square proportion and medium bone. Its gait at a trot is quick stepping, but neither far reaching nor mincing. It is of utmost importance that the Puli be able to change directions instantly, and it is quick, agile, and even acrobatic. Its weatherproof coat consists of a soft, wooly, dense undercoat and a wavy or curly outer coat. This coat will form round or flattened cords, but it may also be brushed out.

Illustrated Standard

1. Almond-shaped eyes
2. Skull slightly domed
3. Ears V-shaped, hanging, medium size
4. Back level
5. Tail carried over back, blending into backline
6. Feet round

❏ **Color:** solid black, rusty black, gray, and white
❏ **DQ:** none

At a Glance

Energy level:	▨▨▨▢
Exercise requirements:	▨▨▨
Playfulness:	▨▨▨
Affection level:	▨▨
Friendliness toward dogs:	▨
Friendliness toward other pets:	▨▨▨
Friendliness toward strangers:	▨
Ease of training:	▨▨
Watchdog ability:	▨▨▨▨▨
Protection ability:	▨▨▨▨▨
Grooming requirements:	▨▨▨▨▨
Cold tolerance:	▨▨▨▨
Heat tolerance:	▨▨

Weight:	25–35 lb*
Height:	male: ideally 17"; female: ideally 16"

Shetland Sheepdog

History

The ancestors of the Shetland Sheepdog were the herding dogs of Scotland that also provided the root stock for the Collie and Border Collie. Some of these dogs were quite small, measuring only about 18 inches in height. The Shetland Sheepdog almost certainly is derived from these early Collie type dogs, which then were further developed on the Shetland Islands. Some Iceland dogs may have also played a role, and perhaps even a black and tan King Charles Spaniel. The paucity of vegetation favored smaller livestock, and the animals needed to herd them were proportionately smaller. In a land with few fences, an adept herder was essential to keep livestock away from cultivated land. As an all-around farm dog, they herded not only sheep but also ponies and chickens. In some remote areas, it was customary to keep all animals in the family's home building during winter, and the amiable herding dog no doubt worked its way right into the family part of the home.

AKC Ranking: 15
Family: Livestock, Herding
Area of Origin: Scotland (Shetland Islands)
Date of Origin: 1800s
Original Function: Sheep herder
Today's Function: Sheep herding, herding trials
Other Name: None

Because of their isolation from the rest of the world, the breed was able to breed true in a comparatively short time. The British naval fleet used to frequent the islands for maneuvers, and often bought puppies to take home to England. Early dogs were referred to as Toonie dogs (Toon being the local Shetland word for farm), but they were initially shown (around 1906) as Shetland Collies. Collie fanciers objected to the name, so it was changed to Shetland Sheepdog. The breed is far more often referred to by its nickname of "Sheltie," however. In the early years in England breeders often discreetly crossed Shelties with rough-coated Collies in an attempt to improve on their Collie characteristics. This practice led to oversized Shelties, however, and has long since stopped. Following the immense popularity of the Collie, the Sheltie became the answer to the family wanting a loyal striking pet of smaller size, and is one of the most popular breeds in the world.

Temperament

The Shetland Sheepdog is extremely bright, extremely sensitive, and extremely willing to please. This combination makes for a dog that is very obedient, quick to learn, and utterly devoted to its family. It is not only gentle, playful, amiable, and companionable, but also excellent with children, although it can nip at heels in play. It is reserved and often timid toward strangers. It barks a lot.

Upkeep

The Sheltie is energetic, but its exercise needs can be met with a good walk, short jog, or active game and training session. It can live outdoors in a temperate climate, but it is strongly advised that the Sheltie be a housedog. It is too attached to its family to do well separated from them. Its thick coat needs brushing or combing every other day.

Health

- Major concerns: dermatomyositis
- Minor concerns: CEA, PRA, trichiasis, cataract, CHD, hemophilia, Legg–Perthes, patellar luxation

Illustrated Standard

1. Head forms a long blunt wedge viewed from front or side
2. Almond-shaped eyes
3. Skull flat
4. Small ears, carried erect with top fourth tipping forward
5. Tail carried low
6. Feet oval

❏ **Color:** black, blue merle, and sable, marked with varying amounts of white and/or tan
❏ **DQ:** above or below 13–16", brindle color

- Occasionally seen: PDA, deafness, epilepsy, vWD
- Suggested tests: eye, hip, DNA for vWD
- Life span: 12–14 years
- Note: May be sensitive to ivermectin. Merles should not be bred to merles because homozygous merle is lethal or detrimental to health.

Form and Function

The Shetland Sheepdog is a small, agile dog, longer than it is tall. Its gait is smooth, effortless, and ground covering, imparting good agility, speed, and endurance essential in a herding dog. It has a double coat, with a short, dense undercoat and a long, straight, harsh outer coat. The hair of the mane, frill, and tail is abundant. Its expression is gentle, intelligent, and questioning. Although it resembles a Rough Collie in miniature, subtle differences distinguish the breeds.

At a Glance

Energy level:	☐☐☐
Exercise requirements:	☐☐☐
Playfulness:	☐☐☐
Affection level:	☐☐☐
Friendliness toward dogs:	☐☐☐☐
Friendliness toward other pets:	☐☐☐☐
Friendliness toward strangers:	☐
Ease of training:	☐☐☐☐☐
Watchdog ability:	☐☐☐☐☐
Protection ability:	☐
Grooming requirements:	☐☐☐☐
Cold tolerance:	☐☐☐
Heat tolerance:	☐☐☐

Weight:	about 20 lb*
Height:	13–16"

Cardigan Welsh Corgi

History

One of the earliest breeds to come to the British Isles, the Cardigan Welsh Corgi was brought from central Europe to Cardiganshire, South Wales centuries ago. Its derivation is unknown, though it may have been influenced by the extinct English turn-spit dog, a short-legged, low-bodied dog used to turn spits in kitchens. Initially used as a family protector and even helper in the hunt, it was only later that the Corgi found its true forte. In a time when the land available to tenant farmers was determined by how much acreage their cattle occupied, it was to the farmer's advantage to have scattered, far-ranging stock. Thus, a dog that would drive, rather than herd, the cattle was an invaluable aid, and the Corgi stepped right into this role, nipping at the cattle's heels and ducking their kicks. In fact the word *Corgi* probably is derived from *Cor* (to gather) and *Gi* (dog). The original Corgis were supposed to measure a Welsh yard (slightly longer than an English yard) from nose to tail-tip, and in parts of Cardiganshire the breed was called the yard-long Dog or Ci-llathed. When the Crown lands were later divided, sold, and fenced, the need for drovers was lost, and the Corgi lost its job. Kept by some as a

AKC Ranking: 88
Family: Livestock, Herding
Area of Origin: Wales
Date of Origin: Ancient times
Original Function: Cattle drover
Today's Function: Cattle drover,
   herding trials
Other Name: None

guard and companion, nonetheless, it became a luxury that few could afford, and it became perilously close to extinction. Crosses with other breeds had been tried, but most were not particularly successful. The exception was the cross with the brindle herder, and present-day Cardigans are the products of this slight herder influence. The first Cardigans were shown around 1925. Until 1934, the Cardigan and Pembroke Welsh Corgis were considered one breed, and interbreeding between the two was common. The first Cardigans came to America in 1931, and AKC recognized the breed in 1935. For some unknown reason, the Cardigan has never enjoyed the popularity of the Pembroke Corgi, and remains only modestly popular.

Temperament

Fun-loving and high spirited, yet easygoing, the Cardigan is a devoted and amusing companion. This is a hardy breed, capable of a day dodging kicks, so it is agile and tireless. At home it is well mannered, but it is inclined to bark. It tends to be reserved with strangers and can be scrappy with other dogs.

Upkeep

The Cardigan needs a surprising amount of exercise for its size. Its needs can best be met with a herding session, but a moderate walk or vigorous play session will also suffice. It can live outside in temperate to cool weather, but it is a very good housedog and best when it is allowed access to both house and yard. Its coat needs brushing once a week to remove dead hair.

Health

- Major concerns: CHD
- Minor concerns: PRA
- Occasionally seen: urolithiasis, PRA
- Suggested tests: hip, (eye), (DNA test for PRA)
- Life span: 10–12 years

Form and Function

The Cardigan is a low-set dog, approximately 1.8 times longer than it is tall, with moderately heavy bone. It is a small but powerful dog capable of the agility, speed, and endurance necessary to drive cattle for extended periods. Its small size allowed it to duck under the cattle's hooves should they kick at the dog.

Illustrated Standard

1. Medium to large eyes
2. Moderately flat skull
3. Large ears, slightly rounded at tip
4. Level topline
5. Tail set and carried fairly low, not curled over back
6. Feet large and round, front feet pointing slightly outward

- ❏ **Color:** all shades of red, sable, and brindle; also blue merle or black, both with or without tan or brindle points; white flashings common
- ❏ **DQ:** blue or partially blue eyes in non-merle dogs; drop ears; non-solid black nose in non-merle dogs; color predominantly white; any color other than specified

Its gait is free, smooth, effortless, and ground covering. Its double coat consists of a soft thick undercoat and slightly harsh outer coat of medium length. Its expression is alert, gentle, and watchful, yet friendly.

At a Glance

Energy level:	◻◻◻
Exercise requirements:	◻◻
Playfulness:	◻◻◻
Affection level:	◻◻◻
Friendliness toward dogs:	◻
Friendliness toward other pets:	◻◻◻◻
Friendliness toward strangers:	◻◻◻
Ease of training:	◻◻◻◻
Watchdog ability:	◻◻◻◻◻
Protection ability:	◻◻◻◻
Grooming requirements:	◻
Cold tolerance:	◻◻◻
Heat tolerance:	◻◻◻

Weight:	male: 30–38 lb; female: 25–34 lb
Height:	10.5–12.5"

Pembroke Welsh Corgi

History

The Corgi was an essential helper to the farmers of South Wales. Although these little dogs specialized in herding cattle, nipping at their heels and then ducking under their kicking hooves, they were almost certainly also used in herding sheep and even Welsh ponies. Despite claims for the antiquity of the breed, it is difficult to trace its origins or even authenticate its existence in early times. A Welsh cattle dog is mentioned in a book of the eleventh century, however. Although it certainly shares its past with the Cardigan Welsh Corgi, the Pembroke was developed separately, in Pembrokeshire, Wales. As a hard-working dog, the Corgi was out in the fields when many of the early dog shows were being held. Only in 1926 did a club form and the breed enter the show ring. The first exhibits were straight from the farm and aroused only modest attention. Breeders subsequently strove to improve upon the breed's inherent good looks and were rewarded with increased popularity. The obvious differences between the Pembroke and Cardigan were troublesome to judges—the Pembroke is smaller,

AKC Ranking: 37
Family: Livestock, Herding
Area of Origin: Wales
Date of Origin: 1110s
Original Function: Cattle drover
Today's Function: Cattle drover,
  herding trials
Other Name: None

with sharper features, a more foxlike expression, and characteristically no tail. In 1934, the Cardigan and Pembroke Corgis were divided into two separate breeds, after which the Pembroke soared in popularity. Its appeal was heightened when it became the favorite of King George VI and, subsequently, Queen Elizabeth II. By the 1960s, the Pembroke had become one of the most popular pet breeds all over the world, but especially in Britain. This popularity has since waned slightly, but far more Pembrokes can be found herding in backyards than in farmyards today.

Temperament

Quick and quick-witted, the Pembroke Welsh Corgi has an active mind and body. It needs daily physical and mental exercise to be at its best in the house. It is devoted and willing to please, fun loving, amiable, and companionable. It is very good with children, although it can nip at heels in play. It is usually reserved with strangers. Many bark a lot.

Upkeep

The Pembroke loves to herd, and a daily herding session would be ideal to meet its exercise requirements. It can do fine without herding, however, as long as it gets a moderate walk on leash or a good play and training session off leash. It is physically able to live outdoors in temperate climates, but it is mentally far better suited to share its family's home and have access to a yard. Coat care consists only of brushing once a week to remove dead hairs.

Health

- Major concerns: intervertebral disc disease, CHD
- Minor concerns: epilepsy
- Occasionally seen: vWD, skin fragility, PRA, lens luxation, urolithiasis
- Suggested tests: hip, eye, (blood)
- Life span: 11–13 years

Form and Function

The Pembroke Welsh Corgi is moderately long and low, less heavily boned than the Cardigan Welsh Corgi. Its movement is free and smooth, with good reach and

drive. This is a breed that needs to be quick and agile, even after herding all day, in order to avoid the cattle's kicking hooves. It combines a weather-resistant undercoat of medium length with a coarser outer coat of slightly longer length. Its expression is intelligent and interested, foxy, but not sly.

At a Glance

Energy level:	▢▢▢
Exercise requirements:	▢▢▢
Playfulness:	▢▢▢
Affection level:	▢▢▢▢
Friendliness toward dogs:	▢▢▢
Friendliness toward other pets:	▢▢▢▢
Friendliness toward strangers:	▢▢▢▢
Ease of training:	▢▢▢▢
Watchdog ability:	▢▢▢▢▢
Protection ability:	▢▢▢▢
Grooming requirements:	▢
Cold tolerance:	▢▢▢
Heat tolerance:	▢▢▢

Weight:	ideally, male: 27 lb, female: 25 lb
Height:	10–12"

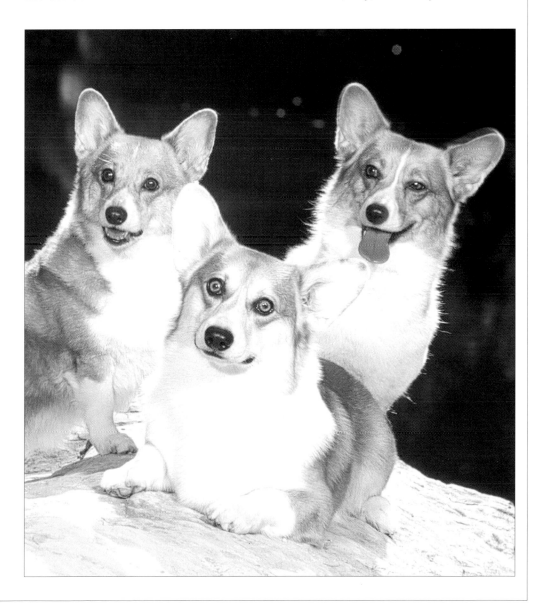

Definitions of Medical Conditions

ABBREVIATIONS USED IN THIS BOOK
ASD: Atrial septal defects
CEA: Collie eye anomaly
CHD: Canine hip dysplasia
CPRA: Central progressive retinal atrophy
CTP: Thrombocytopenia
HOD: Hypertrophic osteodystrophy
KCS: Keratoconjunctivitis sicca
MVI: Mitral valve insufficiency
OCD: Osteochondritis dissecans
PDA: Patent ductus arteriosus
PK: Pyruvate kinase deficiency
PPM: Persistent pupillary membrane
PRA: Progressive retinal atrophy
VKH: Vogt-Koyanagi-Harada-like syndrome
vWD: von Willebrand's disease

DEFINITIONS
Achondroplasia: (Skeletal) Type of dwarfism with shortened limbs.

Acute moist dermatitis (pyotraumatic dermatitis): (Skin) Also called "hot spots." An area of extremely itchy and inflamed skin that is exacerbated by the animal licking at it.

Addison's (hypoadrenocorticism): (Endocrine) Insufficient secretions by the adrenal cortex. Special Diagnostics: blood test.

Albinism: (Multiple sites) Deficiency of pigmentation, resulting in white fur color, pink skin, and pink or blue eyes.

Amyloidosis: Abnormal deposits of a type of protein (amyloid) in various tissues or organs, resulting in progressive organ dysfunction. In renal amyloidosis (which is the most common type in some breeds) the kidney is the site of amyloid accumulation. Special Diagnostics: biopsy.

Ataxia: (Neural) Incoordination.

Atrial septal defects (ASD): (Heart) Hole in the wall separating the right and left atria of the heart. Special Diagnostics: ultrasound of heart.

Basenji enteropathy: (Digestive) Also called immunoproliferative small intestinal disease. Severe progressive intestinal malabsorption resulting in protein loss, intractable diarrhea, and loss of body weight.

Canine hip dysplasia (CHD): (Skeletal) Abnormal development of the hip assembly wherein the head of the femur does not fit snugly into the pelvic socket. Special Diagnostics: hip radiograph.

Cardiomyopathy: (Heart) Enlargement of the heart resulting from dysfunction of the heart muscle. Special Diagnostics: heart ultrasound.

Cataract: (Eye) Opacities of the lens of the eye; juvenile cataracts are present in young dogs and have a hereditary basis. Special Diagnostics: ophthalmoscopic exam.

Cauda equina syndrome: (Neural) Group of neurological signs resulting from compression of the spinal nerves of the lumbosacral vertebral region. Special Diagnostics: radiographs.

Central progressive retinal atrophy (CPRA): (Eye) Degeneration of retinal cells beginning with those serving central areas of vision. Special Diagnostics: retinoscopic exam, electroretinogram.

Cerebellar abiotrophy: (Brain) Degeneration of brain neurons in the cerebellum, resulting in progressively worsening incoordination. Caused by a recessive gene.

Ceroid lipofuscinosis: (Neural) Metabolic disorder in which a waste product (ceroid lipofuscin) accumulates in the cells, eventually destroying brain cells and leading to abnormal neurologic function.

Cherry eye: (Eye) Tear gland protrudes beyond the "third eyelid," resulting in bright red bulge in the inner corner of the eye.

Chondrodysplasia: (Skeletal) Type of dwarfism that is also associated with anemia. Special Diagnostics: radiograph of foreleg.

Ciliary dyskinesia: Deformation and rigidity of cells that normally have cilia, small hair-like appendages that aid in movement of the cells themselves (such as sperm) or mucous (such as in the lungs and nose).

Colitis: (Digestive) Inflammation of the large bowel, often resulting in diarrhea.

Collie eye anomaly (CEA): (Eye) Congenital abnormalities of varying degrees found in the posterior part of the eye. Special Diagnostics: ophthalmoscopic exam.

Colonic disease: (Digestive) Disease of the large bowel.

Copper toxicosis: (Liver) Accumulation of copper in the liver, resulting in chronic hepatitis. Special Diagnostics: DNA test.

Corneal erosion: (Eye) Loss of the outer layers of the cornea; if progressive, can lead to ulceration of the cornea.

Corneal opacities (corneal dystrophy): (Eye) Deposits of white or silver spots on the central area of the cornea.

Craniomandibular osteopathy: (Skeletal) Abnormal development of the jaw involving excessive bone formation. Due to a recessive gene.

Deafness: (Ear) Inability to hear in either one or both ears. Special Diagnostics: BAER test (Brainstem Auditory Evoked Potential).

Demodicosis: (Skin) Generalized demodectic mange, a condition caused by the *Demodex* mite to which certain breeds are more susceptible. Special Diagnostics: skin scraping.

Dermatomyositis: (Skin and muscle) Systemic connective disease causing inflammation of both skin and muscles.

Dermoid sinus: (Skin) Tubular indentation leading from the skin along the midline of the back, sometimes extending into the spinal canal. Special Diagnostics: visual exam.

Diabetes mellitus: (Endocrine system) Deficiency in insulin production or utilization causing glucose to be utilized abnormally.

Digital hyperkeratosis: (Skin) Thickening of the foot pads leading to cracked, infected, and painful pads.

Distichiasis: (Eye) Abnormal origin of eyelashes along the lid margin, often resulting in irritation to the eye.

Ectropion: (Eye) Eversion of the eyelids, so that they roll out from the eye, leaving a gap between the lid and eye.

Elbow dysplasia (ununited anconeal process): (Skeletal) Elbow joint laxity resulting from improper development, and eventually leading to arthritic changes. Special Diagnostics: elbow radiograph.

Elongated soft palate: (Respiratory) Abnormal extension of the soft palate, such that it interferes with breathing.

Entropion: (Eye) Inversion of the eyelids, so that they roll inward, often irritating the eye.

Epilepsy: (Neural) Brain disorder resulting in periodic seizures.

Esophageal achalasia: (Digestive) Failure of the walls of the esophagus to relax enough to allow food to pass into the stomach, resulting in regurgitation of ingested food. Special Diagnostics: radiograph or endoscopic exam.

Familial nephropathy: (Kidney) Hereditary impaired kidney function.

Fanconi's syndrome: (Kidney) Reabsorptive defects resulting in kidney failure. Special Diagnostics: urine test, renal clearance test.

Fragmented coronoid process: (Skeletal) Developmental flaw in which a fragment of the ulnar bone of the foreleg never fuses, leaving a chip floating in the region of the elbow, resulting in lameness. Special Diagnostics: radiograph of elbow.

Gastric torsion (gastric dilation-volvulus): (Digestive) Often called "bloat"; twisting of the stomach that traps the stomach contents and gases, and can lead to death if untreated. It is most common in large, deep-chested breeds.

Glaucoma: (Eye) Increased intraocular pressure, most often due to an abnormality in the drainage of aqueous fluid from the eye. Special Diagnostics: tonometry (eye pressure measurement).

Globoid cell leukodystrophy: (Neural) Gradual destruction of white matter in the brain, eventually fatal.

Glycogen storage disease: (Metabolic) Deficiency of enzymes required for normal glycogen metabolism, resulting in variable symptoms including weakness. Special Diagnostics: blood test.

Hemivertebra: (Skeletal) Partially formed wedge-shaped vertebrae. Special Diagnostics: radiographs.

Hemophilia A (factor VIII deficiency): (Blood) Deficiency in clotting factor VIII leading to excessive bleeding. Special Diagnostics: blood test.

Hemophilia B (factor IX deficiency): (Blood) Deficiency in clotting factor IX leading to excessive bleeding. Special Diagnostics: blood test.

Histiocytosis: (Multiple sites) Rapidly progressive malignant cancer infiltrating many parts of body, often including the lungs, liver, spleen, and central nervous system. Special Diagnostics: radiograph and biopsy.

Hydrocephalus: (Brain) Increased accumulation of cerebrospinal fluid in the ventricles of the brain. Highest incidence in toy and brachycephalic breeds. Special Diagnostics: radiograph of skull; also MRI or CT scan.

Hypertrophic osteodystrophy (HOD): (Skeletal) Inflammation of the bone growth plates during periods of rapid growth in large breeds, resulting in lameness. Special Diagnostics: radiographs.

Hypoglycemia: (Metabolic) Abnormally low level of glucose in the blood. Special Diagnostics: blood test.

Hypomyelination: (Neural) Abnormally low amounts of myelin (the insulator surrounding nerve fibers) in peripheral nerves, resulting in weakness of limbs. Special Diagnostics: nerve conduction tests.

Hypothyroidism: (Endocrine) Decreased production of thyroid hormone, often caused by an auto-immune response. One of the most wide-spread disorders in dogs. Special Diagnostics: blood test.

Inguinal hernia: (Body wall) Protrusion of abdominal contents through the inguinal canal.

Intervertebral disk disease: (Skeletal) Abnormality of the cartilaginous disks that normally provide cushioning between the vertebra. Special Diagnostics: radiograph of spine.

Iris coloboma: (Eye) Pits in the iris (colored portion) of the eye.

Keratoconjunctivitis sicca (KCS): (Eye) Decreased tear production of the eye causing a dry eye and damage to the cornea. Special Diagnostics: tear test.

Lacrimal duct atresia: (Eye) Abnormally small or malformed duct that normally drains tears from the eye. Special Diagnostics: tear drainage test.

Legg–Perthes disease (Legg–Calvé–Perthes): (Skeletal) Destruction of the head of the femur bone due to decrease in blood supply. Special Diagnostics: radiograph of hip.

Lens luxation: (Eye) Displacement of the lens of the eye. Special Diagnostics: retinoscopic exam.

Lip fold pyoderma: (Skin) Infection of the skin around the folds of the lips due to moisture and bacteria.

Lumbar-sacral syndrome: (Neural) Group of neurological signs resulting from compression of the spinal nerves of the lumbosacral vertebral region. Special Diagnostics: radiographs.

Lymphedema: (Lymph system) Swelling due to improper drainage of the lymph system.

Megaesophagus: (Digestive) Paralysis and enlargement of the esophagus, resulting in regurgitation of food. Special Diagnostics: radiograph of throat.

Meningitis: Inflammation of the membranes surrounding the brain and spinal cord.

Mitral valve insufficiency (MVI): (Heart) Degeneration of the mitral valve of the heart, allowing blood to flow backward into the left atrium and resulting in enlargement of the heart. Special Diagnostics: auscultation (listening to heart), radiographs or ultrasound of heart.

Muscular dystrophy: (Muscles) Progressive degeneration of skeletal muscles. Special Diagnostics: blood test and electromyography.

Narcolepsy: (Neural) Condition in which the dog has episodes of sudden deep sleep.

Narrow palpebral fissure: (Eye) Abnormally small opening between the eyelids.

Nasal solar dermatitis: (Skin) Inflammation of the nose surface from exposure to sunlight.

Necrotic myelopathy: (Neural) Loss of insulating myelin from the spinal cord, resulting in paralysis.

Open fontanel: (Skeletal) Incomplete closure of the bones of the skull, resulting in a soft spot on top of the head.

Osteochondritis dissecans (OCD): (Skeletal) Degeneration of bone underlying the cartilage of joint areas, most often seen in young, fast growing dogs of larger breeds. Special Diagnostics: radiographs of suspected joints; often inconclusive.

Osteosarcoma: (Skeletal) Malignant bone cancer. More common in large and giant breeds. Special Diagnostics: radiograph and biopsy of suspected area.

Otitis externa: (Ear) Infection of the outer ear, including the ear canal. Most common in dogs with long, hanging ears receiving little ventilation.

Pancreatic insufficiency: (Digestive) Inadequate digestive enzyme production by the pancreas, resulting in poor nutrient absorption. Special Diagnostics: blood test.

Pannus (chronic superficial keratitis): (Eye) Potentially blinding inflammation of the cornea, including abnormal growth of vascularized pigment over the cornea.

Panosteitis: (Skeletal) Excessive formation of bone growth of different maturity around some joints of young dogs resulting in intermittent lameness. Special Diagnostics: radiograph of suspected joints.

Patellar luxation: (Skeletal) Abnormally shallow groove in the knee, so that the knee cap (patella) slips in and out of position, causing lameness. Though seen in many breeds, it is most common in small dogs. Special Diagnostics: radiograph of stifle (knee)—though not always necessary.

Patent ductus arteriosus (PDA): (Heart) Failure of the embryonic blood vessel connecting the pulmonary artery to the aorta to go away in the postnatal dog, resulting in improper circulation of blood. Special Diagnostics: auscultation (listening to the heart), radiographs or ultrasound of heart.

Pelger–Huet: (Blood) Abnormal development of neutrophils. Special Diagnostics: blood test.

Pemphigus: (Skin) Auto-immune disease of the skin.

Perianal fistula: (Skin) Draining tract in the area around the anus.

Persistent pupillary membrane (PPM): (Eye) Developmental abnormality in which a few strands of iris tissue may be stretched over the pupillary opening.

Persistent right aortic arch: (Heart) Failure of the embryonic right aorta to go away in the postnatal dog, resulting in constriction of the esophagus. Special Diagnostics: radiograph of esophagus.

Phosphofructokinase deficiency: (Blood) Deficiency in a red blood cell enzyme (phosphofructinase), causing a type of anemia. Special Diagnostics: blood test; DNA test (English Springer Spaniel).

Polyneuropathy: (Neural) Weakness or paralysis of limbs due to problems in peripheral nerves.

Portacaval shunt (portasystemic shunt): (Liver) Failure of embryonic blood vessel within the liver to go away in the postnatal dog, allowing blood to bypass the liver processing, resulting in neurological and other symptoms. Special Diagnostics: radiograph or ultrasound of liver, ammonia tolerance test.

Premature closure of distal radius: (Skeletal) One side of the radius bone of the foreleg stops growing before the other, resulting in malformation of the leg. Special Diagnostics: radiograph.

Progressive posterior paresis: (Neural) Paralysis of one or both hind limbs.

Progressive retinal atrophy (PRA): (Eye) A family of diseases all involving gradual deterioration of the retina. Symptoms begin with night blindness and progress to total blindness. Special Diagnostics: retinoscopic exam or electroretinogram; DNA test in some breeds.

Prolapse of nictitans gland: (Eye) Hypertrophy of the gland of the third eyelid.

Protein wasting disease: (Digestive) Loss of protein through the kidneys (protein-losing nephropathy: PLN) or intestines (protein-losing enteropathy: PLE) resulting in diarrhea and weight loss. Special Diagnostics: blood and urine tests, including urine protein creatinine ratio.

Pulmonic stenosis: (Heart) Congenital narrowing of the opening in the heart between the right ventricle and pulmonary artery, eventually causing right-sided heart failure. Special Diagnostics: auscultation (listening to heart), ultrasound or angiography.

Pyruvate kinase deficiency (PK): (Blood) Deficiency of a particular red blood cell enzyme (pyruvate kinase), causing premature destruction of red blood cells and resulting in anemia. Special Diagnostics: blood test; DNA test (Basenji).

Rage syndrome: (Neurological) Sudden episode of unprovoked aggression, thought to be a form of epilepsy.

Renal cortical hypoplasia: (Kidney) Failure of both kidneys to function normally. Special Diagnostics: urine test.

Renal disease: (Kidney) Unspecified kidney disease.

Renal dysplasia: (Kidney) Abnormal development and function of the kidneys.

Retinal detachment: (Eye) Detachment of the retina from the back of the eye, leading to partial visual loss. Special Diagnostics: retinoscopic exam.

Retinal dysplasia: (Eye) Abnormal development of the retina. Special Diagnostics: retinoscopic exam, electroretinogram.

Retinal folds: (Eye) Folds in the retinal layer, often caused by differences in growth of different layers of the eye. Many disappear with maturity.

Schnauzer comedo syndrome (follicular dermatitis): (Skin) Skin disease characterized by blackhead formation.

Scotty cramp: (Neuromuscular) Periodic generalized cramping of the muscles, usually precipitated by excitement; associated with problem with metabolism of a neurotransmitter (serotonin).

Sebaceous adenitis: (Skin) Inflammation of the sebaceous glands, resulting in scaly debris, hair loss, and infection. Special Diagnostics: skin biopsy.

Shoulder luxation: (Skeletal) Dislocation of the shoulder. Special Diagnostics: radiograph of shoulder.

Skin fold dermatitis: (Skin) Skin infection caused by moisture and bacteria trapped within deep folds of skin.

Skin fragility (Ehlers-Danlos syndrome, cutaneous asthenia): (Skin) Tissue disease causing extremely fragile skin. Special Diagnostics: skin biopsy.

Spiculosis: (Skin) Abnormally bristle- or spike-like hairs interspersed among normal hairs.

Stenotic nares: (Respiratory) Abnormally small nostrils, sometimes interfering with breathing.

Subvalvular aortic stenosis: (Heart) Abnormally narrow connection between the left ventricle and the aorta, eventually leading to heart failure. Special Diagnostics: auscultation (listening to heart), ultrasound of heart.

Tail fold dermatitis: (Skin) Infection of the skin around the tail due to excessive skin folds or an "inset" tail.

Tetralogy of Fallot: (Heart) Pulmonic stenosis combined with a defect in the ventricular septum results in de-oxygenated blood being pumped throughout the body. Special Diagnostics: blood test, blood gas measurements, and ultrasound of heart.

Thrombocytopenia (CTP): (Blood) Lowered platelet number in the blood, leading to excessive bleeding. Special Diagnostics: blood test.

Tracheal collapse: (Respiratory) Loss of rigidity of the trachea, leading to weakness of the trachea and susceptibility to collapse. Most common in small breeds. Special Diagnostics: radiograph or endoscopic exam of trachea.

Trichiasis: (Eye) Eyelashes arising from normal origin are misdirected into the eye, causing irritation.

Urethral prolapse: (Urinary) Protrusion of part of the mucosal lining of the urethra through the external urethral orifice.

Uric acid calculi: (Urinary) Bladder stones resulting from an abnormality in the excretion of uric acid. Special Diagnostics: radiograph.

Urolithiasis: (Urinary) Formation of urinary stones. Special Diagnostics: radiograph.

Vaginal hyperplasia: (Reproductive) Vaginal tissue becomes overly enlarged, especially with estrogen stimulation, sometimes protruding through the vulva. More common in giant breeds.

Vogt-Koyanagi-Harada-like syndrome (VKH) (uveodermatologic syndrome): (Many structures) Auto-immune disease leading to progressive destruction of melanin containing tissues, including those in the eye and skin.

Von Willebrand's disease (vWD): (Blood) Defective blood platelet function resulting in excessive bleeding, caused by a deficiency in clotting factor VIII antigen (von Willebrand factor). Special Diagnostics: blood test.

White dog shaker syndrome: (Neural) Episodic diffuse muscular tremors and incoordination, seen mostly in some white dogs.

Wobbler's syndrome (cervical vertebral instability): (Skeletal) Abnormality of the neck vertebrae causing rear leg incoordination or paralysis.

Guide to Hereditary Health Problems

Hip Dysplasia

Canine hip dysplasia is one of the most well known and widespread of hereditary health problems. The Orthopedic Foundation for Animals (OFA) has collected data on breed incidence of CHD since 1974. The following lists their ranking of breeds for which at least 100 dogs have been submitted. Those breeds listed with a prevalence of 10% or more are considered to have CHD as a major concern; those with a prevalence of 5 to 10% are listed as having CHD as a minor concern.

Breed—incidence (%)

Bulldog—71
Otterhound—54
Clumber Spaniel—49
St. Bernard—47
Newfoundland—27
American Staffordshire Terrier—27
Bullmastiff—26
Bloodhound—26
Chesapeake Bay Retriever—23
Gordon Setter—22
Golden Retriever—22
Chow Chow—22
Field Spaniel—21
Staffordshire Bull Terrier—21
Rottweiler—21
Kuvasz—21
Norwegian Elkhound—21

Mastiff—21
Giant Schnauzer—21
Old English Sheepdog—21
German Shepherd Dog—20
Bernese Mountain Dog—20
English Setter—19
Spinone Italiano—19
Beagle—18
Welsh Corgi, Pembroke—17
Welsh Springer Spaniel—17
Black and Tan Coonhound—17
Shih Tzu—17
Briard—17
Brittany—17
Greater Swiss Mountain Dog—17
Welsh Corgi, Cardigan—17
Bouvier des Flandres—17
English Springer Spaniel—16
Irish Water Spaniel—16
Portuguese Water Dog—15
Curly Coated Retriever—15
Akita—15
Chinese Shar-Pei—15
Australian Cattle Dog—14
Airedale Terrier—14
Poodle—14
Komondor—13
Labrador Retriever—13
Irish Setter—13
Alaskan Malamute—12
Great Dane—12
Border Collie—12
Anatolian Shepherd—12

Boxer—12
Samoyed—12
Cavalier King Charles Spaniel—11
Puli—10
Great Pyrenees—10
German Wirehaired Pointer—10
Weimaraner—9
Standard Schnauzer—9
Pointer—9
Kerry Blue Terrier—8
American Water Spaniel—8
American Eskimo Dog—8
Vizsla—8
Shiba Inu—8
Lhasa Apso—7
Wirehaired Pointing Griffon—7
Petit Basset Griffon Vendeen—7
Keeshond—7
Bearded Collie—7
Cocker Spaniel—7
Rhodesian Ridgeback—7
Tibetan Terrier—6
Doberman Pinscher—6
Australian Shepherd—6
Belgian Malinois—6
Irish Wolfhound—6
English Cocker Spaniel—6
German Shorthaired Pointer—6
Afghan Hound—6
Dalmatian—5
Shetland Sheepdog—5
Finnish Spitz—5
Flat Coated Retriever—5
Border Terrier—4
Soft Coated Wheaten Terrier—4
Belgian Tervuren—4
Greyhound—4
Canaan Dog—3
Basenji—3
Collie—3
Belgian Sheepdog—3
Ibizan Hound—3
Schipperke—2
Pharaoh Hound—2
Siberian Husky—2

Saluki—2
Borzoi—2

Elbow Dysplasia
Elbow dysplasia also occurs in many breeds of dogs. The following list represents the percentage of dysplastic dogs in breeds in which at least 75 individuals have been evaluated. Information is from the OFA. The absence of a breed from this list does not imply that elbow dysplasia is not found in that breed; it merely implies that sufficient numbers of that breed have yet to be registered with the OFA. At this writing OFA has recorded elbow dysplasia in 78 breeds.

Breed—incidence (%)

Chow Chow—50
Rottweiler—41
Chinese Shar-Pei—31
Bernese Mountain Dog—29
Newfoundland—20
German Shepherd Dog—20
Bloodhound—19
Bullmastiff—19
English Springer Spaniel—16
Mastiff—14
English Setter—14
Greater Swiss Mountain Dog—13
Labrador Retriever—12
Golden Retriever—11
Belgian Malinois—10
Gordon Setter—9
Rhodesian Ridgeback—6
Bouvier des Flandres—5
Belgian Sheepdog—5
German Wirehaired Pointer—5
Chesapeake Bay Retriever—4
Belgian Tervuren—4
Samoyed—4
Australian Shepherd—3
Great Dane—2

Great Pyrenees—2
Doberman Pinscher—1
Portuguese Water Dog—1
Weimaraner—1
Akita—1
Brittany—1
Border Collie—0
German Shorthaired Pointer—0
Flat Coated Retriever—0

Gastric Torsion

Gastric torsion is a potentially fatal emergency to which some breeds—most notably large, deep chested breeds—are predisposed. In a comparison of 24 popular breeds, the following ranking was established in *Bloat Notes* (School of Veterinary Medicine, Purdue University).

Ranked from greatest to least risk:

Great Dane
St. Bernard
Weimaraner
Irish Setter
Gordon Setter
Standard Poodle
Basset Hound
Doberman Pinscher
Old English Sheepdog
German Shorthaired Pointer
Newfoundland
Airedale Terrier
German Shepherd Dog
Alaskan Malamute
Chesapeake Bay Retriever
Boxer
Collie
Labrador Retriever
English Springer Spaniel
Samoyed
Dachshund
Golden Retriever
Cocker Spaniel

Deafness

The information on deafness in this section was supplied by Dr. George Strain of Louisiana State University Veterinarian School (personal communication).

Breeds with a high prevalence of unilateral or bilateral deafness:

Breed—incidence (%)

Australian Cattle Dog—12
Bull Terrier (white)—19
English Cocker Spaniel (parti-colors)—8
English Setter—15
Dalmatian—30

Other breeds in which congenital deafness has been reported:

Akita
American Eskimo Dog
American Staffordshire Terrier
Australian Shepherd
Beagle
Bichon Frise
Border Collie
Boston Terrier
Boxer
Bulldog
Bull Terrier (colored)
Welsh Corgi, Cardigan
Cavalier King Charles Spaniel
Chihuahua
Chow Chow
Cocker Spaniel
Collie
Dachshund (dappled)
Doberman Pinscher
Foxhound
Fox Terrier
French Bulldog
German Shepherd Dog
Great Dane
Great Pyrenees

Ibizan Hound
Italian Greyhound
Jack Russell Terrier
Kuvasz
Labrador Retriever
Maltese
Miniature Pinscher
Miniature Poodle
Old English Sheepdog
Papillon
Pointer
Puli
Rhodesian Ridgeback
Rottweiler
Saint Bernard
Schnauzer
Scottish Terrier
Sealyham Terrier
Shetland Sheepdog
Siberian Husky
Soft Coated Wheaten Terrier
Springer Spaniel
Sussex Spaniel
Tibetan Spaniel
Tibetan Terrier
Toy Poodle
West Highland White Terrier
Whippet
Yorkshire Terrier

Cardiomyopathy

Breeds with the highest incidence of cardiomyopathy. Prevalence of cardiomyopathy determined as percentage of dogs admitted to a veterinary teaching hospital according to D. Sisson and W. Thomas ("Myocardial Diseases," in *Textbook of Veterinary Internal Medicine,* edited by S. Ettinger and E. Feldman. W.B. Saunders Co. Philadelphia, 1995).

Scottish Deerhound
Doberman Pinscher
Irish Wolfhound
Great Dane
Boxer
St. Bernard
Afghan Hound
Newfoundland
Old English Sheepdog
English Cocker Spaniel
Cocker Spaniel
Labrador Retriever
Golden Retriever

Glossary

GENERAL TERMS

Balance Overall proportion and symmetry of conformation.

Conformation Physical make-up.

High in rear A dog that is higher over its rear quarters than over its front quarters.

High-stationed Tall and long-legged.

Plucking Pulling out loose hair by hand.

Racy Long-legged with a slight build.

Rangy Long-bodied with a shallow chest.

Square-proportioned Height at withers equal to length from point of sternum to point of croup.

Standard The official blueprint for a breed.

Stripping Removal of the undercoat and dead outercoat without losing the harsh texture; plucking.

Substance Fairly heavy bone and musculature.

Typey Displaying important essential characteristics of the breed, especially of the head.

Variety A subtype of a breed that is shown separately, but that can be interbred with other varieties of the same breed.

Weedy Lacking sufficient bone and musculature.

Wicket Device for measuring the height of a dog, consisting of two vertical bars joined by a horizontal bar that can be adjusted for height.

COAT TERMS

Corded Coat that is intertwined in the form of long, narrow mats giving a mop-like appearance (example: Komondor).

Feather Long hair on the ears, backs of legs, and beneath the tail.

Flag Long fringe on the tail.

Jacket Tight body coat of a terrier.

Mane Profuse growth of hair on the rear of the neck.

Plume Profusely feathered tail carried over the back.

Ruff Profuse growth of hair on the front of the neck, or that surrounds the entire neck.

Stand-off coat Coat that sticks out from the body rather than lying flat (example: Norwegian Elkhound).

Topknot Tuft of hair on top of the head.

COLOR TERMS

Belton Intermingled colored and white hairs.

Brindle Irregular vertical bands of dark hair overlaid on lighter hair.

Harlequin Spotted coloration, used specifically for the Great Dane.

Hound colored Black, tan, and white, with a black saddle.

Merle Dark patches overlaid on a lighter background of the same pigment type; also called dapple.

Parti-color Spotted.

Piebald Black patches on a white background.

Sable Black-tipped hairs in which the undercoat is of lighter color.

Saddle Dark patch over the back.

Spectacles Dark markings around the eyes.

Ticking Small flecks of coloring on a white background.

Wheaten Pale yellow color.

HEAD TERMS
Apple head Extremely domed skull.
Brachycephalic Broad head with short-muzzle (example: Pekingese).
Butterfly nose Spotted or partially unpigmented nose.
Chiseled Clean-cut muzzle and foreface.
Dish-face Nose tipped up.
Dolichocephalic Narrow head with long-muzzle (example: Collie).
Down-faced Muzzle curved downward.
Dudley nose Liver- or flesh-colored nose.
Fill Fullness beneath the eyes, not chiseled.
Flews Upper lips, especially those that are pendulous.
Haw Exposed nictitating membrane (third eyelid), especially if unpigmented.
Mesatacephalic Medium-width head with medium-length muzzle (example: Beagle).
Occiput Highest point at the back of the skull, above where the neck joins the head; in many breeds it forms a crest and is quite prominent.
Stop Transition area from backskull to muzzle, often demarcated by an abrupt depression.
Snipey Weak, pointed muzzle lacking underjaw.

TEETH TERMS
Bite Occlusion; relationship of the upper and lower jaws when the mouth is closed.
Full dentition No missing teeth.
Level bite When upper and lower incisors meet evenly.
Overshot bite When upper incisors overlap lower incisors, leaving a gap between the teeth.
Scissors bite When upper incisors just overlap lower incisors, such that the rear surface of the upper incisors touches the outer surface of lower incisors.
Premolars Small teeth situated just to the rear of the fangs (canines).

Punishing mouth Strong, powerful jaws.
Undershot bite When lower incisors extend beyond upper incisors

EAR TERMS
Button ears Semi-prick ears in which the top portion folds forward (example: Fox Terrier).
Bat ears Large, erect ears (example: French Bulldog).
Drop ears Long, hanging ears.
Rose ears Small ears folded back in repose (example: Greyhound).
Prick ears Ears that stand upright (example: German Shepherd Dog).

NECK TERMS
Bull-neck Thick, muscular, often short neck.
Crest Arched area near the top of the neck.
Ewe neck Neck that is arched so that the top line of the neck is concave and the bottom is convex.
Goose neck Overly long, thin neck lacking strength and shape.
Throaty neck Neck with loose skin.

BODY TERMS
Barrel chest Rounded ribcage.
Brisket Chest or sternum area.
Cobby Compact.
Herring gutted Gradual slope from a fairly shallow chest to tuck-up.
Loin Region between the ribcage and croup.
Rib spring Arch formed by the ribcage; more spring refers to more arch.
Roach back An overly arched, convex topline.
Shelly Narrow, shallow chest and body.
Short-coupled Short loin area.
Slab-sided Flat-ribbed.
Swayback A sunken, concave topline.
Topline Line formed by the withers, back, loin, and croup.
Tuck-up Area under the loin in a small-waisted dog.

FOREQUARTER TERMS

Bowed front Forelegs that curve out between the elbows and pasterns.

Down in pastern Weak, overly sloping pastern.

East-west front When feet turn out to the sides, pointing away from each other.

Fiddle front East-west front combined with a bowed front, so that the assembly looks like a fiddle.

Lay back Angle at which the shoulder is set on the dog's body.

Knuckled over Steep pastern, or with a reverse slope.

Loaded shoulders Overly muscled or lumpy forequarters.

Out at elbow Elbows that stick out from the sides of the ribcage.

Return Set-back of the upper arm under the dog's body.

Shoulder Scapula; also used (incorrectly) to refer to both the scapula and upper arm (humerus) region.

Shoulder angulation Angle formed between the scapula and humerus.

Toed-in front Pigeon toed; feet pointing toward each other.

REARQUARTER TERMS

Bandy-legged Wide, bowed-legged rear quarters.

Cow-hocked Viewed from behind, the point of hocks point toward each other, resulting in the rear feet pointing outward.

Lower thigh Area from stifle to hock, also called second thigh.

Rear angulation Angles formed between the pelvis, thigh bone (femur), and second or lower thigh bone (tibia/fibula).

Sickle-hocked Viewed from the side, an over-angulated joint between the lower thigh and hock; an inability to straighten this joint when moving.

Well let-down Short hocks.

FOOT TERMS

Cat foot Short, round foot.

Dew claws Extra toes on the insides of the front, and sometimes, rear legs.

Hare foot Long, narrow foot.

Paper foot Flat foot.

Splay foot Toes that are not close together.

TAIL TERMS

Bob tail Very short, almost stump-like tail (Example: Pembroke Welsh Corgi).

Brush tail Tail covered in hair in such a manner as to give it a bottle-brush appearance (Example: Siberian Husky).

Docked tail Tail cut to a shorter length.

Gay tail Tail carried above the level of the back.

Saber tail Slightly curved, low-carried tail.

Screw tail Short, twisted tail.

MOVEMENT TERMS

Close behind Moving with hocks close together.

Crabbing Side-winding.

Crossing-over When viewed from the front (or rarely, the rear), the legs converge beyond the midline.

Drive Strong thrust from the hindquarters.

Gait Way of moving.

Hackney High-stepping front movement.

Loose movement Erratic movement suggestive of poor muscle development.

Lumbering Heavy, ungainly movement.

Pacing Moving both legs on the same side of the body in unison, as though hobbled together.

Pounding Front feet hitting the ground with a jarring reaction.

Reach Length of forward stride.

Single tracking As viewed from the front or rear, the legs converge toward the center line of balance as the dog trots.

Sound Good movement viewed from the front and rear.

Trotting Moving diagonal legs in unison.

Dog Anatomy

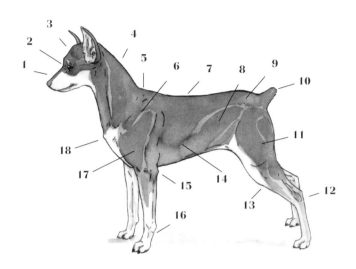

The External Anatomy of the Dog
1. Foreface or muzzle
2. Stop
3. Skull
4. Neckline
5. Withers
6. Shoulder
7. Back
8. Loin
9. Croup
10. Tail
11. Thigh
12. Hock
13. Knee
14. Rib cage
15. Elbow
16. Pastern
17. Upper arm
18. Forechest

The Skeleton of the Dog

The Musculature of the Dog

Two Extreme Skull Types

The dolichocephalic skull (Borzoi).   The brachycephalic skull (Bulldog).

Four Types of Bites

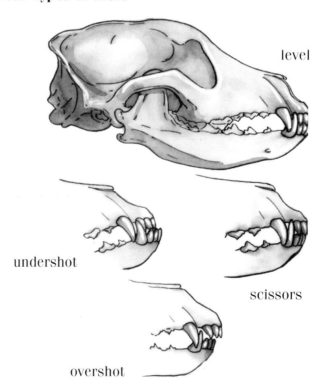

level

undershot

scissors

overshot

LEG AND FEET POSITIONS

The Front

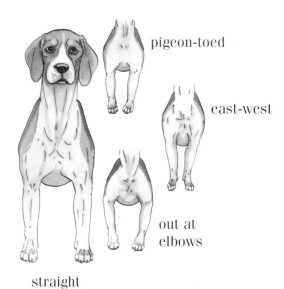

pigeon-toed

east-west

out at elbows

straight

In most breeds, the front should be straight and the same width as the chest, when viewed from the front.

The Rear

cow-hocked

bow-legged

straight

In most breeds, the rear should be straight and fairly wide as viewed from behind.

Degree of Angulation

moderately angulated

underangulated

overangulated

Although the preferred degree of angulation will vary between breeds, in most dogs a moderate degree is desirable, with either under- or over-angulated dogs faulty.

Index of Breed Entries

(AKC names in bold)